The WTO and Economic Development

The WTO and Economic Development

Edited by Ben Zissimos

CESifo Seminar Series

The MIT Press
Cambridge, Massachusetts
London, England

This book was set in Palatino by Westchester Publishing Services.

Library of Congress Cataloging-in-Publication Data

Names: Zissimos, Ben, 1970– editor.
Title: The WTO and economic development / edited by Ben Zissimos.
Description: Cambridge, MA : MIT Press, [2019] | Series: CESifo seminar series | Includes bibliographical references and index.
Identifiers: LCCN 2019006863 | ISBN 9780262043106 (hardcover : alk. paper) ISBN 9780262552103 (paperback)
Subjects: LCSH: World Trade Organization. | Economic development.
Classification: LCC HF1385 .W778726 2019 | DDC 382/.92--dc23
LC record available at https://lccn.loc.gov/2019006863

Contents

Series Foreword

This book is part of the CESifo Seminar Series. The series aims to cover topical policy issues in economics from a largely European perspective. The books in this series are the products of the papers and intensive debates that took place during the seminars hosted by CESifo, an international research network of renowned economists organized jointly by the Center for Economic Studies at Ludwig-Maximilians-Universität, Munich, and the Ifo Institute for Economic Research. All publications in this series have been carefully selected and refereed by members of the CESifo research network.

Introduction

Ben Zissimos

Motivation

What role does the World Trade Organization (WTO) play in facilitating economic development? The intent expressed in the Marrakesh Agreement, which established the WTO in 1995, is clear enough: "The Parties to the Agreement [recognize] that there is need for positive efforts designed to ensure that developing countries, and especially the least developed among them, secure a share in the growth in international trade commensurate with the needs of their economic development" (General Agreement on Tariffs and Trade 1994).

The intention that the WTO should support economic development is self-evident. However, the fact that the WTO's current round of world trade talks, aimed at implementing the "Doha Development Agenda," has taken far longer than planned and achieved far less than projected has called into question the WTO's credentials in this regard.[1] This outcome has created an opportunity to reflect on what is reasonable to expect from the WTO in supporting economic development, and how this expectation might be realized, given the WTO's institutional purpose and design.

This book brings together a collection of perspectives on different aspects of the purpose and institutional design of the WTO, and how these relate to economic development, from a group of leading scholars in the economics of international trade. The role that the WTO and its progenitor, the General Agreement on Tariffs and Trade (GATT), have played to date in facilitating economic development, and the role the WTO can reasonably be expected to play in the future, is the unifying theme.

To set the framework for this collection, in this section I review the historical evolution of ideas regarding the relationship between trade liberalization and development, and how this interacted with the evolution of the GATT and later the WTO. This review makes an original contribution to the literature by providing a fresh perspective on how the ideas and GATT/WTO policies toward development evolved, and how this evolution can be understood in terms of the literature on international trade agreements. In turn, this motivation provides a unifying framework that I use in the next section to interpret the contributions to this volume. In the final section, I synthesize the new insights that emerge.

The review deliberately omits many of the fine institutional details of the GATT and the WTO in order to highlight the main features of the evolution of ideas and policies. Throughout the review, I aim to include useful references so that further details can be obtained where desired.

The primary purpose of the WTO has always been to ensure that international trade flows as freely as possible. Yet the WTO's institutional framework allows for the possibility that freely flowing international trade may not be as beneficial for developing countries as it is for advanced ones. Hence, the WTO's institutional framework embodies special and differential treatment (SDT) of developing countries, which forms the cornerstone of the WTO's approach to facilitating economic development.

SDT is effectively a set of exemptions from Most Favored Nation (MFN) treatment, which is the principle that any terms agreed to between two parties to a trade agreement will automatically be extended to all others and is a central pillar of the GATT/WTO. As Whalley (1999) explains, SDT has two components: an access component, whereby developing countries are granted access to developed-country markets, and a "right to protect" component, whereby they do not have to reciprocate market access concessions that the developed countries make.

The intellectual underpinnings of SDT were (1) that under the gold standard poor countries would tend to suffer from balance of payments problems that could be remedied through protection; (2) the Prebisch-Singer thesis that developing countries would face a secular decline in their terms of trade, which could be remedied by preferential access to developed-country markets; and (3) the logic of infant industry protection, whereby fledgling industries need an initial period of protection to grow in a secure domestic market before eventually competing abroad. These underpinnings supported the policy initiative of "import substitution industrialization" (ISI), which aimed to achieve industrialization by substituting domestic production for imports of manufactured goods known to be in local demand.

Ironically, there was no SDT during the 1950s and 1960s, when the research community was broadly sympathetic to the idea that development could be achieved through ISI. But ISI gained momentum among developing-country policymakers throughout that time period, and SDT measures were formally adopted, mainly in the Tokyo Round of 1973–1979.[2] This happened right around the time that the research community was beginning to argue that development should be supported by outward-looking trade regimes to enhance economic efficiency.

Little, Scitovsky, and Scott (1970) were particularly influential in turning the tide toward outward-oriented development strategies.[3] On behalf of the Organization for Economic Cooperation and Development (OECD), they assessed the effects of trade policies on the economic growth and efficiency of seven countries where industrialization was under way: Argentina, Brazil, India, Mexico, Pakistan, the Philippines, and Taiwan. Their overarching conclusion was that ISI was severely wanting. They argued that, ultimately, ISI itself limits the scope for growth through exports. Their logic follows from the Lerner symmetry theorem, which demonstrates that a tariff on imports in trade equilibrium can be equivalent to a tax on exports.[4] Their conclusion was also based on the development successes of the so-called Asian Tigers, such as Taiwan, whose development strategies had been outward oriented.

As a result of this history, there is an awkward mismatch between what mainstream economics would prescribe, an outward-oriented development strategy, and the protectionism that is allowed for under SDT to this day. This mismatch can be seen through the lens of the "terms-of-trade theory," which is the oldest and most established economic theory of trade agreements, both theoretically and empirically (Mayer 1981; Bagwell and Staiger 1999, 2002, 2011). According to this theory, a trade agreement enables countries to escape from a terms-of-trade driven prisoner's dilemma, whereby they have a collective incentive to liberalize trade to maximize efficiency globally, but each has an individual incentive to adopt protection in order to improve their own terms of trade. Therefore, the benefits of a trade agreement are based on the exchange of balanced concessions, and developing countries can only expect to gain market access abroad if they concede it at home. By allowing developing countries to concede less, SDT holds back what they can expect to gain from participation in the multilateral trade rounds of the GATT and the WTO.

According to the terms-of-trade theory, developing countries have historically been hurt by high protection of agriculture in developed countries because, under SDT, in past trade rounds developing countries did not offer concessions of their own for industrial goods.[5] A key implication of this theory is that if developing countries do not make any tariff concessions while developed countries do make reciprocal and nondiscriminatory tariff cuts, the terms of trade will adjust so that trade flows will not change at all for developing countries. Consequently, developing countries cannot gain from any market access concessions that only developed countries make. This, again, is an implication of the Lerner symmetry theorem (Bagwell and Staiger 2014). Under this view, developing countries should eschew SDT to enable developed-country trade liberalization to support their development.

The same kind of recommendation arises from the most established alternative to the terms-of-trade theory of trade agreements, known as the "commitment theory" (Staiger and Tabellini 1987; Maggi and Rodríguez-Clare 1998). This theory holds that the purpose of a trade agreement is to enable governments to tie their hands against protectionist interests in their own countries. The imperative for developing-country governments to escape from such domestic commitment problems has become greater since the 1980s for two reasons. First, supply chains have become more internationalized (Baldwin 2016), and second, with the fall of the Berlin Wall in 1989, developing countries have become more market oriented as opposed to planning oriented (Ostry 2002). Both innovations have given developing countries a greater interest in international trade, the flip side of which is a greater interest in resisting domestic protectionist pressures. Motivated by this, in the Uruguay Round, developing countries committed to taking on unprecedented obligations to reduce trade barriers.[6]

The WTO was formed as an outcome of the Uruguay Round from 1986 to 1994. Any country that wished to become a member of the WTO, including any developing country, was required to sign onto all elements of the Uruguay Round agreement via a "single undertaking." In line with the single undertaking, new contracting parties that joined the GATT during the Uruguay Round were required to join under significantly stricter accession rules than those that had joined previously. Since developed countries were already contracting parties to the GATT, the new contracting parties overwhelmingly tended to be developing countries. Using the rationale put forward by Maggi and Rodríguez-Clare (1998), Tang and Wei (2009) show econometrically that WTO accession after the Uruguay Round has a commitment value strong enough to have a positive impact on growth. Indeed, they find that the effects are particularly large in countries with weak governance, where external policy commitments have a more important role to play.

Taking the implications of the established theories of trade agreements together, a basic recommendation would be that, while trade agreements under the WTO have a role to play in economic development, developing countries should eschew SDT altogether. However, there are two main alternative perspectives that could provide potential roles for SDT in economic development. The first comes from the trade-and-development literature, which recognizes a role for government involvement in the process of industrialization. The second comes from the commitment-based literature on trade agreements, which attempts to rationalize the use of SDT to phase in trade agreement obligations that developing countries chose to take on in the Uruguay Round. Let us now consider each of these in turn.

Regarding the perspective from the trade-and-development literature, here again Little, Scitovsky, and Scott (1970) is a useful reference point. While the authors argue strongly against ISI, they contend that government promotion of industrial exports can play an important role in development strategy based on the approach and successes of the Asian Tigers. What made the arguments that Little, Scitovsky, and Scott advanced distinctive at the time was their advocacy of a shift away from government attempts to take a planning approach to development and toward a greater reliance on the price mechanism. For example, they advocated subsidizing firm entry into industrial activity where external benefits were thought to exist.[7]

The GATT Agreement on Safeguards and Countervailing Measures (ASCM) allowed developing countries to use subsidies to promote industrial firm entry along the lines envisaged by Little, Scitovsky, and Scott. The GATT ASCM was an outcome of the Tokyo Round, which prohibited the use of subsidies that were conditional on export performance, referred to as "export subsidies." It also prohibited subsidies contingent on the use of domestic goods over imported goods, referred to as "local content subsidies." The reasoning was that these types of subsidy were the most likely to have adverse effects on the trade flows of other contracting parties. Other types of subsidy were not prohibited outright but could be subject to countervailing duties (CVDs) or a "nullification-and-impairment complaint" if other contracting parties thought that they were compromising benefits expected from an earlier agreement. Developing countries secured exemption from the ASCM in the Tokyo Round as part of the formal introduction of SDT.

Developing countries' exemption from the ASCM ended when they agreed to comply with the terms of the WTO ASCM upon creation of the WTO, with an allowance for compliance to be phased in over a period of five years (GATT 1994, annex 1A), so provided that subsidies are not made conditional on exporting, or on the use of domestic content, there is still some scope under the WTO to use them to promote entry along the lines envisaged by Little, Scitovsky, and Scott.[8]

The established theories of trade agreements do not identify an explicit role for government promotion of industrialization or export sectors. When the trade agreements literature considers SDT, it tends to be in its traditional role of import protection rather than to support the development of industrial sectors, but researchers have recently questioned the result, based on the Lerner symmetry theorem outlined earlier, that developing-country trade flows will not change at all if they do not make concessions of their own under SDT.

Econometric research has found evidence (though not conclusive) that developing-country exports have increased significantly for trade agreements involving SDT (Rose 2004; Subramanian and Wei 2007; Gil-Pareja, Llorca-Vivero, and Martínez-Serrano 2014). However, the basis for this increase is not yet clear. Has the surge in exports resulting from SDT facilitated the internalization of externalities that could underpin an export-led growth strategy? Or has it merely allowed exporters to collect rents as the terms of trade adjust? Ornelas (2016) provides a detailed discussion of this literature, outlining its main findings and its limitations.

Regarding the perspective where developing countries take on tariff commitments voluntarily in the Uruguay Round, the emphasis in SDT changed. It shifted away from obtaining outright exemptions from tariff commitments and toward granting developing countries phase-in periods to meet the commitments that they had taken on. Conconi and Perroni (2012, 2015) have developed a theory to rationalize this new role for SDT. They show that a reciprocal trade agreement in which a large, developed country lowers its tariffs conditional on a small, developing country doing the same creates a "carrot and stick" mechanism that helps the small-country government overcome its commitment problem. Moreover, if capacity in the small-country import-competing sector can only be reduced gradually, the agreement may need to allow the small country to delay the implementation of its trade liberalization commitments.[9]

We have already observed that developing countries took on unprecedented obligations to reduce trade barriers in the Uruguay Round. In addition, the Uruguay Round addressed areas not covered by previous rounds, and this extended coverage has created "new issues" regarding the WTO's institutional structure and how this might relate to economic development. Ostry (2002) has described the outcome of the Uruguay Round as a "grand bargain" between developed and developing countries. In this bargain, developed countries committed to open their markets to agriculture and labor-intensive manufacturing goods, especially textiles and clothing. These would generally be regarded as standard "market access" commitments, which simply involve developed countries lowering tariffs and hence reducing local price distortions. Some of the commitments that the developing countries took on, which will be detailed later, would not be regarded as standard market access commitments, and for this reason the "new issues" have arisen.

As part of the grand bargain of the Uruguay Round, developing countries agreed to include in the trading system trade in services (GATS), intellectual property (TRIPS), and (albeit to a lesser extent than originally demanded) investment (TRIMS). The outcome also included "the creation of the WTO, with the strongest dispute settlement system (DSS) in the history of international law" (Ostry 2002). These new features have created four different types of issue in the way developing countries interact with others over international trade and trade policy.

First, since the GATS focuses on trade in services, the relevant barriers to trade are measures such as laws, regulations, and administrative actions that impede cross-border flows. These are referred to as "behind-the-border" measures. This contrasts markedly with the GATT, which focused on goods trade, where relevant barriers to trade, such as trade taxes and quotas, are applied at the border and are therefore called "border measures." The measures associated with services are considerably less visible than those associated with goods, so transparency became more of a concern in fulfilling negotiated commitments. Consequently, countries must now publish all relevant laws, regulations, and administrative procedures. Implicit in this shift embodied in the GATS is a move away from GATT "negative regula-tion," what governments *must not* do, to "positive regulation," what governments *must* do. Two types of concern have arisen from this out-come: implementation is likely to be costly, amounting to as much as a year's development budget for the least developed countries, and there is a sense that the implementation of regulation is being imposed on developing countries by developed countries, which risks being inappropriate and even "imperialistic" (Finger and Schuler 2000).

Second, while the GATS behind-the-border measures might reason-ably be characterized as enhancing market access, like GATT border measures do, TRIPS commitments are not market access commitments. Instead, TRIPS commitments set down minimum standards for the reg-ulation by national governments of many forms of intellectual property as applied to nationals of other WTO member nations. Consequently, their implementation would not be expected to reduce local-price dis-tortions in developing countries in the way that traditional market access commitments would.

Bagwell and Staiger (2014) discuss this issue in detail. They argue that SDT has resulted in the WTO now facing a "latecomer problem" integrating its developing-country members. That is, because develop-ing countries have come to the trade negotiation table relatively late, they still have many distortions created by trade policies, while devel-oped countries have already eliminated their domestic distortions in previous GATT rounds. The potential solution for developing coun-tries, which Bagwell and Staiger (2014) describe as "setting a place at the table," is to try to identify new areas where they can offer market access to developed countries. This would in turn create the opportu-nity for developed countries to respond with new reciprocal market access concessions themselves. But because the TRIPS agreement does not entail market access commitments, its inclusion in the Uruguay Round may actually have exacerbated the latecomer problem. Specif-ically, because TRIPS does not involve having developing countries come up with market access concessions that can be exchanged with developed countries, it cannot be used as a way to encourage devel-oped countries to liberalize markets beneficial to developing countries, such as agriculture.

Third, TRIPS has been bitterly opposed by developing countries because it is seen as now-advanced countries "pulling up the develop-ment ladder," making it harder for developing countries to follow. In the past, most now-advanced countries used an absence of intellectual property protection within their own economies to learn to innovate by first imitating (but not compensating) foreigners. With TRIPS making this approach illegal, many developing countries believe that the imitation route to industrial development is now closed off to them.

Saggi (2016) undertakes a balanced and comprehensive discussion of this issue, weighing the point just made against its counterarguments. One counter is that, with the dramatic growth of a number of middle-income countries over the last few years, developing countries now account for half the world economy. This is a large enough scale to affect incentives to innovate across all countries, including those in middle-income developing countries themselves, so an international regime to defend intellectual property rights (IPRs) is warranted. A second counter is that since developing countries now have stronger IPR regimes, this will provide greater incentives for developed countries to invest in developing-country markets through foreign direct investment (FDI). This should in turn promote the transfer of technology to developing countries, providing a more direct route through which they will be able to start innovating.

To date, the empirical evidence on TRIPS is limited, but it seems to show small effects, both bad and good. Prices of patented products have risen in developing countries because the imitation channel has been closed off, but the price rises have been smaller than feared. On the other hand, while the pace of technology transfer through FDI has increased, there is as yet no evidence that this has had a positive impact on the pace of indigenous innovation in the developing world.[10]

Fourth, the new DSS could be good for developing countries because it reinforces the operation of the world trading system as "rules based," but it can only be beneficial to developing countries if they can access it. In principle, even the smallest developing countries can hold the largest and most powerful accountable for the concessions they have agreed to. But the absolute marginal cost of access to each small developing country of managing a dispute will in general be higher than for a developed country, because the former tend to maintain smaller missions to the WTO Secretariat in Geneva. A developing-country mission will therefore become overstretched by a dispute more quickly, given their existing workload.

In recognition of the higher marginal costs of managing a dispute faced by developing countries, SDT makes available to them additional privileged procedures. Moreover, in 2001, the Advisory Centre on WTO Law (ACWL) was established to make advice and subsidies available to poorer countries to help them with the costs of mounting a WTO dispute. Developing countries may choose a faster procedure, request longer time limits, or request legal assistance. Some of these provisions are applied very frequently, while others have not yet had any practical relevance (Bown 2009).

Given that SDT helps developing countries access the DSS, the main overarching issue raised by the system for developing countries is that it is "self-enforcing." That is, the only way for a country to enforce a violation of an agreement against it is to withdraw equivalent concessions that it has made in the agreement. This means that the reciprocal exchange of concessions on an MFN basis is at the core of the functioning of the dispute settlement system and indeed the entire GATT/WTO-based system of trade agreements. However, as Bown (2009) explains in detail, because SDT extends concessions to developing countries on a preferential and hence nonreciprocal basis, they may have nothing to withdraw in order to hold those violating an agreement accountable. This provides yet another reason why developing countries should consider eschewing SDT in order to take full advantage of the DSS.[11]

This Book

As discussed in the previous section, the historical evolution of ideas regarding the relationship between trade liberalization and development has seen a shift from endorsement of a planning-based approach toward an approach based on markets and institutions. Under the planning-based approach, economic development is an exercise in "conscious design," whereby the government is directly involved in a deliberate process of deciding which firms and industries to promote, using trade policy to further this process. The approach based on markets and institutions aims to set institutions and government policies, including those relating to trade, such that, in the language of North and Thomas (1973), "individuals capture the social returns to their actions as private returns, so that development emerges spontaneously through the efforts of individuals." The approach based on markets and institutions has come to be the dominant paradigm in the literature on international trade agreements, and this is reflected in the contributions to this volume.

The chapters that follow are generally about getting institutions and prices right, leaving implicit the assumption that promoting the process of economic development does not necessarily require further government intervention. From a planning-based perspective, which is still prevalent in some quarters of the literature on international development, the contributions to this volume would be regarded as lacking in their disregard for the government's role in promoting a deliberate process of economic development.

In defense of our approach, it has proved remarkably difficult to find concrete evidence of which policies consistently promote economic development, leaving some to conclude that basing development on "conscious design" is a fruitless exercise (Cohen and Easterly 2009). At the same time, the literature on misallocation and productivity has demonstrated that the removal of distortions, including those created by trade policies, as well as establishing institutions that support international trade, does play a demonstrable role in promoting productivity and hence economic development (Hall and Jones 1999; Waugh 2010).[12]

Past attempts to study the scope of the WTO to promote economic development in the Doha Round have tended to focus on which developed-country sectors could be opened to the benefit of developing countries. The focus has been on agriculture, textiles, and other low-skilled manufactured products, as well as services.[13] However, as we have seen, a key insight from the "terms-of-trade" theory of trade agreements is that countries can only expect to gain from a trade agreement in proportion to the market access concessions that they themselves make. Accordingly, rather than focusing on sectors where developing countries could benefit from being granted greater access, the first four chapters of this book aim to identify areas where developing countries have in the past, and could in the future, potentially offer concessions. Hence, the aim is to see how developing countries could create the greatest scope for themselves to gain from current and possible future trade rounds under the WTO.

Chapter 1 of this book, by Robert Staiger, sets out a comprehensive framework for formally incorporating nontariff measures (NTMs) into a model for analyzing a multilateral trade agreement, taking account of the presence of tariffs as well. There appears to be broad recognition that the existence of NTMs is making it difficult for developing countries to gain reliable access to developed-country markets. At the same time, there is recognition that developing countries set numerous NTMs of their own, so there appears to be scope here for a mutually beneficial agreement between developed and developing countries that involves NTMs. The main issue with reaching such an agreement seems to be that NTMs have become increasingly complex and multifaceted, encompassing a dense web of rules and regulations across countries that are proving difficult to understand and disentangle systematically (UNCTAD 2013).

Chapter 1 first categorizes NTMs, taking the initial step of defining as NTMs all trade interventions that are not tariffs. It then breaks down NTMs into two subcategories: "border NTMs," such as import quotas and export restrictions, and "behind-the-border NTMs," such as food safety standards and other standards aimed at protecting consumers.[14] Drawing on UNCTAD (2013), the chapter notes that while developing countries tend to impose border NTMs on imports from developed countries, developed countries tend to impose behind-the-border NTMs on imports from developing countries.

Although the framework developed in chapter 1 is general and allows for a broad spectrum of possibilities, the policy prescriptions turn out to be surprisingly clear-cut. With regard to border NTMs, the chapter argues that some form of international cooperation may be needed to bring international trade flows up to efficient levels. A key question is whether the fact that NTMs do not necessarily generate any revenues prevents an agreement on border NTMs from being subject to the same terms-of-trade motivation as tariffs. The concern is that tariff revenues apparently play a critical role in the terms-of-trade motivation for a trade agreement, while there may be no revenues with NTMs.

A key contribution of chapter 1 is to show that an agreement involving border NTMs is indeed amenable to a terms-of-trade motivation. Since border NTMs can exert a negative terms-of-trade externality on trade partners by causing a reduction in demand for their exports, an agreement over border NTMs has the same motivation of escaping from a terms-of-trade externality as in the tariff-based theory of trade agreements discussed earlier. As the chapter points out, this provides a rationale for the WTO's Trade Facilitation Agreement (TFA), reached at the 2013 Bali Ministerial Conference. The TFA focuses on trade facilitation, improving administrative procedures at the border.

Turning to behind-the-border measures, chapter 1 identifies a critical distinction between whether international prices are determined through a Walrasian process or instead involve an element of bilateral bargaining. International prices are determined through a Walrasian process when the production of each traded good takes place within a country. On the other hand, Antras and Staiger (2012) argue that offshoring may be seen as changing the nature of international price determination from one governed by a standard Walrasian market-clearing mechanism to one that is described by a collection of bilateral bargains between foreign suppliers and domestic buyers. In that case, the rise in offshoring will require fundamental changes in the WTO's approach to trade liberalization if that institution is to remain effective.

In the case of behind-the-border NTMs under Walrasian international price determination, import tariffs and export taxes are the only policies that are distorted in the Nash equilibrium. All other (NTM) policies are set at their efficient, Pigouvian levels conditional on (inefficiently low) Nash trade volumes. Hence, chapter 1 shows that the only job for an international trade agreement is to liberalize tariffs and hence expand trade volumes to efficient levels, just as in an agreement without NTMs.

If, on the other hand, international prices are determined partly through bilateral bargaining, then domestic policies such as a domestic consumption tax have not only a Pigouvian role but take on a terms-of-trade role as well. This means that to attain efficiency, in addition to a tariff component, an agreement must involve "deep integration" that addresses behind-the-border measures such as consumption taxes.

This insight provides a possible rationale for why, as trade has become based more on the supply chain in recent years, countries have increasingly pursued deep integration through preferential trade agreements (PTAs) rather than shallow integration through multilateral trade rounds. It also suggests that developing countries have a stake in developed countries agreeing to adopt further behind-the-border NTMs, and could encourage this by offering concessions over border NTMs in exchange.

Chapter 2, by Chad Bown, adopts a more traditional focus on tariffs. The motivation is compelling, arguing that there are 3.5 billion people in the world who have yet to benefit from an agreement to lower tariffs under the GATT/WTO, the overwhelming majority of whom are in developing countries. This chapter uses the terms-of-trade theory to identify, in the data, scope for further efficiency gains through trade liberalization facilitated by the WTO. It does so by testing a key implication of the terms-of-trade theory, focusing on tariff bindings. Tariff bindings are levels above which countries are not permitted to raise tariffs, except under extenuating circumstances. In practical terms, agreements reached in GATT/WTO negotiations are over bindings rather than tariffs themselves. The implication focused on in the chapter is that, through WTO negotiations, members are requested to take on lower tariff binding commitments on products for which they have higher market power and thus where their tariffs (if left unchecked) would result in larger terms-of-trade externality losses for trade partners.

Chapter 2 assesses this implication for three groups of countries: those that recently acceded to the WTO, because they approximate countries who have yet to join; WTO members with unbound tariffs; and WTO members with bound tariffs but substantial tariff overhang. (Tariff overhang is the gap between the tariff binding that a country has agreed to and the tariff that it actually applies.) The chapter uses established theoretical and econometric methodologies to investigate a new dataset that incorporates detailed evidence on a number of developing countries. We know from the prior literature that the terms-of-trade theory of trade agreements has provided motivation for tariff agreements between developed countries. The main contribution of this chapter is to assess the extent to which the same motivation holds for developing countries.

The results for recently acceding countries suggest that future accessions could be motivated by the terms-of-trade theory, yielding further efficiency gains through trade liberalization. The same is not found to be true of countries whose tariffs are unbound. This second group is concentrated in sub-Saharan Africa and tends to be poorer. For these countries, the general finding is that there is no evidence that market power considerations are driving applied tariff rates for unbound products. This finding is consistent with the idea that unbound tariffs in the WTO system allow countries flexibility to raise their applied rates in response to shocks, and poor countries put a high premium on such flexibility in raising tariff revenues, because they lack domestic fiscal alternatives.

The approach used in chapter 2 to study countries with substantial tariff overhang follows Nicita, Olarreaga, and Silva (2018). This approach makes two predictions. First, as per the key implication noted earlier, when applied tariffs are constrained by WTO binding commitments, there is a negative relationship between importer market power and the applied tariff. Second, when applied tariffs are unconstrained by WTO binding commitments, there is a positive relationship between importer market power and the applied tariff.

It is the second of these predictions that chapter 2 investigates in detail for countries with substantial tariff overhang. The findings are that products for countries, and in particular developing countries, that have taken on WTO bindings but for which substantial tariff overhang remains have applied MFN import tariffs that continue to reflect importer market power considerations. So this may constitute an area where additional WTO-facilitated negotiations for applied MFN tariff reductions would be consistent with the motivation provided by the terms-of-trade theory of trade agreements.

Chapter 3, by Rodney Ludema, Anna Maria Mayda, and Jonathon McClure, studies the evolution of the MFN free-rider problem, an implication of the terms-of-trade theory. Ludema and Mayda (2009, 2013) show that an exporting country's benefit from an MFN tariff concession by another country is proportional to exporter concentration. An exporting country's willingness to pay for an MFN tariff concession on the product it exports with tariff concessions of its own depends on how much its refusal to offer concessions would reduce the MFN tariff concession. The smaller the exporter, the less its refusal would mitigate the tariff cut and thus the less costly it would be for the exporter to refuse to make a concession. The fact that any tariff concession that others make must be extended to all on an MFN basis then means that smaller exporters have an incentive to free ride on other countries' tariff concessions. Ludema and Mayda have termed this phenomenon the "MFN free-rider problem." The MFN free-rider problem is most severe when there is a relatively large number of small countries exporting a product (i.e., exporter concentration is low), so that each country has a low willingness to pay for an MFN tariff reduction with tariff concessions of its own.

Ludema and Mayda (2009, 2013) show that an exporter's maximum willingness to pay for a tariff cut is proportional to the square of its export share. Summing over all exporters, the collective willingness to pay of all MFN exporters is proportional to the Herfindahl-Hirschman index (HHI) of exporter concentration. The higher the HHI is, the less severe the MFN free-rider problem will be.

Chapter 3 focuses on the period since 1993. This covers the period since the Uruguay Round was completed in 1994 and the WTO was formed in 1995. The evolution of the MFN free-rider problem is analyzed in two steps. First, the chapter analyzes how much of the trade liberalization that has taken place since 1947 is attributable to the GATT. Alternative channels could be unilateral trade liberalization and through the formation of preferential trade agreements (PTAs). Particularly useful, given the focus of this book, is that the chapter decomposes the changes according to whether countries are developed or developing.

The results show that through negotiations under the GATT up to the conclusion of the Uruguay Round, developing countries were able to internalize 78% of the terms-of-trade effects of their tariff reductions, while developed countries were only able to internalize 70%. The difference results from the fact that each developed country tends to account for a larger share of the goods that it exports, which is reflected in a higher HHI, motivating developed countries to offer larger tariff concessions. For developing countries, each country is responsible for a lower share of the good that it exports, resulting in a lower HHI, so they are more inclined to free ride on MFN.

With regard to specific sectors, a particularly interesting finding is that while developing countries tend to export manufactured goods such as footwear and textiles, which have relatively high potential for negotiated liberalization, this potential goes unrealized. This is because these products are produced by a relatively large number of small countries, so the HHI is low and the free-rider problem more acute for these products.

In addition, chapter 3 examines the prospects for future multilateral trade liberalization by decomposing changes in exporter concentration into three components: the creation of PTAs, the accession of new countries to the WTO, and the change in trade patterns resulting from emerging economies' high growth rates. The results show that the increase in PTAs over the last 20 years has increased exporter concentration. When countries form a PTA, they extend MFN treatment to fewer countries than they did before. Theoretically, this could increase or decrease the HHI of the remaining exporters to those countries, but chapter 3 shows that in the data the HHI has increased. So surprisingly, the chapter identifies a new way in which PTAs create "building blocks" in the path to multilateral trade liberalization. Similarly, the accession of new members has also increased the HHIs of existing members.[15] This is because, before acceding, the new members were observers and so already received MFN treatment, but because they were observers, they were not able to participate in negotiations. Thus, the accession of new members to the WTO increases exporter concentration by adding new participants to the negotiations.

However, crucially, through the growth of trade with emerging economies such as China, the MFN free-rider effect is found to have gotten worse. For some countries, such as Brazil and India, the total HHI of industrial exporters with whom they negotiate decreased between 1993 and 2012 because the increase in exports of industrial goods by China has eroded the export market shares of existing exporters such as the United States and European countries. This may be one reason why Brazil and India have apparently become more reluctant to make tariff reductions during the Doha Round. In other words, this effect may contribute to the "latecomer problem" discussed by Bagwell and Staiger (2014). Yet the overarching finding is that there has been an average increase in exporter concentration consistent with the trade liberalization, however modest, that has been realized through the Doha Round.

While the discussion so far has focused on developing-country GATT/WTO members, chapter 4, by Xuepeng Liu, considers a puzzle concerning so-called nonmember participants (NMPs). NMPs consist of three groups: colonies and overseas territories of GATT members, newly independent states, and provisional members. NMPs are relevant here because they tend overwhelmingly to be developing countries.

Recognition that NMPs may be important in understanding the benefits of the GATT emerged with the inception of the econometric literature on the GATT/WTO. This literature was launched by a controversial paper by Rose (2004) that apparently found "little evidence that countries joining or belonging to the GATT/WTO have different trade patterns than outsiders." Rose described his finding as an "interesting mystery." This has also been referred to in the literature as the GATT/WTO "ineffectiveness puzzle."

On the face of it, this puzzle was resolved by Tomz, Goldstein, and Rivers (2007) when they took another look at the way Rose classifies countries into GATT "insiders" and "outsiders." Rose classifies NMPs as outsiders when in fact they often formally adopt many of the rights and obligations of members. By more reasonably classifying these countries as insiders, Tomz, Goldstein, and Rivers find that insiders trade more than outsiders do.

Perplexingly, in resolving the ineffectiveness puzzle, Tomz, Goldstein, and Rivers create a new one. Their preferred results imply that two formal GATT members trade 61% more than the baseline case of neither country being a formal member nor an NMP, while two NMPs trade 140% more than the baseline. It is difficult to understand why the

NMPs should trade even more than formal members do. Chapter 4 is directed at understanding this finding, which Liu refers to as the "NMP puzzle."

Chapter 4 addresses the NMP puzzle in two ways. The first is to incorporate zero bilateral trade flows in the dataset, something that Tomz, Goldstein, and Rivers do not do. So while Tomz, Goldstein, and Rivers are able to account for the effect of GATT participation on the intensive margin, they fail to take account of its effect on the extensive margin. Chapter 4 shows that full GATT membership was more effective in stimulating new trading relationships, possibly because only full members could initiate negotiations. While this approach addresses the NMP puzzle overall, the puzzle still remains at the intensive margin when the zeros are introduced.

The second way that chapter 4 addresses the NMP puzzle is to adopt a Poisson quasi-maximum likelihood estimation (PQML) approach in the regressions. This addresses a bias to estimates introduced by the standard gravity equation approach, known from the prior literature, that arises when taking the logarithm of trade flows.

The main finding of chapter 4 is that under the PQML approach, with both positive and zero trade, two formal GATT members trade 60% more than the baseline case of neither being a formal member nor an NMP, while two NMPs trade 10% less than the baseline case. While there is no necessary reason to expect NMPs to trade less than the baseline case, overall this finding is more in line with what we would expect, in that NMPs trade less than members do. In sum, the main contribution of the chapter is to show that the "NMP puzzle" can be addressed by undertaking two relatively simple modifications to the original gravity equation approach of Rose (2004) and Tomz, Goldstein, and Rivers (2007).

Chapters 5 through 7 of the book develop new theoretical and econometric approaches to better understand key aspects of trade liberalization under the GATT/WTO, with applications that can help us understand the implications of SDT. Chapter 5 develops a new model of how nations can achieve cooperation in eliminating prohibitive trade barriers, which is useful because SDT has been used in the past to support autarky in some sectors. Chapter 6 studies export subsidies in China and asks whether they have been responsible for China's remarkable growth in exporting. This will shed light on whether government promotion of industrial development through SDT can form a useful part of a development strategy. Chapter 7 develops a framework for thinking about how to optimally set trade policy to facilitate the movement of productive resources between sectors when this is costly, thus providing a different rationale for SDT.

In chapter 5, David DeRemer develops a model for analyzing a trade agreement when autarky is the (unique) outcome of noncooperation over trade policy. While the canonical model of trade agreements with perfect competition and political economy (Bagwell and Staiger 1999, 2002) has proved to be powerful and flexible in explaining many aspects of trade liberalization under the GATT/WTO, it cannot motivate a trade agreement of the kind that DeRemer considers. Specifically, in the canonical model, if each government has a unilateral preference for autarky, then they must have a joint preference for autarky as well. This limits the scope for studying situations where developing countries have adopted autarkic trade policies for specific sectors through SDT but where there may nevertheless be scope to open these sectors as part of a trade agreement.

Chapter 5 adopts a familiar "Brander-Spencer" type model in which to explore the scope for a trade agreement when autarky is the noncooperative outcome. The basic setting is one of two countries, with one firm in each producing the same homogeneous product. Strategic interaction in production between the firms is captured via Cournot competition. The government in each country sets a specific tariff on imports coming from the other country. There is a standard rent-shifting motive for setting tariffs, familiar from Brander and Spencer (1981).

Under this setup, each government has a dominant strategy to set its tariff at a certain positive level determined by underlying parameters, and tariffs are strategically independent. The main parameter of interest in the basic setup is the weight that each government places on the profits made by its nation's firm. The first main result identifies an interval for the weight in which Nash equilibrium tariffs are prohibitive but free trade is globally optimal. Consequently, governments and each nation as a whole can benefit from a trade agreement. This is the main idea of chapter 5, and the rest is devoted to exploring other conditions under which this basic result holds.

The extensions considered show that cooperation over trade liberalization is more likely for lower levels of trade costs, sufficiently large cross-industry differences in productivity, weaker levels of competition between nations, and intermediate ranges of firm heterogeneity. An extension of this framework could be used to highlight the "latecomer problem" identified by Bagwell and Staiger (2014) in a particularly stark way. That is, while developed countries liberalized a particular sector through past GATT rounds, some developing countries may have remained autarkic in that sector. As chapter 5 notes, this seems to have been particularly true for the production of buses and trucks, where even to this day many developing countries' markets are dominated exclusively by inefficient domestic goods produced behind high tariff walls. Fully understanding this problem may be the first step toward finding an appropriate solution.

Chapter 6, by Fabrice Defever and Alejandro Riaño, looks specifically at the export promotion policies implemented by China and how they have promoted China's transition from autarky in the 1970s to the world's largest exporting economy today. Previously we noted that the literature on international trade and development admits a potential role for the promotion of industrialization as part of a development strategy, to the extent that this internalizes externalities associated with industrial development. The literature's recognition of this role was originally based on successful government interventions in development of the Asian Tigers, and this success appears to be ongoing with the "rise of China."

The point of departure for chapter 6 is a set of stylized facts on firms' exporting behavior that have been established in the economics literature for the world's major trading economies. The first aim of the chapter is to see the extent to which Chinese exporting firms conform to these stylized facts. The stylized facts are that relatively few firms engage in exporting, that exporting firms tend to be more productive and hence larger, and that most firms that do export sell only a small fraction of their output abroad. As the chapter notes, it is particularly interesting to compare the characteristics of Chinese exporters against these stylized facts, partly because export growth has been so rapid in China and partly because the approach China has taken has been somewhat heterodox, based on the "distinctive traits of a centrally planned economy."

Key features of China's approach to promoting exports have been the formation of free trade zones (FTZs), the use of duty drawback schemes in the form of processing trade zones, and the provision of tax concessions and subsidies based on export share requirements. Since all of these policies are likely to distort economic incentives, the question is whether the standard stylized facts still prevail in this type of environment.

Chapter 6 reveals that, on the face of it, the characteristics of Chinese exporters fit the stylized facts listed. The chapter notes that the most striking difference is that one-third of firms export almost all of their output. These firms are referred to as "pure exporters." Moreover, pure exporters are found to be less productive than "regular exporters," for which a large share of their output serves the domestic market. This goes against a pervasive feature found elsewhere, that a firm's productivity and its export share are positively correlated. On this basis, the chapter characterizes China as having a "dual export sector."

The second aim of chapter 6 is to assess whether the export promoting policies that China has adopted have given rise to the dual nature of the export sector. The chapter uses a detailed dataset to characterize, in a number of dimensions, the sense in which Chinese export promotion policies have created a clear incentive to export where otherwise the firms might not have done so.

The overall conclusion is that China's export promotion policies have been responsible for creating its dual export sector and have been instrumental in making China the world's largest exporter. Now that these policies are being challenged under the WTO ASCM, chapter 6 speculates that perhaps the dual nature of China's export sector will recede. Yet the results seem to imply that export subsidies have played an important role in China's industrial development. Understanding China's experience in this regard may be helpful for anticipating future outcomes for a large number of other developing economies that use export subsidies. But the fact that the WTO ASCM outlaws such policies raises an open question of how future industrialization might be promoted in ways that are consistent with WTO rules.

Chapter 7, by Eric Bond, considers whether an efficient trade agreement should allow for gradual trade liberalization to mitigate adjustment costs. Recent research has shown that the adjustment costs of moving productive resources between sectors in response to trade liberalization are significantly higher than previously thought. These costs are likely to be particularly high for developing countries, where adjustment is likely to involve geographical relocation between rural and urban settings. For example, Dix-Carneiro (2014) finds that in response to the Brazilian trade liberalization episode of 1988–1994, labor migration costs could be as high as 42% of the gains from trade, and that adjustment can take five years or longer. The chapter pays particular attention to whether there should be an allowance for adjustment to be longer in developing countries, providing a potential role for SDT.

Recent agreements demonstrate the relevance of these issues. For example, developed countries were given five years to implement the tariff schedules negotiated in the Uruguay Round, but developing countries were allowed longer phase-in periods in some sectors, notably textiles and agriculture.

The analytical approach taken in chapter 7 is to examine the optimal liberalization path between two large countries, where workers face the adjustment costs of moving between sectors. The respective governments would like to be able to provide compensation to workers in their import-competing sectors but do not have a lump-sum tax instrument to redistribute funds in a nondistorting way. The government's desire to compensate workers for trade liberalization in the import-competing sector results in tariff reductions being spread over the entire adjustment period until wage rates are equalized between sectors.

Having set up the analytical framework, chapter 7 is able to address several issues having to do with gradual trade liberalization to mitigate adjustment costs. These include whether developing countries should be encouraged to front-load tariff reductions, so that the majority of reductions are achieved at the beginning of the adjustment period, or back-load them to occur largely at the end.

The results show that if tariffs are the only policy instruments available, then developing countries should be allowed longer phase-in periods if their marginal costs of adjustment are higher than those in developed countries. Longer phase-in periods are also justified if initial employment levels are further from free trade levels, which will be true for developing countries if their initial tariffs are higher. Hence, the analysis shows that there may be a normative justification for SDT of developing countries.

Surprisingly, these results can break down when governments in developed countries have access to more policy instruments than in developing countries. Then, under an optimal agreement, developing countries should actually liberalize more rapidly than developed countries. The reason is that, to achieve efficiency, tariffs must be used more intensively by developing countries to encourage the movement of labor out of import-competing sectors when alternative instruments are unavailable.

The final two chapters of the book address the most important "new issues" that arose from the grand bargain between developed and developing countries in the Uruguay Round. These centered mainly on the TRIPS agreement and the DSS, which are considered in chapters 8 and 9, respectively.

Chapter 8, by Eric Bond and Kamal Saggi, contrasts the roles of price controls and compulsory licensing (CL) to improve consumer access to patented foreign products in developing countries. While the TRIPS agreement created a storm of controversy, the eye of the storm was over the implication that, as a result of the agreement, it became more difficult for poor people in developing countries to access medicine at affordable prices. The TRIPS agreement extended the reach of the monopoly power granted to pharmaceutical companies by the patents that they held, with the overall expectation that this would increase the prices of pharmaceuticals. It comes as no surprise that governments across the world use price controls and other such regulations to combat the monopoly power of firms selling patented pharmaceuticals. A second instrument that governments can use to manage the monopoly power of firms granted through patents is CL.

While the issue of affordability of patented pharmaceuticals takes on a special urgency in the context of poor developing countries, it is also relevant within the developed world. Under the terms of the TRIPS agreement, if a patent holder refuses to grant access to its product on "reasonable" commercial terms, then a government may grant a CL to a different firm to produce the product. This may even be granted to a firm in a third country in order to allow for the possibility that the domestic country lacks the capacity to produce pharmaceuticals locally.

In the model, a developing country sets the level of the price control while the patent holder chooses between direct entry and the voluntary licensing (VL) of its technology to a local firm. The model assumes a trade-off: the licensee has a lower fixed cost relative to the patent holder, but the licensee's product is of inferior quality. Chapter 8 compares two scenarios, one where the developing country attempts to improve consumer access via the use of a price control and another where it resorts to CL if the patent holder refuses to grant a VL locally.

The analysis shows that the option to use CL ensures that at least a lower-quality version of the patented good is available locally if the patent holder decides not to issue a VL in the developing country. However, the possibility of CL also makes it less likely that the patent holder will choose to sell in the developing country. The logic is as follows. The threat of CL reduces the patent holder's profits under VL by lowering the fee that the licensee in the developing country is willing to pay, knowing that a CL would eventually be granted. Similarly, since the royalty payments under CL provide the patent holder a return from the developing-country market when it chooses to stay out, entry there becomes less attractive as well. When CL replaces entry, it can lower a developing country's welfare because it delays consumer access to the patented good.

The main lesson of chapter 8 is that the social value of CL is context dependent. If the fixed cost of entry is high relative to the size of the developing-country market, CL plays a socially useful role that can be to the advantage of both the developing country and the patent holder. The reason is that the developing country obtains access to the pharmaceutical product, while the patent holder receives royalties from a market it would not have entered in the absence of CL. On the other hand, when fixed costs are at an intermediate level such that the patent holder prefers to wait for the CL to be issued rather than entering itself, the developing country is made worse off by the fact that CL is an option. Finally, when fixed costs are so small that the patent holder chooses to enter regardless of whether the developing country has the option to issue a CL, the threat of CL does not affect market outcomes and welfare. This context dependency seems to be a feature of outcomes under the TRIPS agreement more broadly, making it difficult to assess the extent to which it is beneficial or harmful overall.

The ninth and final chapter, by Mostafa Beshkar and Mahdi Majbouri, tests the outcomes of disputes empirically, focusing on whether they lead to litigation, taking explicit account of whether the dispute involves developed and/or developing countries. The chapter focuses on the fact that developing and developed countries show divergent behaviors in the dispute settlement process. More than half of all initiated disputes are resolved without litigation, meaning without the establishment of a dispute panel. This probably reflects the parties' desire to avoid the costs of litigation. Of those cases that do go to litigation, they are more likely to involve developed countries, probably because the marginal costs of going to litigation tend to be lower for them.

A surprising pattern uncovered in chapter 9 is that, in a dispute between a developed country and a developing country, litigation is more likely if the developed country is the defending party. As detailed in the chapter, 62% of disputes in which a developed country presses charges against a developing country are settled without establishing a dispute panel. In contrast, only 44% of disputes are settled without establishing a dispute panel if a developing country mounts a dispute against a developed country.

Chapter 9 investigates this pattern as follows. It first develops a signaling model of "direct breach" of a trade agreement and a signaling model of "indirect breach." As the name suggests, in a direct breach, the complainant claims that a term of an agreement has been breached. An indirect breach occurs where there is a disagreement over a policy that is not explicitly limited by an agreement but where its use may nullify or impair the benefits to a party that were intended under the agreement. Based on these models, the chapter derives two propositions. The first states that the equilibrium settlement rate is increasing in the litigation costs of either party. The second states that the equilibrium settlement rate is more sensitive to changes in the defendant's costs than to changes in the complainant's costs.

In the empirical section, these two theoretical propositions are then translated into two testable hypotheses. The first is that the settlement rate is positively correlated with the measures of litigation costs. The second is that the settlement rate is more sensitive to changes in the litigation costs of the defending party than to changes in the litigation costs of the complaining party. The empirical section also introduces a third testable hypothesis, which says that the settlement rate is negatively correlated with the trade volume between the disputing parties in the disputed sector before the violation.

Support is found in the data for all three of these hypotheses prior to 2001. After 2001, the difference in settlement behavior between developed and developing countries disappears. This is interesting and important because, as noted previously, it was in 2001 that the ACWL was established to provide subsidized expertise to poorer countries to help them with the costs of mounting or defending a WTO dispute. The disappearance of the difference in behavior suggests that the subsidized legal assistance made available by the ACWL has been effective in addressing the potential denial of developing countries' access to the dispute settlement system as a result of their relatively low incomes.

Basic Insights

Classical economics provides a useful frame for the insights of this book. Among the most important points made by Smith (1776) was that economic prosperity rests on free international trade because this facilitates an efficient allocation of resources. To the extent that the process of economic development can be seen as synonymous with a nation's pursuit of economic prosperity, the GATT/WTO need do nothing more to promote economic development than to facilitate international trade. This perspective chimes well with the literature on misallocation and productivity, which has shown that the removal of distortions, including those created by trade policies, has been instrumental in increasing productivity and hence economic development. This perspective also chimes well with the view through the lens of the terms-of-trade theory of trade agreements that to benefit from a multilateral trade agreement each country must come to the table ready to make concessions of their own. This couches the gains from a trade agreement in terms of enhancing economic efficiency by removing domestic distortions, which is a critical part of exploiting the gains from specialization and trade through comparative advantage.

It had traditionally been thought that the case for developing countries exploiting the gains from trade was essentially a unilateral one, especially because they were thought not to have sufficient power on world markets to affect their own terms of trade. Yet the econometric evidence presented in this book (and elsewhere) suggests that even many developing countries' trade policies have an effect on international prices. So they too need the kinds of agreements facilitated by the GATT/WTO to be able to fully exploit these gains.

One set of insights that emerges from the contributions to this book is that there are still a number of areas where concessions could be made in future trade agreements under the GATT/WTO. Developed countries, which have largely exhausted the scope for further liberalization over industrial tariffs, could come to the table ready to make substantial concessions over behind-the-border NTMs. At the same time, developing countries have the opportunity to make concessions not just over tariff measures but also over nontariff border measures. Crucially, we have come to understand that possible agreements involving NTMs could follow the same basic logic based on terms-of-trade as the agreements of the past based only on tariffs, and this in itself offers motivation for future agreements to be made.

Equally important to understanding where future concessions could be made is the question of why possible gains may have gone unrealized in the Doha Round. The "latecomer problem" has emerged in this book as a useful way to think about this issue. A key finding in the data was that the "rise of China" has discouraged key emerging economies such as Brazil and India from coming to the table to offer concessions in agriculture. This finding corroborates the suspicions of many that the reluctance of Brazil and India to offer concessions in agriculture contributed to the disappointing outcomes of the Doha Round. Also exacerbating the latecomer problem is the fact that commitments taken on by developing countries as part of the TRIPS agreement cannot be regarded as standard market access concessions that could be exchanged for developed-country concessions in agriculture.

These insights help to reconcile disagreements in the literature as to why the Doha Round proved to be so disappointing. Some argue that, after encouraging progress had been made in developing-country trade liberalization during the Uruguay Round, the narrative surrounding the Doha Round has been one of developing-country backsliding based on SDT (Ornelas 2016). Others suggest that the broadening of the policy space into new areas such as TRIPS has created a perceptibly more coercive, imperialistic policy environment of "what countries must do" and that this created reluctance among developing countries to come to the table (Rodrik 2011).[16] The insight we gain from this book is that both can be seen in terms of the latecomer problem. In part, the findings presented here offer hope for the future in that there is scope to resolve the latecomer problem by identifying market access concessions based on new policy instruments, particularly NTMs. In part, the findings are more cautionary because if the rise of China is making the MFN free-rider problem worse, the continued industrial development of Asia may further entrench the latecomer problem.

Regarding the new issues concerning the TRIPS agreement and the DSS, there appear to be two insights. The implication of the TRIPS agreement itself seems to be that its effects, both positive and negative, have been smaller than expected. However, it is early in terms of the timespan that the agreement has had to make a meaningful impact, and there appears to be scope for the effects to become larger in either direction over the coming years. Regarding the DSS, the findings were quite encouraging in that assistance made available to developing countries through the WTO ACWL appears to have helped them access the system on a more equal footing with developed countries. So even

if the weakness of the Doha Round outcomes is an indication of slowing momentum behind multilateral trade rounds, having an effective
DSS means that members, especially developing-country members,
should be able to effectively access the gains from agreements that have
already been reached.

While the insights of this book endorse the consensus that developing countries should embrace trade liberalization as part of their
development strategies, they also support a nuanced perspective that
SDT may nevertheless have a role to play in supporting economic
development. They are in line with the view that China's export subsidies have helped to promote the development of its industrial sectors.
While the specific policies that China has used are now illegal under the
WTO's ASCM, the question remains as to whether developing countries might legitimately want to exploit legal SDT measures to promote
industrialization. In addition, there does appear to be a normative
basis for using SDT measures to phase in trade liberalization commitments. The key set of questions that remain on this issue concern
how, and indeed whether, SDT measures can be made robust against
protectionist interests.

Notes

1. The Doha Round has not formally been concluded at the time of this writing, but
there is a growing consensus that it effectively ended with the Ministerial Conference
that took place in Nairobi in December 2015. See Lester (2016) for a discussion of the
accomplishments of the "Nairobi Ministerial," the Doha Round overall, how this relates
to the outcomes that were planned, and what should be the focus of WTO negotiations
in the future.

2. Formal recognition among GATT parties that allowances might be made for developing countries' less favorable experiences with trade can be traced to 1957. At the Twelfth
Session of the contracting parties to the GATT, they decided to appoint a Panel of Experts
to report on trends in international trade: "in particular the failure of the trade of less
developed countries to develop as rapidly as that of industrialized countries." This led
to "GATT Part IV" being introduced in 1965, adding three articles (XXXVI, XXXVII,
and XXXVIII) that recognize the development needs of developing countries and state
the principle of nonreciprocity. Article XVIII was the GATT's first attempt, in 1954, to
accommodate developing-country initiatives for infant industry protection, but only on
a reciprocal basis: any countries using this were expected to offer compensation or face
retaliation (GATT 1994 Analytical Index, Part IV; Whalley 1999). Also see Srinivasan
(1999).

3. See Corden (1994) and Wolf (2004) on Little, Scitovsky, and Scott (1970).

4. In addition, they argued that ISI tended to be highly distortionary. For example, while
industrial finished products were protected, imported capital goods and other imports

were encouraged, so much so that industrialization became excessively capital intensive and value added in some instances turned negative.

5. Some agricultural liberalization has now been agreed at the Nairobi Ministerial Conference of the Doha Round. See Lester (2016) for details.

6. While the obligations that developing countries as a group agreed to take on in the Uruguay Round were significantly greater than before, and have widely been described as unprecedented, it is important to keep their commitments in perspective. As will be discussed later in this introduction and in chapter 2 of this book, a number of developing countries did not take on any commitments in the Uruguay Round, and a number did so for only a limited number of products. While a number of countries did take on notional commitments for some products, the levels at which they capped, or "bound," their tariffs were so far above the rates at which their tariffs were applied that these commitments had no effect on the openness of their economies.

7. See, for example, the various references to Little, Scitovsky, and Scott (1970) in Corden (1994).

8. Under ASCM, subsidies may be judged "actionable" if they cause adverse effects of "injury" and "serious prejudice" in addition to nullification-and-impairment (Article V). But unlike prohibited subsidies, for which a dispute settlement panel would recommend "withdraw without delay" (Article IV.7), countries can achieve compliance for actionable subsidies by removing their adverse effects (Article VII.8).

9. For an in-depth discussion of this perspective, see Ornelas (2016). Whalley (1999) discusses the change in approach to SDT adopted in the Uruguay Round.

10. See Saggi (2016) for a comprehensive and nuanced discussion of the theoretical issues raised about TRIPS and the empirical studies of the effects of TRIPS.

11. TRIMS has attracted less attention than the other new features of the WTO (such as the GATS and TRIPS), both in practice and in research. See UNCTAD (2007) for a useful discussion.

12. See Restuccia and Richardson (2013) for a review of the literature on misallocation and productivity. See Easterly (2013, part 2) for a discussion of the two views of development as planning based (which he refers to as "conscious design") versus market-and-institutions based (which he refers to as "spontaneous solutions"), in which he argues in favor of an approach based on markets and institutions. See Rodrik (2007) for a view that recognizes the idea that markets and institutions must be organized to align individual incentives toward development but at the same time sees a fairly extensive role for government to internalize externalities in support of development.

13. See, for example, Brown, Deardorff, and Stern (2003) and Hertel and Winters (2006).

14. These are more formally referred to as sanitary and phytosanitary (SPS) measures and technical barriers to trade (TBTs), respectively.

15. The terminologies of GATT "contracting party" and "member" are used interchangeably for consistency with the fact that the terminology of "member" is used with reference to the WTO.

16. Rodrik (2011) refers to the new approach to trade negotiations that developed from the Uruguay Round onward as "hyperglobalization."

References

Antras, P., and R. W. Staiger. 2012. Offshoring and the Role of Trade Agreements. *American Economic Review* 102(7): 3140–3183.

Bagwell, K., and R. W. Staiger. 1999. An Economic Theory of the GATT. *American Economic Review* 89:215–248.

Bagwell, K., and R. W. Staiger. 2002. *The Economics of the World Trading System*. Cambridge, MA: MIT Press.

Bagwell, K., and R. W. Staiger. 2011. What Do Trade Negotiators Negotiate About? Empirical Evidence from the World Trade Organization. *American Economic Review* 101(4): 1238–1273.

Bagwell, K., and R. W. Staiger. 2014. Can the Doha Round Be a Development Round? Setting a Place at the Table. In *Globalization in an Age of Crisis: Multilateral Economic Cooperation in the Twenty-First Century*, edited by R. C. Feenstra and A. M. Taylor, 91–124. Chicago: University of Chicago Press for the NBER.

Baldwin, R. 2016. *The Great Convergence: Information Technology and the New Globalization*. Cambridge, MA: Harvard University Press.

Bown, C. P. 2009. *Self-Enforcing Trade: Developing Countries and WTO Dispute Settlement*. Washington, DC: Brookings Institution Press.

Brander, J. A., and B. Spencer. 1981. Tariffs and the Extraction of Foreign Monopoly Rent under Potential Entry. *Canadian Journal of Economics* 14:371–384.

Brown, D. K., A. V. Deardorff, and R. M. Stern. 2003. Developing Countries' Stake in the Doha Round. Discussion Paper No. 495. Ann Arbor: Gerald R. Ford School of Public Policy, University of Michigan.

Cohen, J., and W. Easterly. 2009. Introduction: Thinking Big versus Thinking Small. In *What Works in Development?*, edited by J. Cohen and W. Easterly, 1–23. Washington, DC: Brookings Institution Press.

Conconi, P., and C. Perroni. 2012. Conditional versus Unconditional Trade Concessions for Developing Countries. *Canadian Journal of Economics* 45:613–631.

Conconi, P., and C. Perroni. 2015. Special and Differential Treatment of Developing Countries in the WTO. *World Trade Review* 14:67–86.

Corden, M. 1994. *Trade Policy and Economic Welfare*, 2nd edition. Oxford: Clarendon Press.

Dix-Carneiro, R. 2014. Trade Liberalization and Labor Market Dynamics. *Econometrica* 82(3): 825–885.

Easterly, W. 2013. *The Tyranny of Experts: Economists, Dictators, and the Forgotten Rights of the Poor*. New York: Basic Books.

Finger, J. M., and P. Schuler. 2000. Implementation of Uruguay Round Commitments: The Development Challenge. *World Economy* 23(4): 511–525.

General Agreement on Tariffs and Trade (GATT). 1994. Marrakesh Agreement Establishing the World Trade Organization. Geneva. Available online at https://www.wto.org /english/docs_e/legal_e/04-wto_e.htm.

Gil-Pareja, S., R. Llorca-Vivero, and J. A. Martínez-Serrano. 2014. Do Nonreciprocal Preferential Trade Agreements Increase Beneficiaries' Exports? *Journal of Development Economics* 107:291–304.

Hall, R. E., and C. I. Jones. 1999. Why Do Some Countries Produce So Much More Output per Worker than Others? *Quarterly Journal of Economics* 114(1): 83–116.

Hertel, T. W., and L. A. Winters. 2006. *Poverty and the WTO: Impacts of the Doha Development Agenda.* Washington, DC: World Bank and Palgrave Macmillan.

Lester, S. 2016. Is the Doha Round Over? The WTO's Negotiating Agenda for 2016 and Beyond. *Free Trade Bulletin* 64 (February 11). Available online at https://object.cato.org/sites/cato.org/files/pubs/pdf/ftb64.pdf.

Little, I. M. D., T. Scitovsky, and M. Scott. 1970. *Industry and Trade in Some Developing Countries: A Comparative Study.* London: Oxford University Press for the Organization of Economic Cooperation and Development.

Ludema, R., and A. M. Mayda. 2009. Do Countries Free Ride on MFN? *Journal of International Economics* 77(2): 137–150.

Ludema, R., and A. M. Mayda. 2013. Do Terms-of-Trade Effects Matter for Trade Agreements? Theory and Evidence from WTO Countries. *Quarterly Journal of Economics* 128(4): 1837–1893.

Maggi, G., and A. Rodríguez-Clare. 1998. The Value of Trade Agreements in the Presence of Political Pressures. *Journal of Political Economy* 106:574–601.

Mayer, W. 1981. Theoretical Considerations on Negotiated Tariff Adjustments. *Oxford Economic Papers* 33(1): 135–153.

Nicita, A., M. Olarreaga, and P. Silva. 2018. Cooperation in WTO's Tariff Waters. *Journal of Political Economy* 126(3): 1302–1338.

North, D. C., and R. P. Thomas. 1973. *The Rise of the Western World.* Cambridge: Cambridge University Press.

Ornelas, E. 2016. Special and Differential Treatment for Developing Countries. In *Handbook of Commercial Policy*, volume 1B, edited by K. Bagwell and R. W. Staiger, 369–432. Amsterdam: Elsevier/North Holland.

Ostry, S. 2002. The Uruguay Round North-South Grand Bargain: Implications for Future Negotiations. In *The Political Economy of International Trade Law: Essays in Honor of Robert E. Hudec*, edited by D. L. M. Kennedy and J. D. Southwick, 285–300. Cambridge: Cambridge University Press.

Restuccia, D., and R. Richardson. 2013. Misallocation and Productivity. *Review of Economic Dynamics* 16:1–10. (Introduction to special issue on Misallocation and Productivity.)

Rodrik, D. 2007. *One Economics, Many Recipes: Globalization, Institutions, and Economic Growth.* Princeton, NJ: Princeton University Press.

Rodrik, D. 2011. *The Globalization Paradox: Why Global Markets, States, and Democracy Can't Coexist.* Oxford: Oxford University Press.

Rose, A. 2004. Do We Really Know That the WTO Increases Trade? *American Economic Review* 94(1): 98–114.

Saggi, K. 2016. Trade, Intellectual Property Rights, and the World Trade Organization. In *Handbook of Commercial Policy*, volume 1B, edited by K. Bagwell and R. W. Staiger, 433–512. Amsterdam: Elsevier/North Holland.

Smith, A. 1776. *An Enquiry into the Nature and Causes of the Wealth of Nations*. London: Strahan and Cadell.

Srinivasan, T. N. 1999. Developing Countries in the World Trading System: From GATT, 1947, to the Third Ministerial Meeting of the WTO, 1999. *World Economy* 22(8): 1047–1064.

Staiger, R. W., and G. Tabellini. 1987. Discretionary Trade Policy and Excessive Protectionism. *American Economic Review* 77(5): 823–837.

Subramanian, A., and S.-J. Wei. 2007. The WTO Promotes Trade Strongly but Unevenly. *Journal of International Economics* 72:151–175.

Tang, M.-K., and S.-J. Wei. 2009. The Value of Making Commitments Externally: Evidence from WTO Accessions. *Journal of International Economics* 78:216–229.

Tomz, M., J. L. Goldstein, and D. Rivers. 2007. Do We Really Know That the WTO Increases Trade? Comment. *American Economic Review* 97(5): 2005–2018.

United Nations Conference on Trade and Development (UNCTAD). 2007. *Elimination of TRIMS: The Experience of Selected Developing Countries*. UNCTAD Current Studies on FDI and Development. New York and Geneva: United Nations.

United Nations Conference on Trade and Development (UNCTAD). 2013. *Non-tariff Measures to Trade: Economic Policy Issues for Developing Countries*. Developing Countries in International Trade Studies. New York and Geneva: United Nations.

Waugh, M. E. 2010. International Trade and Income Differences. *American Economic Review* 100(5): 2093–2124.

Whalley, J. 1999. Special and Differential Treatment in the Millennium Round. *World Economy* 22(8): 1065–1093.

Wolf, M. 2004. *Why Globalization Works*. New Haven, CT: Yale University Press.

1   Nontariff Measures and the WTO

Robert W. Staiger

1.1   Introduction

In this chapter, I consider how the World Trade Organization (WTO) might best approach the issue of nontariff measures (NTMs). The General Agreement on Tariffs and Trade (GATT) adopted a particular minimalist approach to handling NTMs. That approach evolved over time, and with the creation of the WTO, the GATT's successor organization, the handling of NTMs has evolved still further, with the latest example of this evolution provided by the recently concluded negotiations over the Trade Facilitation Agreement emerging from the Doha Round. Was there an economic logic to the GATT's approach? Do the changes in the treatment of NTMs ushered in with the creation of the WTO mark an improvement from the perspective of the economic theory of trade agreements? Is the GATT/WTO approach to the treatment of NTMs adequate for the world economy of today? I survey and extend the economic theory of trade agreements to provide answers to these questions, and I use the theory to characterize the central issues with which the WTO must contend in regard to NTMs.

The issue of NTMs may have particular relevance for developing countries. As I will describe further, a central question faced by the WTO regarding NTMs is whether continued evolution away from a primary focus on border measures ("shallow integration") to greater emphasis on behind-the-border measures ("deep integration") is warranted. While the use of policy measures that could be classified as NTMs is widespread across all countries (see, for example, UNCTAD 2013), the NTMs typically employed in developing countries tend to take the form of border measures (e.g., quantitative restrictions), while in developed countries behind-the-border measures (e.g., technical regulations) receive greater emphasis. Hence, the NTMs that are most important for developing-country exporters in their attempts to export into developed-country markets are those NTMs that are at the heart of the shallow versus deep integration question.

Moreover, the issue of NTMs and the WTO's approach to them are at the center of rising concerns about the clash between international trade agreements and national sovereignty. While the WTO and deeper forms of integration are not mutually inconsistent, an important question is this: Can the WTO continue to emphasize a shallow-integration approach and deliver internationally efficient policy outcomes while avoiding unnecessary intrusions into national sovereignty? Or instead, does achieving internationally efficient policies require that the WTO evolve further toward deep integration, with the increasing erosion of the national sovereignty of WTO members that this implies?

The subsequent sections of the chapter sketch out the rough contours of the challenge faced by the WTO in dealing with NTMs from the perspective of the economic theories of trade agreements. I conclude that, when it comes to handling NTMs, there appear to be two key questions for the WTO: (1) Is it the terms-of-trade problem or the commitment problem (or both, or neither) that WTO member governments seek to solve with their WTO membership?; and (2) Is it market clearing or offshoring/bilateral bargaining that is now the most prominent mechanism for determining international prices? As I will describe, answers to these questions help to indicate whether shallow or deep integration with regard to NTMs is warranted.

Regarding the first question, the empirical evidence as surveyed by Bagwell and Staiger (2010) and most recently by Bagwell, Bown, and Staiger (2016) offers support for the terms-of-trade theory as identifying the main purpose of the GATT/WTO, though more evidence on this important question is needed. Regarding the second question, there is as yet no systematic body of evidence that would help provide an answer, but as I will argue, it seems likely that answering this second question will be a key input for identifying the best way forward on NTMs for the WTO.

The rest of the chapter proceeds as follows. Section 1.2 considers the definition of nontariff measures. Section 1.3 then describes the evolving approach to NTMs in existing trade agreements. In section 1.4, I describe what the various economic theories of trade agreements have to say about the treatment of NTMs, and along the way I provide a novel terms-of-trade interpretation of the WTO's Trade

Facilitation Agreement. Finally, section 1.5 concludes with a summary of the challenge faced by the WTO regarding the treatment of NTMs as that challenge is suggested by the material in the preceding sections.

1.2   Nontariff Measures

In this section, I consider the definition of nontariff measures and thereby frame the scope of my discussion for the remainder of the chapter. After describing in broad terms the available evidence on the landscape of nontariff measures in practice, I then turn briefly to a discussion of the quantification of trade effects associated with nontariff measures.

1.2.1   Defining Nontariff Measures

What are "nontariff measures" (NTMs)? As the term suggests, NTMs may include any policy measures other than tariffs that can impact trade flows. At a broad level, NTMs can usefully be divided into three categories.

The first category of NTMs are those imposed on imports. This category includes import quotas, import prohibitions, import licensing, and customs procedures and administration fees, as well as the nontariff features associated with various forms of administered protection (e.g., price undertakings resulting from antidumping actions). The second category of NTMs are those imposed on exports. These include export taxes, export subsidies, export quotas, export prohibitions, and voluntary export restraints. These first two categories encompass NTMs that are applied at the border, either to imports or to exports. The third and final category of NTMs are those imposed internally in the domestic economy. Such behind-the-border measures include domestic legislation covering health, technical, product, labor, and environmental standards, internal taxes or charges, and domestic subsidies.

It is difficult to obtain a comprehensive picture of the catalog of possible NTMs, but an impressive collection of studies compiled by the Organization for Economic Cooperation and Development (OECD 2005) provides a view of the range, complexity, and diversity of NTMs in practice. One study contained in this collection sets out to assess the relative importance for the post–Uruguay Round landscape of the various kinds of behind-the-border measures and NTMs (or equivalently, nontariff barriers, NTBs) imposed on imports as these measures are perceived by foreign exporters and recorded in various survey results. Summarizing the survey findings, the study reports:

The ten and seven surveys that report technical measures and customs rules and procedures, respectively, rank these barriers high. They are always among the five most reported categories of barriers. ... Where internal taxes or charges and competition-related restrictions on market access are reported, these are also often among the top five. Although less often mentioned, restrictions for services in general rank high in three out of the five surveys that report them. The relatively consistent high ranking observed for these items does not hold in the case of other NTB categories, such as government procurement practices or subsidies, although they are reported by a substantial number of the surveys. Finally, although respondents in almost half of the 12 surveys mention problems related to intellectual property protection and finance measures and a smaller number report price control measures, import charges and other para-tariff measures, these categories of barriers are not among the most reported. (OECD 2005, p. 23)

Another study in the OECD collection focuses on NTMs that are of particular importance to developing countries, including technical barriers to trade (TBTs) and sanitary and phytosanitary (SPS) measures, and paints a more complicated, dynamic, and somewhat mixed picture of the evidence in this regard:

The existing literature describes a few key findings and trends pertaining to developing countries. Most analysts observe that the utilization of certain types of NTBs affecting developing countries, such as quantitative restrictions, has decreased markedly in the post–Uruguay Round (UR) setting. ... The remaining post-Uruguay NTBs, according to frequency ratio analyses ... appear to be more prevalent in developing-country than in developed-country markets, although they have decreased over time. Michalopoulos (1999) notes that frequency ratios of quantity and price control measures tend to be higher in countries with lower levels of per capita income and lower degrees of openness. A seemingly greater prevalence of these NTBs in trade among developing countries is however difficult to demonstrate given that the literature focuses predominantly on barriers to developing-country trade in their major export markets, which are generally OECD markets. ...

    Although the literature takes a range of approaches to identifying measures of concern to developing countries, it frequently focuses on quantity control measures: nonautomatic import licensing, quotas and tariff rate quotas. These measures may also attract attention because their effects are by nature easier to quantify and analyze than most other types of NTBs. Researchers report that post-UR NTBs are far more frequent for processed goods than for primary commodities.

    Laird (1999) finds that the primary NTBs affecting developing-country access to both OECD and non-OECD markets are essentially the same, primarily import licensing systems (including allocation of tariff quotas); variable levies and production and export subsidies (in the agricultural sector); import/export quotas (in textiles and clothing sector) and local content and export balancing requirements (automotive industry); export subsidies to develop non-traditional manufacturers (administered as tax breaks or subsidized finance, as direct subsidies have almost disappeared under fiscal pressures); and state trading operations.

Another perspective comes from research that identifies the prevalence of various types of NTBs differently, according to whether developing countries trade with developed countries or among themselves. ... The literature suggests that technical regulations, price control measures and certain other measures are very often subject to concerns about access to developed-country markets. ...

A more systematic account of developing countries' perceptions of non-tariff barriers comes from the notification process established under the auspices of NAMA [nonagricultural market access negotiations]. ... TBTs represent the NTB category with the highest incidence of notifications with 530 entries, or almost half of the total, followed by Customs and Administrative Procedures (380 entries) and SPS measures (137 entries). Quantitative restrictions, trade remedies, government participation in trade, charges on imports, as well as other barriers amount to less than 5% of total NTB entries. (OECD 2005, pp. 230–234)

Finally, two of the OECD studies focus specifically on export NTMs, in the form of export duties and export restrictions. Regarding export duties, a natural question is why these duties should be defined as nontariff measures rather than as tariffs. This and related questions are addressed in one of the OECD studies in this way:

The question also arises whether export duties should be considered a tariff or a nontariff measure. In the Doha Declaration of 2001, paragraph 16 on market access for nonagricultural products states that negotiations aim to reduce, or as appropriate eliminate, tariffs as well as non-tariff barriers. In discussions on the organisation of these negotiations, the definition of the scope of non-tariff barriers to be included has been a primary concern, while for tariffs (particularly reduction of import tariffs), the coverage and issues for discussion have been well defined. Export duties are sometimes equated with tariffs (and even called export tariffs), perhaps reflecting the fact that they are normally levied by customs in a manner similar to import tariffs. For example, the EU-Mexico free trade agreement (FTA) includes "customs duties on exports" in the chapter on customs duties, rather than in the chapter on "non-tariff measures." However, the GATT and a number of regional trade agreements (RTAs) tend to consider export duties as non-tariff measures. The "Indicative List of Notifiable Measures" annexed to the Decision on Notification Procedures adopted at the conclusion of the Uruguay Round puts "export taxes" in the category of non-tariff measures. The NAFTA also puts "export taxes" in the section "Nontariff Measures." A well-known case book uses the term "export taxes" in the chapter entitled "Export Controls under the GATT and National Law" (Jackson et al. 1995).

A further question is the relationship between export duties and fees and formalities. Export duties are explicitly excluded from the application of Article VIII(a) of the GATT 1994, which deals with fees and formalities and prohibits fees and other charges rendered in connection with exportation (or importation) that exceed the costs of the service rendered. The article stipulates that fees and other charges shall not represent an indirect protection to domestic products or a taxation of imports or exports for fiscal purposes. It applies to all fees and formalities of whatever character, but it explicitly states that "export duty" is excluded from the scope of application. Therefore, a distinction should be drawn between export duties and fees or charges, even though in specific cases the substance of the measures may be similar. (OECD 2005, p. 179).

In short, we may think of NTMs as all the measures that governments might take, other than import tariffs, that can impact trade flows. And as the passages just quoted make clear, NTMs comprise an extremely diverse set of policy measures, which individually can be as different from each other as they are collectively different from import tariffs.

This raises an important question: Why should measures impacting nontariff trade be separated conceptually from import tariffs and lumped together as NTMs? For example, for the purpose of discussing measures impacting trade, why not adopt an alternative categorization strategy, in which all measures impacting trade are divided into tax and nontax measures or in which they are categorized in terms of border and nonborder measures? In some sense, these alternative ways of categorizing measures impacting trade would reflect a more natural and obvious intellectual coherence.

But in the context of the institutional features of the GATT/WTO, NTMs *are* usefully separated from import tariffs, because while both tariff and nontariff measures may impact trade, import tariffs stand out as the central policy measure with which negotiated market access commitments are made—through negotiated tariff "bindings"—and in this way tariffs have a special place relative to all nontariff measures in the GATT/WTO. A fundamental question is whether the GATT/WTO's asymmetric treatment of tariff versus nontariff measures is warranted on economic grounds. As we will see, the answer to this question is complex, offering strong support for the GATT/WTO treatment of some NTMs but less support for others, and importantly, as I will describe, the answer itself depends in part on the nature of trade, so it may evolve as the nature of trade evolves.

1.2.2   Quantifying the Impact of NTMs on Trade

In light of the diversity of NTMs described, it should come as no surprise that quantifying the impact of NTMs on trade is a challenging exercise. For example, as the Executive Summary of the 2005 OECD study described observes:

Not only do these measures take often non-transparent forms, analysis also has to take into account whether and how they are linked to non-trade policy objectives. Some NTBs serve important regulatory purposes and are legitimate under WTO rules under clearly defined conditions even though they restrict trade. For example, import licences may be used to control the importation of products carrying potential health risks. Countries may ban imports of farm products for food safety reasons or impose labelling requirements in response to consumer demands for information. The issue here is whether governments, in pursuing legitimate goals, are restricting imports more than is necessary to achieve those goals. Under multilateral rules, the objective is not to remove these measures but to ensure that they are set at an appropriate level to achieve legitimate objectives with minimum impact on trade. However, because legitimacy claims are typically associated with the introduction of these measures, they are hard to assess.
   All this makes the issues that arise in connection with determining the economic impact of NTBs very different from those surrounding the use of tariffs. As far as trade and the economic impact of NTBs are concerned, much depends on the specific circumstances of their application. To understand the effect of a specific measure requires a case-by-case examination. (OECD 2005, p. 13)

The validity of these concerns notwithstanding, various attempts using different methodologies and data have been undertaken to estimate the impact of NTMs on imports, including frequency/coverage measures, price comparison measures, and quantity impact measures, as well as residuals of gravity-type equations (see Deardorff and Stern 1997 for a review). The most ambitious attempt to date, in terms of both theoretical grounding and country/tariff line coverage, is contained in Kee, Nicita, and Olarreaga (2009), who seek a consistent measure of the trade restrictiveness of NTMs that can be compared to tariffs.[1] They motivate their approach as follows:

Trade policy can take many different forms: tariffs, quotas, non-automatic licensing, antidumping duties, technical regulations, monopolistic measures, subsidies, etc. How can one summarize in a single measure the trade restrictiveness of a 10% tariff, a 1000-ton quota, a complex non-automatic licensing procedure and a $1 million subsidy? Often the literature relies on outcome measures, e.g., import shares. The rationale is that import shares summarise the impact of all these trade policy instruments. The problem is that they also measure differences in tastes, macroeconomic shocks and other factors which should not be attributed to trade policy. Another approach that is often followed is to simply rely on tariff data or collected customs duties and assume that all other instruments are positively (and perfectly) correlated with tariffs. These are obviously unsatisfactory solutions. A more adequate approach ... is to bring all types of trade policy instruments into a common metric. (Kee, Nicita, and Olarreaga 2009, p. 173)

The approach taken by Kee, Nicita, and Olarreaga is to estimate ad valorem equivalents of NTMs for each country at the tariff line level that can then be compared directly to (ad valorem) tariffs.

Despite all these difficulties in measurement, most estimates of the trade impacts of NTMs suggest that they can be substantial. For example, Kee, Nicita, and Olarreaga (2009) find that for a majority of tariff lines the ad valorem equivalent of the NTMs in their sample of 78 countries is higher than the actual tariff. The mechanism by which NTMs impact trade can be subtle. For instance, Staiger and Wolak (1994) find that the mere filing of US antidumping claims can significantly reduce trade flows during the period of investigation of these claims, even though no antidumping duties are in place over the period of investigation and even if the investigation ends in a finding of no dumping and no duties are ever imposed.

1.3 The Evolving Approach to NTMs in Trade Agreements

In this section, I briefly describe the evolving approach to NTMs taken first by the GATT and then by the WTO. I also briefly describe the approaches to NTMs taken increasingly by countries when they create preferential trade agreements. In each case, I first consider border (import and export) NTMs and then turn to behind-the-border NTMs.

1.3.1 The GATT Approach
The GATT took a minimalist approach to NTMs in general. I begin by briefly describing the GATT's approach to NTMs applied at the border and then describe in broad terms the GATT approach to behind-the-border NTMs.

1.3.1.1 Border NTMs
The GATT approach to border NTMs differs on the import side and the export side. The approach can be loosely characterized as follows.

First, on the import side, the GATT was designed to serve as a negotiating forum in which reciprocal, voluntary, and nondiscriminatory

(MFN) tariff bargaining among member governments would lead to tariff bindings that defined maximum allowable tariff levels. Of course, tariff bindings in themselves are not likely to be valued by governments, but it was anticipated that these bindings would imply meaningful increases in market access and trade volumes for foreign exporters, and for this reason they would be valued by the participating governments.

However, as Hudec (1990) describes, the drafters of the GATT were acutely aware that policies other than tariffs could easily substitute for tariffs and might become tempting in this role once a country bound its tariffs as a result of a negotiation. The drafters also understood that if left unchecked these NTMs could undermine the market access value of a negotiated tariff binding and hence the foundation of the negotiating framework they sought to create. For this reason, while member governments did not negotiate directly over the level of NTMs in the GATT as they did over tariffs, the GATT contains numerous provisions, such as Articles V (freedom of transit), VIII (fees and formalities connected with importation and exportation), X (publication and administration of trade regulations), and XI (general elimination of quantitative restrictions), that are designed to induce "tariffication" of import-protective border measures and prevent the substitution of alternative forms of import protection for tariffs. This is the essence of the GATT's approach to border NTMs on the import side.

On the export side, the GATT was far more permissive (although the GATT rules on fees and formalities and prohibition on quantitative restrictions apply to both imports and exports), in part because it was not anticipated that GATT member governments would actively engage in negotiations over export-sector liberalization commitments (say, on export taxes or export subsidies), so the issues regarding NTMs that arise on the import side as described earlier do not arise symmetrically on the export side. In addition, at least with regard to developed countries (which were the major actors in GATT-sponsored negotiated liberalization), export taxes were used less often than import tariffs, so they may have been seen as a less pressing issue for the world trading system at the time of the GATT's creation.[2] With regard to the particular issue of export subsidies, early GATT disciplines were very permissive, though they have tightened over time. For example, originally the GATT contained only a loose reporting requirement regarding export subsidies (and granted affected importing countries the authority to impose countervailing duties).

1.3.1.2 Behind-the-border NTMs The GATT approach to dealing with behind-the-border NTMs can also be described as a minimalist or "shallow-integration" approach. The essence of this approach follows the logic described for the GATT's approach to border NTMs on the import side, though the tactics differ. In particular, as observed, the drafters of the GATT were well aware that policies other than tariffs could easily substitute for tariffs and might become attractive if a country bound its tariffs as a result of a negotiation, but in the case of behind-the-border NTMs, issues of national sovereignty precluded the kind of approach to this issue that was taken with border NTMs (e.g., the prohibition on quantitative restrictions). Hudec (1990) describes this problem as it was perceived by the drafters of the GATT:

The standard trade policy rules could deal with the common types of trade policy measure governments usually employ to control trade. But trade can also be affected by other "domestic" measures, such as product safety standards, having nothing to do with trade policy. It would have been next to impossible to catalogue all such possibilities in advance. Moreover, governments would never have agreed to circumscribe their freedom in all these other areas for the sake of a mere trade agreement. (Hudec 1990, p. 24)

To address this problem, the GATT essentially took a two-pronged approach to behind-the-border NTMs. First, it requires that all domestic taxes, charges, and regulations satisfy a basic nondiscrimination rule (national treatment). This rule in principle prevents the simplest and most direct method of substituting behind-the-border NTMs for tariffs—discriminating in taxes and/or regulations against imported products.

But it was also recognized by the drafters of the GATT that even nondiscriminatory domestic taxes and regulations could be a partial substitute for tariffs, and it was therefore thought that something more unusual might be needed to guard against the substitution of behind-the-border NTMs for import tariffs. Hudec (1990) continues in this regard:

The shortcomings of the standard legal commitments were recognized in a report by a group of trade experts at the London Monetary and Economic Conference of 1933. The group concluded that trade agreements should have another more general provision which would address itself to any other government action that produced an adverse effect on the balance of commercial opportunity. (Hudec 1990, p. 24)

As Hudec explains, these additional concerns eventually led to the inclusion of a second line of defense against the substitution of behind-the-border NTMs for import tariffs, which is contained in the "nonviolation" nullification-or-impairment provision of the GATT. According to the nonviolation clause, a GATT member is entitled to compensation from another GATT member if the two countries had originally negotiated an exchange of tariff bindings, and if one of the countries subsequently introduces a new measure—any new measure, even one on which no GATT commitments exist—that erodes the market access value of its original tariff binding and that the other country could not reasonably have anticipated at the time of their original market access negotiation.

Hence, as with border NTMs, member governments did not negotiate directly over behind-the-border NTMs in the GATT. But there are several provisions that are meant to protect the value of negotiated market access agreements against erosion by behind-the-border NTMs. This is the essence of the GATT's approach to behind-the-border NTMs.

1.3.2 The WTO Approach
The approach to NTMs has evolved from the GATT to the WTO. As described, the GATT's approach to NTMs was minimalist, although, as mentioned, in the later GATT years some of the obligations regarding NTMs (e.g., export subsidies) became more stringent. With the creation of the WTO, this trend was continued and extended in a number of important ways.

1.3.2.1 Border NTMs
The WTO approach to border NTMs represents a significant tightening of obligations relative to the GATT in a number of dimensions. For example, the WTO Safeguard Agreement prohibits the use of various forms of border NTMs administered on the export side, such as Orderly Marketing Arrangements (OMAs) and Voluntary Export Restraints (VERs), that were considered "grey-area" measures under the GATT and had become popular in the last decade of the GATT before the creation of the WTO. The WTO Subsidies and Countervailing Measures (SCM) Agreement significantly strengthened the prohibition against export subsidies. And most recently in the context of the Doha Round, the conclusion of the negotiations of the Trade Facilitation Agreement (TFA) at the Bali Ministerial Conference marks a similar tightening and clarification of the rules related to border NTMs contained in GATT Articles V, VIII, and X.

1.3.2.2 Behind-the-border NTMs   The WTO approach to behind-the-border NTMs also represents a significant tightening of obligations relative to the GATT in a number of dimensions. For example, the WTO Technical Barriers to Trade (TBT) and Sanitary and Phytosanitary (SPS) Measures agreements represent a significant strengthening of the nondiscrimination and national treatment obligations regarding certain kinds of domestic regulations.[3] In addition, the WTO SCM Agreement contains substantial commitments regarding domestic subsidies that were not included in the GATT. In essence, while the overall approach of the WTO with respect to behind-the-border NTMs can still be characterized as one of shallow integration, there has been some evolution over the history of the GATT/WTO in the direction of "deep integration."

1.3.3   The PTA Approach

I close this section by simply noting that many recent preferential trade agreements (PTAs) include commitments on behind-the-border NTMs that are substantially more stringent than those contained in the GATT or the WTO. In particular, a growing number of PTAs go significantly beyond eliminating tariffs on a preferential basis and focus instead on negotiating specific commitments on behind-the-border NTMs. A recent and comprehensive documentation of this development, including a discussion of the circumstances under which countries seem to prefer this kind of deep integration from their negotiated agreements rather than the shallow integration that characterizes traditional GATT market access agreements, is provided in WTO (2011), while Bagwell, Bown, and Staiger (2016) survey the relevant economics literature. I will return to the issue of deep versus shallow integration in later sections.

1.4   The Economics of the Approach to NTMs in Trade Agreements

In this section, I review the two major established economic theories of trade agreements, the terms-of-trade theory and the commitment theory, and consider what each theory has to say about the treatment of border NTMs and the treatment of behind-the-border NTMs in trade agreements. Motivated by the recent rise in "offshoring" of specialized inputs, I then consider a world in which international prices are determined by bilateral bargaining between buyers and sellers, and I show that a key result from the terms-of-trade theory with regard to the treatment of behind-the-border NTMs is reversed. I use these contrasting findings to interpret the implications of the rise in offshoring for the treatment of NTMs in trade agreements.

1.4.1 The Terms-of-Trade Theory

According to the terms-of-trade theory of trade agreements, governments are attracted to trade agreements as a means of escape from a terms-of-trade driven Prisoners' Dilemma (see Bagwell and Staiger 1999, 2002). The "problem" that arises in the absence of an agreement, and that a trade agreement can then "fix," can be easily understood in intuitive terms as follows.

Suppose a government is unconstrained by a trade agreement and unilaterally chooses the level of a tariff it will impose. This government will naturally consider the various costs and benefits of a slightly higher or lower tariff when coming to its decision on the preferred level of import protection, but there is one cost that the government will inevitably leave out of its calculation: the cost of its import protection that is borne by foreign exporters. And, in ignoring this cost, the unilateral trade policy choices of the government will then be too protective relative to internationally efficient choices. According to the terms-of-trade theory of trade agreements, the purpose of a trade agreement is to give foreign exporters a "voice" in the tariff choices of their trading partners, so that through negotiations they can make their trading partners responsive to this cost. In accomplishing this, a trade agreement then naturally leads to lower tariffs and an expansion of market access and trade volumes.

1.4.1.1 Border NTMs The description of the basic prediction of the terms-of-trade theory that I have provided is focused on tariffs as the instrument of protection. What does the terms-of-trade theory say about border NTMs? Regarding border NTMs on the export side, and in particular export subsidies, there is some tension between the terms-of-trade theory and the negotiated restrictions on export subsidies that are observed, especially as those commitments are structured in the WTO, in effect because negotiated restrictions on export subsidies would tend to reduce trade volumes and therefore work against the basic goal of trade agreements according to the terms-of-trade theory (see Bagwell and Staiger 2001b, 2012a).[4] However, regarding border NTMs on the import side, the observed treatment in the GATT and the WTO resonates strongly with the terms-of-trade theory. In particular, the logic of tariffication as emphasized by the GATT and described here finds support in the terms-of-trade theory. For example, the prohibition of quantitative measures contained in GATT Article XI facilitates the implementation of nondiscriminatory (MFN) import protection, which the terms-of-trade theory supports (see Bagwell and Staiger 1999), and the evolving GATT/WTO approach to issues of "trade facilitation" in relation to GATT Articles V, VIII, and X can also be usefully interpreted from the perspective of the terms-of-trade theory.

This last point is not well appreciated in the literature. Therefore, I sketch a simple model to illustrate the rationale for the TFA from the perspective of the terms-of-trade theory. I emphasize three related points. First, the terms-of-trade theory provides a simple framework for interpreting the purpose of an agreement on trade facilitation. Second, the terms-of-trade theory indicates that the inefficiencies associated with unilateral investments in trade facilitation arise only once tariffs are constrained through international agreement. And third, in principle these inefficiencies can be addressed by either shallow or deep integration approaches.[5]

A model of trade facilitation   At the broadest level, the issue of trade facilitation encompasses any measure that impacts the cost of international trade, including both border measures and behind-the-border measures. In the context of the WTO TFA, however, the focus on trade facilitation is decidedly narrow, restricted to improving administrative procedures at the border. I capture this focus by considering a simple partial equilibrium setting, in which a home country imports a competitively produced good from the foreign country, and I let I and I^* denote respectively home and foreign investments in border management processes (e.g., IT) that determine the efficiency of import and export transactions. In particular, I assume that the per-unit (specific) trade cost for exports from foreign to home, t, can be represented by the function $t(I, I^*)$, where $t(0,0)$ is nonprohibitive and with $t(I, I^*)$ decreasing and convex in both its arguments and nonnegative for all I and I^*.

With the (specific) import tariff set by the home government denoted by τ, and the (specific) export tax set by the foreign government denoted by τ^*, the arbitrage relationship between the home-country price of this good (P) and the foreign-country price of the good (P^*) that must hold as long as strictly positive trade occurs is given by

$$P = P^* + t(I, I^*) + \tau + \tau^*. \tag{1.1}$$

I then define the *foreign world price* by

$$P^{w*} \equiv P^* + \tau^*,$$

and I define the *home world price* by

$$P^w \equiv P - \tau.$$

The foreign and home world prices P^{w*} and P^w are measures of the foreign-country and home-country terms of trade—the foreign terms of trade improve when P^{w*} rises, and the home terms of trade improve when P^w falls—and through (1.1) they are related by

$$P^w - P^{w*} = t(I, I^*).$$

A drop in transport costs t brings P^w and P^{w*} closer together, and when $t = 0$ the home and foreign world prices are equated.

To complete the model, I denote by $D(P)$ and $D^*(P^*)$ respectively the home and foreign demands for the product under consideration, and I assume that each demand function is a decreasing function. For simplicity, I assume that the product is supplied only by the foreign country, and I denote the foreign supply function by $S^*(P^*)$, which I assume is an increasing function. Using the pricing relationship (1.1) and denoting foreign export supply by $E^*(P^*) \equiv S^*(P^*) - D^*(P^*)$ and home import demand by $M(P) \equiv D(P)$, the market-clearing condition may be written as

$$M(P^* + t(I, I^*) + \tau + \tau^*) = E^*(P^*),$$

yielding the market-clearing foreign price $\hat{P}^*(t(I, I^*) + \tau + \tau^*)$, from which the market-clearing home price and foreign and home world prices also follow:

$$\hat{P}(t(I, I^*) + \tau + \tau^*) \equiv \hat{P}^*(t(I, I^*) + \tau + \tau^*) + t(I, I^*) + \tau + \tau^*,$$

$$\hat{P}^{w*}(t(I, I^*) + \tau, \tau^*) \equiv \hat{P}^*(t(I, I^*) + \tau + \tau^*) + \tau^*,$$

$$\hat{P}^w(t(I, I^*) + \tau^*, \tau) \equiv \hat{P}(t(I, I^*) + \tau + \tau^*) - \tau.$$

As is standard, the world prices depend on the levels of both τ and τ^*, but the home and foreign prices depend only on the sum $\tau + \tau^*$ (and on the trade facilitation investment levels I and I^*).

With the market-clearing price expressions just given, the terms-of-trade impacts of policy choices can now be assessed. Regarding the terms-of-trade impacts of trade taxes, direct calculations yield (with a prime denoting the derivative of the function with respect to its argument)

$$\frac{\partial \hat{p}^w}{\partial \tau} = \frac{\partial \hat{p}^{w*}}{\partial \tau} = \frac{M'}{E^{*\prime} - M'} < 0,$$

$$\frac{\partial \hat{p}^{w*}}{\partial \tau^*} = \frac{\partial \hat{p}^w}{\partial \tau^*} = \frac{E^{*\prime}}{E^{*\prime} - M'} > 0.$$

As expected, an increase in the home-country tariff improves the home terms of trade and worsens the foreign terms of trade, while an increase in the foreign-country tariff has the opposite impact, improving the foreign terms of trade and worsening the home terms of trade. These familiar terms-of-trade effects of tariff intervention provide the basis for the inefficient Prisoners' Dilemma situation that according to the terms-of-trade theory arises in the absence of a trade agreement.

The terms-of-trade impacts of investments in trade facilitation are more novel. For home-country investments in trade facilitation, these impacts are given by

$$\frac{\partial \hat{p}^w}{\partial t} \frac{\partial t}{\partial I} = \frac{E^{*\prime}}{E^{*\prime} - M'} \cdot \frac{\partial t}{\partial I} < 0,$$

$$\frac{\partial \hat{p}^{w*}}{\partial t} \frac{\partial t}{\partial I} = \frac{M'}{E^{*\prime} - M'} \cdot \frac{\partial t}{\partial I} > 0,$$

(1.2)

while for foreign-country investments in trade facilitation, these impacts are given by

$$\frac{\partial \hat{p}^{w*}}{\partial t} \frac{\partial t}{\partial I^*} = \frac{M'}{E^{*\prime} - M'} \cdot \frac{\partial t}{\partial I^*} > 0,$$

$$\frac{\partial \hat{p}^w}{\partial t} \frac{\partial t}{\partial I^*} = \frac{E^{*\prime}}{E^{*\prime} - M'} \cdot \frac{\partial t}{\partial I^*} < 0.$$

(1.3)

Evidently, home-country investments in trade facilitation improve the home-country terms of trade *while at the same time improving the terms of trade of the foreign country*, and similarly for foreign-country investments in trade facilitation. Such a "win-win" prospect for investments in trade facilitation makes it tempting to conjecture that the terms-of-trade theory cannot explain why countries would need an international agreement to encourage such investments.[6] As I will demonstrate, however, this conjecture turns out to be false. Intuitively, the key is to note from the derivative expressions in (1.2) and (1.3) that each country's investment in trade facilitation imparts a positive terms-of-trade externality on the other country, providing a possible reason for under-investment in trade facilitation when countries are guided only by their unilateral interests (i.e., in the absence of an international agreement that covers trade facilitation).

I now define the welfare functions for the home- and foreign-country policymakers. I abstract from political economy motives, though the results I report are easily generalized to include such motives. With no home-country production, home welfare is then given by the sum of consumer surplus plus tariff revenue minus the cost of home investment in trade facilitation. Letting c denote the unit cost of investment in trade facilitation for the home country, with the total cost of home-country investment in trade facilitation then given by $c \cdot I$, and with CS denoting the home-country consumer surplus and using $\tau = P - P^w$, home welfare is given by

$$
\begin{aligned}
W = {} & CS(\hat{P}(t(I,I^*)+\tau+\tau^*)) \\
& + [\hat{P}(t(I,I^*)+\tau+\tau^*) - \hat{P}^w(t(I,I^*)+\tau^*,\tau)] \\
& \cdot M(\hat{P}(t(I,I^*)+\tau+\tau^*)) - c \cdot I \\
\equiv {} & W(I, \hat{P}(t(I,I^*)+\tau+\tau^*), \hat{P}^w(t(I,I^*)+\tau^*,\tau)).
\end{aligned}
$$

Taking account of production in the foreign country and with PS^* denoting the foreign producer surplus and c^* denoting the unit cost of investment in trade facilitation for the foreign country, foreign welfare is similarly defined as the sum of consumer and producer surpluses plus export tax revenue minus the cost of foreign investment in trade facilitation, or

$$
\begin{aligned}
W^* = {} & CS^*(\hat{P}^*(t(I,I^*)+\tau+\tau^*)) + PS^*(\hat{P}^*(t(I,I^*)+\tau+\tau^*)) \\
& + [\hat{P}^{w*}(t(I,I^*)+\tau,\tau^*) - \hat{P}^*(t(I,I^*)+\tau+\tau^*)] \\
& \cdot E^*(\hat{P}^*(t(I,I^*)+\tau+\tau^*)) - c^* \cdot I^* \\
\equiv {} & W^*(I^*, \hat{P}^*(t(I,I^*)+\tau+\tau^*), \hat{P}^{w*}(t(I,I^*)+\tau,\tau^*)).
\end{aligned}
$$

Finally, the sum of home and foreign welfare, which I refer to as "world welfare" and denote by W^w, is given by

$$
\begin{aligned}
W^w = {} & CS(\hat{P}(t(I,I^*)+\tau+\tau^*)) + CS^*(\hat{P}^*(t(I,I^*)+\tau+\tau^*)) \\
& + PS^*(\hat{P}^*(t(I,I^*)+\tau+\tau^*)) + [\hat{P}(t(I,I^*)+\tau+\tau^*) \\
& - \hat{P}^*(t(I,I^*)+\tau+\tau^*) - t(I,I^*)] \cdot E^*(\hat{P}^*(t(I,I^*)+\tau+\tau^*)) \\
& - c \cdot I - c^* \cdot I^* \\
\equiv {} & W^w(I, I^*, \hat{P}(t(I,I^*)+\tau+\tau^*), \hat{P}^*(t(I,I^*)+\tau+\tau^*)).
\end{aligned}
$$

Notice that while home welfare and foreign welfare each depend on their respective world prices and hence on the levels of both τ and τ^*, world welfare is independent of world prices—because movements in these prices only serve to redistribute surplus between the home country and foreign country—and hence world welfare depends only on the sum of home and foreign tariffs $\tau + \tau^*$ (in addition to trade facilitation investment levels I and I^*).

Efficient policies   I define efficient policies as those that maximize world welfare (and thereby I implicitly assume that lump sum transfers are available to distribute surpluses across the two countries as desired). As just noted, world welfare depends on the sum of the home and foreign tariffs, $\tau + \tau^*$, and on home and foreign investment levels in trade facilitation, I and I^*. The first-order conditions that define the sum of efficient tariffs, $\partial W^w / \partial [\tau + \tau^*] = 0$, can be simplified to yield[7]

$$[\tau + \tau^*] \cdot \frac{\partial E^*}{\partial P^*} \frac{\partial \hat{P}^*}{\partial [\tau + \tau^*]} = 0,$$

which immediately implies

$$\tau^e + \tau^{*e} = 0, \tag{1.4}$$

where a superscript e denotes efficient policies. Hence, as should come as no surprise in this perfectly competitive setting, there is no efficiency role for tariff intervention, and this is true independent of the setting of investment levels for trade facilitation (and hence independent of trade costs t).

Next consider the efficient levels of home and foreign investment in trade facilitation, denoted by I^e and I^{*e}, respectively. The first-order condition that defines I^e can be manipulated to yield

$$\left\{ [\tau + \tau^*] \cdot \frac{\partial E^*}{\partial P^*} \frac{\partial \hat{P}^*}{\partial [\tau + \tau^*]} - E^* \right\} \frac{\partial t}{\partial I} = c,$$

which, evaluated at the efficient tariffs $\tau^e + \tau^{*e}$, simplifies to

$$M^e \cdot \left[-\frac{\partial t}{\partial I} \right] = c, \tag{1.5}$$

where M^e denotes the home import volume evaluated under efficient policies. In words, the efficient level of home investment in trade facilitation I^e equates the marginal benefit of the last unit of this investment undertaken by the home country (the marginal savings in total trade costs $M^e \cdot [-\frac{\partial t}{\partial I}]$) with the marginal cost to the home country of the last unit of this investment (c). The efficient level of foreign investment in trade facilitation, I^{*e}, is similarly characterized as

$$E^{*e} \cdot \left[-\frac{\partial t}{\partial I^*}\right] = c^* \tag{1.6}$$

with E^{*e} denoting the foreign export volume evaluated under efficient policies.

Nash policies Next consider the Nash policies adopted by the two countries in the absence of a trade agreement. The first-order conditions for the home country that define its best-response levels of τ and I are given by

$$\frac{\partial W}{\partial \tau} = -M(\hat{P})\frac{\partial \hat{P}}{\partial \tau} + \tau \frac{\partial E^*}{\partial P^*}\frac{\partial \hat{P}^*}{\partial \tau} + M(\hat{P}) = 0,$$

$$\frac{\partial W}{\partial I} = \left[-M(\hat{P})\frac{\partial \hat{P}}{\partial t} + \tau \frac{\partial E^*}{\partial P^*}\frac{\partial \hat{P}^*}{\partial t}\right]\frac{\partial t}{\partial I} - c = 0. \tag{1.7}$$

Similarly, the first-order conditions for the foreign country that define its best-response levels of τ^* and I^* are given by

$$\frac{\partial W^*}{\partial \tau^*} = -E^*(\hat{P}^*)\frac{\partial \hat{P}^*}{\partial \tau^*} + \tau^* \frac{\partial M}{\partial P}\frac{\partial \hat{P}}{\partial \tau^*} + E^*(\hat{P}^*) = 0,$$

$$\frac{\partial W^*}{\partial I^*} = \left[-E^*(\hat{P}^*)\frac{\partial \hat{P}^*}{\partial t^*} + \tau^* \frac{\partial M}{\partial P}\frac{\partial \hat{P}}{\partial t^*}\right]\frac{\partial t^*}{\partial I^*} - c^* = 0. \tag{1.8}$$

The Nash policies, which I denote by τ^N, I^N, τ^{*N}, and I^{*N}, satisfy the four first-order conditions in (1.7) and (1.8) simultaneously.

Now notice from the preceding pricing relationships that $\frac{\partial \hat{P}}{\partial \tau} = \frac{\partial \hat{P}}{\partial t}$ and $\frac{\partial \hat{P}^*}{\partial \tau} = \frac{\partial \hat{P}^*}{\partial t}$ and that $\frac{\partial \hat{P}^*}{\partial \tau^*} = \frac{\partial \hat{P}^*}{\partial t^*}$ and $\frac{\partial \hat{P}}{\partial \tau^*} = \frac{\partial \hat{P}}{\partial t^*}$. Using this, substituting the first first-order condition in (1.7) into the last first-order condition in (1.7), further simplifying the first condition in (1.7), and performing the analogous steps for the first-order conditions in (1.8), it follows that the Nash tariffs are characterized by

$$\tau^N = \frac{\hat{P}^{w*N}}{\eta^{E*N}} \quad \text{and} \quad \tau^{*N} = \frac{\hat{P}^{wN}}{\eta^{MN}}, \tag{1.9}$$

while the Nash investment levels satisfy

$$M^N \cdot \left[-\frac{\partial t}{\partial I}\right] = c \quad \text{and} \quad E^{*N} \cdot \left[-\frac{\partial t}{\partial I^*}\right] = c^*, \tag{1.10}$$

with η^{E*N} the elasticity of foreign export supply evaluated under Nash policies and η^{MN} the elasticity of home import demand (defined positively) evaluated under Nash policies, and where $\hat{p}^{w*N}$, $\hat{p}^{wN}$, M^N, and E^{*N} denote their respective previously defined magnitudes evaluated under Nash policies. The Nash tariffs in (1.9) represent the usual inverse trade-elasticity formulas for the Johnson (1953–1954) optimal tariff, and the Nash investments in trade facilitation described by (1.10) equate the marginal benefit of investment with its marginal cost, just as described previously in the context of efficient policy choices.

A trade facilitation agreement With the Nash and efficient policies characterized, I now offer an interpretation of the evolving GATT/ WTO approach to issues of trade facilitation from the perspective of the terms-of-trade theory. An initial pair of observations come directly from a comparison of the conditions for Nash and efficient policies. First, as (1.4) and (1.9) make clear, Nash tariffs are too high relative to efficient tariffs: $\tau^N + \tau^{*N} = \frac{\hat{p}^{w*N}}{\eta^{E*N}} + \frac{\hat{p}^{wN}}{\eta^{MN}} > 0 = \tau^e + \tau^{*e}$. And second, as (1.5), (1.6), and (1.10) make clear, conditional on the Nash trade volume, the Nash investments in trade facilitation are *efficient* (i.e., they equate the marginal savings in total trade costs with the marginal cost of investment).

These initial observations reflect a hallmark prediction of the terms-of-trade theory of trade agreements that I will emphasize again in later sections: as the import tariff or export tax is the best policy for manipulating the terms of trade, and as terms-of-trade manipulation is the only problem for a trade agreement to fix, import tariffs and export taxes will be the only policies that are distorted in the Nash equilibrium, with all other policies set at their efficient levels conditional on (inefficiently low) Nash trade volumes. Hence, the job of a trade agreement is to liberalize tariffs and thereby expand trade volumes to efficient levels, without introducing inefficiencies in the other policy choices—once tariffs are constrained by the agreement—as a second-best means of terms-of-trade manipulation.

To interpret an agreement on trade facilitation through the lens of the terms-of-trade theory, it is then necessary to consider the incentive each country would have to distort its investment in trade facilitation unilaterally as a second-best means of terms-of-trade manipulation once its tariffs are bound below their best-response levels in a trade agreement and are therefore no longer set to optimally manipulate the terms of trade from a unilateral perspective. To this end, suppose countries begin from an efficient set of policies ($\bar{\tau}$, $\bar{\tau}^*$, $\bar{I}$, and $\bar{I}^*$) such that $\bar{\tau} + \bar{\tau}^* = \tau^e + \tau^{*e}$, $\bar{I} = I^e$, and, $\bar{I}^* = I^{*e}$ and both countries are positioned below their best-response tariffs.[8] From this starting point, if it can be shown that $\frac{\partial W}{\partial I} < 0$ and $\frac{\partial W^*}{\partial I^*} < 0$, so that the home and foreign countries would each have a unilateral incentive to back away from efficient levels of investment on trade facilitation, then it may be concluded that if left unconstrained in this dimension the home and foreign countries would underinvest in trade facilitation relative to the efficient level, indicating that some form of international cooperation on trade facilitation would be needed to bring investments in trade facilitation up to their efficient levels.

Beginning from the efficient policies outlined, we have

$$\frac{\partial W}{\partial I} = \left[-M^e \frac{\partial \hat{P}}{\partial t} + \bar{\tau} \frac{\partial E^*}{\partial P^*} \frac{\partial \hat{P}^*}{\partial t} \right] \frac{\partial t}{\partial I} - c, \tag{1.11}$$

where all magnitudes in (1.11) are evaluated under these efficient policies. But it follows from the first condition in (1.7) that

$$\frac{\partial W}{\partial \tau} = -M^e \frac{\partial \hat{P}}{\partial \tau} + \bar{\tau} \frac{\partial E^*}{\partial P^*} \frac{\partial \hat{P}^*}{\partial \tau} + M^e > 0 \tag{1.12}$$

when all magnitudes in (1.12) are evaluated under these efficient policies. Manipulating (1.12) and substituting into (1.11) then implies

$$\frac{\partial W}{\partial I} = \left[-M^e \frac{\partial \hat{P}}{\partial t} + \bar{\tau} \frac{\partial E^*}{\partial P^*} \frac{\partial \hat{P}^*}{\partial t} \right] \frac{\partial t}{\partial I} - c < M^e \cdot \left[-\frac{\partial t}{\partial I} \right] - c = 0, \tag{1.13}$$

where the last equality follows from (1.5) which implies that $\left[-\frac{\partial t}{\partial I} \right] = \frac{c}{M^e}$ when evaluated under efficient policies. Using the first condition in (1.8), analogous steps lead to

$$\frac{\partial W^*}{\partial I^*} = \left[-E^*(\hat{P}^*) \frac{\partial \hat{P}^*}{\partial t^*} + \tau^* \frac{\partial M}{\partial P} \frac{\partial \hat{P}}{\partial t^*} \right] \frac{\partial t^*}{\partial I^*} - c^* < E^{*e} \cdot \left[-\frac{\partial t}{\partial I^*} \right] - c^* = 0, \tag{1.14}$$

where the last equality follows from (1.6) which implies that $[-\frac{\partial t}{\partial I^*}] = \frac{c^*}{E^{*e}}$ when evaluated under efficient policies.

Hence, according to (1.13) and (1.14), beginning from a position on the efficiency frontier as described and if left unconstrained in their investment decisions, the home and foreign countries would choose to underinvest in trade facilitation relative to the efficient level. This implies that, according to the terms-of-trade theory of trade agreements, some form of international cooperation on trade facilitation would be needed to bring investments in trade facilitation up to their efficient levels.

Finally, while I will develop closely related points further in the context of later sections, it is worth observing here that the terms-of-trade theory points to two interesting and potentially viable forms of international cooperation on trade facilitation: (1) a "shallow" form of cooperation, in which integration is accomplished with negotiated tariff bindings combined with "tariffication" rules to prevent the erosion of implied market access commitments through the use of border NTMs, reminiscent of the GATT's reliance on negotiated tariff bindings plus associated rules such as GATT Articles V, VIII, X, and XI as described earlier; and (2) a "deeper" form of cooperation, in which integration is accomplished with direct negotiations over tariff bindings *and* specific border NTMs. The first approach places minimal restrictions on border NTMs and hence raises fewer issues of national sovereignty than the second, but in placing constraints on specific border NTMs directly, the second approach may be more straightforward to implement.[9] An interpretation of the WTO's TFA according to the terms-of-trade theory is that the TFA represents an evolution of approaches on border NTMs in the GATT/WTO from shallow to deeper forms of integration over border measures.[10] As with the terms-of-trade theory more generally, an interesting implication of this interpretation is that TFA commitments should reflect the presence of market power, with truly small countries essentially left unconstrained to make unilateral investment decisions regarding trade facilitation.[11]

1.4.1.2 Behind-the-border NTMs Some of the terms-of-trade theory's most interesting and provocative predictions regarding the treatment of NTMs are associated with behind-the-border NTMs. To illustrate the implications of the terms-of-trade theory for the treatment of behind-the-border NTMs in trade agreements, I now present a variant of the basic model of Staiger and Sykes (2011) and confirm the findings of that paper (which in turn confirms the original findings of Bagwell and Staiger 2001a and extends those findings to a setting with product standards), that in the noncooperative Nash equilibrium from which countries would begin in the absence of a trade agreement, tariffs are set inefficiently high but behind-the-border NTMs are set at efficient levels. After establishing these findings, I then offer an interpretation of their implications for the treatment of behind-the-border NTMs in trade agreements.

The basic model Following Staiger and Sykes (2011), I consider a simple partial equilibrium two-country model of trade between a domestic country and a foreign country. Throughout, I denote foreign-country variables with a "$*$". For simplicity, I assume that the good under consideration is produced in both countries but only demanded in the domestic country, where its demand can be represented by the demand curve $D(P)$, with P the consumer price of the good in the domestic market. I assume that D is decreasing in P, with "choke price" α (possibly infinite) such that $D(\alpha) = 0$.[12]

To provide a possible rationale for government intervention with domestic policies, I assume that consumption of the good under consideration generates a negative externality. This externality is not internalized by individual consumers, and therefore it does not impact demand for the product. I assume as well that it does not affect production. Hence, I am considering an "eyesore" pollutant whose impact is simply to detract from aggregate national welfare in the domestic country (and I assume the externality does not cross borders).

The domestic government has the capability to impose a regulatory standard that specifies a (maximum) level of pollution generated per unit of the good consumed, and in principle the standard may discriminate between domestically produced and imported units of the good. I denote by r the standard imposed on domestically produced units of the good, with $\theta(r)$ the associated per-unit pollution level generated by consumption of domestically produced units under the standard r. Analogously, I denote by ρ the standard imposed on imported units of the good, with $\theta^*(\rho)$ the associated per-unit pollution level generated by consumption of imported units under the standard ρ. I assume that θ and θ^* are decreasing and convex in their respective arguments.

Meeting a regulatory standard of course has a cost. I assume that to meet the standard r, domestic producers must incur the per-unit compliance cost $\phi(r)$, and similarly, I assume that to meet the standard ρ, foreign producers must incur the per-unit compliance cost $\phi^*(\rho)$. I also assume that ϕ and ϕ^* are increasing and convex in their respective arguments. For simplicity, I take domestic and foreign supplies to be linear in the price faced by producers. In particular, for any regulatory standards r and ρ, I assume that domestic and foreign supplies are given respectively by $S = q - \phi(r)$ for $q \geq \phi(r)$ and $S^* = q^* - \phi^*(\rho)$ for $q^* \geq \phi^*(\rho)$, where q and q^* are the respective domestic and foreign producer prices.

The domestic government also has at its disposal an import tariff τ and a consumption tax t (both expressed in specific terms), in addition to the regulatory standards that I have just described. For simplicity and to keep focused on the main points, I assume that the foreign government is passive in this industry.[13] Assuming that all taxes are set at nonprohibitive levels, the domestic consumer and producer prices must satisfy

$$P = q + t,\tag{1.15}$$

while the domestic and foreign producer prices must satisfy

$$q = q^* + \tau.\tag{1.16}$$

Note that all units of the product sell in the domestic country at the same price P regardless of the standard to which they are produced. This feature derives from my assumption that individual consumers do not differentiate across units of the good on the basis of how much pollution it generates when they consume it, so their willingness to pay for the good is independent of the good's pollution-generating characteristics.

I also define the price at which the good is available for sale in international markets once it clears customs in the exporting country—which hereafter I call the "world" price—as

$$q^w \equiv q^* = q - \tau.\tag{1.17}$$

Given my assumption that the foreign government has no export policy, the world price is simply the foreign exporter price in this setting, as (1.17) reflects. However, more generally the world price will differ from the foreign exporter price as a result of foreign export tax policies (as in the model of trade facilitation that I presented earlier, or in the analysis of Staiger and Sykes 2011). To reflect this distinction and avoid confusion, where appropriate I will continue to use the notation q^w for the world price and the notation q^* for the foreign price, even though in this setting they happen to be the same.

I am now ready to use the model to determine equilibrium prices. Equilibrium in this market is determined by the market-clearing condition that the volume of domestic imports must equal the volume of foreign exports:

$$D - S = S^*. \tag{1.18}$$

Employing the expressions for demand and supply as well as the pricing relationships in (1.15)–(1.17), the market-clearing condition (1.18) implicitly determines the market-clearing world price—which I denote by $\tilde{q}^w(\tau, t, r, \rho)$—as a function of the tax and regulatory policies:

$$D(\tilde{q}^w + \tau + t) = 2\tilde{q}^w + \tau - \phi(r) - \phi^*(\rho). \tag{1.19}$$

With (1.15)–(1.17), I may also derive expressions for the market-clearing levels of each of the other prices as functions of the tax and regulatory policies:

$$\begin{aligned}
\tilde{P}(\tau, t, r, \rho) &= \tilde{q}^w(\tau, t, r, \rho) + \tau + t, \\
\tilde{q}(\tau, t, r, \rho) &= \tilde{q}^w(\tau, t, r, \rho) + \tau, \\
\tilde{q}^*(\tau, t, r, \rho) &= \tilde{q}^w(\tau, t, r, \rho).
\end{aligned} \tag{1.20}$$

It will also be useful to record how the equilibrium world price is impacted by policies. Implicit differentiation of (1.19) yields

$$\begin{aligned}
\frac{\partial \tilde{q}^w}{\partial \tau} &= \frac{-[D'(\tilde{P}) - 1]}{[D'(\tilde{P}) - 2]} < 0, \\[2mm]
\frac{\partial \tilde{q}^w}{\partial t} &= \frac{-D'(\tilde{P})}{[D'(\tilde{P}) - 2]} < 0, \\[2mm]
\frac{\partial \tilde{q}^w}{\partial r} &= \frac{-\phi'(r)}{[D'(\tilde{P}) - 2]} > 0, \\[2mm]
\frac{\partial \tilde{q}^w}{\partial \rho} &= \frac{-\phi^{*\prime}(\rho)}{[D'(\tilde{P}) - 2]} > 0.
\end{aligned} \tag{1.21}$$

And, using (1.20), the following derivative properties are direct (and, as is clear from (1.20), all other price derivatives are the same as those for $\tilde{q}^w$ as reported earlier):

$$\begin{aligned}
\frac{\partial \tilde{P}}{\partial \tau} &= \frac{-1}{[D'(\tilde{P}) - 2]} > 0, \\[2mm]
\frac{\partial \tilde{P}}{\partial t} &= \frac{-2}{[D'(\tilde{P}) - 2]} > 0, \\[2mm]
\frac{\partial \tilde{q}}{\partial \tau} &= \frac{-1}{[D'(\tilde{P}) - 2]} > 0.
\end{aligned} \tag{1.22}$$

I now define the market-clearing foreign producer price of the "raw" *un*regulated good—prior to bringing it into compliance with the prevailing regulatory standard—as a function of the tax and regulatory policies, and the associated world price of the foreign-produced unregulated good. These are given by

$$\tilde{q}_0^*(\tau, t, r, \rho) \equiv \tilde{q}^*(\tau, t, r, \rho) - \phi^*(\rho),$$

$$\tilde{q}_0^w(\tau, t, r, \rho) \equiv \tilde{q}^w(\tau, t, r, \rho) - \phi^*(\rho). \tag{1.23}$$

Following Staiger and Sykes (2011), I will refer to $\tilde{q}_0^w$ rather than $\tilde{q}^w$ as the terms of trade, although for any ρ there is a one-to-one mapping between the two notions of world price, as the last line of (1.23) indicates. Note that $\tilde{q}_0^*$ also happens to be the market-clearing volume of foreign exports (production, S^*). This this will simplify some of the following calculations, but it does not drive any of the results. The following derivative properties are direct (and, as (1.23) makes clear, all other price derivatives are the same as those for $\tilde{q}^*$ and $\tilde{q}^w$ respectively as reported earlier):

$$\frac{\partial \tilde{q}_0^*}{\partial \rho} = \frac{\phi^{*\prime}(\rho) \cdot [1 - D'(\tilde{P})]}{[D'(\tilde{P}) - 2]} < 0,$$

$$\frac{\partial \tilde{q}_0^w}{\partial \rho} = \frac{\phi^{*\prime}(\rho) \cdot [1 - D'(\tilde{P})]}{[D'(\tilde{P}) - 2]} < 0.$$

I can now write expressions for domestic and foreign welfare. Domestic -country welfare is given by first calculating the usual partial equilibrium measure of consumer surplus plus producer surplus plus tax revenue and then subtracting from this measure the disutility of the consumption-generated pollution. Domestic consumer (CS) and producer (PS) surpluses are defined as

$$CS = \int_{\tilde{P}}^{\alpha} D(P)dP \equiv CS(\tilde{P}) \text{ and } PS = \int_{\phi(r)}^{\tilde{q}} [q - \phi(r)]dq \equiv PS(r, \tilde{q}).$$

Using the preceding pricing relationships and the definition of $\tilde{q}_0^w$, the tax revenue collected by the domestic government (TR) can be written as

$$TR = [\tilde{P} - \tilde{q}] \cdot D(\tilde{P}) + [\tilde{q} - \tilde{q}_0^w - \phi^*(\rho)] \cdot [D(\tilde{P}) - (\tilde{q} - \phi(r))]$$

$$\equiv TR(r, \rho, \tilde{P}, \tilde{q}, \tilde{q}_0^w),$$

and the utility cost of domestic pollution (Z) is given by

$$Z = \theta(r) \cdot [\tilde{q} - \phi(r)] + \theta^*(\rho) \cdot [D(\tilde{P}) - (\tilde{q} - \phi(r))] \equiv Z(r, \rho, \tilde{P}, \tilde{q}).$$

With these definitions, I may write domestic welfare as

$$W = CS(\tilde{P}) + PS(r, \tilde{q}) + TR(r, \rho, \tilde{P}, \tilde{q}, \tilde{q}_0^w) - Z(r, \rho, \tilde{P}, \tilde{q})$$
$$\equiv W(r, \rho, \tilde{P}, \tilde{q}, \tilde{q}_0^w). \tag{1.24}$$

Note that (1.24) expresses domestic welfare as a function of prices (in addition to nontax regulations). As Bagwell and Staiger (1999, 2001a) have emphasized and as I confirm, writing government objectives as functions of prices rather than tax policies directly can help to illuminate the basic structure of the terms-of-trade theory of trade agreements.

Using the definition of $TR(r, \rho, \tilde{P}, \tilde{q}, \tilde{q}_0^w)$, notice that (1.24) implies $W_{\tilde{q}_0^w} = -[D(\tilde{P}) - (\tilde{q} - \phi(r))] < 0$ (where here and in what follows I use a subscripted variable to denote a partial derivative with respect to the variable). This captures the welfare reduction suffered by the domestic country when its terms of trade deteriorate (i.e., when $\tilde{q}_0^w$ rises) while holding all regulatory standards and domestic local prices fixed, and it is simply the income effect of a small terms-of-trade deterioration for the domestic country, which amounts to the domestic import volume.

Now turning to foreign welfare, the fact that the foreign government is passive in the industry under consideration, combined with the absence of foreign demand for the product in this industry and the absence of foreign pollution, makes the foreign welfare measure very simple. Specifically, foreign welfare is given by foreign producer surplus. Using the preceding pricing relationships and the definition of $\tilde{q}_0^*$, foreign producer surplus (PS^*) can be defined as

$$PS^* = \int_{\phi^*(\rho)}^{\tilde{q}_0^* + \phi^*(\rho)} [q^* - \phi^*(\rho)]dq^* = \int_0^{\tilde{q}_0^*} q^* dq^* \equiv PS^*(\tilde{q}_0^*).$$

Hence, foreign welfare may be expressed as

$$W^* = PS^*(\tilde{q}_0^*) \equiv W^*(\tilde{q}_0^*). \tag{1.25}$$

Notice from $W^*(\tilde{q}_0^*)$ that foreign welfare does not depend directly on the standard ρ to which foreign producers must comply (though it does depend on ρ indirectly through the impact of ρ on $\tilde{q}_0^*$). As Staiger and

Sykes (2011) explain, this feature derives from the fact that the production of the unregulated good has been modeled as an increasing -cost (upward-sloping supply) industry, while for a given standard level ρ the per-unit cost of coming into compliance with the standard is then assumed to be constant (and equal to $\phi^*(\rho)$) regardless of how many units of the unregulated good must be altered to meet the standard. For this reason, foreign producer surplus is impacted by the standard level ρ only to the extent that ρ impacts the market-clearing foreign supply decisions for the unregulated good (through $\tilde{q}_0^*$).[14]

Efficient policies With my variant of the basic Staiger and Sykes (2011) model described, I first characterize the jointly efficient policy choices (i.e., the policies that maximize $W + W^*$).[15] I will subsequently compare these policies to the noncooperative policy choices that the domestic government would make absent any international agreement, and in this way I will identify and characterize the problem that a trade agreement must solve if it is to move governments from inefficient noncooperative ("Nash") choices to the efficiency frontier.[16]

Recalling that the domestic government has at its disposal four policy instruments (and the foreign government has none), the first-order conditions that must hold for the choices of these policies that maximize the sum of domestic and foreign welfare are given by[17]

$$W_{\tilde{P}}\frac{d\tilde{P}}{d\tau} + W_{\tilde{q}}\frac{d\tilde{q}}{d\tau} + W_{\tilde{q}_0^w}\frac{d\tilde{q}_0^w}{d\tau} + W_{\tilde{q}_0^*}^*\frac{d\tilde{q}_0^*}{d\tau} = 0,$$

$$W_{\tilde{P}}\frac{d\tilde{P}}{dt} + W_{\tilde{q}}\frac{d\tilde{q}}{dt} + W_{\tilde{q}_0^w}\frac{d\tilde{q}_0^w}{dt} + W_{\tilde{q}_0^*}^*\frac{d\tilde{q}_0^*}{dt} = 0,$$

$$W_r + W_{\tilde{P}}\frac{d\tilde{P}}{dr} + W_{\tilde{q}}\frac{d\tilde{q}}{dr} + W_{\tilde{q}_0^w}\frac{d\tilde{q}_0^w}{dr} + W_{\tilde{q}_0^*}^*\frac{d\tilde{q}_0^*}{dr} = 0, \qquad (1.26)$$

$$W_\rho + W_{\tilde{P}}\frac{d\tilde{P}}{d\rho} + W_{\tilde{q}}\frac{d\tilde{q}}{d\rho} + W_{\tilde{q}_0^w}\frac{d\tilde{q}_0^w}{d\rho} + W_{\tilde{q}_0^*}^*\frac{d\tilde{q}_0^*}{d\rho} = 0.$$

But, as previously noted and as (1.20) and (1.23) confirm, the foreign country's lack of an available policy instrument in this industry implies that $\tilde{q}_0^w = \tilde{q}_0^*$. Moreover, observe that

$$\left[W_{\tilde{q}_0^w} + W_{\tilde{q}_0^*}^*\right] = -[D(\tilde{P}) - (\tilde{q} - \phi(r))] + \tilde{q}_0^w = 0,$$

where the second equality follows from market clearing. Hence, I may write the first-order conditions for efficiency in (1.26) as

$$W_{\tilde{P}}\frac{d\tilde{P}}{d\tau} + W_{\tilde{q}}\frac{d\tilde{q}}{d\tau} = 0,$$

$$W_{\tilde{P}}\frac{d\tilde{P}}{dt} + W_{\tilde{q}}\frac{d\tilde{q}}{dt} = 0,$$

$$W_r + W_{\tilde{P}}\frac{d\tilde{P}}{dr} + W_{\tilde{q}}\frac{d\tilde{q}}{dr} = 0,$$

$$W_\rho + W_{\tilde{P}}\frac{d\tilde{P}}{d\rho} + W_{\tilde{q}}\frac{d\tilde{q}}{d\rho} = 0.$$

(1.27)

Using the expressions in (1.19)–(1.25) to evaluate the first-order conditions for efficiency contained in (1.27), and letting the efficient policy choices be denoted by τ^E, t^E, r^E, and ρ^E, it follows that

$$\tau^E = [\theta^*(\rho^E) - \theta(r^E)],$$

$$t^E = \theta(r^E),$$

$$-\theta'(r^E) = \phi'(r^E),$$

$$-\theta^{*\prime}(\rho^E) = \phi^{*\prime}(\rho^E),$$

(1.28)

where here I have used primes to denote derivatives.

There are a number of notable features of the efficient policies as described by (1.28). First, notice that $t^E = \theta$, so the efficient domestic consumption tax is set at a Pigouvian level that reflects the externality associated with consumption of a unit of the *domestically produced* good, even if this externality differs from the externality associated with consumption of a unit of the imported good. As the first expression of (1.28) indicates, the efficient way to respond to any difference in the externality generated by consumption of the domestically produced and imported goods is via the *tariff*: τ^E is positive (a net tax on imports) if consumption of a unit of the imported good generates more pollution than a unit of the domestically produced good, and τ^E is negative (a net subsidy to imports) if consumption of a unit of the imported good generates less pollution than a unit of the domestically produced good. This feature admits a natural interpretation once it is observed that a tariff can equivalently be thought of as a (discriminatory) domestic tax on the consumption of the imported good. Thus these two policies together represent the usual Pigouvian intervention to address the (possibly distinct levels of) consumption externality associated with consumption of the domestically produced and imported goods.

Second, notice that r^E, the efficient standard on domestically produced goods, equates the marginal benefit per unit of pollution reduction that is associated with a slightly tighter standard $(-\theta'(\cdot))$ with the marginal cost per unit of domestic compliance with the tighter standard $(\phi'(\cdot))$. A similar observation holds for ρ^E, the efficient standard on imported goods, which must equate the marginal benefit per unit of pollution reduction that comes with a slightly tighter standard $(-\theta^{*\prime}(\cdot))$ with the marginal cost per unit of foreign compliance with the tighter standard $(\phi^{*\prime}(\cdot))$. In general, the efficient regulatory standards for domestic and imported goods, and the efficient level of the externality produced by each type of good, will not be the same.[18]

This raises a third and related point: it is interesting to consider the efficient policies for a symmetric benchmark case in which both domestic and foreign producers face the same compliance cost for any (common) standard level (i.e., the functions ϕ and ϕ^* are identical), and consumption of both the domestically produced and imported goods generate the same level of pollution per unit for any (common) standard level (i.e., the functions θ and θ^* are identical). In this case, because of symmetry in the compliance cost functions ϕ and ϕ^*, (1.28) implies $\rho^E = r^E$, and given that $\rho^E = r^E$, symmetry in the pollution functions θ and θ^* then implies by the first condition in (1.28) that $\tau^E = 0$. Hence, in the symmetric benchmark case, the efficient policies are given by

$$\tau^E = 0,$$
$$t^E = \theta(r^E),$$
$$-\theta'(r^E) = \phi'(r^E), \tag{1.29}$$
$$\rho^E = r^E.$$

As (1.29) indicates, efficient policy intervention in the case of identical technologies across countries takes the intuitive form of free trade, a nondiscriminatory regulatory standard that equates the marginal benefit of pollution reduction to the marginal compliance cost, and a Pigouvian consumption tax set at the level of the consumption externality.

Noncooperative policies I now characterize the noncooperative (Nash) policy choices of the domestic country (recall that the foreign country is assumed passive in this industry). Using the domestic welfare expression given in (1.24), the noncooperative policy choices are the choices of τ, t, r, and ρ that satisfy the following four first-order conditions:

$$W_{\tilde{P}}\frac{d\tilde{P}}{d\tau} + W_{\tilde{q}}\frac{d\tilde{q}}{d\tau} + W_{\tilde{q}_0^w}\frac{d\tilde{q}_0^w}{d\tau} = 0,$$

$$W_{\tilde{P}}\frac{d\tilde{P}}{dt} + W_{\tilde{q}}\frac{d\tilde{q}}{dt} + W_{\tilde{q}_0^w}\frac{d\tilde{q}_0^w}{dt} = 0,$$

$$W_r + W_{\tilde{P}}\frac{d\tilde{P}}{dr} + W_{\tilde{q}}\frac{d\tilde{q}}{dr} + W_{\tilde{q}_0^w}\frac{d\tilde{q}_0^w}{dr} = 0,$$

$$W_\rho + W_{\tilde{P}}\frac{d\tilde{P}}{d\rho} + W_{\tilde{q}}\frac{d\tilde{q}}{d\rho} + W_{\tilde{q}_0^w}\frac{d\tilde{q}_0^w}{d\rho} = 0.$$

(1.30)

Using the expressions in (1.19)–(1.25) to evaluate the first-order conditions contained in (1.30), and denoting the noncooperative volume of foreign export supply by S^{*N} and the noncooperative policy choices by τ^N, t^N, r^N, ρ^N, and τ^{*N}, the following expressions for the Nash policy levels may be derived:

$$\tau^N = [\theta^*(\rho^N) - \theta(r^N)] + S^{*N},$$

$$t^N = \theta(r^N),$$

$$-\theta'(r^N) = \phi'(r^N),$$

$$-\theta^{*\prime}(\rho^N) = \phi^{*\prime}(\rho^N).$$

(1.31)

Finally, in the symmetric benchmark case of identical technologies, Nash policies reduce to

$$\tau^N = S^{*N},$$

$$t^N = \theta(r^N),$$

$$-\theta'(r^N) = \phi'(r^N),$$

$$-\theta^{*\prime}(\rho^N) = \phi^{*\prime}(\rho^N).$$

(1.32)

The problem for a trade agreement to solve I now turn to a comparison of the efficient policies and the noncooperative policies as characterized earlier, in order to identify and understand the problem that a trade agreement must solve if it is to move governments from inefficient Nash choices to the efficiency frontier. This comparison turns out to be illuminating, and in the context of the present model and the terms-of-trade theory more generally (see Bagwell and Staiger 2001a), it leads to a striking result.

Specifically, a comparison of the last two conditions in (1.28) and (1.31) reveals that the Nash standards choices satisfy the same conditions as the efficient standards choices, and indeed the Nash standards correspond to the efficient standards: $r^N = r^E$ and $\rho^N = \rho^E$. And with $r^N = r^E$, it also follows from a comparison of the middle conditions in (1.28) and (1.31) that the Nash consumption tax corresponds to the efficient consumption tax: $t^N = t^E$. Hence, all behind-the-border NTMs are left undistorted from their internationally efficient levels in the noncooperative Nash equilibrium.

Given that $r^N = r^E$ and $\rho^N = \rho^E$, it is then also apparent from a comparison of the first condition in (1.28) with the first condition in (1.31) that $\tau^N > \tau^E$.[19] It is also easily shown that the difference between Nash and efficient tariffs is driven by the home country's incentive to manipulate the terms of trade $(\tilde{q}_0^w)$ with its unilateral tariff choice.[20] Finally, the same statements apply in the case of identical technologies. This can be seen by comparing the efficient policies for the symmetric benchmark case in (1.29) to the Nash policies in the symmetric benchmark case given in (1.32).

The inefficiencies of noncooperative policies in this model can thus be traced to a single source: the Nash tariff is too high, and the Nash trade volume is correspondingly too low, because the domestic country seeks to manipulate its terms of trade with its tariff. In fact, this interpretation of the problem for a trade agreement to solve can be confirmed at a more general level by following Bagwell and Staiger (1999, 2001a) and defining *politically optimal* policies as those policies that would hypothetically be chosen by governments unilaterally if they did not value the terms-of-trade implications of their policy choices.[21]

In particular, with the foreign government passive by assumption in the model I have developed here, to define politically optimal tariffs in the present setting I need only suppose hypothetically that when choosing its politically optimal policies the domestic government acts as if $W_{\tilde{q}_0^w} \equiv 0$. I can then ask whether politically optimal policies so defined are efficient when evaluated in light of the governments' actual objectives, and I can thereby explore whether the Nash inefficiencies identified earlier can in fact be given the terms-of-trade interpretation I have just outlined. But comparing (1.30) when $W_{\tilde{q}_0^w} \equiv 0$—which yields the first-order conditions that define the politically optimal policies in this setting—with the conditions for efficiency in (1.27), it is immediately clear that politically optimal policies are indeed efficient. Hence, if governments could be induced to make policy choices free from motives reflecting terms-of-trade manipulation, there would be nothing left for a trade agreement to do.

As a consequence, the fundamental inefficiency for a trade agreement to correct in this setting—and therefore the problem that gives rise to the need for a trade agreement to exist in this setting—is the unilateral incentive for the domestic government to manipulate the terms of trade $\tilde{q}_0^w$ with its tariff choice. But, as (1.23) makes clear, the domestic country can alter $\tilde{q}_0^w$ with *any* of its policies, both tariffs and behind-the-border NTMs. Why, then, are all behind-the-border NTMs left undistorted from their internationally efficient levels in the noncooperative Nash equilibrium, with all of the distortions contained in the level of the tariff? The simple reason is that the tariff is the first-best instrument for manipulating the terms of trade in this setting, and hence with the domestic country's Nash tariff set to achieve this purpose, there is no need for it to distort any other policy choices to engage in terms-of-trade manipulation.[22]

This leads to an important point: according to the terms-of-trade theory, even in the context of a complex policy environment, there is no need for member governments of a trade agreement to negotiate directly over the levels of their behind-the-border NTMs. Rather, according to the terms-of-trade theory, the central task of a trade agreement is simply to reduce tariffs and raise trade volumes without *introducing* distortions into the unilateral choices of domestic regulatory and tax policies as a result of the negotiated constraints on tariffs.

For my purposes here, the important implication of this point is what it means for the approach to negotiations in a world where governments have a myriad of policies at their disposal: in principle, negotiations over tariffs alone, in combination with an effective "market access preservation rule" that prevents governments from subsequently manipulating their domestic policy choices to undercut the market access implications of their tariff commitments, can bring governments to the efficiency frontier. The key feature of such a market access preservation rule, which in practice, as discussed further in Bagwell and Staiger (2001a) and Staiger and Sykes (2011), has its closest conceptual analogue in the GATT's nonviolation clause, is that, in principle, by securing market access against erosion from future unilateral changes in domestic policies, such a rule also secures the terms of trade $\tilde{q}_0^w$ against such changes.[23]

To illustrate this point, consider its application to the setting I have analyzed here, where there are no political economy considerations.

In this case, efficiency can be achieved in the presence of a market access preservation rule by a simple commitment to free trade from the domestic country and no negotiated commitments on its behind-the-border NTMs.[24] To see that this must be true, note that efficiency will be achieved under the free trade agreement only if the domestic government does not alter its domestic tax and regulatory policies from their Nash levels. Note as well that the market access preservation rule, by preserving $\tilde{q}_0^w$, must also preserve $\tilde{q}_0^*$ given that $\tilde{q}_0^w = \tilde{q}_0^*$, and hence must preserve the level of foreign welfare $W^*(\tilde{q}_0^*)$.[25] But then, with the elimination of tariffs and beginning from the Nash domestic tax and regulatory policies, the efficiency of this starting point ensures that it is impossible for the domestic government to find domestic tax and regulatory policy alternatives to the Nash policies that would satisfy the market access preservation rule (and thereby preserve the level of foreign welfare) and yet make itself better off.

Evidently, the terms-of-trade theory of trade agreements provides strong support for shallow integration as the most direct means to solve the policy inefficiencies that would arise absent a trade agreement. At a conceptual level, this resonates with the GATT approach to behind-the-border NTMs described earlier, where negotiators emphasize tariff reductions as a means to expand market access, and where various GATT provisions serve to protect the value of negotiated market access agreements against erosion by behind-the-border NTMs.[26]

1.4.2 The Commitment Theory

Thus far I have described an "international externality" theory of trade agreements that emphasizes the control of the beggar-my-neighbor motives associated with terms-of-trade manipulation. A distinct though possibly complementary theory of trade agreements turns the focus away from international policy externalities that one government imposes on another and posits instead that the purpose of a trade agreement is to tie the hands of its member governments in their interactions with private agents in the economy and thereby offer an external commitment device.[27]

With a few exceptions, two of which I discuss briefly, most research adopting the commitment approach to trade agreements has focused on tariffs, and specifically on the possibility that governments might benefit from a trade agreement that could help them commit to a policy of free trade. As a result, the implications of the commitment approach for the treatment of NTMs in trade agreements is less well understood than for the terms-of-trade theory. Nevertheless, a basic feature of the commitment approach to trade agreements is worth emphasizing here: unlike the terms-of-trade theory, which offers a robust reason to expect that trade agreements ought to be trade *liberalizing*, there is no presumption one way or the other under the commitment theory as to whether trade agreements should increase or reduce trade. Hence, a basic anchor of the terms-of-trade theory that resonates broadly with observed trade agreements and provides structure for understanding the treatment of NTMs is absent from the commitment theory.

A simple way to see this is to note that government commitment problems typically arise when governments are forced to use policy instruments that are "second best" for the task to which they are put. A tariff, which, as is well known, is equivalent to a combination production subsidy and consumption tax, will almost always be a second-best instrument for any goal (aside from terms-of-trade manipulation), because it distorts two margins: a production margin and a consumption margin. Consider, then, a developing-country government that would like to offer a production subsidy to firms that invest in a new import-competing industry (i.e., it would like to distort the production margin) but cannot feasibly raise the funds for the production subsidy by independent means and so employs an import tariff in the industry instead (which distorts both the production margin and the consumption margin).

In this case, the commitment problem faced by the government could be described as follows: announcing the import tariff in order to stimulate firm entry and import-competing production will not be credible for the government, because if firm entry were to occur and investments in production processes were made, it would then be optimal for the government to renege on the promise of a tariff in order to avoid the consumption distortion that would be associated with the tariff. But, anticipating this, domestic firms will not enter the import-competing industry in the first place, and the government will therefore be unable to carry out its desired plan on account of a credibility ("time consistency") problem. In principle, a trade agreement could help supply the needed credibility for the government by credibly threatening to punish the government if it reneges on its import-tariff plan, but notice that in this case the purpose of a trade agreement would be to enable higher tariffs, not lower ones. In general, as noted, there is no presumption either way as to the trade effects of trade agreements in a world where governments use trade agreements as commitment devices.

Still, commitment theories may offer important insights into features of the treatment of NTMs in real-world trade agreements that the terms-of-trade theory fails to explain. Next, I will briefly describe two papers that provide insights into the trade-agreement treatment of border and behind-the-border NTMs, respectively.

1.4.2.1 Border NTMs I first discuss the implications of the commitment theory of trade agreements for the treatment of border NTMs in trade agreements, focusing specifically on export subsidies. A paper that uses the commitment theory to offer an explanation for features of the observed treatment of export subsidies in the GATT/WTO is Potipiti (2012).

In particular, Potipiti (2012) employs the commitment theory to offer an explanation of the asymmetric treatment of tariffs and export subsidies in the WTO where, as described previously, tariffs are the subject of negotiated limits, while export subsidies are banned outright. To focus on the distinct non-terms-of-trade elements, commitment theories of trade agreements typically adopt a small-country assumption, a convention that Potipiti follows. In Potipiti's model, the anticipation of protection generates inefficient investment ex ante, for which the government is not compensated in its (ex post) political relationship with the industry, along the lines of Maggi and Rodriguez-Clare (1998). A government can join an agreement that bans tariffs and/or an agreement that bans export subsidies, and doing so will eliminate this anticipation and generate a social welfare gain. On the downside, commitment to such an agreement means that the government must forfeit the political contributions it would otherwise collect for the protection it offers. In Potipiti's model, the government therefore commits to a trade agreement on a particular policy (import tariff and/or export subsidy) if the social welfare gain from liberalizing that policy is greater than the government's valuation of the associated loss in political contributions.

The asymmetry in treatment across import tariffs and export subsidies in Potipiti's (2012) model stems from an underlying asymmetry in the growth prospects of the two sectors. As Potipiti demonstrates, in an environment where trade and transportation costs are decreasing over time, export sectors grow and import-competing sectors decline. Therefore, in export sectors, export subsidies attract new entrants and investment that erodes the protection rent associated with the export subsidies. The political contributions that the government receives from providing export subsidies is therefore small, and Potipiti establishes conditions under which the government would opt to ban export subsidies for the social welfare gain as a result. On the other hand, in declining import-competing sectors, the return on capital drops and capital is therefore sunk and cannot exit. As Potipiti argues, this sunk capital allows protection to raise the rate of return in these sectors at least somewhat without attracting entry. Here the rent from protection is not eroded by new entrants, and the government can extract large political contributions for offering protection. Potipiti shows that under the same conditions that lead the government to ban export subsidies, it will opt for the political rents and not ban import tariffs.

Hence, as Potipiti (2012) demonstrates, the asymmetric treatment of export subsidies and import tariffs in the WTO, which is difficult to explain from the perspective of the terms-of-trade theory, may be understood from the perspective of the commitment theory as reflecting underlying differences in the rent-generating capacity of protection in export and import-competing sectors.

1.4.2.2 Behind-the-border NTMs Turning to the treatment of behind-the-border NTMs in trade agreements, Brou and Ruta (2013) adopt a small-country political economy setting similar to Potipiti (2012) and more specifically Maggi and Rodriguez-Clare (1998), but they introduce domestic production subsidies as well as import tariffs to study what they term the "policy substitution problem."[28] Taxation is assumed to be distortionary, so that a tariff is not dominated by a production subsidy for achieving production goals. Rather, as Brou and Ruta show, in the setting that they study, optimal intervention will typically include a mix of tariffs and production subsidies.

In the model of Brou and Ruta (2013), the fundamental reason for signing a trade agreement that commits a government to free trade is the same as that in Maggi and Rodriguez-Clare (1998) and in Potipiti (2012), but the novel twist in the model of Brou and Ruta is that a commitment to free trade by itself will simply induce the government to turn more intensively to production subsidies in its political relationship with the import-competing lobbies—the policy substitution problem—and the resulting distortions are welfare reducing (and recall that the country is assumed to be small, so there is no terms-of-trade reason for the government to distort its domestic subsidy once its tariff is constrained and no sense in which a "market access preservation rule" could fix this problem). As Brou and Ruta show, relative to an agreement that simply commits the government to free trade, the government is better off under an agreement that also imposes explicit rules on the use of domestic subsidies, because only under such a more complete trade agreement can policy credibility with respect to special interests be achieved.

As Brou and Ruta (2013) demonstrate, their model is capable of providing an explanation based on commitment theory of some of the important features for handling domestic subsidies that are contained in the WTO SCM agreement and that the terms-of-trade theory has difficulty explaining. In particular, the findings of Brou and Ruta can provide a rationale for the need to pursue deep integration with regard to behind-the-border NTMs.[29]

1.4.3 The Offshoring Theory

It is well documented that modern trade flows are dominated by trade in intermediate inputs, many of which appear to be highly specialized to their intended use, and that this has not always been so (see, for example, the discussion in Antras and Staiger 2012a). This rise in prominence of "offshoring" raises the question of whether the traditional approach to trade liberalization as embodied in the rules and norms of the GATT/WTO, crafted at a time when the nature of trade was quite different than it is today, is still appropriate in the world of today.

Recently, Antras and Staiger (2012a, 2012b) asked this question and suggested a provocative answer: if offshoring can be seen as changing the nature of international price determination from one governed by a standard market-clearing mechanism to one that is described by a collection of bilateral bargains between foreign suppliers and domestic buyers, then the rise in offshoring will require fundamental changes in the WTO's approach to trade liberalization if that institution is to remain effective. In the next two subsections, I discuss the implications of offshoring for the treatment of border and behind-the-border NTMs in trade agreements.

1.4.3.1 Border NTMs Whether offshoring has strong implications for the treatment of border NTMs (such as export subsidies) that would differ from those of the terms-of-trade theory is not known at this time. However, as I demonstrate in the next subsection, some striking implications of offshoring for the treatment of NTMs in trade agreements come in the context of behind-the-border measures. In light of these implications, exploring the treatment of border NTMs in the presence of offshoring seems like a promising area for further research.

1.4.3.2 Behind-the-border NTMs

To illustrate the implications of offshoring for the treatment of behind-the-border NTMs in trade agreements, I now introduce further changes to the variant of the model of Staiger and Sykes (2011) developed in subsection 1.4.1.2 above. Specifically, I now assume that individual pairs of foreign exporters and domestic importers bargain over the international price at which the traded good is exchanged between them, along the lines of Antras and Staiger (2012a, 2012b). As in Antras and Staiger, the model I describe here is meant to highlight and capture in a simple way the growing importance of the relationship-specific nature of trade between importers and their specialized suppliers.

Antras and Staiger (2012a) work in a setting in which the supply of a specialized input is offshored, providing a natural environment for the study of relationship-specific trade. Here, in order to make minimal changes to the framework of Staiger and Sykes (2011) within which the findings presented in earlier sections were derived, I follow Antras and Staiger (2012b) and do not introduce trade in inputs but instead simply assume that a domestic importer imports a specialized good from abroad for sale on the domestic market and that the international price at which this good is exchanged is determined through bilateral bargaining between the domestic importer and the foreign exporter/supplier. In this setting, I show that now both the tariff *and* behind-the-border NTMs are set inefficiently in the Nash equilibrium (confirming related findings by Antras and Staiger). I then offer an interpretation of the implications of these findings for the treatment of behind-the-border NTMs in trade agreements when offshoring is present.[30]

In particular, I continue to assume that domestic demand ($D(P)$) and domestic supply ($S = q - \phi(r)$) are exactly as in the model of subsection 1.4.1.2 above, and I continue to make the same assumptions about the available policies (i.e., the domestic country has τ, t, r, and ρ at its disposal, while the foreign country is passive in this industry). But now I assume that there is a single domestic importer, who acts like a monopolist in the domestic market, facing a "competitive fringe" of domestic suppliers. As for the foreign exporters faced by the monopoly importer, there are now two interesting possibilities that might be considered.

The first possibility is that the monopoly importer faces a competitive foreign export supply, given by $S^* = q^* - \phi^*(\rho)$, just as in
the model of subsection 1.4.1.2. In this case, there is domestic market power, but otherwise nothing has changed from the earlier setup. It
can be confirmed (along the lines of Bagwell and Staiger 2002, chapter
9; Bagwell and Staiger 2012b; and Antras and Staiger 2012b) that all the
results from subsection 1.4.1 continue to apply in this setup augmented
by market power.

The second possibility is that the monopoly importer faces a single
foreign exporter. It is this possibility that I focus on here. Specifically, I adopt an incomplete contracts setting (along the lines of Antras
and Staiger 2012a), and I assume that to successfully make sales in
the domestic market, the foreign exporter must first invest in production and then (Nash) bargain over the price—the *international* price—at
which it sells its production to the domestic importer. I take the good
under consideration to be specialized for the domestic market and
worthless if not sold there, and I assume that the importer has no
alternative source of supply. Hence, the outside option of both the
importer and the exporter is zero. For simplicity, I also now assume
that the unit cost of foreign production is $1 + \phi^*(\rho)$. The decisions of
this importer-exporter pair imply an import quantity x^* that together
with the domestic competitive-fringe supply response then determines
total supply in the domestic market.

I now describe the structure of the bilateral importer-exporter relationship in detail. I assume that all government policies are fixed in
advance of the start of the following sequence of events:

Stage 1. The foreign exporter decides on the amount x^* to be produced
(at a marginal cost of $1 + \phi^*(\rho)$).
Stage 2. The foreign exporter and the domestic importer (symmetric
Nash) bargain over the price at which the good will change hands.
Failure to reach agreement leaves both partners with their zero outside
option.
Stage 3. The domestic importer imports the quantity x^* from the foreign exporter, payments agreed to in stage 2 are settled, and the
domestic importer sells x^* on the domestic market at the domestic
market-clearing price (with taxes collected at the time of importation
and sale on the domestic market).

To analyze the outcome of this three-stage game, first I consider
the determination of the domestic producer price q given a level of

imports x^*. With the supply of the domestic competitive fringe given by $q - \phi(r)$, domestic demand given by $D(P)$, and the relationship between the domestic consumer price P and the domestic producer price q given by $P = q + t$, domestic market clearing determines the domestic producer price according to

$$x^* + q - \phi(r) = D(q + t), \tag{1.33}$$

which implicitly defines $\tilde{q}(x^*, r, t)$. The following derivative properties may be obtained from total differentiation of (1.33):

$$\frac{\partial \tilde{q}}{\partial x^*} = \frac{1}{D'(\tilde{q}(x^*, r, t) + t) - 1} < 0,$$

$$\frac{\partial \tilde{q}}{\partial t} = \frac{-D'(\tilde{q}(x^*, r, t) + t)}{D'(\tilde{q}(x^*, r, t) + t) - 1} < 0, \tag{1.34}$$

$$\frac{\partial \tilde{q}}{\partial r} = \frac{-\phi'(r)}{D'(\tilde{q}(x^*, r, t) + t) - 1} > 0.$$

Consider now the subgame perfect equilibrium of the three-stage game outlined here. First, if the domestic importer and foreign exporter reach agreement in stage 2, the importer can offer the quantity x^* for sale on the domestic market and make revenues net of trade taxes equal to $[\tilde{q}(x^*, r, t) - \tau] \cdot x^*$, whereas disagreement in stage 2 results in both the importer and the exporter receiving their outside option of zero. Hence, given the quantity x^*, it follows that in the symmetric Nash bargain of stage 2, the domestic importer and the foreign exporter split the bargaining surplus and each receives $\frac{1}{2}[\tilde{q}(x^*, r, t) - \tau] \cdot x^*$. For the domestic importer, its share of the bargaining surplus is also its profit, and I record this profit (conditional on x^*) for future use:

$$\pi = \frac{1}{2}[\tilde{q}(x^*, r, t) - \tau] \cdot x^*. \tag{1.35}$$

Now consider the foreign exporter's output choice in stage 1. Recalling that the unit cost of production for the foreign exporter is $1 + \phi^*(\rho)$, the foreign exporter chooses x^* to maximize its profits, which are given by

$$\pi^* = \left(\frac{1}{2}[\tilde{q}(x^*, r, t) - \tau] - [1 + \phi^*(\rho)] \right) \cdot x^*. \tag{1.36}$$

Using (1.36) and (1.34), the chosen $\hat{x}^*(r, \rho, t, \tau)$ is therefore implicitly defined by the first-order condition

$$\frac{1}{2}\left[\tilde{q}(x^*,r,t) - \tau + \frac{x^*}{D'(\tilde{q}(x^*,r,t)+t)-1}\right] - [1+\phi^*(\rho)] = 0. \qquad (1.37)$$

It is straightforward to confirm that the second-order condition implies $2(D'-1)^2 - \hat{x}^* \cdot D'' > 0$, which is satisfied provided that demand is not too convex (i.e., D'' is not too large and positive). In fact, for simplicity, I impose the stronger assumption that demand is neither too convex nor too concave (i.e., $|D''|$ is not too large), thereby ensuring that each policy's impact on $\hat{x}^*$ takes the intuitive sign, as I now record:

$$\frac{\partial \hat{x}^*}{\partial r} = \phi'\left[\frac{(D'-1)^2 - \hat{x}^* \cdot D''}{2(D'-1)^2 - \hat{x}^* \cdot D''}\right] > 0,$$

$$\frac{\partial \hat{x}^*}{\partial \rho} = \frac{2\phi^{*\prime} \cdot (D'-1)^3}{2(D'-1)^2 - \hat{x}^* \cdot D''} < 0,$$

$$\frac{\partial \hat{x}^*}{\partial t} = \frac{D' \cdot (D'-1)^2 - \hat{x}^* \cdot D''}{2(D'-1)^2 - \hat{x}^* \cdot D''} < 0, \qquad (1.38)$$

$$\frac{\partial \hat{x}^*}{\partial \tau} = \frac{(D'-1)^3}{2(D'-1)^2 - \hat{x}^* \cdot D''} < 0.$$

Using $\hat{x}^*(r,\rho,t,\tau)$ as implicitly defined by (1.37), I can now express the equilibrium domestic producer price as a function of government policies:

$$\hat{q}(r,\rho,t,\tau) = \tilde{q}(\hat{x}^*(r,\rho,t,\tau),r,t).$$

For future use, I record the following derivatives, whose signs are intuitive and again follow from my assumption that $|D''|$ is not too large:

$$\frac{\partial \hat{q}}{\partial r} = -\phi'\left[\frac{(D'-1)}{2(D'-1)^2 - \hat{x}^* \cdot D''}\right] > 0,$$

$$\frac{\partial \hat{q}}{\partial \rho} = \frac{2\phi^{*\prime} \cdot (D'-1)^2}{2(D'-1)^2 - \hat{x}^* \cdot D''} > 0,$$

$$\frac{\partial \hat{q}}{\partial t} = -\left[\frac{D' \cdot (D'-1) - \hat{x}^* \cdot D''}{2(D'-1)^2 - \hat{x}^* \cdot D''}\right] < 0, \qquad (1.39)$$

$$\frac{\partial \hat{q}}{\partial \tau} = \frac{(D'-1)^2}{2(D'-1)^2 - \hat{x}^* \cdot D''} > 0.$$

Finally, using (1.35) and (1.36), the home and foreign profits may be written as functions of government policies:

$$\pi(r,\rho,t,\tau) = \frac{1}{2}[\hat{q}(r,\rho,t,\tau) - \tau] \cdot \hat{x}^*(r,\rho,t,\tau),$$

$$\pi^*(r,\rho,t,\tau) = \left(\frac{1}{2}[\hat{q}(r,\rho,t,\tau) - \tau] - [1 + \phi^*(\rho)]\right) \cdot \hat{x}^*(r,\rho,t,\tau).$$

The *international ("world") price* of the product under consideration (i.e., the untaxed price negotiated in stage 2 for the exchange between the foreign exporter and the domestic importer), which I now denote by $\hat{q}^w$, is given by $\hat{q}^w = \pi^*/\hat{x}^* + (1 + \phi^*(\rho))$, which can in turn be written as

$$\hat{q}^w = \frac{1}{2}[\hat{q}(r,\rho,t,\tau) - \tau] \equiv \hat{q}^w(r,\rho,t,\tau). \tag{1.40}$$

The remaining equilibrium prices may then be defined as

$$\hat{P}(r,\rho,t,\tau) = \hat{q}(r,\rho,t,\tau) + t,$$

$$\hat{q}^*(r,\rho,t,\tau) = \hat{q}^w(r,\rho,t,\tau) = \frac{1}{2}[\hat{q}(r,\rho,t,\tau) - \tau],$$

where the absence of a foreign trade tax instrument again ensures $\hat{q}^* = \hat{q}^w$ as in the model of subsection 1.4.1.2. And analogously to the earlier case, I now define the "raw" prices of the foreign export good by

$$\hat{q}_0^*(r,\rho,t,\tau) \equiv \hat{q}^*(r,\rho,t,\tau) - \phi^*(\rho),$$
$$\hat{q}_0^w(r,\rho,t,\tau) \equiv \hat{q}^w(r,\rho,t,\tau) - \phi^*(\rho). \tag{1.41}$$

Welfare in the domestic country is again given by the usual partial equilibrium measure of consumer surplus plus producer surplus—and now also domestic profits—plus tax revenue and then subtracting the disutility of the consumption-generated pollution. Domestic consumer surplus (CS) and producer surplus (PS), are given by

$$CS = \int_{\hat{P}}^{\alpha} D(P)dP \equiv CS(\hat{P}(r,\rho,t,\tau)) \text{ and}$$

$$PS = \int_{\phi(r)}^{\hat{q}} [q - \phi(r)]dq \equiv PS(r,\hat{q}(r,\rho,t,\tau)),$$

while tax revenue is given by

$$TR = t \cdot D(\hat{P}(r,\rho,t,\tau)) + \tau \cdot \hat{x}^*(r,\rho,t,\tau) \equiv TR(r,\rho,t,\tau).$$

Finally, the utility cost of domestic pollution (Z) is given by

$$Z = \theta(r) \cdot [\hat{q}(r,\rho,t,\tau) - \phi(r)] + \theta^*(\rho) \cdot \hat{x}^*(r,\rho,t,\tau) \equiv Z(r,\rho,t,\tau).$$

With these definitions, domestic welfare W may now be expressed as[31]

$$CS(\hat{P}(r,\rho,t,\tau)) + PS(r,\hat{q}(r,\rho,t,\tau)) + \pi(r,\rho,t,\tau) + TR(r,\rho,t,\tau)$$
$$- Z(r,\rho,t,\tau) \equiv W(r,\rho,t,\tau). \tag{1.42}$$

Turning now to foreign welfare, recall that the absence of foreign demand for the product under consideration and of foreign pollution, together with the assumed policy passivity of the foreign government, makes the foreign welfare measure very simple: foreign welfare is given by the profits of the foreign exporter. Hence

$$W^* = \pi^*(r,\rho,t,\tau) \equiv W^*(r,\rho,t,\tau). \tag{1.43}$$

Efficient policies With the "offshoring" variant of the model of subsection 1.4.1.2 described, I now turn to characterizing the jointly efficient policy choices in this environment. As before, after characterizing and interpreting the efficient policy choices, I will compare these policies to the noncooperative policy choices that the domestic government would make absent any international agreement and thereby shed light on the problem that a trade agreement must solve in this environment if it is to move governments from inefficient Nash choices to the efficiency frontier.

Recalling once more that the domestic government has at its disposal four policy instruments (and the foreign government has none), there are four first-order conditions that must hold under the choices of these policies that maximize the sum of domestic and foreign welfare as given in (1.42) and (1.43), respectively. Using the derivatives in (1.38) and (1.39) and solving these four equations for the efficient levels of the four policies yields

$$\tau^E = \frac{\hat{x}^{*E}}{D'(\hat{P}^E) - 1} - [1 + \phi^*(\rho^E)] + [\theta^*(\rho^E) - \theta(r^E)],$$

$$t^E = \theta(r^E),$$

$$-\theta'(r^E) = \phi'(r^E), \tag{1.44}$$

$$-\theta^{*'}(\rho^E) = \phi^{*'}(\rho^E),$$

where I use $\hat{x}^{*E}$ and $\hat{P}^E$ to denote the equilibrium magnitudes of these variables evaluated under efficient policies. And in the symmetric benchmark setting in which the functions ϕ and ϕ^* are identical and the functions θ and θ^* are identical, (1.44) reduces to

$$\tau^E = \frac{\hat{x}^{*E}}{D'(\hat{P}^E) - 1} - [1 + \phi^*(\rho^E)],$$

$$t^E = \theta(r^E), \tag{1.45}$$

$$-\theta'(r^E) = \phi'(r^E),$$

$$\rho^E = r^E.$$

Comparing the efficient policies in (1.44) and (1.45) with those of subsection 1.4.1.2 as contained in (1.28) and (1.29), where the international price is determined by market clearing, it is apparent that the only difference in efficient policies when international prices are determined by bilateral bargaining is in the efficient setting of the tariff. In particular, as the first line of (1.44) indicates, in addition to serving a Pigouvian role ($[\theta^*(\rho^E) - \theta(r^E)]$) as in (1.28), the efficient tariff now also offsets the market power wielded by the foreign exporter when it chooses its export volume (a subsidy to imports in the amount $\frac{\hat{x}^{*E}}{D'(\hat{P}^E)-1}$) and corrects the "holdup" problem associated with the foreign exporter's ex ante investment decision (a subsidy to imports in the amount $-[1 + \phi^*(\rho^E)]$). Facing the efficient tariff τ^E, the foreign export volume is then determined by (1.37) to satisfy $\hat{q}^E = [1 + \phi^*(\rho^E)] + [\theta^*(\rho^E) - \theta(r^E)]$. In words, the efficient tariff level induces a level of foreign exports $\hat{x}^{*E}$ such that the marginal cost of the last unit produced by the competitive fringe of domestic suppliers ($\hat{q}^E$) is equal to the cost of foreign supply ($[1 + \phi^*(\rho^E)]$) adjusted for any difference in per-unit pollution level generated by consumption of the foreign and domestically produced goods $[\theta^*(\rho^E) - \theta(r^E)]$.

Aside from the differences in the levels of the efficient tariff, the efficient levels of intervention for the other instruments as depicted in (1.44) and (1.45) are all unchanged relative to (1.28) and (1.29) by the presence of bilateral bargaining between the domestic importer and the foreign exporter/supplier. In particular, as before, the efficient domestic consumption tax is set at a Pigouvian level that reflects the externality associated with consumption of a unit of the domestically produced good and, as before, the efficient standards applied to domestic and imported goods must equate the marginal benefit per unit of pollution reduction that comes with a slightly tighter standard with the marginal cost per unit of compliance with the tighter standard.

Noncooperative policies Next I characterize the noncooperative (Nash) policy choices of the domestic country (recall again that the foreign country is assumed passive in this industry). Using the domestic welfare expression given in (1.42) and the derivatives in (1.38) and (1.39), the noncooperative choices of τ, t, r, and ρ must satisfy the four first-order conditions for maximization of W. Denoting by $\hat{x}^{*N}$ and $\hat{P}^N$ the equilibrium magnitudes of these variables evaluated under noncooperative (Nash) policies, these first-order conditions can be manipulated to yield

$$\tau^N = -\frac{\pi^N}{\hat{x}^{*N}} - \frac{\hat{x}^{*N}}{D'(\hat{P}^N) - 1} + [\theta^*(\rho^N) - \theta(r^N)],$$

$$t^N = \theta(r^N) + \frac{\hat{x}^{*N} \cdot D''(\hat{P}^N)}{2D'(\hat{P}^N) \cdot (D'(\hat{P}^N) - 1)^2}, \tag{1.46}$$

$$-\theta'(r^N) = \phi'(r^N),$$

$$-\theta^{*\prime}(\rho^N) = \phi^{*\prime}(\rho^N)$$

and in the symmetric benchmark setting (1.46) reduces to

$$\tau^N = -\frac{\pi^N}{\hat{x}^{*N}} - \frac{\hat{x}^{*N}}{D'(\hat{P}^N) - 1},$$

$$t^N = \theta(r^N) + \frac{\hat{x}^{*N} \cdot D''(\hat{P}^N)}{2D'(\hat{P}^N) \cdot (D'(\hat{P}^N) - 1)^2}, \tag{1.47}$$

$$-\theta'(r^N) = \phi'(r^N),$$

$$\rho^N = r^N.$$

Comparing (1.46) and (1.47) to their analogues (1.31) and (1.32) in subsection 1.4.1.2, it is apparent that the conditions determining the Nash regulatory policies are the same, but the conditions determining the Nash tariff and domestic consumption tax are now different.

Referring to the general case of (1.46), the level of the Nash tariff now reflects three forces. First, τ^N is lower when the importer's profit per unit imported $\left(\frac{\pi^N}{\hat{x}^{*N}}\right)$ is higher, because with $\frac{\partial \hat{x}^*}{\partial \tau} < 0$ by (1.38) a marginally higher tariff is then more costly to the domestic country in terms of reduced domestic profits. Second, τ^N is higher when the market power wielded by the foreign exporter $\left(-\frac{\hat{x}^{*N}}{D'(\hat{P}^N) - 1}\right)$ is higher, because more of the tariff can then be imposed on the foreign country and extracted as tariff revenue. Finally, τ^N serves the now familiar Pigouvian role ($[\theta^*(\rho^N) - \theta(r^N)]$).

Turning to the Nash domestic consumption tax, its level is now determined by two forces: first, its Pigouvian role ($\theta(r^N)$), and second, an add-on term $\left(\frac{\hat{x}^{*N} \cdot D''(\hat{P}^N)}{2D'(\hat{P}^N) \cdot (D'(\hat{P}^N)-1)^2}\right)$, whose sign is opposite the sign of D''. This second term can be understood intuitively as follows.

First, note from (1.37) that the domestic country can alter its tariff and domestic consumption tax in a manner that leaves the equilibrium trade volume $\hat{x}^*$ unaffected. Using (1.37), the precise adjustment in τ that must accompany a small increase in t to hold $\hat{x}^*$ fixed is given by

$$\frac{d\tau}{dt}\Big|_{d\hat{x}^*=0} = -\left[\frac{D' \cdot (D'-1)^2 - \hat{x}^* \cdot D''}{(D'-1)^3}\right] < 0,$$

where the inequality follows under my maintained assumption that the magnitude of D'' is not too large. Next, observe that these tax adjustments impact foreign profits according to

$$\frac{d\pi^*(r, \rho, t, \tau(t)|_{d\hat{x}^*=0})}{dt} = -\frac{(\hat{x}^*)^2 \cdot D''}{2(D'-1)^3},$$

whose sign is the same as the sign of D''. Finally, it is straightforward to confirm that, beginning from the efficient domestic consumption tax $t^E = \theta(r^E)$, the impact of these tax adjustments on domestic welfare is given by

$$\frac{dW(r, \rho, t, \tau(t)|_{d\hat{x}^*=0})}{dt}\Big|_{t^E=\theta(r^E)} = \frac{(\hat{x}^*)^2 \cdot D''}{2(D'-1)^3},$$

which takes a sign opposite to the sign of D''. Evidently, when D'' is positive and beginning from t^E, the domestic country can reduce foreign profits and convert this foreign loss into its own welfare gain by reducing the domestic consumption tax from its efficient level and adjusting the tariff so as to preserve the equilibrium volume of foreign exports $\hat{x}^*$. When D'' is negative, it can accomplish this by increasing the domestic consumption tax and adjusting the tariff. As (1.46) indicates, what eventually stops this adjustment in t away from its efficient level is the cost of the domestic demand distortion (as reflected in the magnitude of $D'(\hat{P})$) that is induced by the changes in t.

Finally, notice from (1.40) and (1.41) that foreign profits may be written as $\pi^* = [\hat{q}_0^w - 1] \cdot \hat{x}^*$, so the maneuver I have just described, wherein the domestic country uses adjustments in t and τ to hold $\hat{x}^*$ fixed while reducing π^* for domestic benefit, amounts to a maneuver to manipulate the terms of trade in its favor (i.e., to reduce $\hat{q}_0^w$). However, while again this points to terms-of-trade manipulation as the root of the problem that leads to inefficiencies in the noncooperative Nash equilibrium, it should nevertheless be clear that the policies used to manipulate the terms of trade in presence of offshoring are more complex than would be expected according to the terms-of-trade theory.[32]

The problem for a trade agreement to solve I now turn to a comparison of the efficient policies characterized in subsection 1.4.3.2 with the noncooperative policies characterized there, in order to identify and understand the problem that a trade agreement must solve in this "offshoring" environment if it is to move governments from inefficient Nash choices to the efficiency frontier. This comparison again turns out to be illuminating, and in the context of the present model (as in Antras and Staiger 2012a, 2012b), it leads to a striking result.

First, consider the tariff. It can be shown that $\tau^N > \tau^E$: the Nash tariff is again inefficiently high. Simply put, it is not in the unilateral interests of the domestic country to offer import subsidies to counter the inefficiencies associated with foreign market power and the holdup problem, as international efficiency concerns would dictate. On the contrary, as (1.46) indicates, the domestic country has a unilateral incentive to tax imports and shift some of this tax onto the foreign exporter, an incentive that is kept in check only by the trade volume reductions that come with the higher tariff. This finding is analogous to that derived in the context of the terms-of-trade theory in subsection 1.4.1.2.

Now consider the domestic consumption tax. Recalling that, according to the terms-of-trade theory, in the Nash equilibrium the domestic consumption tax is not distorted from its efficient level, we now have a striking finding: in the presence of offshoring, where international prices are determined by bilateral bargaining rather than through market-clearing conditions, the Nash level of the domestic consumption tax is distorted from its internationally efficient level. That is, as a comparison of (1.44) and (1.46) reveals, t^N is greater than or less than its efficient Pigouvian level when D'' is negative or positive, respectively.[33] Hence, behind-the-border NTMs can no longer be presumed to be set at efficient levels in the noncooperative Nash equilibrium in the presence of offshoring.

Recalling now that it was the terms-of-trade theory's prediction of efficient Nash choices for behind-the-border NTMs that I interpreted as lending support to the kind of shallow integration that characterizes the GATT approach, the result just given indicates that by changing the nature of international price determination, the rise of offshoring undercuts this support, and it points instead to the possibility that effective trade agreements now require deep integration. In this way, the rise in offshoring may necessitate fundamental changes in the WTO's approach to behind-the-border NTMs.[34]

Interestingly, at least in the model considered here, the inefficiency of noncooperative behind-the-border NTMs in the presence of offshoring is contained to domestic tax policies and does not spread to domestic nontax regulations. This can be seen by noting from the last two lines in (1.44) and (1.46) that the Nash standards choices continue to satisfy the same conditions as the efficient standards choices, and indeed the Nash standards correspond to the efficient standards: $r^N = r^E$ and $\rho^N = \rho^E$. Hence, at least in this model and where product-level consumption taxes are available, the presence of offshoring and the implications for international price determination that offshoring implies lead to inefficient noncooperative choices for domestic tax instruments but not for domestic nontax policies.

A finding that is somewhat related to this last point is reported by Staiger and Sykes (2011) in the context of the terms-of-trade theory. They show that when the tariff is constrained in a trade agreement and when domestic taxes and nontax regulations are constrained to satisfy a "national treatment" restriction, the domestic consumption tax will be distorted but the nontax regulations will not.[35] However, as Staiger and Sykes observe, for a variety of reasons, the ability of governments to impose product-specific consumption taxes appears to be quite limited in practice. Hence, it is important to note that this last point depends on the availability of such taxes. I will now show that when a (product-specific) consumption tax is unavailable to the domestic government, the inefficiency of noncooperative Nash behind-the-border NTMs spreads to nontax regulatory policies.

Consumption tax unavailable Thus far, I have adopted the view that product-specific consumption taxes are available to the domestic government. As might be expected, the ability to impose product-specific consumption taxes at the same level of detail as the tariff and product standards is important for the formal results given earlier, and in particular for the result that in the presence of offshoring, among all possible behind-the-border NTMs, only domestic tax instruments are distorted in the noncooperative Nash equilibrium.

In practice, however, governments are not typically observed to impose detailed and distinct product-specific consumption taxes across a wide swath of products (gasoline is an obvious exception). Rather, the norm in practice tends to be uniform sales (or value-added) taxes at various levels of government. Motivated by this observation, I now illustrate briefly how the "offshoring" results reported earlier must be altered if the domestic government does not have a (product-specific) consumption tax at its disposal.[36] For simplicity, and because it will not impact the point that I emphasize here, I also assume that consumption of the domestically produced good no longer has an externality associated with it and that there is no regulatory policy imposed on the (clean) domestic production. That is, I now assume $t \equiv 0$, $r \equiv 0$, and $\theta \equiv 0$, so that I may concentrate on the domestic-country policies τ and ρ. In this context, I repeat my comparison of efficient and noncooperative policies to assess the efficiency properties of the nontax behind-the-border regulatory policy ρ in the noncooperative Nash equilibrium.

Proceeding as earlier, it is straightforward to demonstrate that when $t \equiv 0$, $r \equiv 0$, and $\theta \equiv 0$, the efficient domestic tariff and regulatory policies (recall once more that the foreign government is passive) satisfy

$$\tau^E = \frac{\hat{x}^{*E}}{D'(\hat{P}^E) - 1} - [1 + \phi^*(\rho^E)] + \theta^*(\rho^E),$$

$$-\theta^{*\prime}(\rho^E) = \phi^{*\prime}(\rho^E). \tag{1.48}$$

The interpretation of (1.48) is analogous to that of (1.44) as described in subsection 1.4.3.2, and, proceeding as before, it can be shown that the noncooperative Nash policies are now described by

$$\tau^N = -\frac{\pi^N}{\hat{x}^{*N}} - \frac{\hat{x}^{*N}}{D'(\hat{P}^N) - 1} + \theta^*(\rho^N) + \frac{(\hat{x}^{*N})^2 \cdot D''}{(D' - 1)^3},$$

$$-\theta^{*\prime}(\rho^N) = \phi^{*\prime}(\rho^N) \left[1 - \frac{(D' - 1)^2}{2(D' - 1)^2 - \hat{x}^{*N} \cdot D''} \right]. \tag{1.49}$$

Notice that relative to (1.46), (1.49) implies that the Nash tariff is adjusted by an add-on term $\left(\frac{(\hat{x}^{*N})^2 \cdot D''}{(D' - 1)^3} \right)$ whose sign is opposite the sign of D''. This compensates for the lack of an available domestic consumption tax t. But the important difference to note is revealed by comparing the second lines of (1.48) and (1.49). It can be confirmed that this comparison implies $-\theta^{*\prime}(\rho^N) < -\theta^{*\prime}(\rho^E)$, which in turn indicates that $\rho^N > \rho^E$. In words, in the presence of offshoring and when product-level domestic consumption taxes are unavailable to the domestic government, the noncooperative level of domestic regulation applied to foreign exports is set higher than would be efficient. Hence, in this setting with limited domestic tax instruments, offshoring and the bilateral bargaining over international prices that is associated with it results in inefficiencies in the noncooperative Nash equilibrium that extend beyond border measures (tariffs) to apply also to behind-the-border nontax regulatory policies.

1.5   Conclusion

In this chapter, I have attempted to sketch the rough contours of the challenge faced by the WTO in dealing with the NTMs. As I have described, the GATT adopted a particular and minimalist "shallow-integration" approach to handling NTMs. That approach evolved over time, and with the creation of the WTO, the handling of NTMs evolved still further. I have considered the economic logic of the GATT's shallow-integration approach from the perspective of three theories of trade agreements: the terms-of-trade theory, the commitment theory, and the offshoring theory. I have shown that, subject to certain caveats, the GATT's approach resonates well with the terms-of-trade theory of trade agreements. Along the way, I have provided a terms-of-trade interpretation of the WTO's Trade Facilitation Agreement. Some of the changes in the treatment of NTMs toward a deeper form of integration that were ushered in with the creation of the WTO are less supported by the terms-of-trade theory but may find some support in the commitment theory of trade agreements. Finally, I have asked: Is the GATT/WTO approach to the treatment of NTMs adequate for the world economy of today? Viewed through the lens of the offshoring theory of trade agreements, I have suggested that the answer to this question may be "No" if the rise in offshoring can be taken to imply that the predominant mechanism for international price determination has changed.

From this perspective, I have suggested that when it comes to handling NTMs, and specifically the choice between shallow and deep approaches to integration, there appear to be two key questions for the WTO: (1) Is it the terms-of-trade problem or the commitment problem (or both, or neither) that WTO member governments seek to solve with their WTO membership?; and (2) Is it market clearing or offshoring/bilateral bargaining that is now the most prominent mechanism for the determination of international prices?

Regarding the first question, empirical evidence seems to support the terms-of-trade theory as identifying the main purpose of the GATT/WTO (see Bagwell, Bown, and Staiger 2016 for a recent review of this evidence), but more evidence on this important question is needed. Regarding the second question, I am not aware of any systematic evidence that would help provide an answer,[37] but it seems likely that answering this second question will be a key step in identifying the best way forward on NTMs for the WTO.

Finally, as I noted in my introduction, the appropriate handling of NTMs in trade agreements may have particular importance for developing countries in light of evidence that the most prevalent forms of NTMs faced by developing-country exporters in their attempts to export into developed-country markets are behind-the-border measures. These are the NTMs that are at the heart of the shallow versus deep integration question, and in this sense developing countries may have the biggest stake in getting the right answer to this question. In this light, extending the simple frameworks I have outlined to better reflect the particular experience of developing countries seems an especially important goal for future research.

Notes

An earlier draft of this chapter was written in 2011 as a background paper for the WTO's World Trade Report 2012, "Shining the Light on NTMs." I thank Kyle Bagwell, Robert Gulotty, Patrick Low, and Michele Ruta for very helpful discussions on the earlier draft, and I thank my discussant Swati Dhingra and participants at the July 20–21, 2015, CESifo Venice Workshop on The World Trade Organization and Economic Development, as well as Kyle Bagwell, Chad Bown, and Ben Zissimos, for helpful discussions and comments that led to improvements in the final draft. Financial support from the WTO and from CESifo is gratefully acknowledged.

1. Recent papers that focus more narrowly on the trade effects of specific nontariff measures include Martincus, Carballo, and Graziano (2015), who estimate the effects of customs-related delays on Uruguay's firm-level exports, and Fontagne et al. (2015), who estimate the effects of SPS measures on the exports of French firms.

2. That said, Irwin, Mavroidis, and Sykes (2008, pp. 69–70, 136) observe that in the negotiations leading up to the creation of the GATT, the United States pushed for a prohibition on export taxes. While no such prohibition was ultimately included in the GATT, this observation does indicate that in the pre-GATT era export taxes were an important trade policy concern to at least some of the major trading countries.

3. The WTO TBT Agreement can also be seen as complementing the ongoing international standardization process, as embodied for example in the International Organization for Standardization (ISO) and the International Electrotechnical Commission (IEC). I do not emphasize this standardization process in what follows, because my focus is on the international cooperation (e.g., prisoners' dilemma) problems that I will argue the WTO is designed to solve rather than on the international coordination problems that the standardization process seeks to address.

4. A comprehensive assessment of the treatment of export subsidies (and of border NTMs more generally) in the GATT and the WTO and an evaluation of this treatment from the perspective of the terms-of-trade theory is provided in Bagwell, Staiger, and Sykes (2013).

5. Bond (2006) also provides an analysis of agreements on trade facilitation from the perspective of a terms-of-trade model, thereby also demonstrating that the terms-of-trade theory can account for the purpose of a trade facilitation agreement. His focus is somewhat different from my focus here, however, and he does not consider the second and third points that I will emphasize.

6. Indeed, the view that the rationale for international agreements regarding trade facilitation (such as the TFA) falls outside the purview of the terms-of-trade theory of trade agreements seems to have gained traction recently in policy circles. Although it appears in various writings, the clearest expression of this view of which I am aware is in Hoekman (2014, p. 5), which also emphasizes that investments in trade facilitation improve the terms of trade of both importing and exporting countries and concludes:

> The puzzle therefore is that a government can unilaterally take actions that will improve its terms of trade without in the process creating an adverse impact on its trading partners. While the foreign country will benefit from a trading partner's trade facilitation, it does not do so at the expense of the country concerned. There is therefore no prisoner's dilemma situation of the type that often drives cooperation on trade policy. The TFA cannot be motivated by the terms-of-trade rationale that has become the staple of the formal economic literature on trade agreements.

7. Here and throughout, I assume that second-order conditions for the relevant maximization problems hold.

8. It is possible to be on the efficiency frontier and yet have one country strictly above its tariff reaction curve (because, as I have noted, only the sum of the tariffs matters for efficiency, not the individual tariff levels), but it is standard to restrict attention to points on the efficiency frontier where both countries are strictly below their tariff reaction curves (see the discussion, for example, in Bagwell and Staiger 2005).

9. For a formal analysis of the implications of international agreements for national sovereignty, with a particular emphasis on trade agreements and the GATT/WTO, see Bagwell and Staiger (2018).

10. As I later discuss, the degree of the GATT/WTO's evolution toward deeper forms of integration on behind-the-border NTMs has been much less significant than it has been for border NTMs, as embodied especially in the recently negotiated TFA. A possible reason is that the sovereignty issues that arise with the TFA are minor compared to those that would arise with deep integration over behind-the-border NTMs.

11. In this regard, it is also interesting to note that the negotiations leading to the WTO's TFA seemed to feature a distinctly more multilateral structure than that typical of GATT/WTO bargains over tariffs. In the latter, a more decentralized approach is often

emphasized, featuring bilateral bargaining in the presence of norms such as reciprocity and the principal supplier rule. It is not clear from the terms-of-trade perspective I have described here why the TFA negotiations featured such a different approach, though one possibility might be that the extreme nature of the free-rider potential associated with investments in trade facilitation as compared to tariff cuts on particular goods (it would be difficult to design improvements in ports or customs procedures that would selectively benefit some foreign exporters but not others) made the more decentralized bargaining approach infeasible in the context of the TFA. In any case, I thank Chad Bown for bringing this issue to my attention, and I view it as an interesting open question for future research.

12. Staiger and Sykes (2011) adopt a linear demand assumption, and the more general demand function that I work with here is the main difference between the model of Staiger and Sykes and the model I develop in this section. As I will establish later, allowing for generalized demands is important once I introduce offshoring.

13. Staiger and Sykes (2011) allow the foreign government to choose an export tax for the industry. They show that all the results that I emphasize in this section apply with a policy-active foreign government of this kind. As none of the results depend on whether the foreign government is policy active, I simplify here by abstracting from foreign government policies altogether.

14. If there were a separate increasing-cost industry in the foreign country that took unregulated goods as inputs and provided a service that transformed these goods to achieve compliance for a given regulatory standard, then there would be an additional foreign-producer-surplus consequence of the domestic regulatory choice ρ, but again the impact would travel through market-clearing prices, in this case the price of the service performed. As long as this new price is introduced into the measure of welfare in the appropriate way, the added complication would not alter the basic findings I present.

15. As before, by focusing on the policy choices that maximize this joint welfare measure, I am thereby assuming implicitly that lump sum transfers are available to distribute surpluses across the two countries as desired.

16. I will sometimes refer to the noncooperative policy choices of the domestic country as "Nash" policies even though the foreign country has no policies of its own so there is no strategic interaction between the countries, because all the findings that I emphasize here would apply also when the foreign country is allowed to have policies as well and such strategic interaction between countries is present (see note 13).

17. I assume throughout that policy choices correspond to interior solutions of the relevant maximization problems. It is easily confirmed that the second-order conditions associated with the maximization problems considered here and throughout this section are satisfied under the convexity assumptions for θ, θ^*, ϕ, and ϕ^*.

18. This observation is also made in Staiger and Sykes (2011), where a discussion of its implications for the desirability of the GATT "national treatment" clause is included as well. See also Gulati and Roy (2008).

19. This follows from my focus on nonprohibitive intervention, which ensures that the Nash export volume S^{*N} is strictly positive.

20. To see this, notice that the elasticity of foreign export supply in this model can be written as $\frac{\partial S^*}{\partial \tilde{q}^w} \frac{\tilde{q}^w}{S^*} = \frac{\tilde{q}^w}{S^*}$. Dividing τ^N by $\tilde{q}^w$ to convert the specific import tariff of the domestic

country into its ad valorem equivalent yields $\frac{\tau^N}{\bar{q}^w} = \frac{[\theta^*(\rho^N)-\theta(r^N)]}{\bar{q}^w} + \frac{S^*}{\bar{q}^w}$. Evidently, the second term in this expression is the inverse of the foreign export supply elasticity, which is the Johnson (1953–1954) "optimal" terms-of-trade-manipulating ad valorem tariff.

21. The terminology used by Bagwell and Staiger (1999, 2001a) reflects the fact that they work with government objective functions that allow for general political economy motives. I have abstracted from political economy motives here, but it is convenient nevertheless to adopt their terminology (and it can be shown that the results I emphasize here extend to a setting with political economy motives, as Staiger and Sykes 2011 also observe).

22. With this interpretation, it can also be seen that the international efficiency of the behind-the-border NTMs in the noncooperative Nash equilibrium does not hinge on the nature (e.g., completeness) of the set of behind-the-border instruments that are available to a government.

23. The importance of the nonviolation clause in practice is difficult to assess, because it can shape GATT/WTO policy outcomes through both on-equilibrium and off-equilibrium impacts. Staiger and Sykes (2017) consider the implications of the observed (on-equilibrium-path) performance of the nonviolation clause in GATT/WTO disputes for the implied importance of the clause in shaping GATT/WTO policy outcomes.

24. See Bagwell and Staiger (2001a) and Staiger and Sykes (2011) for a demonstration that the same desirable properties of a market access preservation rule of the kind described in the text extends to the case of governments with political economy motives. Bagwell and Staiger (2006) establish related themes in the context of domestic subsidies.

25. In a more general setting where the foreign government also had a trade tax instrument at its disposal so that a distinction between $\tilde{q}_0^*$ and $\tilde{q}_0^w$ could arise as a result of this foreign trade tax, the same conclusion would hold, because changes in domestic-country policies that hold $\tilde{q}_0^w$ fixed would also hold $\tilde{q}_0^*$ fixed given the (unchanged) level of the foreign trade tax (see Staiger and Sykes 2011).

26. This is not to imply that this support is without caveats. For example, important qualifications to some of the results I emphasize here have been shown to arise in the presence of private information (see Bagwell, Bown, and Staiger 2016 for a recent review of the relevant literature).

27. The commitment role for trade agreements has been formalized in a large number of papers. In addition to the papers I discuss here, see Carmichael (1987), Staiger and Tabellini (1987), Matsuyama (1990), and Maggi and Rodriguez-Clare (1998, 2007), to name a few.

28. Limão and Tovar (2011) also study the role of trade agreements as commitment devices when governments have both tariffs and behind-the-border NTMs at their disposal, but their focus is on the possibility that international commitments to lower tariffs will impact the use of behind-the-border NTMs, and on whether tariff agreements can still be attractive to governments when these impacts are present. Unlike Brou and Ruta (2013), Limão and Tovar do not consider the possibility that international commitments might be extended to cover behind-the-border NTMs, and the way in which this extension might best be designed.

29. DeRemer (2011) provides an alternative "international externality" rationale for deep integration, and in particular for the evolution of GATT/WTO subsidy rules in this direction. Working in a setting characterized by monopolistic competition, trade taxes, and

trade costs, where entry is fixed except for an entry subsidy from the government, DeRemer argues that the kinds of market access assurance rules incorporated in the GATT do not prevent international policy externalities from being transmitted in this setting and so cannot enable countries to achieve efficient policies with shallow integration.

30. As Antras and Staiger (2012b) emphasize, the key feature of the economy needed for results of the kind I describe is that international prices are determined by bilateral bargaining rather than by market-clearing mechanisms, and the rise of offshoring is just one plausible way in which the former method of price determination may have become increasingly prominent in recent decades.

31. I do not express welfare in terms of nontax policies and prices as I did in subsection 1.4.1.2, because, as I will show, the terms-of-trade structure that such a representation of welfare was useful for illuminating does not apply in the offshoring environment that I consider here.

32. In fact, Antras and Staiger (2012a) establish formally that when political economy motivations are absent (as is the case here), the problem for a trade agreement to fix in the presence of offshoring can be given a terms-of-trade interpretation. However, they also show that this interpretation no longer applies once political economy motives are introduced.

33. The role of my generalization of the model of Staiger and Sykes (2011) to nonlinear demands can now be appreciated, since with linear demands $D'' = 0$ and the inefficiency identified here would not arise. The role of the curvature of demand in the model of offshoring I develop here is analogous to the role of the curvature of the final-good production function in Antras and Staiger (2012a).

34. See Antras and Staiger (2012a) for a discussion of this point and additional ways in which offshoring may change the role for trade agreements, as well as the possibility that the recent proliferation of PTAs may in part be an institutional response to offshoring triggered by the WTO's inability to facilitate deep integration for its member governments.

35. Nontax regulatory policies are not considered in Antras and Staiger (2012a, 2012b), so there is no analogous result reported in those papers.

36. No changes would result in the (non-consumption-tax) findings I report from the terms-of-trade theory if the consumption tax is assumed unavailable to the domestic government (see note 22).

37. That said, some indirect evidence that hints at the growing relevance of the offshoring/bilateral bargaining perspective is provided in Antras and Staiger (2012a).

References

Antras P, Staiger RW. 2012a. Offshoring and the Role of Trade Agreements. *American Economic Review* 102(7): 3140–3183.

Antras P, Staiger RW. 2012b. Trade Agreements and the Nature of International Price Determination. *American Economic Review Papers and Proceedings* 102(3): 470–476.

Bagwell K, Bown C, Staiger RW. 2016. Is the WTO Passé? *Journal of Economic Literature* 54(4): 1125–1231.

Bagwell K, Staiger RW. 1999. An Economic Theory of GATT. *American Economic Review* 89:215–248.

Bagwell K, Staiger RW. 2001a. Domestic Policies, National Sovereignty and International Economic Institutions. *Quarterly Journal of Economics* 116:519–562.

Bagwell K, Staiger RW. 2001b. Strategic Trade, Competitive Industries and Agricultural Trade Disputes. *Economics and Politics* 13:113–128.

Bagwell K, Staiger RW. 2002. *The Economics of the World Trading System*. Cambridge, MA: MIT Press.

Bagwell K, Staiger RW. 2005. Multilateral Trade Negotiations, Bilateral Opportunism and the Rules of GATT/WTO. *Journal of International Economics* 67:268–294.

Bagwell K, Staiger RW. 2006. Will International Rules on Subsidies Disrupt the World Trading System? *American Economic Review* 96(3): 877–895.

Bagwell K, Staiger RW. 2010. The World Trade Organization: Theory and Practice. *Annual Review of Economics* 2:223–256.

Bagwell K, Staiger RW. 2012a. The Economics of Trade Agreements in the Linear Cournot Delocation Model. *Journal of International Economics* 88(1): 32–46.

Bagwell K, Staiger RW. 2012b. Profit Shifting and Trade Agreements in Imperfectly Competitive Markets. *International Economic Review* 53(4): 1067–1104.

Bagwell, K, Staiger RW. 2018. National Sovereignty in an Interdependent World. In *World Trade Evolution: Growth, Productivity and Employment*, edited by Lili Yan Ing and Miaojie Yu (pp. 12–59). London: Routledge.

Bagwell K, Staiger RW, Sykes AO. 2013. Border Instruments. In *Legal and Economic Principles of World Trade Law*, edited by H Horn, PC Mavroidis (pp. 68–204). Cambridge: American Law Institute and Cambridge University Press.

Bond, EW. 2006. Transportation Infrastructure Investments and Trade Liberalization. *Japanese Economic Review* 57(4): 483–500.

Brou D, Ruta M. 2013. A Commitment Theory of Subsidy Agreements. *BE Journal of Economic Analysis and Policy* 13(1): 239–270.

Carmichael C. 1987. The Control of Export Credit Subsidies and Its Welfare Consequences. *Journal of International Economics* 23:1–19.

Deardorff AV, Stern RM. 1997. Measurement of Non-tariff Barriers. University of Michigan Economics Department Working Paper No. 179. Ann Arbor: University of Michigan.

DeRemer DR. 2011. The Evolution of International Subsidy Rules. Mimeo, Columbia University. November.

Fontagne L, Orefice G, Piermartini R, Rocha N. 2015. Product Standards and Margins of Trade: Firm-Level Evidence. *Journal of International Economics* 97:29–44.

Gulati S, Roy D. 2008. National Treatment and the Optimal Regulation of Environmental Externalities. *Canadian Journal of Economics* 41:1445–1471.

Hoekman B. 2014. The Bali Trade Facilitation Agreement and Rulemaking in the WTO: Milestone, Mistake or Mirage? European University Institute Working Paper No. RSCAS 2014/102. Florence: European University Institute.

Hudec RE. 1990. *The GATT Legal System and World Trade Diplomacy*, 2nd edition. Salem: Butterworth Legal Publishers.

Irwin D, Mavroidis PC, Sykes AO. 2008. *The Genesis of the GATT*. Cambridge: Cambridge University Press.

Jackson JH, Davey WJ, Sykes AO. 1995. *Legal Problems of International Economic Relations: Cases, Materials, and Text.*, 3rd edition. St. Paul, MN: West Publishing.

Johnson HG. 1953–1954. Optimum Tariffs and Retaliation. *Review of Economic Studies* 21:142–153.

Kee HL, Nicita A, Olarreaga M. 2009. Estimating Trade Restrictiveness Indices. *Economic Journal* 119:172–199.

Laird S. 1999. Millennium Round Market Access Negotiations in Goods and Services. Paper prepared for a meeting of the International Economics Study Group, Birmingham, September 14–16.

Limão N, Tovar P. 2011. Policy Choice: Theory and Evidence from Commitment via International Trade Agreements. *Journal of International Economics* 85(2): 186–205.

Maggi G, Rodriguez-Clare A. 1998. The Value of Trade Agreements in the Presence of Political Pressures. *Journal of Political Economy* 106:574–601.

Maggi G, Rodriguez-Clare A. 2007. A Political-Economy Theory of Trade Agreements. *American Economic Review* 97:1374–1406.

Martincus CV, Carballo J, Graziano A. 2015. Customs. *Journal of International Economics* 96(1): 119–137.

Matsuyama K. 1990. Perfect Equilibria in a Trade Liberalization Game. *American Economic Review* 80:480–492.

Michalopoulos C. 1999. *Trade Policy and Market Access Issues for Developing Countries: Implications for the Millennium Round*. Washington, DC: World Bank.

Organization for Economic Cooperation and Development (OECD). 2005. *Looking beyond Tariffs: The Role of Non-tariff Barriers in World Trade*. OECD Trade Policy Studies. Paris: OECD.

Potipiti T. 2012. Import Tariffs and Export Subsidies in the WTO: A Small Country Approach. Unpublished mimeo, Chulalongkorn University.

Staiger RW, Sykes AO. 2011. International Trade, National Treatment and Domestic Regulation. *Journal of Legal Studies* 40(2): 149–203.

Staiger RW, Sykes AO. 2017. How Important Can the Non-violation Clause Be for the GATT/WTO? *American Economic Journal: Microeconomics* 9(2): 149–187.

Staiger RW, Tabellini G. 1987. Discretionary Trade Policy and Excessive Protection. *American Economic Review* 77:823–837.

Staiger RW, Wolak F. 1994. Measuring Industry Specific Protection: Antidumping in the United States. *Brookings Papers on Economic Activity: Microeconomics* 1:51–118

United Nations Conference on Trade and Development (UNCTAD). 2013. *Non-tariff Measures to Trade: Economic and Policy Issues for Developing Countries.* Developing Countries in International Trade Studies, United Nations Publication ISSN 1817–1214. New York and Geneva: United Nations.

World Trade Organization (WTO). 2011. *World Trade Report 2011.* Geneva: World Trade Organization.

2 What's Left for the WTO?

Chad P. Bown

2.1 Introduction

While the WTO may seem ubiquitous, in reality there have been substantial segments of the international trading system that remain seemingly untouched by its reaches. This chapter utilizes the lens of the terms-of-trade theory of trade agreements and insights from recent empirical developments to investigate three of these areas in particular. First, as of 2013, roughly three dozen countries remained WTO non-members. The people living in these countries do not enjoy the basic rights and obligations of the multilateral system for all the products that they might trade. Second, another 25 countries have now been full WTO members for more than 20 years and yet their governments have not taken on even the minimum legal commitment of binding the upper limit of their import tariffs for more than two-thirds of manufactured products. Third, even among the WTO members that have legally bound their tariffs, another 45 countries have committed to binding rates that convey limited economic meaning. On average, the binding commitments are more than 15 percentage points above these countries' applied Most Favored Nation (MFN) tariff rates; put differently, these countries could immediately and permanently raise their applied MFN tariffs by an average of 400% with only minimal notification to other WTO members and with no required compensation. Combined, more than 3.5 billion people live under one of these three sets of conditions in what are predominantly developing countries.

I highlight and choose to investigate these three areas given the crossroads at which the WTO found itself even before the more recent challenges threatening the system.[1] On the one hand, trade negotiators seemed to have moved beyond the WTO. The Doha Round was a failure, albeit its weaknesses may be at least partially laid at the feet of those who established the Doha negotiating agenda in 2001.[2] Many have argued that the agenda and approach were fundamentally unfit to deliver any sort of successful outcome along the lines of the previous institutional and reciprocal negotiating frameworks that the GATT had repeatedly delivered over eight previous rounds and more than 50 years of negotiations (Bagwell and Staiger 2014).[3]

Perhaps more threatening to the stasis that plagued the WTO, however, was that many important WTO members had already turned their negotiating efforts away from the multilateral system and toward something else. This included moving away from the GATT/WTO's historical "shallow" integration approach of negotiating over tariffs and market access in favor of the "deeper" integration and direct negotiation over behind-the-border policy instruments through the "megaregional" negotiations of the Trans-Pacific Partnership (TPP) and Transatlantic Trade and Investment Partnership (T-TIP), as well as a potential Regional Comprehensive Economic Partnership (RCEP) or Free Trade Area of the Asia-Pacific (FTAAP) (Bagwell, Bown, and Staiger 2016).[4] Shifting away from the WTO and toward these megaregional efforts was at least initially led by both historical champions of the multilateral system, such as the United States, European Union, and Japan, and other recent and chief beneficiaries, such as China.[5]

On the other hand, the economics literature has made improved strides toward understanding some of the core microeconomic and institutional underpinnings behind what has facilitated the GATT/WTO's relatively successful achievement of reaching and sustaining levels of import tariffs that were historically low, despite massive macroeconomic shocks to the system (Bown 2011a). In particular, the terms-of-trade literature of trade agreements, most closely associated with the theoretical developments introduced by Bagwell and Staiger (1999, 2002), as well as the inaugural empirical work of Broda, Limão, and Weinstein (2008), has ushered in a number of recent theoretical and empirical advancements. In section 2.2, I survey key aspects of this literature that had significantly helped clarify determinants of trade policy under the multilateral system. Many of these insights interpret the WTO as coordinating policies for countries seeking to address the prisoner's dilemma outcome of terms-of-trade externalities.

One of the primary insights from the theory is that, in order for the GATT/WTO to work at getting significant areas of the global economy to internalize such externalities, it has focused on shallow integration and the reduction of border barriers (tariffs); relied on fundamental principles such as reciprocity, MFN treatment, and national treatment; and secured market access commitments implied by tariff reductions through a legal system of tariff bindings that is backed up by third-party dispute settlement. The research that I review in section 2.2 sheds light on some of the successes of this approach at getting countries to internalize what would otherwise be terms-of-trade *externalities* (i.e., applying tariffs that exert market power and drive down the price exporters receive for sales into the import market). Second, the literature has also begun to reveal specific places where the impact of the historical approach has proven incomplete and potential explanations behind why failures have arisen. My approach is to extend this analysis of the WTO with a particular focus on three areas of tariffs that are particularly critical to the interests of developing countries.

In section 2.3, I begin this chapter's empirical contribution by introducing the applied tariffs for the 36 countries and 500 million people that were not yet a part of the WTO system as of 2013. I choose this as my launch point not only because this is where the WTO has had the least impact to date but also because this is one of the least studied areas of international trade policy. As such, much of my effort here is expositional—a contributing reason why so little has been studied for these countries is a combination of data limitations (some of which I am able to overcome) and that these particular countries have many other economic and social problems to address in the global community that may outweigh the importance of international trade agreements. Nevertheless, this section also provides me the opportunity to compare the applied tariffs and political-economic characteristics of WTO non-member countries with those of a group of nearly 30 other countries that recently acceded to the WTO. Furthermore, I am able to utilize newly available data and newly constructed measures of importer market power by taking advantage of newly available foreign export supply estimates provided by Nicita, Olarreaga, and Silva (2018). I then reassess—and largely confirm—prior evidence in the terms-of-trade literature on the tariff-setting behavior of a subsample of these recently acceded countries, and the role of market power in affecting the changes to their trade policies upon accession to the WTO.

I then turn to a more formal empirical investigation of two areas in which the applied tariffs of WTO members are sometimes alleged to be too high. Section 2.4 focuses on the applied tariffs for the products that are "unbound" in the WTO system. I examine a set of 25 countries (and more than 700 million people), mostly concentrated in sub-Saharan

Africa, that are long-standing WTO members but have nevertheless not yet taken on the legal commitment to bind the upper limit of their tariffs at any level for more than two-thirds of their manufactured import products. Nevertheless, while there may be arguments for the WTO to encourage these countries to bind the tariffs of these unbound products that are not motivated by terms of trade, I fail to find evidence that the applied tariffs for these unbound products are positively related to the importing country's ability to exert market power.

There is, however, evidence linking import market power influences and applied MFN tariffs for countries that have legally bound their tariffs under the WTO and yet retain considerable discretion as to the *level* at which they would be applied because of "tariff overhang." In section 2.5, I note the 45 countries (and more than 2.4 billion people) where substantial tariff overhang still remains in the WTO system, and I provide some evidence identifying this area as potentially one in which the terms-of-trade theory could motivate use of the WTO as a forum to facilitate additional tariff liberalization.

Finally, in section 2.6, I conclude by integrating this evidence alongside related work that highlights the difficulties confronting negotiators seeking to utilize the WTO system to facilitate additional tariff liberalization. I also highlight priority areas and some remaining unanswered questions for policy-related research.

Before delving into the formal theoretical and empirical analysis, it is worth acknowledging two additional points. First, my focus on tariffs and the terms-of-trade theory is limited by design so as to keep the empirical analysis manageable, but it is admittedly incomplete.[6] Second, the role of the WTO in the multilateral trading system goes well beyond its service as a forum for reciprocal tariff cutting. Put differently, even if the evidence were to indicate that the WTO's tariff-liberalization function was now somehow complete—which even the evidence that I review and provide suggests is not yet the case—the WTO *institution* makes other substantive contributions to the system that are not provided by any other entity. These include providing forums for the peaceful resolution of bilateral trade disputes between countries over their commitments and obligations (Maggi and Staiger 2011, 2015; Bown 2009; Bown and Reynolds 2015, 2017) and for transparency and the dissemination of information (e.g., the Trade Policy Review Mechanism and other reporting requirements) regarding how governments make changes to their trade policies in ways that affect trading partners' market access (Maggi 1999).

2.2 The Terms-of-Trade Approach to Trade Agreements

My analysis of where to look for evidence that the WTO's tariff liberalization performance to date may be incomplete is guided by the terms-of-trade theory of trade agreements and a number of recent pieces of empirical evidence. This section provides a brief description of the core insights of the terms-of-trade theory of trade agreements and recent empirical research that searches for evidence of this theory inside and outside the GATT/WTO system. Its main purpose is to survey the state of the art of the existing research literature in this area in order to establish expectations for my formal empirical analysis that follows. I begin with the theory of the terms-of-trade motivations for trade agreements and then turn to evidence on how this affects trade policy determination for countries outside the GATT/WTO, for countries that change their tariffs in order to enter the WTO through accession, and for countries that have been more long-standing participants in the GATT/WTO regarding their applied and binding tariffs.

2.2.1 The Terms-of-Trade Theory of Trade Agreements

Here I review the basics of the terms-of-trade theory of trade agreements introduced in Bagwell and Staiger (1999). In a noncooperative setting characterizing the absence of a trade agreement, two large countries each have a unilateral incentive to impose import tariffs at Nash levels that are too high relative to the jointly efficient outcome. Each Nash tariff is too high because it shifts some of the cost of the tariff—by reducing the price received by the trading partner's exporters of the product—onto the trading partner via a terms-of-trade externality. The result of having each country set its tariff at an excessively high level is the classic prisoner's dilemma outcome driven by terms of trade. Bagwell and Staiger then compare this outcome with an outcome whereby they suppose that each government was not motivated by terms-of-trade considerations in its objective function when setting its tariff but that each government was only (potentially) concerned with the domestic price effects of its tariff choice. In this way, their model allows for the consideration of political economy influences; for example, a government may be interested in using its tariff to redistribute income from one group in the domestic economy to another.[7]

The Bagwell and Staiger (1999) approach generates a number of insights that have subsequently had implications for empirical analysis.[8] First, a trade agreement like the GATT/WTO can be used to coordinate tariff reductions for the governments of two large countries, neither of which would have a unilateral incentive to reduce tariffs because it would suffer losses in economic welfare through a self-imposed worsening of its terms of trade. They interpret the GATT principle of reciprocity as providing a framework for the mutual reduction of import tariffs that serves to expand trade volumes from inefficient levels of market access when under Nash tariffs to jointly efficient levels. Reciprocity allows for the mutual reduction in tariffs that serves to *neutralize* the impact on each country's terms of trade so that neither country experiences a negative price effect from its own tariff liberalization.

A second important insight, and one that often goes overlooked, is that the *only* role for the GATT/WTO in this framework is to reduce tariffs to a level that eliminates the international (terms-of-trade) externality impact of each government's tariff choice. That is, in the trade agreement equilibrium, the "politically optimal" trade agreement tariffs that the government imposes may still be *positive*. In this case, once the terms-of-trade externality has been neutralized, the jointly efficient equilibrium tariffs arising under the trade agreement may still be positive and the GATT/WTO under the terms-of-trade theory will have nothing left "to do" in terms of facilitating additional tariff liberalization.

The key implication of the theory is that when empiricists begin to examine the tariff data, the existence of positive tariffs is not, by itself, evidence that the job performance of the WTO is incomplete. Under a strict interpretation of the terms-of-trade theory, the WTO only has work to be done if any nonzero tariff is positive because the country is exercising its import market power (i.e., if, for some reason, the country is a member of the agreement but the terms-of-trade component to its tariff has not been fully exorcised). Put differently, if the nonzero tariff is positive for political or redistributive purposes (in light of the government's preferences), and all of the import market power exertion motives have been extinguished (e.g., either through reciprocal bargaining under GATT rounds or through WTO accession negotiations), then the terms-of-trade motive for the WTO would indicate that its tariff-reducing job is done.

From the perspective of this basic theory, I use the next two subsections to review recent developments in the empirical literature on trade agreements. A number of recent contributions provide evidence supporting key elements of this basic theory. However, the evidence is also beginning to shed light on particular areas where, within the international trading system, the GATT/WTO has failed to deliver evidence consistent with the baseline theory, thus identifying potential limits as to what the GATT/WTO and the terms-of-trade approach might be able to achieve.

2.2.2 The First Wave of Evidence on Applied and Bound Tariffs for Countries Outside and Inside the WTO

In light of the main predictions of the terms-of-trade theory described, what is the empirical evidence? As this recent and evolving literature covers a number of different trade policy environments, samples of countries, and historical moments in time, I also use table 2.1 to briefly summarize this evidence.

When contemplating whether the terms-of-trade externality is a serious problem that countries seek to solve by establishing a trade agreement like the GATT/WTO, the first questions to consider are: What are the determinants of tariffs that countries set when they are not constrained by such agreements? And is there evidence that tariffs are influenced by import market power, or is the variation in import tariffs driven simply by domestic political economy influences?

Broda, Limão, and Weinstein (2008) were the first to provide an empirical approach to directly examine whether the tariffs set by a number of countries outside the WTO—and thus countries unencumbered by (multilateral) trade agreement constraints—were influenced by market power motives. Their benchmark analysis focused on the applied tariffs set by 15 countries listed in table 2.1 during the 1993–2000 period, when they were not GATT Contracting Parties or (at the time) members of the WTO. They first construct estimates of foreign export supply elasticities facing those importing countries, and then they provide strong evidence that governments impose higher import tariffs on products where they are found to have market power, as captured by the inverse of the foreign export supply elasticity that their consumers face, just as predicted by the canonical optimal tariff formula. Their first round of evidence was thus consistent with the potential terms-of-trade motive for the GATT/WTO (i.e., in the absence of such agreements, governments set import tariffs that reflect their market power, and a result is that some of the externality costs of those higher tariffs are imposed on trading partners through reductions in prices those partners' exporters receive).

Table 2.1
Selected empirical studies of trade agreements, import tariffs, and market power.

Paper	Trade Policy Environment	Countries
Broda, Limão and Weinstein (2008)	Applied tariffs set by 15 non-GATT/WTO countries as a cross section (at some point over 1993–2000)	Algeria, Belarus, Bolivia, China, Czech Republic, Ecuador, Latvia, Lebanon, Lithuania, Oman, Paraguay, Russia, Saudi Arabia, Taiwan (China), Ukraine
	Applied tariffs, statutory tariffs, and nontariff measures set by one major GATT/WTO member	United States
Bagwell and Staiger (2011)	WTO tariff binding levels upon accession for 16 new members that joined over 1995–2005	Albania, Armenia, Cambodia, China, Ecuador, Estonia, Georgia, Jordan, Kyrgyz Republic, Latvia, Lithuania, Macedonia, Moldova, Nepal, Oman, Panama
Ludema and Mayda (2013)	Applied MFN tariffs for 26 WTO members at the conclusion of the Uruguay Round	Argentina, Australia, Bolivia, Brazil, Canada, Chile, Colombia, Ecuador, European Union, Hungary, Iceland, India, Indonesia, Japan, South Korea, Madagascar, Malaysia, Mauritius, Mexico, Morocco, New Zealand, Norway, Peru, Romania, Thailand, United States
Ossa (2014)	Quantification of Nash, unilaterally optimal, and cooperative tariffs for seven countries and the rest of the world	Brazil, China, European Union, India, Japan, United States, and the rest of the world
Nicita, Olarreaga, and Silva (2018)	Applied MFN tariffs for 100 WTO members with and without binding overhang, 2000–2009	100 countries

| Beshkar, Bond, and Rho (2015) | Binding levels and tariff overhang for 108 WTO members, 1995–2007 | 108 countries |
| Bown and Crowley (2013) | Antidumping and safeguard tariffs for a WTO member with applied tariffs at the binding level, 1997–2006 | United States |

This chapter applies the Nicita, Olarreaga, and Silva (2018) export supply elasticities as follows:

Section 2.3	WTO tariff binding levels for 12 countries upon WTO accession (countries acceded 1998–2012)	Albania, Armenia, Cabo Verde, China, Georgia, Jordan, Kyrgyz Republic, Moldova, Nepal, Oman, Russia, Saudi Arabia, Ukraine
Section 2.4	Applied tariffs for unbound products of 25 WTO members that had bound fewer than one-third of nonagricultural products in 2013	25 countries listed in table 2.5
Section 2.5	Applied tariffs for bound products of 45 WTO members with an average of 15 percentage points or more of tariff overhang in 2013	45 countries listed in table 2.7

To further support their analysis, Broda, Limão, and Weinstein (2008) also examine the relationship between these measures of a country's import market power and a number of different trade policy instruments utilized by the United States. The United States is different from the 15 countries in their baseline sample in that it is a country *within* the GATT/WTO and one for which the theory would predict trading partners would have been motivated to seek to extinguish the terms-of-trade component of its tariffs. Indeed, Broda, Limão, and Weinstein (2008) find no statistical evidence of market power affecting MFN import tariffs applied by the United States; this is consistent with an interpretation that decades of GATT/WTO tariff reduction negotiations have eliminated the terms-of-trade cost-shifting component from the applied US tariff. Furthermore, they do find evidence that market power considerations affect US trade policies in two other places: first, the US application of nontariff measures, or the policies less constrained by GATT/WTO negotiations and rules;[9] and second, the United States' statutory (or "column 2") tariffs, which are the tariffs that the United States applied to a number of countries that were not members of the WTO and with which the United States did not have normal trading relations.

Given that countries outside the GATT/WTO agreement may impose import tariffs in a way that reflects their market power, is there other evidence that such market power is neutralized (or at least reduced) when they eventually join the WTO? Bagwell and Staiger (2011) examine this question by empirically examining the determinants of the tariff cuts made by a group of 16 countries that acceded to the WTO between 1995 and 2005, five of which (including China) overlapped with the Broda, Limão, and Weinstein sample of non-GATT countries. Unlike countries that had long been members of the GATT/WTO but whose tariff levels may have gradually been brought to more globally efficient levels over time, the Bagwell-Staiger framework investigates whether these new members brought their tariffs down from unbound (Nash-like) levels to bound (politically optimal and efficient) levels in one shot upon accession and in accordance with the terms-of-trade theory's core predictions.[10] The Bagwell-Staiger evidence is broadly consistent with the theory; that is, there is a strong positive relationship between the magnitude of tariff cuts negotiated under the WTO and the prenegotiation volume of imports. Furthermore, for the five countries with which they have overlap with the Broda-Limão-Weinstein sample, their evidence also holds when specifically controlling for the import market power as measured by Broda-Limão-Weinstein estimated trade elasticities.

While these first two papers present evidence that is consistent with the terms-of-trade theory, the bulk of that evidence admittedly derives from countries either outside the GATT/WTO (Broda, Limão, and Weinstein) or that only recently acceded to the WTO (Bagwell and Staiger). What about the trade policymaking behavior of the major economies that are both "inside" the GATT/WTO system and are the ones that have driven the GATT/WTO through 60 years of reciprocal tariff cutting under multilateral negotiating rounds? Furthermore, with the exception of the Broda-Limão-Weinstein evidence for the United States and the Bagwell-Staiger evidence for China, most of the countries in these samples were not major trading economies in the international system. This has the potential to raise concerns about the external validity for the terms-of-trade theory of trade agreements if, for some reason, these countries did not exhibit behavior consistent with that of the major players.

Ludema and Mayda (2013) provide one approach to address these concerns by examining the applied MFN tariffs under the WTO at the conclusion of the GATT's Uruguay Round of negotiations for a larger sample of 26 countries, including most of the major economies.[11] In particular, they explore whether variation in these countries' applied MFN tariffs is related to variation in these countries' import market power and their trading partners' (exporters') industrial concentration. They find that the concentration of trading partner exporter interests at the product level, as measured by the Herfindahl-Hirschman Index (HHI), helps explain applied MFN tariff variation; that is, products with a combined situation of (1) foreign export suppliers that are less concentrated and (2) an importer with more market power tend to have higher tariffs even after GATT/WTO negotiations.

The Ludema-Mayda evidence is that there is variation in the extent to which the terms-of-trade component of a country's tariff may be negotiated away under the WTO, and that can be linked to the free-rider problem arising from the GATT/WTO's MFN rule. First, this empirical result is intuitive in that it may help to explain the relatively high applied tariffs remaining under the WTO in sectors such as agriculture, textiles, and footwear, which persist because the exporting interests behind these products are diffuse. A limitation of the historical framework for conducting negotiations may have arisen because negotiations were voluntary and the tariff liberalization outcome would be extended to all members under the MFN rule of nondiscrimination. However, because the existence of MFN implied that countries could free ride in the negotiations, sometimes a critical mass of exporting interests may not have bothered to show up at the negotiating table in the first place. Second, an important insight arising from this research is the recognition that not all terms-of-trade effects may be fully neutralized even upon a country's entry into the WTO, a point to which I return. That is, Ludema and Mayda's results identify one potential area in which there may be more tariff-liberalizing work (to neutralize terms of trade) to be "done"; nevertheless, in discovering it, they also identify how the historical GATT/WTO approach of relying on voluntary negotiations and MFN may have contributed to the process by which tariff liberalization (to neutralize terms of trade) remains incomplete.[12]

Finally, given the evidence that the terms-of-trade effects matter for determining trade policy, and that the GATT/WTO system may be working to at least partially neutralize such externalities through negotiations, how economically important is the job that the WTO has done for the major economies of the system? One way to address this issue is to ask how large Nash tariffs (i.e., the combination of best-response tariffs that countries would use) would be in a trade war, and what the economic costs of eliminating trade policy cooperation would be. Using a quantitative approach, Ossa (2014) constructs counterfactual estimates for the size of Nash tariffs in a model featuring seven regions (including the United States, European Union, Japan, China, India, Brazil, and the rest of the world) and finds the median to be 58.1% across countries and industries.[13] The quantitative model suggests substantial gains from the imposition of the tariffs that are in place relative to the levels of welfare that would arise were countries to resort to imposing their Nash tariffs under a trade war.

2.2.3 Additional Evidence on Applied Tariffs, Bindings, and Tariff Overhang for Countries Inside

The next framework that I explore is the recent theoretical and empirical contribution of Nicita, Olarreaga, and Silva (2018), which examines the relationship between a WTO member's applied tariffs and the role of import market power, contingent on whether those tariffs are constrained by WTO tariff binding legal commitments. First, they develop a theoretical model that allows for the political influence of not only import-competing sectors but also exporting sectors. In an environment in which export policies are constrained—as under the WTO, where export subsidies are illegal—they provide a theory that predicts an exporting-country government will negotiate larger tariff reductions exactly where that importing country has the most market power. Their model predicts that in the instances in which applied tariffs are at their WTO binding rates, and countries are cooperating under the WTO, there will actually be a *negative* relationship between the importer's market power and its negotiated tariff. The intuition is that, in these instances, not only does the trade agreement get the country to reduce its tariff cooperatively (to neutralize the terms-of-trade externality) but in equilibrium the negotiation "overshoots" and the tariff ends up even lower to compensate the politically organized exporters in the trading partner. Furthermore, the theoretical prediction of the positive relationship between applied tariffs and market power also arises in the model of Nicita, Olarreaga, and Silva, but it only arises for applied tariffs that are well below tariff binding rates (i.e., applied tariffs in the presence of sufficiently large amounts of tariff binding "overhang").

The second major contribution of Nicita, Olarreaga, and Silva (2018) is empirical. First, they construct estimates of "foreign" export supply elasticities for 100 WTO member economies at the six-digit Harmonized System (HS06) level, resulting in a database of hundreds of thousands of importing-country product-specific elasticities. (I will draw heavily on these elasticities in the formal empirical analysis that I introduce.) Second, Nicita, Olarreaga, and Silva utilize these estimated elasticities to empirically investigate their model's theoretical predictions for applied tariffs imposed between 2000 and 2009. They find evidence that the inverse foreign export supply elasticity has a *negative* relationship with applied MFN tariffs when there is zero tariff overhang (i.e., when countries are "cooperating" in that applied rates are set at binding levels), and they find a *positive* relationship between the importer's market power and the applied tariff when tariff overhang levels are positive. I further empirically investigate this second result; that is, for "tariff overhang" products, are there unchecked terms-of-trade externalities that countries are imposing through their applied tariffs that the WTO could potentially use as a negotiating forum to eliminate?

In related work, Behskar, Bond, and Rho (2015) provide a theory based on terms of trade that explores the question of where a country might set its tariff binding in relation to its applied tariff under a trade agreement. Their theoretical model predicts that governments will seek to retain flexibility and thus bind their tariffs significantly above the applied rates, where the importer has little market power. They conduct an empirical examination of product-level tariff data for a sample of 108 WTO member economies over the period 1995–2007. They also partially rely on the inverse foreign export supply elasticities generated by Nicita, Olarreaga, and Silva (2018) as the measure of import market power in their sensitivity analysis. First, they find that newly acceding WTO members bind a larger share of their product lines than did the historical GATT members under the WTO. Second, their various measures of import market power are negatively related to the level of the bindings that countries take on, as well as the size of the tariff binding overhang.[14]

A final stream of recent research that I briefly highlight explores additional economic implications of countries' failure to constrain their applied tariffs by leaving sufficient tariff overhang between the applied rates and their tariff bindings.[15] Handley and Limão (2015) develop a dynamic, heterogeneous firms model with sunk costs of exporting and show that investment in and entry into export markets is reduced when trade policy is uncertain. Furthermore, they show how a credible commitment implied by a trade agreement (e.g., reducing tariff bindings) can increase trade even if applied trade barriers are already low.[16] Handley (2014) provides an application of some of the key elements of this theory to the context of WTO tariff bindings and the case of Australia, finding that the growth of exporter-product varieties would have been 7% lower between 1993 and 2001 without the binding commitments that Australia took on upon its WTO entry. While Handley's results suggest gains (to the exports) of a trading partner, one would expect that the *reciprocal* reduction of uncertainty (i.e., two countries jointly eliminating uncertainty by simultaneously binding their applied tariffs at low levels) could lead to analogous joint gains that accrue under the distinct exercise of two countries simultaneously lowering those applied rates under a trade agreement that neutralizes terms of trade in the first place.[17]

2.3   WTO Nonmembers (and Recently Acceded Members)

This section focuses attention on WTO nonmember countries in the international trading system as of 2013. One ultimate question of interest—for which I will admittedly only be able to provide very indirect evidence—is whether such countries apply import tariffs that reflect market power motives and whether those would be neutralized should those countries accede to the WTO. First, I introduce the WTO nonmembers and their political-economic characteristics. Then I examine a comparison group of countries that recently acceded to the WTO. I then empirically investigate the implications of the terms-of-trade theory of trade agreements for that second group of countries by applying the Nicita, Olarreaga, and Silva (2018) foreign export supply elasticities to the basic estimation approach introduced by Bagwell and Staiger (2011).

2.3.1 Introduction and Political-Economic Characteristics

As figure 2.1 illustrates, the nonmembers of the WTO are found throughout the world; nevertheless, they are disproportionately concentrated in the Middle East and North Africa, East Africa, and Central Asia. Table 2.2 provides summary data for key economic characteristics of these countries, as well as comparable data for a separate list of important comparison countries that recently acceded to the WTO (i.e., between 1998 and 2014).[18] For ease of exposition, I rank the countries

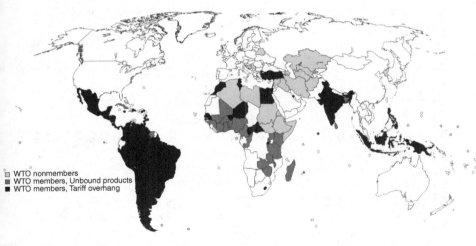

☐ WTO nonmembers
■ WTO members, Unbound products
■ WTO members, Tariff overhang

Figure 2.1
WTO nonmembers, members with substantial unbound products, and members with substantial tariff overhang in 2013. Constructed by the author. For the list of WTO nonmembers, see table 2.2. WTO members with substantial unbound products are defined as countries having fewer than one-third of nonagricultural products with tariff bindings; for the list, see table 2.5. WTO members with substantial tariff overhang are defined as countries having more than one-third of nonagricultural products with tariff bindings but with average tariff overhang of 15 percentage points or more; for the list, see table 2.7.

Table 2.2

Economic characteristics of WTO nonmembers and recently acceded WTO members in 2013.

Low-income countries

WTO Nonmember Country	WTO Observer Status	GNI per Capita (2013 US$)	Population (millions)	Imports (billions, 2013 US$)	Exports (billions, 2013 US$)
Liberia	Observer	410	4.3	1.6	0.6
Ethiopia	Observer	470	94.1	13.8	5.9
Eritrea	No	490	6.3	0.6	0.4
Afghanistan	Observer	690	30.6	10.0	1.3
Comoros	Observer	840	0.7	0.4	0.1
South Sudan	No	950	11.3	5.1	2.1
Sao Tomé and Principe	Observer	1,470	0.2	0.1	<0.1
Sudan	Observer	1,550	38.0	10.7	6.4
Uzbekistan	Observer	1,880	30.2	18.0	15.7
Syria*	Observer	NA	22.8	7.6	1.9
North Korea*	No	NA	24.9	4.8	4.0
Somalia*	No	NA	10.5	0.8	0.6

Recent WTO Accession Country	WTO Accession Year	GNI per Capita (2013 US$)	Population (millions)	Imports (billions, 2013 US$)	Exports (billions, 2013 US$)
Nepal	2004	730	27.8	7.2	2.1
Cambodia	2004	950	15.1	11.2	10.0
Tajikistan	2013	990	8.2	5.8	1.6
Kyrgyz Republic	1998	1,210	5.7	6.9	3.4
Yemen*	2014	1,330	24.4	11.0	8.1
Laos	2013	1,450	6.8	5.2	4.2
Vietnam	2007	1,740	89.7	136.8	143.8

Lower-middle-income countries

WTO Nonmember Country	WTO Observer Status	GNI per Capita (2013 US$)	Population (millions)	Imports (billions, 2013 US$)	Exports (billions, 2013 US$)
Bhutan	Observer	2,330	0.8	1.1	0.7
Kiribati	No	2,620	0.1	0.2	<0.1
Micronesia*	No	3,280	0.1	0.3	0.1
Timor-Leste*	No	3,940	1.2	1.6	0.2
Marshall Islands*	No	4,310	0.1	0.1	<0.1
Bosnia and Herzegovina	Observer	4,780	3.8	9.5	5.7
Algeria	Observer	5,330	39.2	63.6	69.7
Iran*	Observer	5,780	77.4	60.1	93.0
Tuvalu*	No	5,840	0.0	0.2	<0.1
Serbia	Observer	6,050	7.2	23.6	18.6
Nauru	No	NA	<0.1	0.1	0.1

Recent WTO Accession Country	WTO Accession Year	GNI per Capita (2013 US$)	Population (millions)	Imports (billions, 2013 US$)	Exports (billions, 2013 US$)
Moldova	2001	2,470	3.6	6.5	3.5
Vanuatu	2012	3,130	0.3	0.4	0.4
Georgia	2000	3,560	4.5	9.3	7.2
Cabo Verde	2008	3,620	0.5	0.9	0.6
Armenia	2003	3,800	3.0	5.0	2.8
Ukraine	2008	3,960	45.5	98.3	83.2
Samoa	2012	3,970	0.2	0.4	0.2
Tonga	2007	4,490	0.1	0.3	0.1
Albania	2000	4,510	2.9	6.8	4.5
Macedonia	2003	4,870	2.1	7.4	5.5
Jordan	2000	4,950	6.5	24.0	14.3

Middle- and higher-income countries

Iraq	Observer	6,720	33.4	75.0	77.9
Belarus	Observer	6,730	9.5	45.9	43.9
Turkmenistan	No	6,880	5.2	15.6	25.8
Azerbaijan	Observer	7,350	9.4	19.8	35.8
Lebanon	Observer	9,870	4.5	33.8	27.7
Palau	No	10,970	<0.1	0.2	0.2
Kazakhstan	Observer	11,550	17.0	61.9	88.7
Seychelles	No	13,210	0.1	1.3	1.1
Equatorial Guinea	Observer	14,320	0.8	10.7	13.8
Bahamas	Observer	21,570	0.4	4.7	3.5
Andorra*	Observer	NA	0.1	1.5	<0.1
Holy See (Vatican City)	Observer	NA	<0.1	NA	NA
Libya*	Observer	NA	6.2	26.8	34.9
Monaco*	No	NA	<0.1	1.2	1.1
San Marino*	No	NA	<0.1	2.1	2.6
Subtotal (Nonmembers)			490.4	534.3	583.9
World		10,683	7,125.1	22,719.6	23,442.6
Share of world			6.9%	2.4%	2.5%

Middle- and higher-income countries

China	2001	6,560	1,357.4	2,203.6	2,440.5
Montenegro	2012	7,250	0.6	2.7	1.8
Seychelles	2015	13,210	0.1	1.3	1.1
Croatia**	2000	13,420	4.3	24.6	24.9
Russia	2012	13,850	143.5	471.6	594.8
Lithuania**	2001	14,900	3.0	33.9	33.2
Latvia**	1999	15,290	2.0	17.8	16.8
Estonia**	1999	17,780	1.3	21.2	21.4
Oman	2000	25,150	3.6	27.8	48.5
Saudi Arabia	2005	26,260	28.8	229.3	387.6
Taiwan, China*	2002	NA	23.4	267.4	304.6
Subtotal (recently acceded)		10,683	1,814.7	3,644.8	4,170.8
World			7,125.1	22,719.6	23,442.6
Share of world			25.5%	16.0%	17.8%
Share of world (not including China)			6.4%	6.3%	7.4%

Sources: World Bank's World Development Indicators. *Data unavailable so supplemented with estimates from CIA, *The World Fact Book*. GNI=gross national income, NA=not available.

Income classifications *not* based on official World Bank categories. ** Indicates country also acceded to the European Union during this period and adopted the EU's common external tariff.

in each group by gross national income (GNI) per capita, and I split them roughly into three categories based on GNI per capita. I refer to the three groups as low income, lower-middle income, and middle and higher income.[19] For countries that are not yet members of the WTO, I also provide information on whether they have formally been granted "observer" status by the WTO.[20]

Table 2.2 reveals a number of stylized facts about the WTO nonmembers. First, they are disproportionately poor countries—at least 28 of the 38 countries had GNI per capita in 2013 that was less than the world average of $10,683. Second, there is a wide range in population size among these countries. Some are tiny (and relatively wealthy) city-states or islands, with less than a million people. Others are poorer and larger countries in Africa, the largest being Ethiopia, with 94 million people. Combined, 490 million people lived in these WTO nonmember countries, or 6.9% of the total world population.

Most of the WTO nonmember countries had imports that were greater than exports in 2013. The exceptions are mostly made up of major energy (oil and/or natural gas) producers/exporters, such as Algeria, Azerbaijan, Equatorial Guinea, Iran, Iraq, Kazakhstan, Libya, and Turkmenistan. For the rest of the countries with imports substantially larger than exports, this is potentially notable for two reasons. First, the expectation might be that their imports would be limited because their import policies are legally unaffected and undisciplined by the WTO system. Second, many of the nonmembers are relatively poor and are therefore likely (at least in principle) to be beneficiaries of unilateral preference programs offered by WTO member countries. Ceteris paribus, their firms may face lower-than-MFN tariffs for their sales to those markets, which would tend to encourage their exports. Nevertheless, at least at first glance, the data do not suggest this.

Finally, I briefly mention some other geopolitical factors that are likely contributors to the question of why these countries are not (yet) members of the WTO. First, 14 of these countries can be characterized as states in Fragile and Conflict Affected Situations (FCS) (World Bank 2014), which are areas affected by civil war or other forms of violence and strife. Second, while Russia finally acceded to the WTO in 2012 and a handful of former Soviet republics had become members earlier, five of the former Soviet republics (Azerbaijan, Belarus, Kazakhstan, Turkmenistan, and Uzbekistan) have not yet gained entry.

Next compare the WTO nonmembers with the list on the right-hand side of table 2.2, which includes the countries that acceded to the WTO between 1998 and 2014. The recently acceded countries are also disproportionately poor and include a range of small and large countries by population. The list of recently acceded countries also includes countries with geopolitical constraints, such as Russia and other former republics of the Soviet Union (Armenia, Georgia, Kyrgyz Republic, Moldova, Tajikistan, and Ukraine, as well as Estonia, Latvia, and Lithuania, which since then have also acceded to the European Union), and also FCS countries such as Nepal and Yemen. Overall, I conclude that these sets of WTO nonmembers and countries that have recently acceded to the WTO have a number of similarities.

2.3.2   Establishing a Benchmark: The Experience of Recently Acceded WTO Members

What might accession to the WTO mean for nonmember countries? To provide context, in this subsection I benchmark these nonmember countries' applied tariffs against the tariffs of a set of recently acceded WTO member countries. Table 2.3 introduces the most recently available information on the applied tariffs for these WTO nonmember countries. The table documents the mean of their applied rates, as well as their minimum and maximum rates, and the standard deviation of applied tariffs across import products. The average tariff of these countries ranges from a high of 35.1% (Bahamas) to a flat import tariff of 2.5% applied to every imported product (Timor-Leste). Some of these countries do have tariffs that peak at rates higher than 100%.

Table 2.3 also provides important summary statistics for the tariffs of the recently acceded WTO members as a point of comparison. For these recently acceded countries, I present four pieces of information: (1) the tariffs they applied five years before their WTO membership, (2) the share of imported products over which the country agreed to bind its tariffs upon accession to the WTO, (3) the average tariff binding rate that the country committed not to exceed when joining the WTO, and (4) the MFN tariff rate that the country applied to all other WTO members in 2013.

First, table 2.3 indicates that even the poorest recently acceded countries have bound almost 100% of their tariffs at some level. As I will observe in subsection 2.4.1, this is very different from the figure for many developing countries at similar levels of income per capita that joined the WTO upon its inception in 1995 or had previously been a Contracting Party to the GATT and did not similarly bind all of their products' tariffs. (I investigate and address this issue for such countries separately.

Table 2.3

Tariff characteristics of WTO nonmembers and recently acceded WTO members in 2013.

WTO Nonmember Country	WTO Observer Status	MFN Applied Tariff Rate, 2013				Recent WTO Accession Country	WTO Accession Year	MFN Applied Tariff Rate (simple avg.), Pre-WTO‡	MFN Applied Tariff Rate (simple avg.), 2013	WTO Binding Tariff Rate (simple avg.)	WTO Binding Coverage (%)
		Simple Average	Min.	Max.	St. Dev.						
Low-income countries						**Low-income countries**					
Liberia	Observer	10.0	0.0	50.0	6.9	Nepal*	2004	12.3	12.2	26.0	99.4
Ethiopia	Observer	17.3	0.0	35.0	11.8	Cambodia	2004	16.4	10.9	19.1	100.0
Eritrea	No	7.9	0.0	25.0	8.5	Tajikistan	2013	7.6	7.6	7.9	100.0
Afghanistan	Observer	5.9	0.0	40.0	3.9	Kyrgyz Republic*	1998	0.0	4.5	7.4	99.9
Comoros	Observer	15.3	0.0	20.0	7.8	Laos	2013	9.7	9.7	18.8	100.0
Sao Tomé and Principe	Observer	10.2	0.0	20.0	4.1	Vietnam	2007	16.4	9.4	11.4	100.0
Sudan	Observer	21.2	0.0	40.0	15.8						
Uzbekistan	Observer	15.1	0.0	30.0	10.9						
Syria	Observer	16.5	0.0	80.0	23.2						
Lower-middle-income countries						**Lower-middle-income countries**					
Bhutan	Observer	21.9	0.0	100.0	13.7	Moldova*	2001	6.0	8.8	6.7	100.0
Timor-Leste	No	2.5	2.5	2.5	0.0	Vanuatu	2012	14.0	9.1	39.7	100.0
Bosnia and Herzegovina	Observer	6.5	0.0	824.4	13.4	Georgia*	2000	10.6	1.4	7.2	100.0
Algeria	Observer	18.6	0.0	30.0	10.3	Cabo Verde*	2008	10.4	10.3	15.8	100.0
Iran	Observer	26.6	3.0	400.0	28.7	Armenia*	2003	3.0	3.6	8.5	100.0
Tuvalu	No	7.7	0.0	35.0	9.8	Ukraine*	2008	7.0	4.5	5.8	100.0
Serbia	Observer	7.4	0.0	30.0	7.3	Samoa	2012	11.0	11.3	21.1	100.0
						Tonga	2007	11.7	11.7	17.6	100.0
						Albania*	2000	15.9	3.8	7.0	100.0
						Macedonia	2003	14.4	6.5	6.9	100.0
						Jordan	2000	22.1	9.5	16.2	100.0

Middle- and higher-income countries

							Middle- and higher-income countries			
Belarus	Observer	8.8	0.0	100.0	6.6	China*	2001	23.7	9.6	10.0	100.0
Turkmenistan	No	5.1	0.0	150.0	15.4	Montenegro	2012	4.6	4.2	5.1	100.0
Azerbaijan	Observer	9.7	0.0	1478.8	26.0	Croatia**	2000	10.6	4.6	4.1	100.0
Lebanon	Observer	6.3	0.0	334.0	13.7	Russia*	2012	9.0	8.8	7.3	100.0
Palau	No	4.2	0.0	1370.1	29.1	Lithuania**	2001	3.6	4.6	4.1	100.0
Kazakhstan	Observer	8.7	0.0	100.0	6.6	Latvia**	1999	4.3	4.6	4.1	100.0
Equatorial Guinea	Observer	17.9	0.0	30.0	9.5	Estonia**	1999	0.1	4.6	4.1	100.0
Bahamas	Observer	35.1	0.0	75.0	16.2	Oman*	2000	4.7	4.5	13.6	100.0
Libya	Observer	21.3	0.0	3000.0	113.8	Saudi Arabia*	2005	11.9	4.7	10.7	100.0
						Taiwan, China	2002	7.8	5.6	5.7	100.0

Compiled by the author from WTO IDB and CTS and UNCTAD TRAINS made available via the World Bank's World Integrated Trade Solution (WITS) dataset.

† Preaccession data taken from five years prior to WTO accession. **Acceded to the European Union during this period and thus adopted the EU's common external tariff. *Countries utilized in the econometric exercise of table 2.4. Yemen and Seychelles not included because they acceded in 2014 and 2015, respectively.

Second, a number of countries that recently acceded to the WTO were not forced to make substantial cuts (on average) to their applied tariffs upon entry into the agreement. Indeed, for more than half of the 27 recently acceded WTO members listed in table 2.3, their average binding commitment under the WTO is actually higher than the average tariff the country applied five years prior to WTO entry, meaning that the country could (on average) increase its applied tariffs upon entry into the WTO and still be in compliance with its obligations. Major exceptions include a number of large economies, such as China, Saudi Arabia, Taiwan (China), and Ukraine. However, a notable characteristic of all recently acceded WTO members is the relatively limited amount of average tariff overhang between binding rates and applied MFN tariffs in 2013. With the exception of Vanuatu (30.6 percentage points), no newly acceded member had an average level of tariff overhang exceeding 13.8% in 2013 (Nepal). As subsection 2.5.1 reveals, this is also substantially different from that for countries that acceded to the WTO upon its entry into force in 1995—there were 45 WTO members with more than 15 percentage points of average tariff overhang in 2013.

Figure 2.2 illustrates the industry-level variation for these tariff data summarized by table 2.3. The three panels represent the average tariffs by sector for three groupings of countries—low-income countries, lower-middle-income countries, and middle- and higher-income countries. For each sector, there are two sets of bars. The first set reflects the average tariffs for the recently acceded WTO members, and the second set reflects the average tariffs for the WTO nonmembers. Finally, for WTO members, for each sector there are three pieces of information: the gray bar reflects the average MFN applied rate in 2013, the white bar reflects the tariff binding overhang (or water) above the applied rate, and the black star reflects the average applied tariff that was in place five years *prior to* the country's WTO accession. For the WTO nonmember countries, the black bar represents the average tariff in the sector that the countries in that income group applied in 2013.

First, compare the black stars with the black bars (i.e., compare the average applied tariffs for the recently acceded countries five years prior to their WTO membership with the average applied tariffs of the nonmembers). Overall, figure 2.2 suggests that the patterns are quite similar (conditional on income group) across industries; on average at least, the "future" WTO accession countries apply import tariffs that are similar to the applied tariff starting point of the recently acceded countries before they gained WTO entry. And while there is variation across

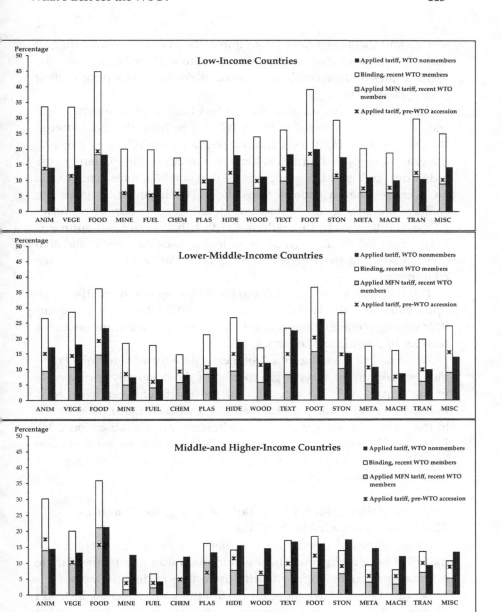

Figure 2.2
Average tariffs for WTO nonmembers versus recently acceded WTO members, by industry and country group. Constructed by the author from tariff data at the HS06 level from the WTO IDB, CTS, and UNCTAD TRAINS and from available data and country groupings provided in table 2.3.

sectors and income groups, if anything, the evidence would suggest that WTO nonmembers apply rates that are slightly higher than the applied rates of the recently acceded countries five years prior to their joining the WTO.

Second, focus attention on the applied tariff *changes* for the countries that recently acceded to the WTO; that is, the difference between the star (applied tariff level five years prior to WTO accession) and the gray bar (applied tariff level in effect in 2013). The pattern across industries and country groupings is that applied rates tend to fall on average when a country joins the WTO. In levels, the average changes are largest for the lower-middle-income group of countries in the middle panel. This reflects the fact that more tariff cutting is likely expected of them (relative to low-income countries) and that they are starting from higher tariff levels (relative to higher-income countries).

Third, consider the differences in tariff binding overhang that result upon entry into the WTO. On average in 2013, there was more tariff overhang remaining upon WTO accession for low-income countries than for higher-income countries.

While table 2.3 and figure 2.2 suggest a path forward for WTO nonmember countries—if what is expected of them roughly corresponds to the impact of WTO accession on the tariffs of recently acceded members—I have not yet provided any evidence that this is linked to the terms-of-trade theory of trade agreements. In subsection 2.3.3, I consider the potential implications of WTO accession for nonmembers through the lens of this theory and drawing from evidence arising from the experience of recently acceded countries.

2.3.3   Empirical Evidence from Tariff Bindings for Countries That Recently Acceded to the WTO

The first empirical question is whether it is likely that accession to the WTO by these nonmembers would neutralize any terms-of-trade externalities that their applied tariffs impose on trading partners.

Because I do not have the ability to test this counterfactual, instead I examine whether there is evidence from the group of recently acceded WTO member countries to suggest that terms-of-trade externalities of their import tariffs were reduced when they joined the WTO. The alternative (i.e., that there is no relationship between their post-WTO accession tariffs and market power influences) would suggest that these countries joined the WTO with something else in mind, and thus some other approach aside from the terms-of-trade theory would be required to motivate why they find the WTO valuable.

In order to specifically investigate this question, I broadly follow the Bagwell and Staiger (2011) estimation approach described earlier. In particular, I examine whether there is a relationship between the binding rate that country c adopts for HS06 product g after WTO accession ($\tau_{gc}^{WTO\ binding}$), and two theoretically motivated determinants: (1) the preaccession applied tariff rate ($\tau_{gc}^{pre-WTO}$) and (2) the inverse of the foreign export supply elasticity ($1/\omega_{gc}^*$). I thus estimate models of the form

$$\ln(1 + \tau_{gc}^{WTO\ binding}) = \alpha_g + \alpha_c + \beta_0\ln(1/\omega_{gc}^*)$$
$$+ \beta_1\ln(1 + \tau_{gc}^{pre-WTO}) + \epsilon_{gc}, \qquad (2.1)$$

where α_c is the importing-country fixed effect, α_g is the HS06 product fixed effect, and ϵ_{gc} is the iid error term. The Bagwell-Staiger theory clearly predicts $\beta_1 > 0$ and $\beta_0 < 0$, or that the post-WTO binding rate will be positively related to $\tau_{gc}^{pre-WTO}$ and negatively related to the measure of the importer's market power ($1/\omega_{gc}^*$).

My estimation exercise serves to complement the original Bagwell-Staiger approach in a number of ways. First, I utilize a slightly different sample of countries (see table 2.1 for the list), though notably my additional countries include a number of relatively large (by population) importers, such as Russia, Saudi Arabia, and Ukraine, that acceded to the WTO only after the Bagwell-Staiger sample period. Second, here I rely heavily on the export supply elasticities provided by Nicita, Olarreaga, and Silva (2018), which were not available at the time of the original study. Third, I utilize fixed effects to address other potential determinants of tariffs.[21]

Before turning to the estimates, I also explain here the general approach that I take throughout to address potential data limitations.[22] For example, one potential concern is that the elasticities are themselves estimates, and some of the estimated values are extreme.[23] First, I winsorize the dataset of the elasticities by setting the extreme values to be the values at the 10th and 90th percentiles of the distribution. Second, in the baseline specifications for each of the regressions, I will take the log of the inverse of foreign export supply elasticity, and I will utilize as a robustness check either an indicator for "high-elasticity" products (defined as those above the median of the distribution) or the *level* of the inverse of foreign export supply elasticity. Third, I will also use as my measure of import tariffs $\ln(1 + \tau)$, though I frequently report as a robustness check a measure of the tariff that is simply the level of the tariff, τ.

Table 2.4 provides evidence of the expected strong negative relationship between the inverse foreign export supply elasticity and the WTO tariff binding commitment taken upon accession for this sample of 12 countries that recently acceded to the WTO. That is, ceteris paribus, newly acceding members are requested (through WTO negotiations) to take on lower tariff binding commitments on products for which they have higher market power and thus where their tariffs (if left unchecked) would result in larger terms-of-trade externality losses for trading partners. Note that I also find a strong positive relationship between the pre-WTO applied tariff and the WTO tariff binding commitment, in line with the theoretical prediction. In column 2, I show the robustness of the results by replacing the log of the inverse foreign export supply elasticity with an indicator that takes on the value of 1 if the elasticity is "high" (above the median value) and 0 otherwise, and again the estimated size of the coefficient is negative. The specification in column 3 substitutes the levels of the tariffs and the elasticities for the log levels that are used in the baseline specification and elsewhere in the table. In column 4, I add importing-country fixed effects. Columns 5 and 6 split the sample in two, depending on whether the importing country was large (by population) (i.e., China, Russia, Saudi Arabia, and Ukraine) or small. While both sets of estimates of the elasticity are negative, as predicted by the theory, the estimate of the elasticity is no longer significant for the small-country (by population) subsample. Nevertheless, even this nonresult is somewhat reassuring, given that I would expect the results to be more likely to break down in the small-country subsample.

Overall, this section suggests evidence consistent with the terms-of-trade theory of trade agreements and that the preexisting WTO membership has negotiated tariff binding commitments for newly acceding WTO nonmembers that serve to reduce the negative (terms-of-trade) externality impact of their tariffs on trading partners. Again, to the extent that there are similarities between the WTO *nonmembers'* applied tariffs and the tariff-setting behavior of these recently acceded WTO members before their WTO accession, any future WTO accession by the nonmembers could also be expected to have them take on lower

Table 2.4
Market power and post-WTO accession import tariff bindings for recently acceded countries.

Regression equation: $\ln(1+\tau_{gc}^{WTO\ binding}) = \alpha_g + \alpha_c + \beta_0\ln(1/\omega_{gc}^*) + \beta_1\ln(1+\tau_{gc}^{pre-WTO}) + \epsilon_{gc}$

	Baseline (1)	High Inverse Elasticity Indicator (2)	Level Inverse Elasticity (3)	Add Importer Fixed Effect (4)	Large Countries Only (5)	Small Countries Only (6)
Log inverse elasticity: $\ln(1/\omega_{gc}^*)$	−2.39*** (0.30)			−0.66** (0.29)	−1.40*** (0.41)	−0.62 (0.65)
Indicator for high inverse elasticity		−0.06*** (0.01)				
Inverse elasticity: $(1/\omega_{gc}^*)$			−1.49*** (0.19)			
Log preaccession tariff: $\ln(1+\tau_{gc}^{pre-WTO})$	0.26*** (0.01)	0.26*** (0.01)		0.31*** (0.01)	0.35*** (0.01)	0.27*** (0.01)
Preaccession tariff: $\tau_{gc}^{pre-WTO}$			0.24*** (0.03)			
Product-level (HS06) fixed effects	Y	Y	Y	Y	Y	Y
Importing-country fixed effects	N	N	N	Y	Y	Y
Observations	26,417	26,417	26,417	26,417	13,659	12,758
R^2	0.48	0.48	0.43	0.62	0.68	0.66

Notes: Robust standard errors are in parentheses. Estimates for the constant term are suppressed. Pre-WTO accession tariffs for HS06 product g were taken five years prior to accession date for 12 countries (c): Albania, Armenia, Cabo Verde, China, Georgia, Jordan, Kyrgyz Republic, Moldova, Nepal, Oman, Russia, Saudi Arabia, and Ukraine. Large countries in column 5 are defined as China, Russia, Saudi Arabia, and Ukraine. ***, **, and * indicate statistical significance at the 1%, 5%, or 10% level, respectively.

tariff binding commitments where they would otherwise have more import market power.

2.4   WTO Members with Unbound Tariffs

This section begins my examination of the tariffs that WTO members apply, and in particular whether there is scope for the WTO to "provide" a forum for additional applied tariff reductions motivated by terms of trade for these countries. Put differently, my approach for the next two subsections will be to examine different areas in the WTO system where speculation has been that applied tariffs remain "too high," and I ask whether the level of applied tariffs in each area remains influenced by measures of import market power. Evidence of such a relationship would be consistent with identification of additional tariff-reduction work for countries to utilize the WTO to potentially pursue under the terms-of-trade theory of trade agreements. However, an alternative may be that, while applied tariffs in one or more areas may appear "too high" (or otherwise unconstrained by the WTO), the applied tariffs are not related to product-level measures of the importing country's market power. If this is the case, there may be little scope to engage the WTO in an attempt to neutralize terms of trade to get the country to reduce its tariffs further.

This section begins by focusing on unbound tariffs. These are the products for which countries have not taken on the legal commitment to set any upper limit for their MFN applied import tariffs. I first introduce where unbound tariffs are most prevalent in the WTO system, and then in Subsection 2.4.2 I investigate whether there is evidence linking import market power motives and applied tariff levels in the areas where tariffs are unbound.

2.4.1   Description of the Countries and Unbound Products

Table 2.5 introduces the WTO member countries with the largest share of products for which their applied import tariffs are unbound. Given that a condition of WTO entry for all countries was the expectation that they would agree to bind all tariffs for their agricultural products, I rank the countries in the table by the share of their *nonagricultural* tariff lines that are bound. The left side of the table lists the 25 WTO member countries ("Group A") that will serve as the main sample for the regression analysis that I describe in subsection 2.4.2; these are countries that have bound fewer than one-third of their nonagricultural import

Table 2.5
Economic and tariff characteristics of WTO members with substantial unbound tariffs in 2013.

Countries with WTO Binding Coverage That Is Less than 33% of All Nonagricultural Products (Group A)						Countries with WTO Binding Coverage That Is between 33% and 95% of All Nonagricultural Products (Group B)					
WTO Member Country	WTO Accession Year	GNI per Capita (2013 US$)	Population (millions)	Binding Coverage, Nonag. (%)	MFN Applied (simple avg.), 2013	WTO Member Country	WTO Accession Year	GNI per Capita (2013 US$)	Population (millions)	Binding Coverage, Nonag. (%)	MFN Applied (simple avg.), 2013
Cameroon	1995	1,290	22.3	1.7	18.0	Turkey	1995	10,980	74.9	35.0	10.8
Tanzania	1995	840	49.3	1.8	12.8	Hong Kong SAR, China	1995	38,520	7.2	35.2	0.0
Gambia	1996	500	1.8	2.2	14.1	Tunisia	1995	4,210	10.9	52.7	15.5
Kenya	1995	1,160	44.4	2.3	12.8	Central African Republic	1995	320	4.6	58.9	18.0
Togo	1995	530	6.8	2.4	11.9	Singapore	1995	54,580	5.4	63.9	0.1
Ghana	1995	1,770	25.9	2.8	12.9	Philippines	1995	3,270	98.4	63.9	3.7
Uganda	1995	600	37.6	4.3	12.7	Thailand	1995	5,360	67.0	68.4	10.4
Bangladesh	1995	1,010	156.6	4.4	14.0	Bahrain	1995	21,330	1.3	71.1	5.4
Congo	1997	2,590	4.4	5.0	18.0	India	1995	1,560	1,252.0	71.2	13.3
Zambia	1995	1,780	14.5	5.5	13.2	Israel	1995	33,930	8.1	72.4	3.4
Zimbabwe	1995	860	14.1	5.7	13.2	Malaysia	1995	10,420	29.7	75.4	5.0
Mauritius	1995	9,570	1.3	6.0	1.5	Korea	1995	25,870	50.2	93.5	12.2
Nigeria	1995	2,690	173.6	8.4	11.7	Brunei	1995	NA	0.4	94.1	1.3
Burundi	1995	260	10.2	12.1	12.8	Iceland	1995	46,650	0.3	94.3	5.9
Macao SAR, China	1995	71,270	0.6	12.7	0.0						
Suriname	1995	9,370	0.5	13.3	10.4						

(continued)

Table 2.5
(continued)

Countries with WTO Binding Coverage That Is Less than 33% of All Nonagricultural Products (Group A)

WTO Member Country	WTO Accession Year	GNI per Capita (2013 US$)	Population (millions)	Binding Coverage, Nonag. (%)	MFN Applied (simple avg.), 2013
Malawi	1995	270	16.4	20.8	12.7
Madagascar	1995	440	22.9	21.2	11.7
Cuba	1995	NA	11.3	21.2	10.3
Cote d'Ivoire	1995	1,450	20.3	23.7	11.9
Sri Lanka	1995	3,180	20.5	28.2	10.5
Guinea	1995	460	11.7	30.9	11.9
Burkina Faso	1995	660	16.9	31.3	11.9
Benin	1996	790	10.3	31.4	11.9
Mali	1995	690	15.3	32.0	11.9
Subtotal (Group A)			709.5		
World		10,683	7,125.1		
Share of world			10.0%		

Countries with WTO Binding Coverage That Is between 33% and 95% of All Nonagricultural Products (Group B)

WTO Member Country	WTO Accession Year	GNI per Capita (2013 US$)	Population (millions)	Binding Coverage, Nonag. (%)	MFN Applied (simple avg.), 2013
Subtotal (Group B)			1,610.5		
World		10,683	7,125.1		
Share of world			22.6%		

Sources: World Bank's World Development Indicators, tariffs constructed by the author with data from WTO CTS, IDB, and UNCTAD TRAINS.
Ranked by binding coverage of nonagricultural products. GNI=gross national income, NA=not available.

products. Cameroon has committed to a legally binding upper limit on the smallest share of imported products, at 1.7%, followed by Tanzania and Gambia.

An examination of the 25 WTO members with less than 33% of bound nonagricultural products suggests a number of common characteristics. First, they are disproportionately poor, as only one (Macao SAR, China) had GNI per capita in 2013 greater than the world average of $10,683. Second, with only a handful of exceptions (Bangladesh, Macao SAR (China), Cuba, Sri Lanka, and Suriname), figure 2.1 reveals that the vast majority of countries with unbound tariffs are located in sub-Saharan Africa. Third, while there are also a range of large and small (by population) countries with substantial unbound tariffs, in total the numbers add up: more than 700 million people—or 10% of the world's population—live in WTO member countries that have bound fewer than one-third of their nonagricultural tariffs at any level. Finally, the last column on the left side of table 2.5 does suggest relatively little variation in average applied tariffs across these countries—with the exception of Macao SAR, China, and Mauritius, the average applied MFN tariff (over all products) for the 23 other WTO member countries ranges between 10% and 20%. A major element of this results from the fact that many of these countries are part of the ECOWAS (Economic Community of West African States), which has been developing a customs union arrangement and thus a common external tariff against nonparticipants, including the MFN tariff that each would apply against imports arising from all other (nonparticipant) WTO members.

The right side of table 2.5 provides similar summary statistics for WTO member countries that have bound between 33% and 95% of their nonagricultural product tariff lines. These 14 countries ("Group B") will be used in robustness checks in the formal regression analysis in subsection 2.4.2, but a cursory examination of their economic characteristics suggests that they are much more diverse. At the extremes, some countries on the list are very poor (Central African Republic) and others very rich (Singapore), and with populations that are very small (Brunei and Iceland) or very large (India). The 2013 average applied MFN tariff also ranges substantially from free trade (Hong Kong SAR, China) to 18% (Central African Republic). Finally, Turkey in particular is also notable in that, while it may have bound relatively few (only 35%) of its nonagricultural products legally at the WTO, it has constrained its applied MFN tariffs through other trade agreement means (i.e., by forming a customs union arrangement with the European Union

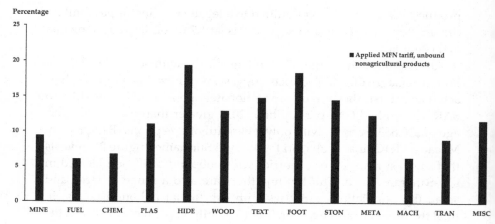

Figure 2.3
Average applied MFN tariffs for WTO members with substantial unbound tariffs in 2013, by industry. Constructed by the author from tariff data at the HS06 level from the WTO IDB, CTS, and UNCTAD TRAINS and from the data for the 25 WTO member countries in table 2.5 ("Group A") with less than 33% of nonagricultural tariffs that are bound.

covering most of its nonagricultural products, with the exception of steel and textiles).

Before moving on, the last note that I make about table 2.5 concerns those countries that are *not* found in the table. The rest of the WTO membership (more than 100 WTO members) that are not listed in the table have bound 95% or more of their nonagricultural products. I have already presented the tariff data for some of these countries (i.e., the recently acceded WTO members) in table 2.3.

Finally, consider figure 2.3 which illustrates the average MFN applied tariffs by sector for the 25 WTO members with less than 33% of their nonagricultural products bound. Much of the cross-industry pattern is similar to what is commonly observed in other settings for low-income countries (again see figure 2.2, for the comparable tariffs for low-income WTO nonmembers and recently acceded members); for example, relatively higher applied tariffs in sectors such as footwear, textiles, hides, and skins, and lower applied tariffs for fuel, chemicals, and machinery.

2.4.2 Empirical Evidence for Unbound Tariffs

To my knowledge, there is no theoretical or empirical work exploring the finer question of why a WTO member would choose to bind some products and yet leave other products unbound. Nevertheless, in this subsection, I use the following model to empirically examine the question of whether measures of importer market power are related to applied tariffs for these *unbound* products:

$$\ln(1 + \tau_{gc}^{WTO\ applied}) = \alpha_g + \alpha_c + \gamma_0 \ln(1/\omega_{gc}^*) + \epsilon_{gc}. \qquad (2.2)$$

If importing countries continue to exert market power over their applied MFN import tariffs ($\tau_{gc}^{WTO\ applied}$) for these unbound products, the theoretical expectation is that γ_0 would be positive.

Table 2.6 presents the results. The general finding is that there is no evidence that market power considerations are driving applied tariff rates for unbound products when the model is estimated on the 25 countries ("Group A") that have committed to bind their tariffs for less than 33% of their nonagricultural products. The first column is the baseline specification, which indicates no statistically significant relationship between the log of the inverse of the foreign export supply elasticity $\ln(1/\omega_{gc}^*)$ and the applied MFN tariff rate, given by $\ln(1 + \tau_{gc}^{WTO\ applied})$. In fact, when I introduce importing-country fixed effects in column 2, there is actually a negative and statistically significant relationship between the measures of import market power and applied MFN tariffs. While, to my knowledge, no one has previously investigated this particular area of unbound tariffs for WTO member countries, these results have some similarities to the pattern of results found by Beshkar, Bond, and Rho (2015), who examine binding tariff levels for 108 WTO members. They find tariff binding levels are negatively related to market power, especially in the presence of substantial amounts of tariff overhang (which they refer to as "weak bindings"). Their theoretical model interprets this negative relationship between import market power and tariff binding levels (in the presence of tariff overhang) as allowing countries flexibility to raise their applied rates in response to shocks. While speculative, a similar motivation could also be at work explaining the applied tariffs for products that are unbound in the WTO system.

Indeed, the last two columns of table 2.6 provide additional evidence of this negative relationship between importer market power and applied MFN tariffs for unbound products by altering the sample of unbound products on which the model is estimated. In column 4, I also include in the sample the unbound products for the 14 WTO member countries (in "Group B") of table 2.5 that had (overall) between 33% and 95% of their nonagricultural products bound. In column 5,

Table 2.6
Market power and WTO members' applied tariffs for unbound products in 2013.

	Regression equation: $\ln\left(1 + \tau_{gc}^{WTO\,applied}\right) = \alpha_g + \alpha_c + \gamma_0 \ln(1/\omega_{gc}^*) + e_{gc}$				
	Baseline (1)	Add Importer Fixed Effect (2)	High Inverse Elasticity Indicator (3)	Add 33% to 95% Bound to Sample (4)	Alternative Unbound Sample (5)
Log inverse elasticity: $\ln(1/\omega_{gc}^*)$	0.44	−1.28***		−0.96***	−2.43***
	(0.63)	(0.45)		(0.34)	(0.70)
Indicator for high inverse elasticity			−0.02		
			(0.02)		
Product-level (HS06) fixed effects	Y	Y	Y	Y	Y
Importing-country fixed effects	N	Y	Y	Y	Y
Observations	25,326	25,326	25,326	36,525	11,199
R^2	0.44	0.71	0.71	0.69	0.70

Notes: Robust standard errors are in parentheses. Estimates for the constant term are suppressed. Columns 1, 2 and 3 include only the 25 WTO member countries (Group A) with less than 33% of nonagricultural products bound, as listed in table 2.5. Column 4 adds 14 countries (Group B of table 2.5) that have bound between 33% and 95% of their nonagricultural products. Column 5 estimates the model on only the 14 Group B countries that have bound between 33% and 95% of their nonagricultural products.

*** , ** , and * indicate statistical significance at the 1%, 5%, or 10% level, respectively.

I estimate the model on only the subsample of data from those 14 WTO member countries. In both cases, the estimate of γ_0 is negative and statistically significant.

To conclude this section, I am unable to find evidence to suggest that the applied MFN tariff levels for unbound products under the WTO are positively associated with importer market power considerations. Under the basic terms-of-trade theory of trade agreements, if countries with unbound tariffs are not applying them to exert market power and impose externalities on trading partners, this suggests little role for the WTO to facilitate applied tariff reductions in this area. While there may be other theories that would motivate welfare improvements arising from countries voluntarily binding these tariffs through the external commitment of a trade agreement, such as the trade policy and uncertainty literature associated with Handley and Limão (2015, 2017), Handley (2014), or Limão and Maggi (2015), in this instance the motivation may not arise from the basic terms-of-trade theory itself.

2.5 WTO Members with Bound Tariffs but Substantial Tariff Overhang

A second contentious area within the WTO system involves countries that, while having taken on the legal commitments to bind their tariffs at some upper limit, have set the upper limit so high relative to the applied MFN tariff that the binding level is economically meaningless. The difference between the legally binding commitment and the applied tariff is again defined as the amount of tariff overhang. In this section, I examine whether applied import tariffs are positively associated with importer market power considerations for products characterized by substantial tariff *overhang*.

My approach in this section follows the theoretical insights and empirical framework introduced by Nicita, Olarreaga, and Silva (2018), described earlier. To summarize, they studied the applied tariffs for roughly 100 WTO member countries and provide two key empirical results. First, when applied tariffs are constrained by WTO binding commitments (e.g., in the extreme, suppose that the applied rate is equal to the binding commitment, so there is zero tariff overhang), then there is a negative relationship between importer market power and the applied tariff. Second, when applied tariffs are unconstrained by WTO binding commitments (e.g., in the extreme, suppose that there is substantial tariff overhang because tariff bindings have *not* been negotiated down close to applied levels), then there is a positive relationship between importer market power and the applied tariff. It is this second result in particular that I investigate in more detail.

2.5.1 The Description of the Countries and Products with Overhang

First, I need to identify the set of WTO member countries with bound tariffs but with significant amounts of tariff overhang remaining between their tariff binding commitments and their applied rates. table 2.7 provides the list of WTO member countries that each have at least 15 percentage points of average tariff overhang. First, it is interesting to note that almost all the countries in table 2.7 acceded to the WTO at the time of its inception in 1995. As is apparent from the data in table 2.3 for countries that acceded to the WTO sometime later (i.e., in 1998 or later), they were only allowed to enter the WTO with much less tariff overhang in place.

Second, it is important to clarify that none of the countries listed in table 2.7 overlap with the "Group A" countries (of table 2.5) that had bound less than 33% of their nonagricultural products (i.e., these two lists are mutually exclusive). However, a handful of countries do appear in both table 2.7 and the "Group B" list of countries in table 2.5 (i.e., those with less than 95% of their nonagricultural products being bound).[24] While these countries' *unbound* products were included as part of the robustness checks provided in columns 4 and 5 of table 2.6, here I only consider the countries' *bound* products. Therefore, because the unbound products are dropped from the analysis here, the country-product pairs included in the robustness check regressions of table 2.6 and those presented next are mutually exclusive.

The countries in table 2.7 share some similarities, but also a number of notable differences, with the WTO nonmembers and recently acceded members (again see tables 2.2 and 2.3) and the list of WTO members with substantial unbound tariffs (again see table 2.5) discussed thus far. Like the earlier lists, the countries with substantial tariff overhang are also developing countries (e.g., nearly three-quarters of the 45 countries had a 2013 GNI per capita at or below the world average). Nevertheless, these developing countries with substantial tariff overhang do have higher GNI per capita on average than the developing countries that are WTO nonmembers, WTO members that recently acceded, or WTO members with substantial unbound products.

Table 2.7

Economic and tariff characteristics of WTO members with substantial tariff overhang in 2013.

WTO Member Country	WTO Accession Year	GNI per Capita (2013 US$)	Population (millions)	Tariff Overhang (simple avg.), 2013	Tariff Binding Rate (simple avg.)	MFN Applied Rate (simple avg.), 2013	Binding Coverage (%)
Panama	1997	10,700	3.9	16.2	23.0	6.8	99.9
Maldives	1995	6,850	0.3	16.2	36.7	20.5	99.1
Israel	1995	33,930	8.1	17.2	20.7	3.4	72.4
Turkey	1995	10,980	74.9	17.5	28.3	10.8	35.0
Brazil	1995	12,550	200.4	17.9	31.4	13.5	100.0
Senegal	1995	1,050	14.1	18.1	30.0	11.9	100.0
Central African Republic	1995	320	4.6	18.1	36.1	18.0	58.9
Argentina	1995	14,590	41.4	18.5	31.9	13.4	100.0
Chile	1995	15,230	17.6	19.1	25.1	6.0	100.0
Egypt	1995	3,140	82.1	20.6	36.1	15.5	99.1
Uruguay	1995	15,640	3.4	21.1	31.6	10.5	100.0
Philippines	1995	3,270	98.4	21.9	25.6	3.7	63.9
Brunei	1995	NA	0.4	22.9	24.2	1.3	94.1
Venezuela	1995	11,730	30.4	23.2	36.5	13.3	100.0
Paraguay	1995	3,980	6.8	23.5	33.5	10.0	100.0
Peru	1995	6,270	30.4	26.1	29.4	3.4	100.0
Honduras	1995	2,120	8.1	26.4	32.1	5.7	100.0
Morocco	1995	3,030	33.0	27.0	41.2	14.3	100.0
Dominican Republic	1995	5,770	10.4	27.0	34.3	7.3	100.0
Papua New Guinea	1996	2,020	7.3	27.1	31.5	4.4	100.0
Mexico	1995	9,880	122.3	27.5	35.2	7.7	100.0
Bolivia	1995	2,550	10.7	28.3	40.0	11.6	100.0
Bahrain	1995	21,330	1.3	28.8	34.2	5.4	71.1
Indonesia	1995	3,760	249.9	29.9	37.1	7.2	96.0
El Salvador	1995	3,720	6.3	30.6	36.6	6.0	100.0
Niger	1996	410	17.8	33.0	44.9	11.9	96.1

(continued)

Table 2.7
(continued)

WTO Member Country	WTO Accession Year	GNI per Capita (2013 US$)	Population (millions)	Tariff Overhang (simple avg.), 2013	Tariff Binding Rate (simple avg.)	MFN Applied Rate (simple avg.), 2013	Binding Coverage (%)
Nicaragua	1995	1,750	6.1	35.3	41.1	5.7	100.0
Colombia	1995	7,610	48.3	35.6	42.3	6.8	100.0
Guatemala	1995	3,340	15.5	35.9	41.6	5.7	100.0
India	1995	1,560	1,252.0	36.2	49.6	13.3	71.2
Costa Rica	1995	9,450	4.9	37.2	42.7	5.6	100.0
Jamaica	1995	5,220	2.7	39.4	49.8	10.4	100.0
Tunisia	1995	4,210	10.9	43.0	58.5	15.5	52.7
Trinidad and Tobago	1995	15,640	1.3	45.3	55.8	10.5	100.0
Guyana	1995	3,750	0.8	45.4	56.6	11.2	100.0
Grenada	1996	7,490	0.1	46.3	56.7	10.4	100.0
Belize	1995	4,510	0.3	47.4	58.1	10.7	100.0
Antigua and Barbuda	1995	13,050	0.1	48.1	58.6	10.5	100.0
Dominica	1995	6,860	0.1	48.4	58.7	10.3	96.4
Saint Lucia	1995	7,060	0.2	51.8	62.1	10.3	100.0
Saint Vincent and the Grenadines	1995	6,540	0.1	52.5	62.7	10.2	100.0
Barbados	1995	NA	0.3	65.6	78.2	12.6	100.0
St. Kitts and Nevis	1996	13,760	0.1	65.7	76.0	10.3	100.0
Lesotho	1995	1,590	2.1	70.8	78.4	7.6	100.0
Rwanda	1996	630	11.8	76.6	89.4	12.8	100.0
Subtotal			2,442.0				
World		10,683	7,125.1				
Share of world			34.3%				

Sources: World Bank's World Development Indicators, tariffs constructed by the author with data from WTO CTS, IDB, and UNCTAD TRAINS. Members with average tariff overhang greater than 15 percentage points, ranked from lowest to highest. GNI=gross national income, NA=not available.

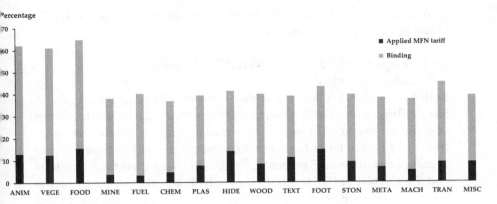

Figure 2.4
Average applied MFN tariffs and tariff bindings for WTO members with substantial tariff overhang in 2013, by industry. Constructed by the author from tariff data at the HS06 level from the WTO IDB, CTS, and UNCTAD TRAINS and from the data for the 45 WTO member countries in table 2.7 with 15 percentage points or more of average tariff overhang.

Next, to the extent that the countries with substantial unbound products were geographically concentrated in sub-Saharan Africa, the countries with substantial tariff overhang tend to be geographically concentrated in Latin America (again see figure 2.1). Nevertheless, there are important exceptions, including countries with substantial overhang arising in South and East Asia and North Africa. Furthermore, while countries with relatively large populations, such as Egypt, Philippines, Brazil, Mexico, Indonesia, and India, are notably on the list of countries with substantial tariff overhang, this list also contains a number of countries with tiny populations (11 of the 45 have less than one million people), including a number of small island economies of the Caribbean. Nevertheless, the combined population of these 45 countries is over 2.4 billion people, or more than one-third of the global population.

Figure 2.4 illustrates the average MFN applied tariffs and tariff bindings by sector for these 45 WTO members that average more than 15 percentage points of tariff overhang. The average applied tariffs exhibit cross-industry patterns similar to the other settings for developing countries (e.g., relatively higher applied tariffs in sectors such as footwear, textiles, hides, and skins, and lower applied tariffs for fuel, chemicals, and machinery. There are significant differences in binding levels across sectors, however. Tariff binding levels average over 60%

in animals, vegetables, and foodstuffs, whereas they are closer to 40% for all other (nonagricultural) sectors.

2.5.2 Empirical Evidence for Bound Tariffs with Substantial Overhang

In this subsection I follow a modified version of Nicita, Olarreaga, and Silva (2018) to empirically examine the question of whether measures of importer market power are related to applied tariffs for the countries identified in table 2.7 as having substantial tariff overhang, or an average of more than 15 percentage points between their tariff bindings and their applied MFN tariffs. In the estimation, I also condition on the country-product pairs that have 15 percentage points or more of tariff overhang as well.[25] The basic model that I estimate is again simply

$$\ln(1 + \tau_{gc}^{WTO\ applied}) = \alpha_g + \alpha_c + \gamma_0 \ln(1/\omega_{gc}^*) + \epsilon_{gc}, \qquad (2.3)$$

where if importing countries continue to exert market power over their applied import tariffs ($\tau_{gc}^{WTO\ applied}$) for this subset of bound products over which there is substantial tariff overhang, I expect γ_0 to be positive. The main difference from the approach described in subsection 2.5.1 is not the model but simply the subsample of countries and products (those with bound tariffs and tariff overhang) over which the model is estimated.

Table 2.8 presents the results. The general finding confirms the evidence from Nicita, Olarreaga, and Silva (2018) for this particular subsample of countries that market power considerations are positively related to applied MFN tariff rates in 2013 for these products.

The first column of table 2.8 is the baseline specification, which indicates a positive and statistically significant relationship between the log of the inverse of the foreign export supply elasticity, given by $\ln(1/\omega_{gc}^*)$, and the measure of the applied MFN tariff rate, given by $\ln(1 + \tau_{gc}^{WTO\ applied})$. In column 2, I introduce importing-country fixed effects, and in column 3 I utilize the high inverse elasticity indicator variable in lieu of the continuous measure. The results are robust to these different specifications.

The next three columns of table 2.8 examine subsamples of these data. Column 4 focuses on where tariff overhang is greatest by changing the threshold from 15 percentage points to 25 percentage points, thereby reducing the sample by almost half.[26] The size of the estimated impact of market power is even larger in the subsample of

Table 2.8

Market power and WTO members' applied tariffs for bound products with substantial tariff overhang in 2013.

	Baseline (1)	Add Importer Fixed Effect (2)	High Inverse Elasticity Indicator (3)	Change to 25 p.p. Subsample (4)	Nonagr. Only (5)	Agr. Only (6)	Recent Accessions Only (7)
			Regression equation: $\ln(1 + \tau_{gc}^{WTO\ applied}) = \alpha_g + \alpha_c + \gamma_0\ln(1/\omega_{gc}^*) + \epsilon_{gc}$				
Log inverse elasticity: $\ln(1/\omega_{gc}^*)$	1.74*** (0.28)	0.49** (0.24)		1.37*** (0.32)	0.55** (0.25)	0.31 (0.66)	−1.25*** (0.38)
High inverse elasticity indicator			0.03*** (0.01)				
Product-level (HS06) fixed effects	Y	Y	Y	Y	Y	Y	Y
Importing-country fixed effects	N	Y	Y	Y	Y	Y	Y
Observations	68,355	68,355	68,355	38,710	60,532	7,823	30,096
R^2	0.33	0.58	0.58	0.65	0.59	0.57	0.48

Notes: Robust standard errors are in parentheses. Estimates for the constant term are suppressed. With the exception of columns 4 and 7, the model estimated on bound products for 45 countries (listed in table 2.7), each with tariff overhang greater than 15 percentage points. Column 4 model estimated on bound products for 30 countries (listed in table 2.7) with tariff overhang greater than 25 percentage points. Column 7 estimated on bound products for 12 recently acceded WTO countries listed in table 2.3. With the exception of Nepal (13.8) and Oman (9.1), the ten other countries have average tariff overhangs of 6 percentage points or less.

***, **, and * indicate statistical significance at the 1%, 5%, or 10% level, respectively.

countries and products where tariff overhang is largest. Columns 5 and 6 split the original baseline sample in two, depending on whether the products fall into agriculture. Interestingly, the potential influence of market power is not found in the agricultural product subsample of the data in column 6, though admittedly this is a much smaller sample of observations.

Finally, and as a last "consistency check" with expectations, the last column of table 2.8 presents estimates from the same model on a completely different subsample of data—the 12 countries that recently acceded to the WTO that were part of the formal econometric analysis of tariff bindings presented in table 2.4. Not surprisingly, the relationship in column 7 between the inverse foreign export supply elasticity and applied import tariffs for these 12 countries is not only not positive but is negative and statistically significant. Recall from table 2.3 that upon entry to the WTO, countries such as China, Russia, and Ukraine not only took on nearly universal tariff binding coverage but also bound their tariffs at relatively low levels compared to their applied rates. The average tariff overhang for the countries and products in the column 7 sample is only 3.6 percentage points, and less than 5% of observations in that sample have 15 percentage points or more tariff overhang.[27] The applied tariffs for the recently acceded WTO members thus have a very different empirical relationship with measures of import market power than the applied tariffs for the WTO members that have been around since the agreement's inception and that continue to have large amounts of tariff overhang.

The evidence from this section suggests that products for countries that have taken on WTO bindings but for which substantial tariff overhang remains have applied MFN import tariffs that continue to reflect import market power considerations. As such, this may constitute an area where additional WTO-facilitated negotiations for applied MFN tariff reductions would be consistent with the insights of the terms-of-trade theory of trade agreements.

2.6   Conclusions and Policy Implications

This chapter uses the lens provided by the terms-of-trade theory of trade agreements, as well as recent empirical and data advances arising in the literature, to assess whether there may be a market power neutralization motive for the WTO to facilitate additional tariff reductions in three distinct areas: (1) applied tariffs for WTO nonmembers,

(2) applied tariffs for members where they are unbound, and (3) applied tariffs for members where there is substantial tariff overhang.

An open policy question is how the WTO could be redeployed to address these areas where additional liberalization motivated by terms of trade might take place. While I have provided a mix of direct and indirect evidence for where there remains a positive relationship between import market power and applied import tariffs, I have nevertheless refrained from assessing why "high" applied import tariffs (that reflect terms-of-trade motives) have yet to be extinguished even by WTO negotiations, as well as whether institutional impediments might be overcome that would allow for their negotiated reduction.

A promising line of research involves the Bagwell, Staiger, and Yurukoglu (2015) examination of the *historical* process of reciprocal trade negotiations that took place product-by-product under the early GATT rounds. There may be lessons to be learned from the details of such experiences for any additional liberalization remaining to be undertaken today.

Nevertheless, one additional possible starting point arises out of the results that I have developed here in subsection 2.5.2. WTO members that retain substantial amounts of tariff overhang and have applied MFN tariffs that continue to reflect market power influences could potentially be grouped with one another to identify reciprocal liberalization matches in the spirit suggested by the Bagwell and Staiger (1999) theory. While obviously these regression results are only suggestive of where negotiators could potentially look in greater detail, the countries in this sample include Argentina, Brazil, India, Indonesia, and Mexico—all members of the Group of 20 (G20) and potential future leaders with a vested interest in sustaining the multilateral trading system.[28] On the other hand, the last set of results of subsection 2.5.2 presents no evidence that, on average, applied MFN tariffs and market power remain positively related for the set of recently acceded WTO members that includes China and Russia. Such evidence would tend to suggest that the countries that recently acceded to the WTO may not be great candidates to lead a new set of reciprocal tariff liberalization negotiations.

Furthermore, I have already noted one particularly important strand of research in the terms-of-trade literature that identifies variation in the concentration of export interests across countries as presenting an additional bottleneck that may mitigate the effectiveness of the

GATT/WTO's reciprocal, shallow-integration approach to tariff cutting (Ludema and Mayda 2013). The Ludema-Mayda evidence was based on a 26-country sample that included a number of high-income countries, and it does suggest that not all of the terms-of-trade motives may have (as yet) been exorcised for the high-income-economy applied MFN tariffs. While this would imply that such countries could also plausibly be part of future reciprocal bargains still to be struck, the difficulty for the WTO and trade negotiators may rest in how to make those matches and strike those bargains. Put differently, the second insight from the Ludema-Mayda evidence is that the real world of trade negotiations is certainly even more complicated than simply getting two large importing countries together to reciprocally reduce their import tariffs. The potential asymmetry of exporters in a many-country world, or the concentration (or lack thereof) of exporting interests for a particular product, may make implementation of the GATT/WTO's historical "principal supplier rule" approach to pairing negotiating interests difficult. To what extent might third-party intermediaries (such as an institution like the WTO) be needed to organize *triangular* liberalization efforts, say, if bilateral trade liberalization opportunities between partners are unlikely because of trade imbalances or other asymmetries? More research is certainly required to further investigate all these questions.

An additional and potentially related concern requiring additional exploration is that the importing countries that continue to impose positive tariffs reflecting their market power incentives may also not face significantly large "foreign" tariffs on their exported products to generate the trade-off necessary for the neutralization of the terms-of-trade cut under the traditional, reciprocal approach. This may be because the importing country receives preferential tariff treatment from trading partners for its exports, either through unilateral preferences such as the Generalized System of Preferences (GSP) or through *reciprocal* preferential trade agreements. Alternatively, "intermediate" (but not "latecomer" nonmember) countries to the system may find that they already receive MFN treatment of very low applied tariffs from the major markets of other WTO members for their exports. While the WTO system has seemingly been able to overcome this hurdle when it comes to neutralizing the terms-of-trade motives behind recently acceded WTO member countries (Bagwell and Staiger 2011; see also the results in subsection 2.3.3), it appears that it may have been much less successful in doing so in the initial tranche of acceding members in 1995, when it did not require these countries especially to take on particularly stringent tariff binding commitments (see the results of section 2.5 and Nicita, Olarreaga, and Silva 2018).

There are other complications to the historical GATT/WTO approach to reciprocal liberalization that the theoretical literature has begun to identify and explore and may also serve as impediments for future liberalization. These include trade in products where prices are determined by bilateral bargaining and not market-clearing conditions (e.g., Antràs and Staiger 2012a, 2012b) and environments characterized by cross-border ownership and foreign direct investment (Blanchard 2007, 2010). While these particular impediments may be more suited to the relatively complex trade in parts and tasks that is commonly associated with high-income countries, nevertheless, as Johnson and Noguera (2017) document, the importance of such trade is increasing almost everywhere over time.

Finally, I conclude by pointing out that even once countries are inside the WTO and the terms-of-trade incentives may have been extinguished from their applied MFN tariffs, significant institutionally provided flexibilities exist so that trade policy is not truly and permanently locked in at levels that may turn out to be too low in the face of political-economic shocks. Bown and Crowley (2013b), for example, provide evidence consistent with the Bagwell and Staiger (1990) theoretical, repeated-game framework of trade agreements that interprets some use of antidumping measures and safeguards as governments managing the terms-of-trade pressure—even once they have bound their applied MFN tariffs at low levels—associated with trade volume shocks.[29] Thus, while the WTO may still have some work to do, so as to more completely exorcise the terms-of-trade incentives from its members' applied MFN tariffs, even after potential completion of those efforts, some trade policy flexibility (and influence of terms-of-trade motives affecting the use of such flexibility) may likely remain.

Data Appendix

The sources of the applied MFN tariff data for WTO members, the tariff binding data for WTO members, and the applied tariff data for WTO nonmembers are a combination of WTO, Integrated Data Base (IBD), Consolidated Tariff Schedules (CTS) data base, and United Nations Conference on Trade And Development Trade Analysis Information System (UNCTAD TRAINS). Some of the tariff data are more disaggregated than the HS06 level, in which case I first construct means at the HS06 level before further employing them.

The data on the inverse export supply elasticities at the HS06 level for 100 WTO member countries are from Nicita, Olarreaga, and Silva (2018).

The sources of the data on the economic characteristics of countries are primarily the World Bank's World Development Indicators. For some countries with missing data, estimates from the CIA's *World Factbook* were used.

Notes

I give special thanks to Kyle Bagwell and Robert Staiger for useful discussions. Maurizio Zanardi, Anna Maria Mayda, Ben Zissimos, Mostafa Beshkar, Rick Bond, Kamal Saggi, and participants at the CESifo Venice Summer Institute provided insightful comments on an earlier draft. I also thank Alessandro Nicita, Marcelo Olarreaga, and Peri Silva for graciously sharing their estimated trade elasticities. I also thank the World Bank's Development Research Group for its hospitality during the period in which most of the work on this chapter was completed, including financial support through the Multidonor Trust Fund for Trade and Development and through the Strategic Research Partnership on Economic Development. Semira Ahdiyyih provided outstanding research assistance. All remaining errors are my own.

1. The United States presented a number of challenges to the WTO by holding up the appointment of WTO Appellate Body members and through the Trump administration's 2018 imposition of tariffs on steel and aluminum under the allegation that they are a threat to American national security (The Economist 2018).

2. The only negotiated tariff reduction taking place under the WTO in the intervening period was for the 201 products arising through the plurilateral Information Technology Agreement in 2015, which involved a critical mass of more than 20 WTO members. Similar negotiations to cut tariffs plurilaterally under an Environmental Goods Agreement have stalled. I will not investigate those products or negotiations here.

3. Other explorations behind the stalled Doha Round and its ineffectiveness include Martin and Mattoo (2011) and Jones (2010). For a behind-the-scenes perspective on many of the personalities involved, see Blustein (2009).

4. Krishna (2014) also provides a skeptical view of the proliferation of preferential trade agreements and its implications for the multilateral trading system. See also Maggi (2014).

5. Even though the United States had negotiated a successful TPP agreement, Donald Trump pulled the country out of it on his third day in office. It has since been renegotiated by the remaining 11 member countries as the Comprehensive and Progressive Agreement for Trans-Pacific Partnership, or CPTPP.

6. In addition to the terms-of-trade theory described in more detail later, there are other prominent theories of trade agreements that I will not integrate into my formal analysis but also deserve mention. The first alternative approach to trade agreements is the commitment theory (Maggi and Rodríguez-Clare 1998, 2007; Staiger and Tabellini 1987;

Limão and Tovar 2011), in which governments may seek an external agreement to tie their own hands in relation to their private sectors. Other recent alternative theories include consideration of other potential international externalities aside from the terms-of-trade externality, such as those that may arise through firm delocation (Ossa 2011, 2012). A third theory is motivated by the rise of offshoring (Blanchard 2007, 2010; Antràs and Staiger 2012a, 2012b). Bagwell, Bown, and Staiger (2016) provide a more extensive survey of theoretical and empirical advances in these areas as well as the terms-of-trade literature. Bown and Crowley (2016) survey the empirical landscape of tariffs and other trade policy instruments in historical perspective and in more detail.

7. In this way, it allows for political economy influences of many different classes of models, including that of Grossman and Helpman (1994).

8. Some of the terms-of-trade externality analysis in the context of trade policy was provided by Johnson (1953–1954). Bagwell and Staiger (2002) provide a book-length treatment that considers a number of alternative applications of the model to trade agreements under different settings, including consideration of some forms of nonpecuniary exernalities and domestic policy instruments.

9. As I will describe in more detail, Bown and Crowley (2013b) provide a separate empirical analysis of a particular class of nontariff barriers for the United States. That study covered a different time period and assessed the terms-of-trade implications of a slightly different theoretical model (Bagwell and Staiger 1990), but it also provides evidence consistent with the terms-of-trade theory.

10. To clarify, Bagwell and Staiger (2011) compare a country's unbound (applied MFN) tariff rates before the country's WTO accession with its legally binding tariff commitment post-WTO accession and not its postaccession applied MFN rate.

11. See also Ludema and Mayda (2009) for an alternative approach focused exclusively on the United States.

12. Bown and Crowley (2013b) provide additional evidence that terms-of-trade motives continue to affect trade policy decisions for WTO members, albeit in a different trade policy setting. They provide evidence consistent with the Bagwell and Staiger (1990) repeated-game model of trade agreements by focusing on the US use of antidumping restrictions and safeguards over 1997–2006. They find for a country like the United States (with applied tariffs virtually at their binding level), the flexibility of antidumping restrictions and safeguards can be seen as allowing the government to raise import protection levels in response to trade volume shocks arising from terms-of-trade motivations.

13. This is notably higher than the estimates of the tariffs applied at the height of the Great Depression in the 1930s, after the US imposition of the Smoot-Hawley tariff in 1930 and international retaliatory response. See Bown and Irwin (2017) for a discussion of the range of tariffs more likely to have been in effect just prior to the GATT's starting point in 1947, which they put at around 22%.

14. To clarify, Beshkar, Bond, and Rho (2015) focus on the determinants of the level tariff bindings (taking applied rates as given), whereas Nicita, Olarreaga, and Silva (2018) focus on the determinants of the level of *applied* tariffs (taking binding rates as given). Nicita, Olarreaga, and Silva do not investigate the impact of import market power on either the level of tariff *bindings* or the *amount of overhang* between the binding and the applied tariff; an instrumental variable for the amount of overhang is interacted with the measure of importer market power.

15. Separately, there is some empirical evidence related to the commitment theory of trade agreements. However, it is much less developed in the literature. Examples include Tang and Wei (2009), which finds some evidence of a positive impact of WTO accession on economic growth. Bown and Crowley (2014) find evidence for some developing countries that WTO entry has committed them to change how they implement increases to their levels of import protection (in response to macroeconomic shocks) by switching to different (and WTO-sanctioned) trade policy instruments, and this is both different from how they operated before the WTO and similar to the commitments and trade policy use of higher-income WTO members. See also Staiger and Tabellini (1999) for evidence on the role of the GATT in allowing the United States to make trade policy commitments during the Tokyo Round of negotiations.

16. Handley and Limão (2015) provide a structural approach to estimate the model and apply it to Portuguese firm-level data. Their policy environment does not entail the binding of tariffs under the WTO. Instead they examine the 1986 Portuguese trade agreement accession to the European Economic Community, which reduced trade policy uncertainty by locking in zero import tariffs from European trading partners. Francois and Martin (2004) provide an alternative theoretical approach examining the role of tariff bindings in reducing the uncertainty associated with market access. Limão and Maggi (2015) provide a more general theory examining when trade agreements can provide gains through the reduction of trade policy uncertainty. Conditional on the level of income risk aversion in a country, gains from reducing trade policy uncertainty are more likely to arise for economies that are more open and specialized and that have lower export supply elasticities.

17. See also Handley and Limão (2017) for an examination of the resolution of trade policy uncertainty facing Chinese firms resulting from accession to the WTO in 2001 and the reduction of uncertainty surrounding tariffs applied by the United States that had persisted during the 1990s through the annual Senate debate on whether to renew China's MFN treatment. They find that the WTO's effect on reducing the threat of a trade war explains 22% of China's export growth to the United States, and that the reduction in policy uncertainty lowered US prices and increased consumers' incomes by the welfare equivalent of an 8 percentage point tariff decrease.

18. I utilize data on accessions starting only in 1998 (instead of, for example, 1996) because some of the initial wave of WTO accession countries in 1996 and 1997 were countries that may simply have waited to begin the domestic legal process to formally ratify WTO membership until after the major WTO members had done so, recalling the US experience of failing to ratify the International Trade Organization (ITO) in the 1940s, which led to the GATT.

19. Note that these three country groupings do not correspond to the World Bank's official categories.

20. Governments with WTO observer status are not members but are granted limited WTO rights, such as access to certain WTO meetings. They are also expected to uphold other obligations, such as making some (minimal) contributions to the WTO's operating budget.

21. Finally, my estimation exercise here and in what follows relies only on ordinary least squares. Unlike the prior literature, I do not estimate instrumental variables, so the estimates reported here should not be interpreted as identifying magnitudes associated with causal effects.

22. The appendix provides a full description of the data and its sources.

23. For a discussion of a variety of potential approaches to adopt for assessing the robustness of results, see Broda, Limão, and Weinstein (2008) and Nicita, Olarreaga, and Silva (2018).

24. These countries are Israel, Turkey, Central African Republic, Philippines, Bahrain, India, and Tunisia.

25. That is, I drop from the sample all products within these 45 countries that have bound tariffs but applied MFN tariffs that are within 15 percentage points (or less) of the binding rate. Because I am therefore conditioning on a sample of countries and products that *only* have tariff overhang, I do not need to include interaction terms as in Nicita, Olarreaga, and Silva (2018) in order to thereby separate out the potential negative relationship between measures of import market power in the absence of such overhang (i.e., when the applied MFN tariff is equal to the binding rate).

26. For the countries involved in this subsample, again see table 2.7, and the bottom two-thirds of the listed countries, beginning with Peru (26.1%).

27. While not presented in the table, I can also confirm another relationship identified by Nicita, Olarreaga, and Silva (2018) for this particular sample of countries: that when applied rates are equal to binding rates (so "cooperation" is the strongest), the relationship between market power and the applied MFN tariff is still negative.

28. However, this is complicated by the fact that many of the countries on this list (e.g., Mexico, Colombia, Peru, and Chile) are actively involved in the formation of preferential tariff agreements with major high-income economies. These agreements may serve as an alternative to neutralizing the terms-of-trade motives associated with certain applied *bilateral* tariffs (with respect to major trading partners at least) if not their applied MFN tariffs.

29. For evidence that macroeconomic shocks—real exchange rate shocks, real GDP and unemployment shocks—also trigger new import protection under such temporary trade barrier policies permitted under the WTO, see Bown and Crowley (2013a, 2014) for cross-country studies on high-income and emerging economies, respectively, in the spirit of the Bagwell and Staiger (2003) theoretical framework. Vandenbussche and Zanardi (2008) describe motivations for the rise of antidumping laws—the most commonly invoked temporary trade barrier policy—across the WTO membership over time, and Bown (2011b) provides a recent empirical account of the use of the policies across countries over time.

References

Antràs, Pol and Robert W. Staiger. 2012a. "Offshoring and the Role of Trade Agreements." *American Economic Review* 102(7): 3140–3183.

Antràs, Pol and Robert W. Staiger. 2012b. "Trade Agreements and the Nature of Price Determination." *American Economic Review: Papers and Proceedings* 102(3): 470–476.

Bagwell, Kyle, Chad P. Bown, and Robert W. Staiger. 2016. "Is the WTO Passé?" *Journal of Economic Literature* 54(4): 1125–1231.

Bagwell, Kyle and Robert W. Staiger. 1990. "A Theory of Managed Trade." *American Economic Review* 80(4): 779–795.

Bagwell, Kyle and Robert W. Staiger. 1999. "An Economic Theory of GATT." *American Economic Review* 89(1): 215–248.

Bagwell, Kyle and Robert W. Staiger. 2002. *The Economics of the World Trading System.* Cambridge, MA: MIT Press.

Bagwell, Kyle and Robert W. Staiger. 2003. "Protection and the Business Cycle." *Advances in Economic Analysis and Policy* 3(1): Article 3 (available at http://www.bepress .com/bejeap/advances/vol3/iss1/art3/).

Bagwell, Kyle and Robert W. Staiger. 2011. "What Do Trade Negotiators Negotiate About? Empirical Evidence from the World Trade Organization." *American Economic Review* 101(4): 1238–1273.

Bagwell, Kyle and Robert W. Staiger. 2014. "Can the Doha Round Be a Development Round? Setting a Place at the Table." In *Globalization in an Age of Crisis: Multilateral Economic Cooperation in the Twenty-First Century,* edited by Robert C. Feenstra and Alan M. Taylor, 91–124. Chicago: University of Chicago Press for the NBER.

Bagwell, Kyle, Robert W. Staiger, and Ali Yurukoglu. 2015. "Multilateral Trade Bargaining: A First Look at the GATT Bargaining Records." NBER Working Paper No. 21488. Cambridge, MA: National Bureau of Economic Research. August.

Beshkar, Mostafa, Eric W. Bond, and Youngwoo Rho. 2015. "Tariff Binding and Overhang: Theory and Evidence." *Journal of International Economics* 97(1): 1–13.

Blanchard, Emily J. 2007. "Foreign Direct Investment, Endogenous Tariffs, and Preferential Trade Agreements." *BE Journal of Economic Analysis and Policy* 7.

Blanchard, Emily J. 2010. "Reevaluating the Role of Trade Agreements: Does Investment Globalization Make the WTO Obsolete?" *Journal of International Economics* 82(1): 63–72.

Blustein, Paul. 2009. *Misadventures of the Most-Favored Nations: Clashing Egos, Inflated Ambitions, and the Great Shambles of the World Trade System.* New York: Public Affairs.

Bown, Chad P. 2009. *Self-Enforcing Trade: Developing Countries and WTO Dispute Settlement.* Washington, DC: Brookings Institution Press.

Bown, Chad P., ed. 2011a. *The Great Recession and Import Protection: The Role of Temporary Trade Barriers.* London: CEPR and World Bank.

Bown, Chad P. 2011b. "Taking Stock of Antidumping, Safeguards and Countervailing Duties, 1990–2009." *World Economy* 34(12): 1955–1998.

Bown, Chad P. and Meredith A. Crowley. 2013a. "Import Protection, Business Cycles, and Exchange Rates: Evidence from the Great Recession." *Journal of International Economics* 90(1): 50–64.

Bown, Chad P. and Meredith A. Crowley. 2013b. "Self-Enforcing Trade Agreements: Evidence from Time-Varying Trade Policy." *American Economic Review* 103(2): 1071–1090.

Bown, Chad P. and Meredith A. Crowley. 2014. "Emerging Economies, Trade Policy, and Macroeconomic Shocks." *Journal of Development Economics* 111:261–273.

Bown, Chad P. and Meredith A. Crowley. 2016. "The Empirical Landscape of Trade Policy." In *The Handbook of Commercial Policy,* edited by Kyle Bagwell and Robert W. Staiger, 3–108. Amsterdam: Elsevier.

Bown, Chad P. and Douglas A. Irwin. 2017. "The GATT's Starting Point: Tariff Levels circa 1947." In *Assessing the World Trade Organization: Fit for Purpose?*, edited by Manfred Elsig, Bernard Hoekman, and Joost Pauwelyn, 45–74. Cambridge: Cambridge University Press.

Bown, Chad P. and Kara M. Reynolds. 2015. "Trade Flows and Trade Disputes." *Review of International Organizations* 10(2): 145–177.

Bown, Chad P. and Kara M. Reynolds. 2017. "Trade Agreements and Enforcement: Evidence from WTO Dispute Settlement." *American Economic Journal: Economic Policy* 9(4): 64–100.

Broda, Christian, Nuno Limão, and David E. Weinstein. 2008. "Optimal Tariffs and Market Power: The Evidence." *American Economic Review* 98(5): 2032–2065.

The Economist. 2018. "The Looming Global Trade War." March 8.

Francois, Joseph F. and William J. Martin. 2004. "Commercial Policy Variability, Bindings, and Market Access." *European Economic Review* 48(3): 665–679.

Grossman, Gene M. and Elhanan Helpman. 1994. "Protection for Sale." *American Economic Review* 84(4): 833–850.

Handley, Kyle. 2014. "Exporting under Trade Policy Uncertainty: Theory and Evidence." *Journal of International Economics* 94(1): 50–66.

Handley, Kyle and Nuno Limão. 2015. "Trade and Investment under Policy Uncertainty: Theory and Firm Evidence." *American Economic Journal: Economic Policy* 7(4): 189–222.

Handley, Kyle and Nuno Limão. 2017. "Policy Uncertainty, Trade and Welfare: Theory and Evidence for China and the U.S." *American Economic Review* 107(9): 2731–2783.

Johnson, Harry G. 1953–1954. "Optimum Tariffs and Retaliation." *Review of Economic Studies* 21(2): 142–153.

Johnson, Robert C. and Guillermo Noguera. 2017. "A Portrait of Trade in Value Added over Four Decades." *Review of Economics and Statistics* 99(5): 896–911.

Jones, Kent. 2010. *The Doha Blues: Institutional Crisis and Reform in the WTO*. Oxford: Oxford University Press.

Krishna, Pravin. 2014. "Preferential Trade Agreements and the World Trade System: A Multilateralist View." In *Globalization in an Age of Crisis: Multilateral Economic Cooperation in the Twenty-First Century*, edited by Robert C. Feenstra and Alan M. Taylor, 131–160. Chicago: University of Chicago Press for the NBER.

Limão, Nuno and Giovanni Maggi. 2015. "Uncertainty and Trade Agreements." *American Economic Journal: Microeconomics* 7(4): 1–42.

Limão, Nuno and Patricia Tovar. 2011. "Policy Choice: Theory and Evidence from Commitment via International Trade Agreements." *Journal of International Economics* 85(2): 186–205.

Ludema, Rodney D. and Anna Maria Mayda. 2009. "Do Countries Free Ride on MFN?" *Journal of International Economics* 77(2): 137–150.

Ludema, Rodney D. and Anna Maria Mayda. 2013. "Do Terms-of-Trade Effects Matter for Trade Agreements? Theory and Evidence from WTO Countries." *Quarterly Journal of Economics* 128(4): 1837–1893.

Maggi, Giovanni. 1999. "The Role of Multilateral Institutions in International Trade Cooperation." *American Economic Review* 89(1): 190–214.

Maggi, Giovanni. 2014. "International Trade Agreements." In *Handbook of International Economics*, edited by Gita Gopinath, Elhanan Helpman, and Kenneth Rogoff, volume 4, 317–390. Amsterdam: Elsevier.

Maggi, Giovanni and Andres Rodríguez-Clare. 1998. "The Value of Trade Agreements in the Presence of Political Pressures." *Journal of Political Economy* 106(3): 574–601.

Maggi, Giovanni and Andres Rodríguez-Clare. 2007. "A Political-Economy Theory of Trade Agreements." *American Economic Review* 97(4): 1374–1406.

Maggi, Giovanni and Robert W. Staiger. 2011. "The Role of Dispute Settlement Procedures in International Trade Agreements." *Quarterly Journal of Economics* 126(1): 475–515.

Maggi, Giovanni and Robert W. Staiger. 2015. "Optimal Design of Trade Agreements in the Presence of Renegotiation." *American Economic Journal: Microeconomics* 7(1): 109–143.

Martin, William J. and Aaditya Mattoo, eds. 2011. *Unfinished Business? The WTO's Doha Agenda*. London: CEPR and the World Bank.

Nicita, Alessandro, Marcelo Olarreaga, and Peri Silva. 2018. "Cooperation in WTO's Tariff Waters?" *Journal of Political Economy* 126(3): 1302–1338.

Ossa, Ralph. 2011. "A 'New-Trade' Theory of GATT/WTO Negotiations." *Journal of Political Economy* 119(1): 122–152.

Ossa, Ralph. 2012. "Profits in the 'New Trade' Approach to Trade Negotiations." *American Economic Review: Papers and Proceedings* 102(2): 466–469.

Ossa, Ralph. 2014. "Trade Wars and Trade Talks with Data." *American Economic Review* 104(12): 4104–4146.

Staiger, Robert W. and Guido Tabellini. 1987. "Discretionary Trade Policy and Excessive Protection." *American Economic Review* 77(5): 823–837.

Staiger, Robert W. and Guido Tabellini. 1999. "Do GATT Rules Help Governments Make Domestic Commitments?" *Economics and Politics* 11(2): 109–144.

Tang, Man-Keung and Shang-Jin Wei. 2009. "The Value of Making Commitments Externally: Evidence from WTO Accessions." *Journal of International Economics* 78(2): 216–229.

Vandenbussche, Hylke and Maurizio Zanardi. 2008. "What Explains the Proliferation of Antidumping Laws?" *Economic Policy* 23(1): 93–138.

World Bank. 2014. "Harmonized List of Fragile Situations FY14." Washington, DC: World Bank.

3 Dragons, Giants, Elephants, and Mice: Evolution of the MFN Free-Rider Problem in the WTO Era

Rodney D. Ludema, Anna Maria Mayda, and
Jonathon C. F. McClure

To be blunt, there is hesitation to make indirect concessions to China, whether or not people are willing to name the dragon in the middle of the room.
—Francois (2008)

For them, the elephant—or rather, the dragon—in the living room was China. Brazil, India, and other emerging economies were reluctant to further reduce industrial tariffs on an MFN basis because market opening towards OECD countries on this basis would also result in market opening towards China, whom they increasingly feared as a competitor.
—Kleimann and Guinan (2011)

3.1 Introduction

Today's World Trade Organization (WTO) oversees a vastly different trading system than the one it inherited 20 years ago, in large part because of three major trends: the accession of new members to the WTO, the rise of emerging economies, and the proliferation of preferential trade agreements (PTAs). The 2012 WTO had 157 members, 45 of which had acceded since the WTO replaced the General Agreement on Tariffs and Trade (GATT) in 1994.[1] Most notable among these new entrants are two of Asia's largest economies, the People's Republic of China (which acceded in 2001) and the Russian Federation (which acceded in 2012). The second trend is the rise of "emerging" economies, most notably Brazil, Russia, India, and China (BRIC). On average, emerging economies have grown far faster than the rest of the world. From 2004 to 2013, the average annual real GDP growth rates of Brazil, China, India, Indonesia, and Russia averaged 6.5%, while growth in Germany, France, Japan, the United Kingdom, and the United States averaged only 1.2% over the same period.[2] Along with this GDP growth has come impressive export growth, which has shaped the trade patterns of all countries. The share of US imports coming from low-income countries, for example, grew from 15% in 2001 to 28% in 2007, with China accounting for 89% of this growth (Autor, Dorn, and Hanson 2013). Emerging countries have also become more assertive in negotiations. The third trend is the proliferation of preferential trade agreements (PTAs). Hundreds of PTAs have been signed since the WTO's creation, such that the majority of world trade now flows between PTA partners and thus is not subject to the WTO's key principle of nondiscrimination.[3] This has led some to question the continuing relevance of the WTO system.

Over the same 20 years, progress toward multilateral trade liberalization through WTO negotiations has ground to a halt. The Doha Round proved largely unsuccessful: the modest package of trade reforms approved at the Bali Ministerial Conference is the only tangible result of 14 years of Doha Round negotiations (2001–2015). This leaves open many questions about the WTO's role as a forum for multilateral trade negotiations. Why were expectations for the Doha Round so high? Why has the divide between developed and developing members grown so wide? Were the trends described here factors in the Doha Round's failure? And, most importantly, in light of these trends, what are the prospects for the WTO as a vehicle for trade liberalization going forward?

Much has already been written in answer to these questions. The ambition of the Doha Round has been linked to the timing of its launch in the wake of the September 11, 2001, attacks on the United States. Doha was seen by WTO members as a means of demonstrating their commitment to international cooperation and to combating terrorism by addressing what is arguably a root cause: poverty and underdevelopment (Blustein 2009; Kleimann and Guinan 2011). The subsequent stalemate has been linked to the rise of "emerging" markets, such as Brazil, India, and China, which challenged the traditional dominance of the "Quad" (United States, European Union, Japan, and Canada) in the negotiations. Standoffs between these groups over agriculture ensued for several years of the round. This gave way to standoffs over nonagricultural market access (NAMA)[4] as the mercurial growth of Chinese exports brought about a hesitance in other countries to make MFN tariff cuts (Francois 2008). This hesitance was reinforced by the global economic downturn late in the first decade of the twenty-first century, which reinforced countries' unwillingness to reduce tariffs and relinquish a tool of protectionism and revenue (Blustein 2009).

Blame for the stalemate has been directed at both sides. Emerging countries have been blamed for using their developing-country status as a pretext for refusing to make or delaying tariff cuts. Former US Trade Representative Susan Schwab has referred to this as "elephants hiding behind mice" (Schwab 2011). Others place the blame on the United States for failing in its traditional leadership role. Jagdish Bhagwati refers to the United States as a "selfish hegemon" suffering from a "diminished giant syndrome" in the face of a rising China (Bhagwati 2008) and has criticized its turn toward regionalism for undermining Doha (Bhagwati 2011). Bagwell and Staiger (2011) fault both developing countries, for seeking special and different treatment, and the United States, for misguided proposals on agriculture. Bagwell and Staiger (2014) argue that the stalemate occurred because developed countries had achieved most of the liberalization they wanted from each other in past rounds, particularly in manufactured goods, while developing countries have not come to the table ready to make sufficient concessions themselves.

This chapter attempts to shed light on the past, present, and future of the GATT/WTO system as a vehicle for multilateral trade liberalization by employing a unified framework, in which both the purpose of trade agreements and the limitations of multilateral negotiations derive from the same source: terms-of-trade externalities. The framework is built on three main claims. The first claim is that governments acting unilaterally will tend to overuse tariffs and other trade restrictions to the extent that they are able to shift the cost of protecting a domestic industry onto foreign producers by altering the terms of trade. The second claim, following the work of Bagwell and Staiger (2002), is that the GATT/WTO serves as a mechanism by which countries internalize the terms-of-trade externalities of their policies and thus move toward efficient policy choices. The third claim, following Ludema and Mayda (2009, 2013), is that terms-of-trade externalities may not be fully internalized if some countries "free ride" on the MFN tariff cuts of others, and the severity of this problem depends on the concentration of MFN exporters across countries and products.

The empirical evidence in favor of these claims has been mounting for some time. Broda, Limão, and Weinstein (2008) provide evidence that the tariffs of non-WTO countries are set on the basis of cost-shifting motives, as are the statutory (nonnegotiated) tariff rates of the

United States. Bagwell and Staiger (2011) find that the pattern of GATT/WTO negotiated tariff cuts for accession countries is consistent with the internalization of terms-of-trade externalities. Bown and Crowley (2013) find that US contingent protection responds to trade shocks in accordance with cooperation based on terms of trade. Ludema and Mayda (2009) find evidence of MFN free riding in the pattern of US MFN tariffs. Finally, Ludema and Mayda (2013) study a sample of 30 WTO countries and find evidence from the MFN tariffs negotiated during the Uruguay Round that countries partially internalized the terms-of-trade effects of their tariff reductions but were limited by MFN free riding.[5]

The novel contribution of this chapter is to examine the evolution of the MFN free-rider problem from 1993 to 2012 by investigating changes in MFN exporter concentration, measured as the Herfindahl-Hirschman Index (HHI) of WTO exporters receiving MFN treatment. We find evidence of an average increase in exporter concentration, which would suggest that negotiated MFN tariffs would decrease if the Doha Round were completed. We also decompose changes in exporter concentration into the three trends noted earlier. First, we find that the main determinant of the average increase in exporter concentration between 1993 and 2012 has been the creation of new PTAs. When two WTO countries form a PTA, they extend MFN treatment to fewer countries than they did before. While this could theoretically increase or decrease the HHI of the remaining exporters to those countries, it has generally increased it in practice, thus reducing the MFN free-rider problem. Thus, we identify a new mechanism through which PTAs can be a "building block" of multilateral trade liberalization. This chapter shows that, far from contributing to the failure of the Doha Round, the creation of new PTAs has actually increased the chances of its success.

Second, we show that accession of new members to the WTO has increased the HHIs of existing members. This is because, before acceding, the new members already received MFN treatment but, at the same time, were not able to participate in the negotiations and thus were not included in the (numerator of the) HHI. Thus, accession of new members to the WTO increases the HHI of existing members by adding new potential participants to the negotiations.[6]

Third, we find that the rapid expansion of exports of emerging markets has generally decreased the concentration of exports across most countries and products, suggesting that the "dragon in the room" problem has merit. Our analysis shows that the HHI of exporters to several developing countries, such as Brazil and India, decreased between 1993 and 2012, mostly because of the growth of trade with other emerging economies, such as China. For these importing countries, the growth of China has eroded the market shares of their principal suppliers, which according to our model undermines the willingness of principal suppliers to reciprocate tariff reductions of the importing country. This reduces the incentive for the importing country to reduce tariffs. Hence, importing countries like Brazil and India have been reluctant to make tariff reductions because of the growth of China—consistent with the quotations at the beginning of the chapter. This also explains why developing countries have not come to the table ready to make significant concessions, as noted by Bagwell and Staiger (2014).[7]

Macro versus micro free riding. Before proceeding with the analysis, it is worth distinguishing between two ways in which free riding on MFN can affect WTO negotiations. The first we call "macro" free riding, which might occur if a country refuses to adopt all or a major part (e.g., services) of an agreement that other countries are willing to sign. For most of GATT history, macro free riding has been practiced, especially by developing countries, and is even enshrined in the special and differential provisions of GATT Part IV. The "Single Undertaking" rule, which requires each country to accept all or none of a negotiated agreement, was employed in both the Uruguay and Doha negotiations as a way to combat macro free riding. Many WTO observers have blamed the Single Undertaking rule for the Doha stalemate and have recommended plurilateral and "critical mass" negotiations as practical ways forward (e.g., Gallagher and Stoler 2009; Hoekman and Mavroidis 2015).

"Micro" free riding refers to free riding that occurs at the importer-product level, when an exporter of a particular product refuses to help other exporters compensate the importer for its tariff cut. It is entirely possible that all countries in a negotiation have perfectly balanced concessions overall (and thus no macro free riding) and yet those concessions will be inefficiently small because of micro free riding. Hence, while a macro free rider is necessarily a micro free rider, the converse is not true. This chapter is aimed at understanding the evolution of conditions under which micro free-riding has been shown to occur. We are interested in whether the world of today is better or worse than the world of 1994 from a micro free-riding perspective, as we believe this is critical to the depth of any agreement that might be reached should a strategy for successful multilateral negotiations at the macro level be found.

Section 3.2 outlines the theoretical framework, while section 3.3 describes the cross-country data used. Sections 3.4 and 3.5 present the results of the empirical analysis. In section 3.4, we bring the theoretical model to the data and, based on our estimates, we explore how successful the GATT/WTO system has been up to the Uruguay Round, in particular in its role of allowing countries to internalize the terms-of-trade effects of their tariff reductions. In section 3.5, we provide evidence on prospects for multilateral trade liberalization during the Doha Round, based on changes in exporter concentration between 1993 and 2012. Finally, we present our conclusions in section 3.6.

3.2   Theoretical Framework

Our theoretical framework is based on the assumption that an importing country is more likely to lower its MFN tariff during GATT/WTO negotiations on a given product if it faces highly motivated exporting countries willing to offer concessions in exchange. What factors motivate the exporting countries? One factor is the extent to which the existing tariff depresses the prices exporting firms can charge in the protected market, otherwise known as the terms-of-trade externality. The more the tariff protection depresses external prices, the more motivated exporting countries will be to see the protection removed. In a competitive market, the terms-of-trade externality is measured by the inverse elasticity of export supply.

A second factor has to do with exporter concentration. Intuitively, a country that is the sole exporter to a given market would be willing to pay more for a tariff cut than would a group of countries sharing the market. Ludema and Mayda (2009) formalize this point and show that it derives from two effects. First, an exporting country's benefit from an MFN tariff reduction is proportional to its share of the total MFN exports destined for that market. However, because MFN implies that the country obtains the benefit whether it offers concessions or not, its willingness to pay also depends on how much its refusal to offer concessions would mitigate the tariff reduction. The larger the exporter, the more its refusal would mitigate the tariff cut and thus the more costly it would be for the exporter to refuse. Together, these two effects imply that an exporter's maximum willingness to pay for a tariff cut is proportional to its squared export share. Summing over all exporters, the collective willingness to pay of all MFN exporters is proportional to the Herfindahl-Hirschman index (HHI) of exporter concentration.

Ludema and Mayda (2009) show that if the HHI is above a certain threshold, then all exporters offer concessions and the outcome is the best. That is, the terms-of-trade externality is fully internalized. In this case, negotiations lead the importer to reduce its tariff (relative to the noncooperative optimal tariff) by the full amount of the terms-of-trade externality. If the HHI is below the threshold, then only a small group of large exporters (principal suppliers) offer concessions and full internalization is not achieved. However, since there is a positive relationship between the export share of the principal suppliers and the HHI, the degree of internalization increases with the HHI. It follows that the size of the negotiated tariff cut (relative to the noncooperative optimal tariff) is some fraction of the terms-of-trade externality, and this fraction is an increasing function of the HHI.

Assuming that governments maximize social welfare and that all trade is governed by MFN, then (1 plus) the ad valorem negotiated MFN tariff rate of country i on product k is given by[8]

$$\tau_{ik}^n (A_{ik}) = 1 + \frac{1}{\varepsilon_{ik}} [1 - \Theta_{ik}(H_{ik})], \tag{3.1}$$

where H_{ik} is the HHI of exporter concentration and $(\frac{1}{\varepsilon_{ik}})$ is the inverse elasticity of foreign export supply (i.e., the market power of country i for product k). The function $\Theta_{ik} (\cdot)$ measures the degree of internalization. Technically, it is equal to the cumulative export market share of the exporters that elect to offer concessions in equilibrium, $\Theta_{ik} \equiv \Sigma_{j \in A_{ik}} \theta_{ik}^j$, where A_{ik} denotes the set of exporting countries participating in negotiations over good k with importing country i. It is an increasing function, with $\Theta_{ik} (0) = 0$ and $\Theta_{ik}(\overline{H}_{ik}) = 1$, where $\overline{H}_{ik}$ is the threshold value of HHI for full participation.

Under noncooperation, $\Theta_{ik} = 0$, and the negotiated tariff reduces to the optimum tariff, which is increasing in importer market power. If $\Theta_{ik} > 0$, the effect of market power is decreasing in Θ_{ik}. At full cooperation ($\Theta_{ik} = 1$), the negotiated tariff equals free trade and importer market power has no effect.

Shifting away from a pure welfare-maximization problem, the model can be extended to include political economy determinants as well as PTAs. The negotiated tariff becomes

$$\tau_{ik}^{n}(A_{ik}) = \frac{1 + \frac{1}{\varepsilon_{ik}}\left(1 - \Theta_{ik} - \Sigma_{j \in MFN_i}\psi_{jk}\theta_{ik}^{j}\right)}{1 - \frac{\lambda_{ik}}{\mu_{ik}}\frac{X_{ik}^{i}}{M_{ik}} - \frac{1 - \Phi_{ik}}{\mu_{ik}}\phi_{ik}}, \tag{3.2}$$

where the values λ_{ik} and ψ_{ik} represent the political power of import-competing and export-oriented firms, respectively. These weights may be indicators of political lobbying as per Grossman and Helpman (1994) or other political economy models (Baldwin 1987; Helpman 1997). ϕ_{ik} denotes country i's concern about the interests of PTA partners (see Limão 2007).

The negotiated tariff (3.2) is increasing in $\frac{\lambda_{ik}}{\mu_{ik}}\frac{X_{ik}^{i}}{M_{ik}}$, the political influence of domestic import-competing firms, and decreasing in $\Sigma_{j \in MFN_i}\psi_{jk}\theta_{ik}^{j}$, the influence of export-oriented firms in countries that are involved in the negotiations. The term $\frac{1 - \Phi_{ik}}{\mu_{ik}}\phi_{ik}$ captures the influence of PTA partners, which is ambiguous in sign, depending on whether a "stumbling block" versus a "building block" effect of PTAs takes place. The tariff complementarity effect of Bagwell and Staiger (1998) and the findings of Estevadeordal, Freund, and Ornelas (2008) suggest that country i's concern for its PTA partners should be small, $\phi_{ik} < 1$, such that the negotiated MFN tariff in the PTA share of imports is decreasing.[9] Instead, Limão (2007) finds evidence from the United States that $\phi_{ik} > 1$, and his interpretation is that PTA countries have an incentive to raise external MFN tariffs to improve their bargaining position with PTA partners over nontrade issues.

Our empirical analysis follows two steps. First, in section 3.4, we begin by asking how successful the GATT/WTO system has been so far. Since 1947, the GATT/WTO system has presided over an unprecedented liberalization of world trade. However, whether this liberalization is entirely attributable to the GATT/WTO system—and in particular to its role in allowing countries to internalize terms-of-trade effects—is an open question. Part of the difficulty in answering this question comes from the various tracks by which trade liberalization occurs. Some trade liberalization has occurred through GATT/WTO negotiations and accessions. At the same time, many countries have liberalized unilaterally and through regional trade agreements. Another difficulty is in knowing the counterfactual of how much trade liberalization would have occurred without the GATT/WTO system. Our theoretical model allows us to address this question based on estimates of the theoretical model in Ludema and Mayda (2013), who use data for the Uruguay Round (i.e., 1993 values for the regressors and 1995–2000 values for the tariff rates). Second, in section 3.5, we examine the prospects for future multilateral trade liberalization through changes in exporter concentration between 1993 and 2012. We decompose the latter changes into the three components discussed in the introduction: the WTO accession of new countries, the creation of PTAs, and the change in trade patterns resulting from emerging economies' high growth rates. Before proceeding to the empirical analysis, we describe the data we use in section 3.3.

3.3   Data

We use the following data sources for the empirical analysis in sections 3.4 and 3.5. In section 3.4, applied MFN tariff rates for the period 1995–2000 are taken from UNCTAD's TRAINS through the World Bank's World Integrated Trade Solution (WITS) dataset. The dataset consists of 135,346 observations across 36 countries and 5,036 product categories. We merge these data with information from Nunn (2007), Broda, Greenfield, and Weinstein (2006), and Rauch (1999) and construct a composite measure of the power of the importing country to affect international prices through its trade policy, which we call the *market power index*. Rauch (1999)'s data consist of dummy variables for product differentiation (*Diff* in Ludema and Mayda 2013). Nunn (2007) supplies an index of contract intensity, and, finally, Broda, Greenfield, and Weinstein (2006) provide values to construct indicators of high inverse elasticity of export supply (*HIEE* in Ludema and Mayda 2013). See section 3.4 for more details about these three variables. This chapter uses the average of these three variables to construct the *market power index* variable. Data on political organization by country and HS four-digit product codes in 1993 were obtained from the World Guide to Trade Associations. For additional details about the variables used in the estimation of section 3.4, see Ludema and Mayda (2013).

For use in section 3.5, data for 1993 and 2012 aggregate and bilateral trade flows were collected from Comtrade through WITS. Each country's bilateral trade flows are merged into a single dataset in order to calculate the Herfindahl-Hirschman Index (HHI) of exporter concentration by importing country and product code (at the HS six-digit level). We construct additional variables at the same level of disaggregation;

for example, the share of imports from PTA partners and the share of imports from non-WTO countries.[10]

3.4 How Successful Was the GATT/WTO System Up to the Uruguay Round?

3.4.1 Estimation of the Theoretical Model Focusing on the Uruguay Round

The empirical strategy employed in this chapter is based on Ludema and Mayda (2013), who estimate a specification closely related to the theoretical model. Taking a first-order Taylor approximation of equation (3.2), we obtain

$$\tau_{ik} = \frac{1}{\varepsilon_{ik}}(1 - \Theta_{ik} - \Sigma_{j\in MFN_i}\psi_{jk}\theta_{ik}^j) + \frac{\lambda_{ik}}{\mu_{ik}}\frac{X_{ik}^i}{M_{ik}} - \frac{1-\Phi_{ik}}{\mu_{ik}}\phi_{ik}. \tag{3.3}$$

There are several challenges to address when carrying out the estimation of equation (3.3). First, the model needs a proxy for Θ_{ik}, which captures the extent to which the terms-of-trade effects of tariff reductions are internalized by the participants in the negotiations over each product. Specifically, Θ_{ik} measures country i's imports of product k from participants in GATT/WTO negotiations as a fraction of total imports of the same product from countries that receive MFN treatment and are not its PTA partners. We do not observe the set of participants, but the theoretical model predicts that there is a positive relationship between Θ_{ik} and the HHI. A larger value of the HHI means a higher concentration of exports of product k to country i (higher *exporter concentration*), meaning the existence of relatively large exporters, which face a greater incentive to participate in the negotiations. Large exporters are deterred from free riding, as they stand to gain more from a given tariff reduction and, also, their participation leads to a greater increase in the importing country's tariff reduction relative to small exporters. Thus, country i having a higher HHI on product k suggests that participants in country i's negotiation of the tariff on product k will cover a higher aggregate share of the exports of that product. Ludema and Mayda (2013) provide the relevant expression to calculate the HHI:

$$H_{ik} = \frac{\Sigma_{j\in MFN_i\cap WTO}(M_{ik}^j)^2}{(\Sigma_{j\in MFN_i}M_{ik}^j)^2} \tag{3.4}$$

This expression excludes the importing country's PTA partners and countries not receiving MFN status. In addition, in the denominator, it accounts for non-GATT/WTO countries that receive MFN treatment. MFN_i is the set of non-PTA-partner countries that are granted MFN status by country i, regardless of GATT/WTO membership, while the numerator considers a subset of MFN_i that only includes GATT/WTO members. This study follows the literature and assumes that the list of countries receiving MFN status is for all importers the same as the US one.[11] M_{ik}^{j} is the value of country i's imports of product k from country j.

The second challenge of the model is in capturing the value of $\frac{1}{\varepsilon_{ik}}$, the inverse elasticity of foreign export supply of product k in country i, which represents country i's market power. The measurement of this variable is difficult because of the unavailability of accurate and standardized estimates. Ludema and Mayda (2013) present two specifications, corresponding to two indicators of market power. First, using data from Broda, Greenfield, and Weinstein (2006) and following Broda, Limão, and Weinstein (2008), they use a categorical variable for "high inverse export elasticity" (HIEE), which is equal to 1 if the inverse export elasticity estimate is in the top two-thirds of all products' estimates within the same country and 0 otherwise. The second indicator used by Ludema and Mayda (2013), based on the Rauch classification, varies by product and provides a value for each product of 1 if the product is differentiated and 0 otherwise (Diff). Rauch (1999) argues that product differentiation interferes with matching in international markets and therefore products categorized as differentiated should have lower export elasticities (higher importer market power) than for homogeneous goods. In this chapter, we also take into account a third measure taken from Nunn (2007), who provides a contract intensity index based on the proportion of each good's intermediate inputs that require relationship-specific investments. In this chapter, we construct a measure of market power that averages the value of the three mentioned measures for each observation (market power index).

In addition to the main independent variables, the analysis includes controls for domestic and foreign political organization. Defining both is necessary to allow import-competing and exporting firms to have different political clout. Domestic political controls follow Goldberg and Maggi (1999) and are defined as $\lambda_{ik} = (\gamma + \delta \cdot PO_{ik})$, where the political organization term PO_{ik} is equal to 1 if a trade association is present for sector k in country i and 0 otherwise. The foreign political economy term is defined symmetrically as $\psi_{jk} = \delta^* \cdot PO_{jk}$.

Based on equation (3.3), we estimate the specification

$$\tau_{ik} = \alpha + \beta_1 MP_{ik} + \beta_2 MP_{ik} H_{ik} + \beta_3 H_{ik} + \omega \frac{\Phi_{ik}}{\mu_{ik}} + \alpha_i + Z_{ik} + \varepsilon_{ik}, \qquad (3.5)$$

where τ_{ik} is the ad valorem MFN tariff rate on product k set by country i, averaged over the years 1995–2000, H_{ik} denotes the HHI of country i's imports on product k in 1993, Φ_{ik} is the PTA share of these imports in 1993, which is divided by the import demand elasticity μ_{ik} in country i on product k, and MP_{ik} is the *market power index* (MPI). α_i and Z_{ik} are controls, α_i comprising country fixed effects and Z_{ik} capturing domestic and foreign political economy effects. ε_{ik} is an idiosyncratic error term.

Based on the theoretical model, we expect $\beta_1 > 0$, as this captures the effect of market power when there is no cooperation (when $H_{ik} = 0$). Optimum tariff theory suggests that the higher country i's market power is in sector k, the higher the tariff it sets (while a small, open economy with $MP_{ik} = 0$ would have an optimum tariff of 0). Second, the effect of market power should decrease in the presence of higher HHI, suggesting $\beta_2 < 0$, as the interaction term captures the effect of the internalization of terms-of-trade effects through negotiations. This term also captures the MFN free-rider effect since, with high market power, the HHI should have a negative effect on MFN tariffs, given that the free-rider problem is less severe when exporter concentration is high. The coefficient β_3 should be 0 or slightly negative as it captures the effect of the HHI when there is no market power. The PTA share term is theoretically ambiguous. Finally, for domestic political economy effects, we expect $\delta > 0$, $\gamma < 0$, and $\gamma + \delta > 0$, as organized domestic producers prefer higher home tariffs on goods they produce and lower tariffs on goods they consume; however, γ may equal zero if lobbying groups are a negligible share of the voting population. We expect $\delta^* < 0$, as organized foreign producers prefer lower home tariffs on the goods they export.

As previously shown in Ludema and Mayda (2013), our results support the theory. In table 3.1, column 1 shows the ordinary least squares (OLS) results of estimating equation (3.5). Column 2, of table 3.1 applies an instrumental variables (IV) approach to address endogeneity concerns, instrumenting for H_{ik}, MPI_{ik}, and foreign

Table 3.1
Regression results.

Dependent Variable	(1)	(2)
Model	OLS	IV
Market Power Indicator (MPI)	4.927***	10.55***
	−0.28	−2.23
Herfindahl-Hirschman Index * MPI	−3.458***	−15.43***
	−0.432	−3.604
Herfindahl-Hirschman Index	0.869***	4.774*
	−0.29	−2.727
Foreign Political Organization * MPI	−1.901***	−1.156**
	−0.157	−0.507
X/Mμ	−0.00715	0.00992
	−0.0233	−0.0115
Domestic Political Organization * X/Mμ	0.119***	0.0722*
	−0.0353	−0.0376
PTA Share/μ	−1.560**	−1.67
	−0.694	−2.546
Constant	13.13***	10.94***
	−0.255	−1.554
Observations	80,207	76,157
R-squared	0.268	0.257

Notes: The F-test statistics for the IV regression are as follows. With regards to the instrumentation of each variable in regression 2: 16.61 for the Herfindahl-Hirschman Index, 390.46 for the Market Power Index, and 72.17 for the interaction term. The instrument for foreign political organization has an F-statistic of 8110.45. The F-statistic for the final 2SLS regression is 1.24. Standard errors are clustered by importing country and HS3 by country. Importing-country fixed effects are included in each regression.
***$p < 0.01$, ** $p < 0.05$, * $p < 0.1$.

political organization (see Ludema and Mayda 2013 for more details on the sources of endogeneity). For each country i, the three countries in the sample with variables most strongly correlated with i's are selected, and their average value of that variable is used as an instrument. The choice of three countries balances a trade-off between losing observations from countries that lack overlapping product imports and decreasing the variance across instrument observations by expanding the selection. The comments that follow are based on the IV estimates. We find that the applied MFN tariff rate increases with market power in the absence of any internalization of terms-of-trade benefits, as demonstrated by the positive and statistically significant coefficient β_1. The effect of market power decreases with the HHI, as shown by the statistically significant and negative β_2. The direct effect of the HHI, β_3, is comparatively small and only slightly significant, consistent with the prediction that concentration in the absence of market power should have no effect. The impact of domestic political organization when interacted with the inverse import penetration ratio is positive and slightly significant, which supports the idea of protection for sale as proposed by Goldberg and Maggi (1999). The negative and significant coefficient on foreign political organization is similarly predictable, as foreign sectors push for lower tariff rates. Finally, the PTA share is negative but insignificant.[12]

3.4.2 Quantification of the Effect of the GATT/WTO System Up to the Uruguay Round

We now quantify the effect of the GATT/WTO system up to the most recently completed round of negotiations, the Uruguay Round, in particular in its role of allowing countries to internalize the terms-of-trade effects of tariff reductions.[13] To do so, we apply the IV regression results of column 2 in table 3.1 to construct the following three estimates. First, we calculate the predicted negotiated MFN tariff rate τ_{ik}^n for each importer i and product k (i.e., the negotiated tariff rate as predicted by the empirical model based on the actual value of the HHI in 1993 at the end of the Uruguay Round). This is the tariff rate that countries are expected to have reached through Uruguay Round negotiations based on their ability in 1993 to internalize terms-of-trade effects. Second, we calculate the predicted noncooperative MFN tariff rate τ_{ik}^u for each importer i and product k (i.e., the tariff rate as predicted by the empirical model when $H_{ik} = 0$), which corresponds to the situation where there is no internalization of terms-of-trade effects and free riding is complete; in other words, when the tariff rate is set in the absence of negotiations. Finally, we calculate the predicted "potential" negotiated MFN tariff rate τ_{ik}^* for each importer i and product k, the tariff rate as predicted by the empirical model when the HHI is high enough ($H_{ik} = \overline{H}_{ik} = -\frac{\beta_1}{\beta_2}$) that market power has no impact on the negotiated tariff rate ($\beta_1 + \beta_2 H_{ik} = 0$; see expression (3.5)). In the last case, internalization of terms-of-trade effects is complete and free riding is absent. Given expression (3.5) and setting $\beta_3 = 0$,[14] the following expressions hold:[15]

$$\tau_{ik}^n = \alpha + \beta_1 MP_{ik} + \beta_2 MP_{ik}H_{ik} + \omega \frac{\Phi_{ik}}{\mu_{ik}} + \alpha_i + Z_{ik}, \qquad (3.6)$$

$$\tau_{ik}^u = \tau_{ik}^n - \beta_2 MP_{ik}H_{ik}, \qquad (3.7)$$

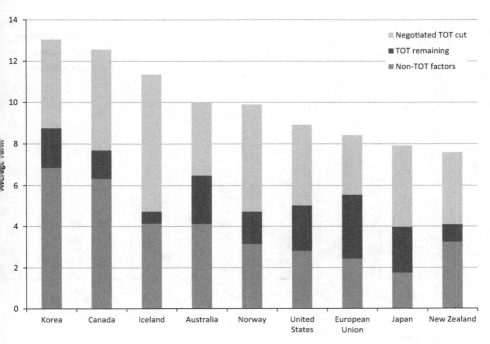

Figure 3.1
Noncooperative versus negotiated tariffs for developed countries (predicted values based on 1993 data).

$$\tau_{ik}^* = \tau_{ik}^u - \beta_1 MP_{ik} = \tau_{ik}^n - \beta_1 MP_{ik} - \beta_2 MP_{ik} H_{ik}. \tag{3.8}$$

Figures 3.1 and 3.2 show the three sets of tariff rates for developed and developing countries, respectively (see also table 3.2). For each country, the height of the overall bar (medium gray plus dark gray plus light gray) gives the predicted noncooperative MFN tariff rate τ_{ik}^u; the height of the medium plus dark gray bar represents the predicted negotiated MFN tariff rate τ_{ik}^n; and finally, the height of the medium gray bar gives the predicted "potential" negotiated MFN tariff rate τ_{ik}^*. Note that the height of the dark plus light gray bar represents the maximum extent of terms-of-trade effects on tariffs absent negotiations (i.e., the "overall" terms-of-trade effects. "Negotiated TOT cut" represents how successful the GATT/WTO system has been so far (up to the Uruguay Round) in its role of allowing countries to internalize the terms-of-trade effects of tariff reductions. "TOT remaining" indicates the noninternalized terms-of-trade effects, representing the magnitude of the free-rider

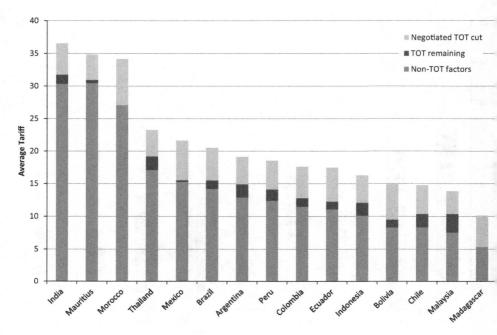

Figure 3.2
Noncooperative versus negotiated tariffs for developing countries (predicted values based on 1993 data).

problem. Finally, "Non-TOT factors" represents the impact on tariff rates of non–terms-of-trade factors such as domestic and foreign political economy effects, PTA effects, and other drivers captured by the country fixed effects. Note that all the tariffs and their components are defined in percentage-points terms.

As table 3.2 shows, for the 24 countries in the sample, in 1993 the average negotiated tariff was 12.20, while the average noncooperative tariff was 16.76, which implies that the internalization of terms-of-trade effects through GATT/WTO negotiations up to the Uruguay Round has lowered the average tariff of these countries by 27% compared to its noncooperative level. For the nine developed countries in the sample, in 1993 the average negotiated tariff was 5.67, which is 43% lower than the average noncooperative tariff of 9.97. The developing countries' average negotiated tariff is 16.11, which is 23% lower than the average noncooperative tariff of 20.84. The difference between developed and developing countries—in terms of percentage change relative to the noncooperative tarif—largely reflects the fact that

Predicted tariff rates and changes, by country (1993–2012).

	1993–2012 Noncoop. Tariff	1993–2012 Potential Negotiated Tariff	1993 Negotiated Tariff	2012 Negotiated Tariff	Change Neg. Tariff from 1993–2012	% TofT Internalized 1993	% TofT Internalized 2012	% Reduction Noncoop. to Neg. 1993	% Reduction Noncoop. to Neg. 2012
All countries	16.76	10.70	12.20	11.62	−0.58	75.31	84.83	27.22	30.66
Developing countries	20.84	14.80	16.11	15.74	−0.37	78.27	84.37	22.68	24.45
Developed countries	9.97	3.87	5.67	4.75	−0.92	70.43	85.58	43.06	52.32
Argentina	19.11	12.89	14.89	13.64	−1.25	67.88	87.92	22.11	28.64
Australia	9.99	4.13	6.48	5.14	−1.34	59.79	82.72	35.10	48.55
Bolivia	14.89	8.33	9.52	8.92	−0.60	81.89	91.09	36.05	40.10
Brazil	20.51	14.21	15.48	15.63	0.15	79.76	77.38	24.50	23.77
Canada	12.56	6.34	7.70	7.88	0.17	78.15	75.35	38.69	37.31
Chile	14.76	8.35	10.38	8.35	−2.02	68.43	100.00	29.69	43.40
Colombia	17.61	11.47	12.77	11.86	−0.91	78.86	93.65	27.50	32.65
Ecuador	17.48	11.07	12.25	12.83	0.58	81.63	72.56	29.92	26.60
European Union	8.42	2.44	5.55	4.30	−1.26	47.94	68.94	34.05	48.97
Iceland	11.35	4.14	4.75	4.42	−0.33	91.62	96.13	58.20	61.07
India	36.57	30.35	31.75	33.02	1.27	77.49	57.08	13.18	9.71
Indonesia	16.27	10.13	12.08	11.53	−0.55	68.20	77.20	25.74	29.14
Japan	7.92	1.74	3.97	2.63	−1.33	63.97	85.59	49.87	66.73
Korea	13.04	6.86	8.75	7.15	−1.60	69.40	95.35	32.89	45.19
Madagascar	9.86	5.34	5.34	6.30	0.97	100.00	78.61	45.86	36.05
Malaysia	13.87	7.58	10.38	9.11	−1.27	55.55	75.74	25.21	34.37
Mauritius	34.85	30.46	30.95	30.99	0.04	88.82	87.99	11.19	11.08
Mexico	21.62	15.28	15.52	15.94	0.42	96.19	89.63	28.21	26.29
Morocco	33.39	27.07	27.07	27.22	0.15	100.00	97.65	18.93	18.48
New Zealand	7.59	3.24	4.09	3.32	−0.77	80.54	98.17	46.12	56.22
Norway	9.90	3.15	4.74	3.75	−0.99	76.38	91.02	52.10	62.09
Peru	18.54	12.39	14.13	12.39	−1.74	71.71	100.00	23.80	33.18
Thailand	23.25	17.08	19.18	18.43	−0.75	66.01	78.15	17.52	20.74
United States	8.92	2.82	5.04	4.18	−0.87	63.56	77.73	43.49	53.19

average noncooperative tariffs are considerably higher for developing countries as a result of domestic factors. However, in the Uruguay Round, the free-rider problem was smaller for developing countries, as "TOT remaining" is 1.80 percentage points for developed countries and 1.31% for developing countries. These values imply that developing countries have been able to internalize around 78% of the terms-of-trade effects of their tariff reductions through the GATT/WTO system up to the Uruguay Round, while developed countries have been able to internalize around 70%.[16] The difference between developed and developing countries results from the fact that developing countries faced higher HHIs in 1993 on average relative to developed countries (0.61 versus 0.5) and thus confronted less of a free-rider problem in negotiations.[17] Regarding specific countries, the United States has been able to internalize around 64% of the terms-of-trade effects, the European Union around 48%, Japan around 64%, Brazil around 80%, and, finally, India around 77%. Figures 3.1 and 3.2 also show that, in developing countries, most of the terms-of-trade effects have been internalized, yet tariffs remain high.

Figure 3.3 and table 3.3 present the results organized by HS section. Figure 3.3 shows that, in percentage points terms, in 1993 the remaining free-rider problem ("TOT remaining") was smallest for goods with high exporter concentration, for example goods in section II (vegetable products), section III (animal or vegetable fats and oils), section V (mineral products), and section XIX (arms and ammunition). These goods were exported by few large, developed countries in 1993 and thus had high HHI. By contrast, the free-rider problem was greatest in sections VIII (raw hides and skins, leather, fur), XXII (footwear, headgear, etc.), and XX (miscellaneous manufactured articles). The latter goods had low HHI (0.48, 0.42, and 0.46, respectively, compared to 0.69 for arms and ammunition and a median of 0.53) because they are low-tech goods produced and exported by a large number of small exporters (largely developing countries). Table 3.3 shows a similar picture (see in particular the column indicating the percentage of terms-of-trade effects that had been internalized through the GATT/WTO system up to 1993).

To conclude, the analysis both across countries and across HS sections points in the same direction. At the end of the Uruguay Round, while developed countries had lower average (negotiated) tariffs, because of lower unilateral motives, in fact they liberalized less relative to potential, because of lower HHIs on the goods they

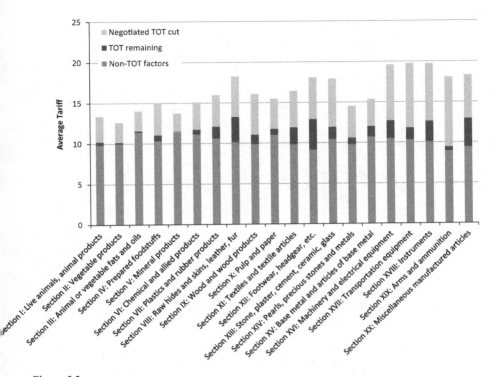

Figure 3.3
Noncooperative versus negotiated tariffs by HS sections (predicted values based on 1993 data).

imported. At the same time, developed countries tended to export advanced manufactured goods, which are relatively concentrated (and thus unencumbered by the MFN free-rider problem) and high in market power, leading to successful negotiated liberalization. On the other hand, while developing countries had higher average (negotiated) tariffs, because of higher unilateral motives, in fact they liberalized more relative to potential, because of higher HHIs on the goods they imported. At the same time, developing countries tended to export manufactured goods, such as footwear, textiles, and other miscellaneous manufactured goods, which had relatively high potential for negotiated liberalization, but because they were produced by so many small countries, this potential went unrealized. The other major class of developing-country exports are agricultural products and raw materials, which are low-liberalization products, mainly because of low estimated levels of market power.

Table 3.3
Predicted tariff rates and changes, by HS section (1993–2012).

HS Sections	1993–2012 Noncoop. Tariff	1993–2012 Potential Negotiated Tariff	1993 Negotiated Tariff	2012 Negotiated Tariff	Change Neg. Tariff 1993–2012	% TofT Internalized 1993	% TofT Internalized 2012	% Reduction Noncoop. to Neg. 1993	% Reduction Noncoop. to Neg. 2012
Section I: Live animals, animal products	13.36	9.82	10.24	9.82	−0.42	88.24	100.00	23.37	26.48
Section II: Vegetable products	12.62	10.00	10.14	10.00	−0.14	94.65	100.00	19.67	20.78
Section III: Animal or vegetable fats and oils	14.02	11.39	11.57	11.51	−0.06	93.02	95.15	17.48	17.88
Section IV: Prepared foodstuffs	14.99	10.35	11.05	10.76	−0.29	84.93	91.20	26.26	28.20
Section V: Mineral products	13.65	11.53	11.53	11.53	0.00	100.00	100.00	15.51	15.51
Section VI: Chemical and allied products	15.07	11.13	11.72	11.53	−0.19	85.11	90.03	22.23	23.52
Section VII: Plastics and rubber products	15.93	10.62	12.06	11.92	−0.14	72.87	75.49	24.30	25.17
Section VIII: Raw hides and skins, leather, fur	18.24	10.15	13.25	10.43	−2.82	61.70	96.52	27.37	42.82
Section IX: Wood and wood products	16.04	9.91	11.05	10.17	−0.88	81.48	95.78	31.16	36.63
Section X: Pulp and paper	15.46	11.03	11.76	11.60	−0.16	83.42	87.00	23.93	24.96

Section XI: Textiles and textile articles	16.41	9.84	11.91	10.38	−1.53	68.51	91.82	27.42	36.75
Section XII: Footwear, headgear, etc.	18.06	9.18	12.93	9.18	−3.75	57.77	100.00	28.43	49.21
Section XIII: Stone, plaster, cement, ceramic, glass	17.90	10.48	11.94	11.10	−0.84	80.26	91.58	33.29	37.99
Section XIV: Pearls, precious stones, and metals	14.50	9.79	10.61	10.31	−0.31	82.60	89.10	26.84	28.95
Section XV: Base metal and articles of base metal	15.35	10.69	12.01	11.24	−0.77	71.68	88.32	21.75	26.80
Section XVI: Machinery and electrical equipment	19.59	10.54	12.70	12.17	−0.53	76.14	82.00	35.18	37.89
Section XVII: Transportation equipment	19.77	10.36	11.80	11.62	−0.18	84.61	86.52	40.29	41.20
Section XVIII: Instruments	19.73	10.10	12.62	12.37	−0.25	73.83	76.46	36.03	37.31
Section XIX: Arms and ammunition	18.04	8.95	9.43	9.07	−0.36	94.76	98.71	47.73	49.72
Section XX: Miscellaneous manufactured articles	18.30	9.45	12.95	10.01	−2.95	60.45	93.77	29.23	45.33

These results shed light on an ongoing debate between developed and developing countries regarding the extent of trade liberalization of each group of countries. Developing countries claim that the GATT/ WTO system serves mainly the export interests of developed countries, since tariffs on products predominantly exported by developing countries are not liberalized as much as tariffs on those exported by developed countries. However, based on our analysis and consistent with Ludema and Mayda (2013), "the lack of progress in cutting tariffs on developing-country exports [in the Uruguay Round] is not so much a question of fairness of negotiations but of their efficiency [which is driven by exporter concentration]; and the solution does not lie in exempting developing countries from reciprocity but attracting them to it" (Ludema and Mayda 2013).[18]

3.5   Prospects for Future Multilateral Trade Liberalization

3.5.1   Trends in Exporter Concentration between 1993 and 2012 by Importing Country

In section 3.4, we analyzed the theoretical role of exporter concentration in determining MFN tariff rates through GATT/WTO negotiations and discussed the state of the free-rider problem up to the end of the Uruguay Round. Next, we examine changes in exporter concentration (HHI) over the following 20 years. These changes will allow us to make predictions on what value negotiated WTO tariff rates might take if a multilateral round were concluded, assuming that the other determinants of tariff rates do not change. As previously shown in equation (3.4), the HHI of importing country i is the sum of squared values of imports from WTO countries receiving MFN treatment divided by the squared sum of imports from countries receiving MFN status, regardless of WTO membership. We exclude from both the numerator and denominator of the HHI imports from importing country i's PTA partners. The change in the HHI between 1993 and 2012 can be decomposed into each of the three channels discussed in our introduction: the accession effect, which is related to accession of new members to the WTO; the PTA effect, which is related to the formation of new PTAs, which include the importing country; and, finally, the trade growth effect, which is related to changes in trade flows during the period, largely resulting from the high growth of emerging economies. We construct the change through each channel by measuring the change in the HHI when that channel was at work between 1993 and 2012, while the

Table 3.4
Decomposition of changes in HHI, by country (1993–2012).

Country	Total HHI Change	Accession Effect	PTA Effect	Trade Growth Effect
All countries	0.07	0.03	0.10	−0.06
Developing countries	0.06	0.02	0.11	−0.07
Developed countries	0.09	0.04	0.08	−0.03
Argentina	0.12	0.01	0.10	0.01
Australia	0.15	0.04	0.11	−0.01
Bolivia	0.07	0.01	0.16	−0.10
Brazil	−0.02	0.01	0.04	−0.07
Canada	−0.04	0.04	0.02	−0.10
Chile	0.39	0.03	0.33	0.02
Colombia	0.12	0.01	0.24	−0.13
Ecuador	−0.06	0.03	0.05	−0.13
European Union	0.14	0.04	0.10	0.00
Iceland	0.02	0.02	0.05	−0.06
India	−0.13	0.03	0.00	−0.16
Indonesia	0.06	0.03	0.06	−0.03
Japan	0.13	0.06	0.04	0.03
Korea	0.18	0.06	0.24	−0.12
Madagascar	−0.14	0.03	0.01	−0.18
Malaysia	0.14	0.03	0.11	0.00
Mauritius	0.00	0.03	0.06	−0.08
Mexico	−0.03	0.01	0.05	−0.08
Morocco	0.08	0.03	0.09	−0.03
New Zealand	0.09	0.05	0.07	−0.04
Norway	0.08	0.03	0.06	−0.01
Peru	0.21	0.02	0.29	−0.10
Thailand	0.09	0.03	0.08	−0.03
United States	0.08	0.03	0.05	0.00

others are shut down. The following expressions give the total HHI change and each of the three components:

$$H_{ik}(T_{12}, PTA_{12}, WTO_{12}) - H_{ik}(T_{93}, PTA_{93}, WTO_{93}) = \quad \textit{(Total HHI Change)}$$

$$H_{ik}(T_{93}, PTA_{93}, WTO_{12}) - H_{ik}(T_{93}, PTA_{93}, WTO_{93}) + \quad \textit{(Accession Effect)}$$

$$H_{ik}(T_{93}, PTA_{12}, WTO_{12}) - H_{ik}(T_{93}, PTA_{93}, WTO_{12}) + \quad \textit{(PTA Effect)}$$

$$H_{ik}(T_{12}, PTA_{12}, WTO_{12}) - H_{ik}(T_{93}, PTA_{12}, WTO_{12}) \quad \textit{(Trade Growth Effect)}$$

Table 3.4 presents the results of this analysis by importing country. The mean change in HHI over this period is positive and equal to 0.07, suggesting that, *if concluded, a new round (or a resurrected Doha Round) would on average lead to greater internalization of terms-of-trade benefits as the result of a smaller free-rider problem.* Note that, for developing countries, the total HHI increase is smaller than for developed countries (0.06 instead of 0.09). Actually, 6 of the 24 countries in the sample experienced declines in HHI—Brazil, Canada, Ecuador, India, Madagascar, and Mexico—and, with the exception of Canada, all are developing countries. These results show that one possible cause for developing countries' reluctance to reduce MFN tariffs during the Doha Round is their inability (or smaller ability) to internalize the benefits of their tariff reductions via negotiations, and not unwillingness for reciprocity. In the case of Canada, the decline in the overall HHI is driven by a particularly small PTA effect (0.02 compared to an average of 0.10).

The WTO accession effect is positive for all countries and on average equal to 0.03, which means that more inclusive membership in the WTO through the accession of 45 countries, including China and Russia, since 1994 helps tariff negotiations. As equation (3.4) shows, a country's accession to the WTO always increases an importing country's HHI if the new WTO member had already been granted MFN status by that importer, since in this case the denominator of the HHI is not affected, while the numerator increases. Note that, for example, the United States had granted MFN ("permanent normal trade relations") status to a number of countries before their WTO accession, including Albania, Bulgaria, Cambodia, China, Estonia, Latvia, and Lithuania (among others) (Pregelj 2005).

The PTA effect also is positive for all countries and on average is equal to 0.10, which is greater than the accession effect. From a theoretical point of view, the formation of new PTAs that include the importing country could either increase or decrease that importing country's HHI. Based on expression (3.4), the imports from the importer's PTA partners need to be removed from both the numerator and the denominator of the HHI, because they are no longer subject to the importer's MFN tariffs. Depending on the size of the PTA partner, measured by its share of the importer's total imports of a product, this could cause the HHI of the importing country to decrease or increase. It is more likely to increase when the PTA partner is smaller.[19] In other words, from a theoretical point of view, the PTA effect through exporter concentration could be either a "stumbling block" or a "building block" for multilateral trade negotiations. Here we find that on average PTAs are building blocks. Note that this is the first time that building or stumbling blocks of this type (i.e., through exporter concentration) have been pointed out in this literature.

In the data, the PTA effect is positive, which means that the formation of PTAs should have had a building block effect on multilateral trade negotiations during the Doha Round. In particular, this means that one way in which exporter concentration increased over time between 1993 and 2012 was through the formation of PTAs with countries that account for a small fraction of exports to the importer in all but a handful of products. Since these new PTA partner countries are pulled out of the HHI calculation for all products once they join the PTA with the importer, they will increase the HHI for most products—those for which they are not major exporters to the importing country—thus raising the likelihood that there will be a critical mass of interested exporters at the negotiating table over time. The building block result we find reinforces the conclusions of Estevadeordal, Ornelas, and Freund (2008), who show that in South America the signing of PTAs led to the reduction of MFN tariffs.

The PTA effect makes a large contribution to the overall HHI change. Absent the PTA effect, the overall HHI change would have been *negative*, at −0.03, instead of 0.07 (on average for all countries in the sample). Absent the PTA effect, the overall HHI change would have been −0.05 instead of 0.06 and 0.01 instead of 0.09, respectively, for developing and developed countries in the sample. In addition, note that the average PTA effect for the six countries with negative changes in overall HHI is only 0.03.

As mentioned, from a theoretical point of view, the PTA effect through exporter concentration could be either a building block or a stumbling block for multilateral trade negotiations for countries joining the PTA, as each PTA member applies its MFN tariff to nonmembers only. This would be true whether the PTA is an FTA or customs union (CU). However, the effect of PTA formation on exporter concentration to nonmember countries depends on the type of PTA. The formation of an FTA will have no effect, because each PTA member continues to maintain and negotiate its own MFN tariffs. Instead, the formation of customs unions unequivocally increases the exporter concentration of countries outside the CU. Indeed, countries that form a CU negotiate MFN tariff rates as a group and thus their exports are grouped together in the calculation of the HHI of other countries, which, as a consequence, increases.[20] Finally, the countries joining the CU might experience either an increase or a decrease in exporter concentration. In this chapter, we do not empirically analyze the CU effect, since no new CUs formed in the period considered.

The trade growth effect is on average equal to -0.06 for all countries in the sample, showing that the increasing multipolarity of global exporters has resulted in a decrease in exporter concentration and thus in a diminished ability of countries to internalize terms-of-trade benefits. Through the trade growth effect, the free-rider problem has worsened on average, with very few countries experiencing increased concentration through this channel over the sample period. These countries are Argentina, Chile, and Japan—interestingly, both the European Union and the United States display a zero trade growth effect. In general, developing countries are characterized by a more negative trade growth effect (-0.07) than for developed countries (-0.03). The countries with the most negative trade growth effect are Madagascar and India.

3.5.2   Implied HHI Impacts on Applied Tariffs

Using the IV coefficient estimates from subsection 3.4.1, the next step is to calculate the implied change in negotiated tariffs were the Doha Round concluded, based on the observed changes in HHI by country and HS section (see tables 3.2 and 3.3). In this exercise, we assume that the only determinant of negotiated tariffs that varies between 1993 and 2012 is the HHI, and that all other variables in equation (3.5) are held constant at their 1993 levels. In other words, the predicted negotiated tariffs only reflect greater internalization of terms-of-trade effects stemming from HHI changes over the observed period. Equation (3.9) shows how the change in the predicted negotiated tariff τ_{ik}^{n} is calculated:

$$\Delta \tau_{ik}^{n} = \beta_2 MP_{ik} \Delta HHI_{1993-2012,ik}. \tag{3.9}$$

Table 3.2 shows that, on average, countries would negotiate lower MFN tariffs as a result of greater internalization of terms-of-trade effects via increased exporter concentration. In percentage-point terms, the reduction in negotiated tariff rates from 1993 to 2012 is greater for developed countries (-0.92) than for developing countries (-0.46). Compared to the optimal noncooperative tariff level, the 2012 negotiated tariffs are 24% lower for developing countries and 52% lower for developed countries (the corresponding percentage differences were 23% and 43%, respectively, in 1993). This implies that if the Doha Round were concluded, increases in exporter concentration between 1993 and 2012 would result in around 85% of the potential tariff liberalization driven by terms of trade being realized (the latter result is approximately the same for developing and developed countries, 84% and 86%, respectively). The remaining 15% would not be realized, as a result of the MFN free-rider problem. Compared to the Uruguay Round, the changes in HHI would result in an increase of 10 percentage points for all countries in the sample, 6 percentage points for developing countries, and 16 percentage points for developed countries with regard to the reduction of the free-rider problem.

3.5.3   Trends in Exporter Concentration between 1993 and 2012 by Industry

So far, we have focused on country averages. We have shown that most countries have become better able to internalize MFN externalities on average, with a few notable exceptions, and these exceptional countries have experienced particularly unfavorable trade growth effects. However, this focus on country averages may mask important industry differences. Thus, we briefly consider the analysis of the three channels across HS sections in table 3.5. We find that the overall HHI increases in all HS sections with the exception of section XIV (pearls, precious stones, and metals), which is unaffected. The evidence across HS sections is similar to what we found across countries. Both the accession effect and the PTA effect are positive for each HS section, while the trade growth effect is negative for all HS sections except section VIII (raw hides and skins, leather, fur), section XII (footwear, headgear, etc.), and section XX (Miscellaneous manufactured articles). We discuss of these exceptions further later. Between the accession effect and the PTA effect, the latter is stronger, (except for section XII (Footwear, headgear, etc.). Absent the PTA effect, the overall HHI change would be negative for 14 of the 20 HS sections. Thus, our findings across HS sections confirm the building block effect of PTAs working through exporter concentration.

Interestingly, the sections facing the largest free-rider problems in 1993, sections VIII (raw hides and skins, leather, fur), XXII (footwear, headgear, etc.), and XX (miscellaneous manufactured articles), are also the ones that show the greatest increases in HHI between 1993 and 2012—the total HHI changes of these three sections are 0.21, 0.33, and 0.22, respectively—owing to a positive trade growth effect. Products in these sections are labor intensive and are largely produced by developing countries, particularly China. For example, China exported US\$ 50.8 billion (40.3% of world exports) of footwear in 2013.

Table 3.5
Decomposition of changes in HHI, by HS section (1993–2012).

HS Classification	Total HHI Change	Accession Effect	PTA Effect	Trade Growth Effect
Section I: Live animals, animal products	0.12	0.04	0.11	−0.03
Section II: Vegetable products	0.08	0.05	0.10	−0.07
Section III: Animal or vegetable fats and oils	0.01	0.01	0.11	−0.11
Section IV: Prepared foodstuffs	0.04	0.03	0.11	−0.09
Section V: Mineral products	0.07	0.06	0.09	−0.07
Section VI: Chemical and allied products	0.04	0.03	0.11	−0.09
Section VII: Plastics and rubber products	0.01	0.01	0.10	−0.10
Section VIII: Raw hides and skins, leather, fur	0.21	0.07	0.08	0.07
Section IX: Wood and wood products	0.11	0.04	0.09	−0.02
Section X: Pulp and paper	0.03	0.01	0.11	−0.09
Section XI: Textiles and textile articles	0.16	0.07	0.09	−0.01
Section XII: Footwear, headgear, etc.	0.33	0.12	0.09	0.13
Section XIII: Stone, plaster, cement, ceramic, glass	0.07	0.02	0.11	−0.06
Section XIV: Pearls, precious stones, and metals	0.00	0.02	0.07	−0.09
Section XV: Base metal and articles of base metal	0.07	0.02	0.10	−0.05
Section XVI: Machinery and electrical equipment	0.03	0.01	0.09	−0.07
Section XVII: Transportation equipment	0.01	0.01	0.09	−0.09
Section XVIII: Instruments	0.04	0.02	0.08	−0.06
Section XIX: Arms and ammunition	0.04	0.01	0.08	−0.05
Section XX: Miscellaneous manufactured articles	0.22	0.04	0.08	0.10

India and Brazil ranked second and third (Bruha 2014). This illustrates the perhaps obvious point that export growth by emerging markets does not always depress exporter concentration. Rather, in products where emerging markets already dominate trade, emerging-market export growth increases exporter concentration and reduces the MFN free-rider problem. This bodes well for the future as emerging markets come to dominate more and more sectors.

3.5.4 The Rise of China

The largest and most rapidly growing of the new economies is China, which had become the second-largest world economy by the end of the period of analysis, dramatically surpassing the other BRIC countries since 2001, when the term *BRIC* was first used (O'Neill 2001). Over the 20 years of this chapter's study, the median growth in exports from China by product category increased by a factor of 27. More importantly, China has become the world's largest exporter in many sectors, meaning its growth has a substantial effect on the trade growth effect. This chapter estimates an OLS regression of the trade growth effect on the change in value of Chinese imports over the 20-year sample, controlling for importing country.[21] The negative and statistically significant coefficient on the change in imports coming from China suggests that growth in exports from China is linked to a reduction in HHI via the trade growth effect. Column 2 of table 3.6 drops outliers below the 10th and above the 90th percentile. The mean value

Table 3.6
Chinese trade growth effect: regression results.

Dependent Variable	(1) Trade Growth Effect	(2)
Change in imports from China	−3.91e-07***	−0.000207***
	(1.49e-07)	(1.21e-05)
Outliers dropped	No	Yes
Observations	33,411	26,739
Adjusted R-squared	0.028	0.040

Note: Standard errors are in parentheses.
*** $p < 0.01$, ** $p < 0.05$, * $p < 0.1$.

Table 3.7
OLS regression HS section results for Chinese trade growth.

Imports from China of HS Section	Coefficient on Trade Growth Effect
Section I: Live animals, animal products	−0.000332
	(0.000387)
Section II: Vegetable products	−0.000422
	(0.000378)
Section III: Animal or vegetable fats and oils	0.000363
	(0.000942)
Section IV: Prepared foodstuffs	−0.000211
	(0.000173)
Section V: Mineral products	−0.000896**
	(0.000391)
Section VI: Chemical and allied products	−0.000346***
	(4.62e-05)
Section VII: Plastics and rubber products	−0.000135***
	(2.50e-05)
Section VIII: Raw hides and skins, leather, fur	0.000346**
	(0.000165)
Section IX: Wood and wood products	−5.06e-05
	(0.000233)
Section X: Pulp and paper	−0.000301***
	(7.21e-05)
Section XI: Textiles and textile articles	6.17e-05
	(6.38e-05)
Section XII: Footwear, headgear, etc.	8.32e-05
	(0.000182)
Section XIII: Stone, plaster, cement, ceramic, glass	−0.000234***
	(6.29e-05)
Section XIV: Pearls, precious stones, and metals	2.97e-05
	(0.000177)
Section XV: Base metal and articles of base metal	−0.000244***
	(3.31e-05)
Section XVI: Machinery and electrical equipment	−9.39e-05***
	(1.12e-05)
Section XVII: Transportation equipment	−0.000127***
	(3.33e-05)
Section XVIII: Instruments	−0.000287***
	(3.40e-05)
Section XIX: Arms and ammunition	−0.000123
	(0.00122)
Section XX: Miscellaneous manufactured articles	−0.000150***
	(5.49e-05)

Note: Standard errors are in parentheses.
*** $p < 0.01$, ** $p < 0.05$, * $p < 0.1$.

for the change in imports from China after the dropping of outliers is 89, suggesting that on average China decreased the HHI of trading partners by 0.018 via the trade growth effect, which is 31% of the overall trade growth effect (-0.0578). The regressions of the trade growth effect on the change in imports from China by HS section are presented in table 3.7.[22]

3.6   Conclusions

The central finding of this chapter is that trends over 20 years have induced an overall increase in HHI across countries and products. The increase has been stronger for the HHI index of exporters to developed countries and for products exported primarily by developing countries. For some countries, such as Brazil and India, the total HHI decreased between 1993 and 2012 This may be one reason why these developing countries have been reluctant to make tariff reductions during the Doha Round. We also find that increasing membership in the WTO and formation of new PTAs have mitigated the free-rider problem over these 20 years. These effects outweigh the dilution effect of emerging economies. Finally, our results show that, were the Doha Round concluded, unrealized potential terms-of-trade liberalization could on average decrease from 25% to 15%. Therefore, the WTO still has a role to play in realizing further trade liberalization.

Appendix

Table 3.A1
HS product classifications.

HS Sections	Two-Digit HS Codes
Section I: Live animals, animal products	1–5
Section II: Vegetable products	6–14
Section III: Animal or vegetable fats and oils	15
Section IV: Prepared foodstuffs	16–24
Section V: Mineral products	25–27
Section VI: Chemical and allied products	28–38
Section VII: Plastics and rubber products	39–40
Section VIII: Raw hides and skins, leather, fur	41–43
Section IX: Wood and wood products	44–46
Section X: Pulp and paper	47–49
Section XI: Textiles and textile articles	50–63
Section XII: Footwear, headgear, etc.	54–67
Section XIII: Stone, plaster, cement, ceramic, glass	78–70
Section XIV: Pearls, precious stones, and metals	71
Section XV: Base metal and articles of base metal	72–83
Section XVI: Machinery and electrical equipment	84–85
Section XVII: Transportation equipment	86–89
Section XVIII: Instruments	90–92
Section XIX: Arms and ammunition	93
Section XX: Miscellaneous manufactured articles	94–96

Notes: The data used include six-digit HS classifications for products. To create HS categories for simple analysis, these classifications are broken down into 20 sections. To do this, the six-digit codes are reduced to two-digit codes (new integers created by dividing the previous code by 10,000). Table 3.A2 displays the arrangement for reference. Sections XXI (97) and XXII (98–99) are dropped from the analysis; 98–99 refer to services rather than goods, and 97 refers to works of art, which is not a category of good that is produced for large-scale export. Section XXI analysis is included in the decomposition of HHI changes for the sake of completeness.

Table 3.A2
Shares of 2012 imports and exports by country economic status.

HS Section	Exports Developing	Imports Developed	Developing	Developed
Section I: Live animals, animal products	41%	59%	34%	66%
Section II: Vegetable products	58%	42%	42%	58%
Section III: Animal or vegetable fats and oils	80%	20%	58%	42%
Section IV: Prepared foodstuffs	51%	49%	27%	73%
Section V: Mineral products	76%	24%	33%	67%
Section VI: Chemical and allied products	31%	69%	37%	63%
Section VII: Plastics and rubber products	44%	56%	48%	52%
Section VIII: Raw hides and skins, leather, fur	67%	33%	28%	72%
Section IX: Wood and wood products	58%	42%	32%	68%
Section X: Pulp and paper	34%	66%	44%	56%
Section XI: Textiles and textile articles	77%	23%	25%	75%
Section XII: Footwear, headgear, etc.	90%	10%	15%	85%
Section XIII: Stone, plaster, cement, ceramic, glass	51%	49%	32%	68%
Section XIV: Pearls, precious stones, and metals	38%	62%	35%	65%
Section XV: Base metal and articles of base metal	46%	54%	44%	56%
Section XVI: Machinery and electrical equipment	51%	49%	40%	60%
Section XVII: Transportation equipment	24%	76%	36%	64%
Section XVIII: Instruments	25%	75%	37%	63%
Section XIX: Arms and ammunition	19%	81%	12%	88%
Section XX: Miscellaneous manufactured articles	77%	23%	15%	85%

Note: Country development statuses are taken from the CIA *World Factbook*.

Notes

The authors would like to thank seminar participants at the CESifo Venice Summer Institute 2015 Workshop on "The World Trade Organization and Economic Development" for comments and suggestions.

1. WTO membership data for 1994 and 2012 are taken from WTO.org.

2. IMF World Economic Outlook Databases.

3. Over 50% of trade flows occur between PTA partners (an increasing trend; see Carpenter and Lendle 2010), but a comparatively small amount (16% in 2011) actually receives preferential treatment (WTO 2011).

4. See Fergusson (2011).

5. The analysis in Ludema and Mayda (2009, 2013) is based on applied rates since the theory in these papers holds for the rates that actually apply to trade flows at any point in time. However, the empirical results are robust to using bound rates as an alternative dependent variable.

6. Most acceding countries already received MFN status before becoming members of the WTO, so their exports already had MFN access to the markets of existing members. But until they became members, existing members could not pressure them to make concessions in exchange. Thus, before acceding, these countries were free riders by construction.

7. While our model and estimates explain why certain key developing countries were unwilling to make tariff reductions in the Doha Round, it does not provide a complete explanation for the stalemate of the round. This is because our model is static. A dynamic model in which countries have the option to postpone the conclusion of the round until a more symmetric result can be achieved could potentially rationalize the stalemate.

8. The model of negotiations applied by Ludema and Mayda (2013) is based on the GATT's most common method of tariff negotiations, an item-by-item request and offer method that saw extensive use in the first five GATT rounds and the Uruguay Round. In this model, four consecutive stages occur: a request of tariff rates, an offer of tariff rates, bilateral bargaining, and the setting of a mutually agreed tariff schedule where the negotiation between countries is solved according to the Nash bargaining solution. The negotiated tariff, chosen in the final stage, is Pareto efficient for the participants in the negotiations for each good.

9. Estevadeordal, Freund, and Ornelas (2008) find that in Latin America the formation of PTAs has a lagged negative effect on the MFN tariff set by the countries involved.

10. Note that the only variable of the estimation that differs between this chapter and Ludema and Mayda (2013) is the measure of the importing country's market power: here we use a composite measure, while in Ludema and Mayda separate specifications were run using, respectively, *Diff* and *HIEE*.

11. From 1996 onward, the only non-MFN countries were Afghanistan, Cuba, Laos, North Korea, Iran, Vietnam, Serbia, and Montenegro. Before that, the United States had granted unconditional MFN to all other countries except communist ones. Communist countries began receiving MFN treatment in the 1990s.

12. The larger the set of averaged country values, the more the instruments overlap. At the extreme, an instrument using the average of all countries would be the same for all

other countries as well. Hence, increasing this number reduces the variance of the data across observations.

13. See also section 4.C and table II in Ludema and Mayda (2013).

14. We set $\beta_3 = 0$ given that the IV estimate of this coefficient is only significant at the 10% level in column 2, of table 3.1 and in several additional robustness checks the estimate is completely insignificant (see table I in Ludema and Mayda 2013).

15. If in the data the actual value of the HHI is higher than $\overline{H}_{ik} = -\frac{\beta_1}{\beta_2}$, we set $\tau_{ik}^n = \tau_{ik}^*$.

16. The apparent asymmetry in internalization between developed and developing countries does not imply that developing countries have given up more concessions than they have received. Generally speaking, developed countries internalize a smaller share of their terms-of-trade externalities, because developing countries are willing to pay them less (in combined concessions) to make MFN tariff reductions, because of free riding.

17. Note that Ludema and Mayda (2013) used different measures of market power, which explains the slight difference in results compared to the results here.

18. This is also in line with the result in Ludema and Mayda (2013) that for the United States the percentage reduction of the negotiated 1993 tariff relative to the noncooperative tariff was 26% for imports from the average developed country in the sample and 11% for imports from the average developing country. Importantly, this calculation accounts for the product mix imported by the United States from each group of countries.

19. Removing an exporter j from the HHI of country i is equivalent to setting j's exports M_i^j equal to 0 in equation (3.4). This decreases both the numerator and denominator of (3.4) and thus produces an ambiguous net effect on i's HHI, H_i. We can show that removal of an exporter causes H_i to increase if j's share in i's total imports, θ_i^j, is less than $2H_i/(1+H_i)$ and decrease if it is greater. Thus, for a given HHI, the smaller θ_i^j is, the more likely it is that removing country j (because of its PTA with country i) will increase i's HHI.

20. Indeed, Ludema and Mayda (2013) find that the average tariff reduction (compared to the noncooperative level) received by the European Union from the United States at the Uruguay Round is 31%, whereas if the European Union were to break apart, the resulting decrease in HHIs of the goods Europe exports would cause the figure to fall to 21%.

21. The change in imports is calculated as $(\text{Imports}_{2012}-\text{Imports}_{1993})/\text{Imports}_{1993}$.

22. Note that China's growth should at some point have an inverse effect on the HHI once the country becomes large enough to concentrate rather than dilute export markets.

References

Abboushi, S. 2014. "Transatlantic Trade and Investment Partnership—Overview." *Competition Forum* 12(1): 107–113.

Autor, David, David Dorn, and Gordon H. Hanson. 2013. "The China Syndrome: Local Labor Market Effects of Import Competition in the United States." *American Economic Review* 103(6): 2121–2168.

Bagwell, Kyle, and Robert W. Staiger. 1998. "Regionalism and Multilateral Tariff Cooperation." NBER Working Paper No. 5921. Cambridge, MA: National Bureau of Economic Research.

Bagwell, Kyle, and Robert W. Staiger. 2002. *The Economics of the World Trading System*. Cambridge, MA: MIT Press.

Bagwell, Kyle, and Robert W. Staiger. 2011. "What Do Trade Negotiators Negotiate About? Empirical Evidence from the World Trade Organization." *American Economic Review* 101(4): 1238–1273.

Bagwell, Kyle, and Robert W. Staiger. 2014. "Can the Doha Round Be a Development Round? Setting a Place at the Table." In Robert C. Feenstra and Alan M. Taylor (eds.), *Globalization in an Age of Crisis: Multilateral Economic Cooperation in the Twenty-First Century*, 91–124. Chicago: University of Chicago Press for the NBER.

Baldwin, Richard E. 1987. "Politically Realistic Objective Functions and Trade Policy: PROFs and Tariffs." *Economics Letters* 24(3): 287–290.

Bhagwati, Jagdish N. 2008. "The Selfish Hegemon Must Offer a New Deal on Trade." *Financial Times*, August 19.

Bhagwati, Jagdish. 2012. "The Broken Legs of Global Trade." *Project Syndicate*, May.

Blustein, Paul. 2009. *Misadventures of the Most Favored Nations: Clashing Egos, Inflated Ambitions, and the Great Shambles of the World Trade System*. New York: PublicAffairs.

Bown, Chad P., and Meredith A. Crowley. 2013. "Self-Enforcing Trade Agreements: Evidence from Time-Varying Trade Policy." *American Economic Review* 103(2): 1071–1090.

Broda, Christian, Joshua Greenfield, and David E. Weinstein. 2017. "From Groundnuts to Globalization: A Structural Estimate of Trade and Growth." *Research in Economics* 71(4): 759–783.

Broda, Christian, Nuno Limão, and David E. Weinstein. 2008. "Optimal Tariffs and Market Power: The Evidence." *American Economic Review* 98(5): 2032–2065.

Bruha, Patrick. 2014. "Footwear Industry in Brazil." *Brazil Business*, October 13.

Carpenter, Theresa, and Andreas Lendle. 2010. "How Preferential Is World Trade?" Working Paper No. 2010-32. Geneva: Center for Trade and Economic Integration.

Estevadeordal, A., C. Freund, and E. Ornelas. 2008. "Does Regionalism Affect Trade Liberalization Towards Non-Members?" *Quarterly Journal of Economics* 123:1531–1575.

Fergusson, Ian F. 2011. "The World Trade Organization: The Non-agricultural Market Access (NAMA) Negotiations." Congressional Research Service.

Francois, Joseph. 2008. "Doha Round Failure: This Is the Way the Round Ends." Center for Economic Policy Research, August 1. http://voxeu.org/article/doha-round-failure -way-round-ends.

Gallagher, Peter, and Andrew Stoler. 2009. "Critical Mass as an Alternative Framework for Multilateral Trade Negotiations." *Global Governance* 15(3): 375–392.

Goldberg, P. K., and G. Maggi. 1999. "Protection for Sale: An Empirical Investigation," *American Economic Review* 89(5): 1135–1155.

Grossman, G., and E. Helpman. 1994. "Protection for Sale." *American Economic Review*, 84(4): 833–850.

Helpman, Elhanan. 1997. "Politics and Trade Policy." In D. M. Kreps and K. F. Wallis (eds.), *Advances in Economics and Econometrics: Theory and Applications*, volume 2. Cambridge: Cambridge University Press.

Hoekman, Bernard M., and Petros C. Mavroidis. 2015. "WTO 'à la carte' or 'menu du jour'? Assessing the Case for More Plurilateral Agreements." *European Journal of International Law* 26 (2): 319–343.

Kleimann, David, and Joe Guinan. 2011. "The Doha Round: An Obituary." Global Governance Program Policy Brief.

Limão, N. 2007. "Are Preferential Trade Agreements with Non-trade Objectives a Stumbling Block for Multilateral Liberalization?" *Review of Economic Studies* 74:821–855.

Ludema, R., and A. M. Mayda. 2009. "Do Countries Free Ride on MFN?" *Journal of International Economics* 77(2): 137–150.

Ludema, R., and A. M. Mayda. 2013. "Do Terms-of-Trade Effects Matter for Trade Agreements? Evidence from WTO Countries." *Quarterly Journal of Economics* 128(4): 1837–1893.

Nunn, N. 2007. "Relationship-Specificity, Incomplete Contracts, and the Pattern of Trade." *Quarterly Journal of Economics* 122(2): 569–600.

O'Neill, Jim. 2001. "Building Better Global Economic BRICs." *Global Economics*, no. 66. New York: Goldman Sachs.

Pregelj, Vladimir N. 1999. "Country Applicability of the U.S. Normal Trade Relations (Most-Favored-Nation) Status." Congressional Research Service.

Rauch, James E. 1999. "Networks versus Markets in International Trade." *Journal of International Economics* 48:7–35.

Schwab, Susan. 2011. "After Doha: Why the Negotiations Are Doomed and What We Should Do About It." *Foreign Affairs* 90(3): 104–117.

World Trade Organization (WTO). 2011. "Changing Face of Trade Pacts Requires Coherence with WTO, Report Says." WTO, July 20.

4 The Impacts of the GATT/WTO on Trade: Formal Members versus Nonmember Participants

Xuepeng Liu

4.1 Introduction

It was often taken for granted that the General Agreement on Tariffs and Trade (GATT), signed in 1947 and replaced by the World Trade Organization (WTO) in 1995, has contributed significantly to the fast growth in international trade during the last several decades. Rose (2004), however, challenges the conventional view on the effectiveness of the GATT/WTO (hereafter the GATT) in promoting world trade. Using a large dataset on bilateral trade covering 175 countries over 50 years, Rose finds little evidence that the trade patterns of GATT members differ from those of nonmembers. A subsequent comment by Tomz, Goldstein, and Rivers (2007) considers the measurement errors in GATT membership. They argue that Rose underestimates the trade impact of the GATT by misclassifying the nonmember participants (NMPs) of the GATT as outsiders. The NMPs include some colonies of formal GATT members, some newly sovereign countries, and provisional applicants to the GATT. They do obtain a stronger trade impact of the GATT after considering the NMPs, but surprisingly, they also find that NMPs are even more liberalized than formal members. Their preferred results imply that two formal GATT members trade 61% more than the baseline case of being neither a formal member nor an NMP, and two NMPs trade 140% more than the baseline case. Their point on the measurement errors in formal membership is well taken, but as they admit, "It is difficult to explain why the effect should be larger for non-member participants than formal members." We consider their finding as another puzzle, the "NMP puzzle," besides the "ineffectiveness puzzle" raised by Rose.

Figure 4.1 displays the shares of total bilateral trade by membership type from 1948 to 2001.[1] Each country pair falls into one of the

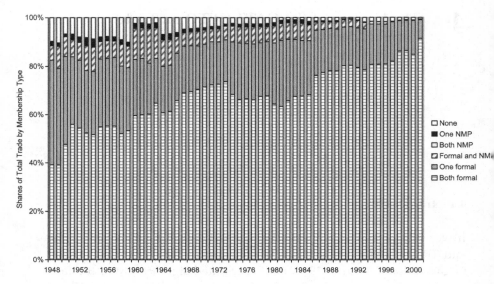

Figure 4.1
Share of total trade by membership type from 1948 to 2001. Each country pair is classified into one of the following six categories: both countries are formal GATT members;
only one country is a formal member and the other is neither a formal member nor
an NMP; one country is a formal member and the other is an NMP; both countries
are NMPs; only one country is an NMP and the other is neither a formal member
nor an NMP; neither country is a formal member or an NMP (the default category in
regressions).

following six categories: both formal, one formal, formal and NMP,
both NMPs, one NMP, and none.[2] World trade is dominated by formal members (i.e., "both formal" and "one formal"). The share of "both
NMPs" is nearly zero, and the sum of "both NMPs" and "one NMP" is
on average less than 1% of the total trade during 1948–2001 (with the
highest share at around 2%–3% in the early 1950s). Similarly, the relative sizes of these NMPs are much smaller than for formal members.
For example, the average real GDP of formal members over 1948–2001
is 31 times larger than that of NMPs, while their average population
size is 14 times larger.[3] With such small trade shares and sizes of NMPs,
it is difficult to understand why NMPs change the results substantially
and why NMPs seem to matter more than formal members.[4]

This chapter provides two solutions to these puzzles by including zero trade flows in the analysis and applying a more appropriate
Poisson method to estimate the gravity regression. First, zero trade
observations are excluded by Rose (2004) and Tomz, Goldstein, and
Rivers (2007).[5] Without zero trade, they lose the information on the

new trading relationships created by the GATT: some country pairs initially did not trade but started to trade after one or both of them joined the GATT. The GATT not only facilitates trade between existing trading partners at the intensive margin but also creates new trading relationships at the extensive margin. Restricting the analysis to positive trade flows can cause underestimation of the GATT's trade-promoting effects. Following the same gravity regression specifications as Rose (2004) and Tomz, Goldstein, and Rivers (2007) but including zero trade, this chapter finds that the GATT has strongly promoted bilateral trade between its formal members, and the formal members are significantly more liberalized than the NMPs. This is to be expected because many colonial economies have established trade relationships with a limited number of countries, and their trading partners usually expand slowly. Therefore, NMPs might not contribute as much as formal members to world trade at the extensive margin. The different roles played by formal member and NMPs are demonstrated graphically in figure 4.2. Based on the trade data used by Liu (2009), figure 4.2 shows the average number of trading partners by membership type over the years of the study.[6] To make sure that the number of partners is not driven by newborn nations, only the country pairs with complete series of trade data over 1948–2001 are used in figure 4.2. This restricted sub-sample covers more than 70% of the total observations and nearly 90% of the total world trade. Although NMPs show an increasing trend in the number of partners before 1980, they trade with fewer countries on average than formal members do and even fewer than outsiders do; the average number of their trading partners stopped increasing and actually decreased after 1980.

Second, this chapter finds that the traditional log-linear gravity regression method should be reconsidered. Zero trade only solves part of the puzzles, because it still cannot explain why we have the puzzles at the intensive margin (i.e., when only positive trade is included). This chapter goes on to show that, even when only positive trade is included, a more appropriate econometric method can address the problems. The Poisson regressions show that formal GATT members are significantly more liberalized than both outsiders and NMPs, with and without zero trade in the regressions. With only positive trade, two formal GATT members on average trade 45% more than the baseline case of being neither a formal member nor an NMP, while two NMPs trade only 22% more than the baseline category. With both positive and zero trade, two formal GATT members trade 60% more than the baseline case of being neither a formal member nor an NMP, while

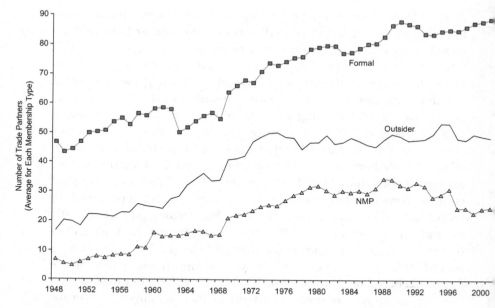

Figure 4.2
Average number of trading partners by membership type from 1948 to 2001.

two NMPs trade even 10% less than the baseline case. In sum, the two puzzles raised by Rose (2004) and Tomz, Goldstein, and Rivers (2007). can be solved by considering zero trade and/or a better econometric method.

This chapter is closely related to Liu (2009) in that it uses the same datasets and econometric methods. Although Liu (2009) also considers NMPs, it treats them the same as formal members. The current chapter, however, distinguishes NMPs from formal members and focuses on their different effects.

The significant impact of formal GATT membership on trade and the larger role it plays compared to being an NMP are what we could reasonably hope for. Since World War II, international trade has been increasing at a much faster rate than national GDP growth, and cross-country trade barriers have been cut substantially, especially in rich countries. During this period, the GATT, as the only international organization governing world trade, should have played a role. Two pillars of the GATT rules, nondiscrimination and reciprocity, are important for their trade-promoting effects. Nondiscrimination, or the most-favored-nation (MFN) clause, requires members to extend their tariff reductions to all the members of the GATT. Reciprocity makes liberalization concessions politically more acceptable. Besides tariff reduction, cooperative and multilateral negotiations under the GATT can avoid the prisoner's dilemma problem arising from the terms-of-trade externality (see, e.g., Bagwell and Staiger 1999, 2003). In addition, the GATT can also alleviate the time-inconsistency problem of trade policy (see, e.g., Staiger and Tabellini 1987, 1999; Maggi and Rodríguez-Clare 1998; Mitra 2002).

The result that NMPs are less liberalized than formal members is consistent with the fact that NMPs are mostly developing countries and only reap part of the benefits of their de facto membership status. Subramanian and Wei (2007) also find that the WTO promotes trade strongly but unevenly, where the unevenness comes from member countries' level of development: developed members appear to have experienced faster growth in trade than in developing members. GATT has many "special and differential treatments" designed for developing countries. These rules make poor countries' participation in the GATT less stringent and allow for many exceptions. For example, former colonies of GATT members are one type of NMP that could avoid offering tariff concessions according to GATT Article XXXVI.8 (see Hoekman and Kostecki 1995, p. 388).[7] Without corresponding concessions, the extent of trade liberalization in those NMPs would likely be more limited than for formal members. Using a multilateral approach based on total trade, openness, and trade policy measures, Rose (2007) also casts doubt on the finding of Tomz, Goldstein, and Rivers (2007) that NMPs are more liberalized than formal members.

There are many further steps that could be taken to further improve the accuracy of the measured effects of the GATT on world trade flows. For instance, a sector-level structural gravity equation with both positive and zero trade flows may help to achieve more precise estimates of these effects, and continued efforts are needed to further improve data quality, refine the measurements of key variables, and investigate the heterogeneity of the impact in various dimensions. Nevertheless, the contribution of the present chapter is to show that the two main puzzles identified in the prior literature, the "ineffectiveness puzzle" and the "NMP puzzle," can both be addressed by undertaking two relatively simple modifications to the original gravity equation approach of Rose (2004).

The rest of the chapter proceeds as follows. Section 4.2 presents the data, methods, and results. Conclusions are presented in section 4.3. A table presenting the results from robustness checks is presented in the appendix.

4.2   Data, Methods, and Results

For ease of comparison, the log-linear gravity regressions in this chapter closely follow Rose (2004) and Tomz, Goldstein, and Rivers (2007).[8]
GATT formal membership and nonmember participant (NMP) data are
from Tomz, Goldstein, and Rivers (2007). Other covariates include the
logarithm of the products of GDP and GDP per capita, the logarithm
of distance, colonial relationship, common language, common country,
regional trade agreement (RTA), customs unions (CU), and Generalized
System of Preferences (GSP). Because zero trade flows have already
been dropped in the dataset used by Rose and Tomz, Goldstein, and
Rivers, their data cannot be used. The dataset used in this chapter is
based on Liu (2009) and has systematic records of zero trade.[9] The panel
dataset includes more than 200 countries or regions for the years 1948–
2001.[10] The number of observations used in regressions can be as large
as 544,000, among which zero trade observations account for 52%. The
number of positive observations (259,433) is larger than that in Rose
and Tomz, Goldstein, and Rivers (234,597) because of the expanded
trade data from various sources.[11]

4.2.1   Traditional Log-Linear Regressions
The traditional log-linear gravity regression is specified as follows:

$$\ln T_{ijt} = \beta_0 + \beta_1 Bothin_{ijt} + \beta_2 Onein_{ijt} + \beta_3 \ln(Y_{it} * Y_{jt})$$
$$+ \beta_4 \ln[(Y_{it}/Pop_{it}) * (Y_{jt}/Pop_{jt})] + \beta_5 Current\ Colonizer_{ijt}$$
$$+ \beta_6 RTA_{ijt} + \beta_7 CU_{ijt} + \beta_8 GSP_{jit} + a_t + a_{ij} + \varepsilon_{ijt},$$

where T_{ijt} is the total trade between i and j in year t; the $Bothin_{ijt}$
dummy equals 1 if both i and j were GATT/WTO members in year
t; the $Onein_{ijt}$ dummy equals 1 if either i or j was a GATT/WTO member in year t; Y is real GDP; Pop is population; the $Current\ Colonizer_{ijt}$
dummy equals 1 if one of the countries in a dyad was currently a
colony of the other country in year t; the RTA_{ijt} dummy equals 1 if
i and j belonged to the same regional trade agreement in year t; the
CU_{ijt} dummy equals 1 if i and j used the same currency in year t;
the GSP_{ijt} dummy equals 1 if one of the countries in a dyad offered
GSP to the other country in year t; a_t is the year dummy variable; a_{ij}
is the country-pair dummy; and ε_{ijt} is the residual. Because country-
dyad fixed effects are included in the regression, the time-invariant
variables at the country or dyad levels are not included, because of

collinearity. More detailed information regarding the data sources and variable construction can be found in Liu (2009).

Table 4.1 reports the traditional log-linear regressions with year dummies and country-pair fixed effects. Alternatively, exporter and importer fixed effects could be used. With country fixed effects, log-linear regressions offer results similar to those of country-pair fixed-effects regressions, but Poisson regressions are sometimes difficult to converge. We therefore report only the results with country-pair fixed effects. Many time-invariant covariates are dropped from the fixed-effects regressions. Regressions (1)–(3) in table 4.1 use only positive trade flows with different GATT membership measures. Considering only formal membership, regression (1) shows a very small and insignificant coefficient on "both formal members" (0.016), consistent with Rose's "ineffectiveness puzzle." In column 2, formal GATT memberships are distinguished from NMPs, so we add three additional variables: formal and NMP, both NMPs, and one NMP. As in Tomz, Goldstein, and Rivers (2007), larger coefficients are obtained for all the GATT variables, and in particular we see a stronger trade-promoting effect for NMPs than for formal GATT members. Column 3 combines the formal members and NMPs and shows that they are significantly more liberalized than outsiders. This is why Tomz, Goldstein, and Rivers (2007) claim that NMPs can help to explain Rose's "ineffectiveness puzzle."

Without accounting for zero trade, Rose (2004) and Tomz, Goldstein, and Rivers (2007) cannot capture the effect of the GATT on trade at the extensive margin. The marginal change (Δ) in trade (T) with respect to the change in a binary covariate (D) such as a GATT dummy can be written as

$$\Delta E(t|x) = t^1 - t^0 = P(T > 0|x) * \Delta E(t|x, T > 0)$$
$$+ \Delta P(T > 0|x) * E(t|x, T > 0),$$

where t^1 and t^0 are estimated $\ln(T)$ measured at $D = 1$ and $D = 0$, respectively, and $P(T > 0)$ is the probability of positive trade, with other covariates usually measured at their mean values. The two terms on the right-hand side of the previous equation account for the changes in trade at intensive and extensive margins, respectively. We would underestimate the impact of the GATT if we ignored the extensive margin and considered only positive trade.

After including zero trade, the two puzzles disappear, as shown in the last three columns of table 4.1. To keep the zero trade values

Table 4.1
Log-linear gravity regressions with country-pair fixed effects.

	T > 0			Full Sample		
	(1)	(2)	(3)	(4)	(5)	(6)
Both in GATT						
Both formal members	0.016	0.515***		1.658***	2.002***	
	(0.011)	(0.021)		(0.028)	(0.051)	
Formal and NMP		0.586***	0.581***		0.423***	0.957***
		(0.022)	(0.021)		(0.050)	(0.048)
Both NMPs		1.143***			0.371***	
		(0.042)			(0.061)	
Only One in GATT						
One formal member	−0.146***	0.266***	0.304***	0.985***	1.236***	0.693***
	(0.011)	(0.019)	(0.019)	(0.027)	(0.045)	(0.043)
One NMP		0.396***			0.158***	
		(0.027)			(0.049)	
Log product of GDP	0.699***	0.716***	0.689***	2.671***	2.679***	2.741***
	(0.015)	(0.015)	(0.015)	(0.031)	(0.031)	(0.031)
Log product of GDP per capita	0.427***	0.413***	0.432***	−0.724***	−0.733***	−0.764***
	(0.015)	(0.015)	(0.015)	(0.030)	(0.030)	(0.030)
Currently colonized	0.545***	0.504***	0.525***	−4.729***	−4.782***	−5.229***
	(0.068)	(0.069)	(0.068)	(0.364)	(0.364)	(0.361)
RTA	0.387***	0.369***	0.371***	0.357***	0.345***	0.298***
	(0.013)	(0.013)	(0.013)	(0.037)	(0.037)	(0.037)
Currency union	0.689***	0.668***	0.667***	5.505***	5.498***	5.562***
	(0.047)	(0.047)	(0.047)	(0.152)	(0.152)	(0.150)
GSP	0.164***	0.171***	0.182***	1.343***	1.368***	1.324***
	(0.009)	(0.009)	(0.009)	(0.028)	(0.028)	(0.028)
Observations	313,695	313,695	313,695	544,195	544,195	544,195

Notes: All the regressions use year dummies and country-pair fixed effects. Robust standard errors are in parentheses
* significant at 10%; ** significant at 5%; *** significant at 1%.

after taking the logarithm, the dependent variable $\ln(T)$ is substituted by $\ln(T + 1)$.[12] In regression (4), we use only formal membership and obtain much larger coefficients on "both formal members" and "one formal member" variables than in regression (1). Regression (5) distinguishes formal members from NMPs and shows that formal members trade much more than NMPs. This is the opposite of what Tomz, Goldstein, and Rivers (2007). find when using only positive trade flows. Results from pooled data analysis, with many time-invariant variables, offer the same conclusions (see table 4.A1).

The economic magnitude of the effect as implied by the log-linear gravity regression results is large, and sometimes seems too large to be true. The results reported in column 5 of table 4.1 imply that two formal GATT members trade 640% (i.e., $\exp(2.002) - 1 = 640\%$) more than the baseline case of neither being a formal member (a large "trade creation" effect)! If only one country in a dyad is a formal GATT member, with the other one being an NMP, they trade 53% (i.e., $\exp(0.423) - 1 = 53\%$) more than the baseline case. The dyads with both countries being NMPs trade 45% (i.e., $\exp(0.371) - 1 = 45\%$) more than the baseline case. If only one country in a dyad is a formal member, with the other being neither a formal member nor an NMP ("outsider"), they actually trade 244% (i.e., $\exp(1.236) - 1 = 244\%$) more than the baseline case (no "trade diversion" effect)! If only one country in a dyad is an NMP, with the other being an outsider, they still trade 17% (i.e., $\exp(0.158) - 1 = 17\%$) more than the baseline case.

Zero trade makes a big difference but still cannot explain the NMP puzzle at the intensive margin (i.e., when only positive trade is included) as in regression (2) of table 4.1. In addition, some unreasonably large coefficients reported in table 4.1 also indicate potential estimation issues with the log-linear specification. To address these concerns, a more appropriate econometric method is considered in subsection 4.2.2.

4.2.2 Poisson Quasi-Maximum Likelihood Estimation

Santos-Silva and Tenreyro (2006) show that taking the logarithm of trade in traditional gravity regressions can create biased estimates because what we are really interested in is the expected trade in levels rather than the expected trade in logarithms. According to Jensen's Inequality, $E(\ln T) \neq \ln E(T)$. The expected value of the logarithm of a random variable depends both on its mean and on the higher-order moments of the distribution. The log-linear gravity regression only picks up the first-order approximation, leaving the higher-order moments in the residual and creating a heteroskedasticity problem. To tackle this problem, Santos-Silva and Tenreyro suggest using the Poisson regression to estimate bilateral trade in levels multiplicatively. This method is also justified by nonparametric tests, as in Henderson and Millimet (2006). The most commonly used conditional mean specification in the Poisson model is $E(T_{ijt}|X_{ijt}) = \exp(X_{ijt}\hat{\beta})$. Note that, to apply the Poisson model, the dependent variable (bilateral trade in this chapter) does not have to be count data. As emphasized by Wooldridge (2002, p. 676), "while the leading application is to count data, the fixed effect Poisson estimator works whenever the conditional mean assumption holds. Therefore, the dependent variable could be a nonnegative continuous variable, or even a binary response if we believe the unobserved effect is multiplicative." Liu (2009) uses this method to show that the GATT has been effective at both intensive and extensive margins.[13]

Based on the Hausman specification test, we choose the country-pair fixed-effect Poisson model as the preferred specification.[14] The results are shown in table 4.2. As in table 4.1, the first three regressions use only positive trade with different GATT membership measures, while the last three regressions use both positive and zero trade.

In table 4.2, regression (1) considers only formal membership. Even with only positive trade, "both formal members" and "one formal member" variables bear positive and negative signs, respectively, as in table 4.1. Unlike table 4.1, the coefficient estimate for "both formal members" is highly significant. The coefficient estimate for "one formal member" is significant in table 4.2, as it was in table 4.1. The results imply that two formal GATT members trade 18.6% (i.e., $\exp(0.171) - 1 = 18.6\%$) more than the baseline case of neither being a formal member ("trade creation" effect). If only one country in a pair is a GATT formal member, they actually trade 11% (i.e., $\exp(0.092) - 1 = 11\%$) less than the baseline case ("trade diversion" effect). These results show that, even at the intensive margin, the GATT has also been effective in promoting world trade when a more appropriate econometric method is used.

Regression (2) distinguishes formal members from NMPs. Even with only positive trade, the Poisson results show that formal members are more liberalized than NMPs at the intensive margin: two formal GATT members on average trade 45% (i.e., $\exp(0.371) - 1 = 45\%$) more than the baseline case of being neither a formal member nor an NMP; formal-NMP dyads trade 30% (i.e., $\exp(0.259) - 1 = 30\%$) more than the baseline category, while two NMPs trade 22% (i.e., $\exp(0.196) - 1 = 22\%$) more than the baseline category. These results indicate a stronger trade-promoting role for formal GATT membership than for NMPs. This is different from what we obtained from the traditional gravity estimation, where NMPs seem to trade even more than formal members (column 2 of table 4.1). The estimated coefficients on the "one formal member" and "one NMP" variables are now both positive, with the former being larger than the latter. The lack of evidence for a trade diversion effect is likely a result of the externalities or a spillover effect of GATT membership.[15]

Table 4.2
Fixed-effect Poisson regressions.

	$T > 0$			Full Sample		
	(1)	(2)	(3)	(4)	(5)	(6)
Both in GATT						
Both formal members	0.171*** (0.000)	0.371*** (0.000)		0.235*** (0.000)	0.467*** (0.000)	
Formal and NMP		0.259*** (0.000)	0.348*** (0.000)		0.303*** (0.000)	0.425*** (0.000)
Both NMPs		0.196*** (0.000)			−0.099*** (0.000)	
Only One in GATT						
One formal member	−0.092*** (0.000)	0.080*** (0.000)	0.073*** (0.000)	−0.010*** (0.000)	0.189*** (0.000)	0.171*** (0.000)
One NMP		0.034*** (0.000)			0.049*** (0.000)	
Log product of GDP	0.243*** (0.000)	0.237*** (0.000)	0.260*** (0.000)	0.409*** (0.000)	0.398*** (0.000)	0.441*** (0.000)
Log product of GDP per capita	0.857*** (0.000)	0.858*** (0.000)	0.841*** (0.000)	0.717*** (0.000)	0.722*** (0.000)	0.688*** (0.000)
Currently colonized	0.533*** (0.000)	0.500*** (0.000)	0.446*** (0.000)	0.299*** (0.000)	0.256*** (0.000)	0.178*** (0.000)
RTA	0.400*** (0.000)	0.398*** (0.000)	0.397*** (0.000)	0.404*** (0.000)	0.401*** (0.000)	0.399*** (0.000)
Currency union	0.710*** (0.000)	0.703*** (0.000)	0.697*** (0.000)	0.780*** (0.000)	0.772*** (0.000)	0.767*** (0.000)
GSP	−0.174*** (0.000)	−0.175*** (0.000)	−0.178*** (0.000)	−0.162*** (0.000)	−0.161*** (0.000)	−0.165*** (0.000)
Observations	312,838	312,838	312,838	533,727	533,727	533,727

Note: All the regressions use year dummies and country-pair fixed effects.
* significant at 10%; ** significant at 5%; *** significant at 1%.

In Poisson regressions, zero trade still matters, as shown by the last three regressions in table 4.2. Regression (4) shows that, with zero trade, the trade creation effect of the GATT is bigger ($\exp(0.235) - 1 = 26.5\%$) than in column 1 (18.6%). Their difference (26.5% − 18.6% = 7.9%) can be taken as the effect of the GATT at the extensive margin, and it is close to one-third of the total impact. When NMPs are considered, column 5 shows that two formal GATT members trade 60% (i.e., $\exp(0.467) - 1 = 60\%$) more than the baseline case of being neither a formal member nor an NMP, formal-NMP pairs trade 35% (i.e., $\exp(0.303) - 1 = 35\%$) more than the baseline case, and two NMPs actually trade 10% (i.e., $\exp(0.099) - 1 = 10\%$) *less* than the baseline case.

Combined with the positive coefficient of "both NMPs" in column 2 at the intensive margin, the negative coefficient of "both" in column 5 is driven primarily by the effect at the extensive margin. It implies that, at the extensive margin, NMPs have experienced even slower growth in new trading relations than the default category (outsiders). This is plausible because NMPs are usually relatively smaller developing countries with less diversified trading relationships (e.g., only with former colonizers), so the expansion of their trading relationships has been slower than for other countries, including outsiders. As shown by figure 4.2, NMPs on average have fewer trading partners than for formal members and even outsiders; their average number of trading partners has actually decreased since the 1980s. In addition, the negative effect of an NMP at the extensive margin might be driven by a trade diversion effect of formal WTO membership. When more and more countries joined the WTO officially, this might have diverted the trade of NMPs from other NMPs to formal members. Finally, another factor behind the result can be limited obligations with respect to other NMPs.[16] Overall, these results from Poisson regressions show that NMPs trade significantly less than formal members at both intensive and extensive margins. This result contrasts sharply with the finding by Tomz, Goldstein, and Rivers (2007).

Some robustness checks are also performed using different subsets of countries. These country-pair fixed-effects Poisson regression results are reported in table 4.3. Regression (1) covers the observations with both countries in a pair as developed countries (IFS country code less than 200) and regression (2) covers the cases when both countries are developing countries (IFS country code greater than 200), while regression (3) covers the rest of the sample (i.e., developed and developing countries in a pair).[17] In all the cases, GATT formal membership is estimated to be effective in promoting world trade. The coefficients of the "both NMPs" variable are always smaller than those of "both formal members." Regression (4) uses a sample without communist and Middle East countries, and regression (5) drops micro states, which are defined as countries with average population during 1948–2001 of less than a half million. Our main conclusions still hold in both cases. China is often considered an outlier in cross-country studies. The last regression drops China from the analysis, but this does not change the results much either. In sum, the regression results using different country subsamples are consistent with those using the whole sample, as in column 5 of table 4.2.

Table 4.3
Fixed-effect Poisson regressions, robustness checks.

	(1)	(2)	(3)	(4)	(5)	(6)
	Developed and Developed	Developing and Developed	Developed and Developed	Without Communist\ Middle East	Without Micro States	Without China
Both in GATT						
Both formal members	0.342***	0.502***	0.980***	0.781***	0.474***	0.464***
	(0.000)	(0.000)	(0.000)	(0.000)	(0.000)	(0.000)
Formal and NMP	0.171***	0.207***	0.774***	0.598***	0.310***	0.282***
	(0.000)	(0.000)	(0.000)	(0.000)	(0.000)	(0.000)
Both NMPs	−0.145***	0.139***	0.073***	0.232***	−0.428***	−0.124***
	(0.000)	(0.000)	(0.000)	(0.000)	(0.000)	(0.000)
Only One in GATT						
One formal member	0.252***	0.302***	0.645***	0.414***	0.191***	0.166***
	(0.000)	(0.000)	(0.000)	(0.000)	(0.000)	(0.000)
One NMP	−0.301***	0.092***	−0.096***	0.354***	−0.076***	−0.014***
	(0.000)	(0.000)	(0.000)	(0.000)	(0.000)	(0.000)
Log product of GDP	−0.177***	1.104***	0.766***	0.104***	0.371***	0.381***
	(0.000)	(0.000)	(0.000)	(0.000)	(0.000)	(0.000)
Log product of GDP per capita	1.547***	−0.097***	0.448***	0.967***	0.760***	0.694***
	(0.000)	(0.000)	(0.000)	(0.000)	(0.000)	(0.000)
Currently colonized			0.167***	0.190***	0.249***	0.265***
			(0.000)	(0.000)	(0.000)	(0.000)
RTA	0.326***	0.227***	0.750***	0.383***	0.399***	0.403***
	(0.000)	(0.000)	(0.000)	(0.000)	(0.000)	(0.000)
Currency union	0.702***	1.547***	0.858***	0.750***	0.763***	0.769***
	(0.000)	(0.000)	(0.000)	(0.000)	(0.000)	(0.000)
GSP	−0.095***	0.133***	−0.160***	−0.207***	−0.167***	−0.188***
	(0.000)	(0.000)	(0.000)	(0.000)	(0.000)	(0.000)
Observations	18,098	324,637	190,992	365,277	398,512	525,505

Notes: Standard errors are in parentheses. Developed countries are those with an IFS country code less than 200, with the rest developing countries. Communist countries are those with an IFS country code greater than 900. Middle East includes Bahrain, Cyprus, Iran, Iraq, Israel, Jordan, Kuwait, Lebanon, Oman, Qatar, Saudi Arabia, Syria, United Arab Emirates, and Yemen. Micro states are defined as countries with an average population of less than a half million from 1948 to 2001. * significant at 10%; ** significant at 5%; *** significant at 1%.

4.2.3 Alternative Econometric Methods

In this subsection, we consider some alternative ways to address zero trade and discuss some recent developments in gravity specification.

Tobit regressions may be used to address zero trade as a corner solution problem, as in Felbermayr and Kohler (2006). This method relies crucially on the assumptions of homoscedastic and normal residuals. If either of these assumptions fails, the entire functional form of the conditional mean in Tobit will change. Nevertheless, we have tried this method to show the robustness of our findings. Table 4.4 shows the results from country-pair random-effects Tobit regression with both positive and zero trade.[18] We also include many time-invariant variables at the country or dyad level. Please refer to the footnote of table 4.4 and Liu (2009) for more details about the construction and data sources of these variables.

The estimation of random-effects Tobit regression is computationally cumbersome because it uses quadrature to approximate the integrals in the likelihood function. To reduce the estimation time, we keep only the data sampled at five-year intervals: 1950, 1955, 1960, 1965, 1970, 1975, 1980, 1985, 1990, 1995, and 2000. For each specification of the GATT variables, we report the marginal effects on the unconditional expected value of $\ln(T)$ in the first three columns and the marginal effects on the probability of positive trade in the last three columns of table 4.4. Although both positive and zero trade observations are covered by these regressions, the sample size is smaller than in previous regressions because only the data at five-year intervals are used.

The results in the first three columns of table 4.4 show that the marginal effects of *"both formal members," "formal and NMP,"* and *"one formal member"* on trade are even bigger than those from the log-linear regressions reported in the last three columns of table 4.1. The marginal effects of *"both NMPs"* and *"one NMP"* on trade, as shown by column 2, are actually negative and significant. These results are consistent with the Poisson regression results in column 5 of table 4.2. As for the marginal effects on the probability of positive trade, the same pattern holds in the last three columns. Column 5 shows that, all other things being equal, two formal GATT members are 10% (i.e., $\exp(0.094) - 1 = 10\%$) more likely to trade with each other than for the baseline case of being neither a formal member nor an NMP, while two NMPs are actually 9% (i.e., $\exp(0.084) = 9\%$) *less* likely to trade with each other compared to the baseline case.

Using separate dummies for each RTA to account for potentially heterogeneous effects of different RTAs, Eicher and Henn (2011) find no

Table 4.4
Random-effects Tobit regressions (marginal effects), full sample.

	$\partial E(\ln T)/\partial X$			$\partial P(T>0)/\partial X$		
	(1)	(2)	(3)	(4)	(5)	(6)
Both in GATT						
Both formal members	2.159*** (0.067)	2.085*** (0.112)		0.100*** (0.003)	0.097*** (0.005)	
Formal and NMP		0.450*** (0.113)	1.090*** (0.103)		0.022*** (0.005)	0.054*** (0.005)
Both NMPs		−1.662*** (0.146)			−0.094*** (0.009)	
Only One in GATT						
One formal member	1.881*** (0.065)	1.671*** (0.104)	0.784*** (0.099)	0.086*** (0.003)	0.078*** (0.005)	0.038*** (0.005)
One NMP		−1.526*** (0.111)			−0.084*** (0.007)	
Log product of GDP	1.791*** (0.021)	1.756*** (0.021)	1.919*** (0.020)	0.088*** (0.001)	0.087*** (0.001)	0.095*** (0.001)
Log product of GDP per capita	0.533*** (0.030)	0.534*** (0.030)	0.439*** (0.030)	0.026*** (0.001)	0.026*** (0.001)	0.022*** (0.001)
Log product of area	−0.349*** (0.017)	−0.339*** (0.017)	−0.362*** (0.017)	−0.017*** (0.001)	−0.017*** (0.001)	−0.018*** (0.001)
Log distance	−2.396*** (0.048)	−2.444*** (0.048)	−2.412*** (0.048)	−0.118*** (0.002)	−0.121*** (0.002)	−0.119*** (0.002)
Land border	0.699** (0.269)	0.741** (0.266)	0.516 (0.268)	0.033** (0.012)	0.035** (0.012)	0.024* (0.012)
Landlocked	−0.792*** (0.070)	−0.833*** (0.070)	−0.707*** (0.070)	−0.039*** (0.003)	−0.041*** (0.003)	−0.035*** (0.003)
Island	0.225** (0.080)	0.222** (0.080)	0.033 (0.080)	0.011** (0.004)	0.011** (0.004)	0.002 (0.004)
Common language	1.232*** (0.119)	1.222*** (0.118)	1.221*** (0.119)	0.057*** (0.005)	0.057*** (0.005)	0.056*** (0.005)
Ever colonized	2.549*** (0.377)	2.323*** (0.375)	2.526*** (0.379)	0.103*** (0.012)	0.096*** (0.013)	0.102*** (0.012)
Currently colonized	−0.916 (0.634)	−1.325* (0.611)	−1.610** (0.599)	−0.049 (0.036)	−0.073 (0.038)	−0.091* (0.039)
Common colonizer	0.707*** (0.119)	0.676*** (0.119)	0.654*** (0.119)	0.034*** (0.005)	0.032*** (0.005)	0.031*** (0.005)
Common country	−0.464 (2.826)	−0.830 (2.731)	−1.530 (2.585)	−0.024 (0.151)	−0.044 (0.155)	−0.086 (0.165)
RTA	−0.063 (0.089)	−0.087 (0.089)	−0.117 (0.089)	−0.003 (0.004)	−0.004 (0.004)	−0.006 (0.004)

(continued)

Table 4.4
(continued)

	$\partial E(\ln T)/\partial X$			$\partial P(T > 0)/\partial X$		
	(1)	(2)	(3)	(4)	(5)	(6)
Currency union	3.978***	3.977***	4.152***	0.145***	0.145***	0.150**
	(0.248)	(0.246)	(0.249)	(0.006)	(0.006)	(0.006)
GSP	0.867***	0.958***	0.878***	0.041***	0.045***	0.041**
	(0.068)	(0.068)	(0.068)	(0.003)	(0.003)	(0.003)
Observations	115,143	115,143	115,143	115,143	115,143	115,143

Notes: Years covered are 1950, 1955, 1960, 1965, 1970, 1975, 1980, 1985, 1990, 1995, and 2000. All the regressions use year dummies and country-pair random effects. *Distance* is the great circle distance between two countries in a dyad; *Area* is the geographic area of a country; the *Land border* dummy equals 1 if two countries in a dyad share a land border; *Landlocked* is the number of landlocked nations in a dyad (0, 1, or 2); *Island* is the number of island nations in a dyad (0, 1, or 2); the *Common language* dummy equals 1 if two countries in a dyad share a common language; the *Ever colonized* dummy equals 1 if one of the countries in a dyad was ever a colony of the other country; the *Common colonizer* dummy equals 1 if two countries in a dyad had ever been colonized by the same colonizer; the *Common country* dummy equals 1 if two countries in a dyad had ever been parts of the same country.
* significant at 10%; ** significant at 5%; *** significant at 1%.

significant trade-promoting effect of the WTO. However, they consider only about a dozen major RTAs, although there are hundreds of others. I have tried adding to the regressions more than 150 separate RTA dummies. The fixed-effect log-linear regression results are reported in table 4.5.[19] The results still suggest that formal WTO membership matters more than informal membership once zero trade flows are included in regressions, despite some quite significant changes in the estimated coefficients.

Helpman, Melitz, and Rubinstein (2008) propose a two-step procedure to consider both firm heterogeneity and selection bias in gravity model estimation. They apply this method primarily to cross-section data in 1986.[20] We apply their method to the panel data sampled at five-year intervals from 1950 to 2000, as well as the cross-section data for each of these years. We include exporter and importer fixed effects in both stages and adopt the same regulation cost variables as instruments, but do not achieve reasonable estimates. Most of the covariates, including the sum of GDPs and distance variables, are surprisingly insignificant. These results are not reported in the tables but are available upon request.[21]

To facilitate the comparisons between our results and those in Rose (2004) and Tomz, Goldstein, and Rivers (2007), this chapter sticks closely to their setup in both data and gravity specification. To control

Table 4.5
Log-linear gravity regressions with country-pair fixed effects (separate RTA dummies).

	$T > 0$			Full Sample		
	(1)	(2)	(3)	(4)	(5)	(6)
Both in GATT						
Both formal members	−0.120	0.257		1.697***	1.596***	
	(0.081)	(0.173)		(0.304)	(0.536)	
Formal and NMP		0.407**	0.407**		−0.096	0.928*
		(0.180)	(0.161)		(0.577)	(0.504)
Both NMPs		0.683***			−0.337	
		(0.264)			(0.783)	
Only One in GATT						
One formal member	−0.389***	−0.035		0.494*	0.412	
	(0.076)	(0.159)	0.071	(0.254)	(0.505)	0.313
One NMP		0.493**	(0.151)		0.014	(0.485)
		(0.231)			(0.691)	
Log product of GDP	0.627***	0.612***	0.541***	0.955	0.974	1.080*
	(0.192)	(0.197)	(0.194)	(0.605)	(0.612)	(0.610)
Log product of GDP	0.230	0.260	0.320	0.527	0.497	0.509
per capita	(0.223)	(0.230)	(0.225)	(0.621)	(0.634)	(0.634)
GSP	−0.124	−0.120	−0.133	−0.472	−0.475	−0.382
	(0.143)	(0.143)	(0.141)	(0.470)	(0.470)	(0.476)
Observations	313,695	313,695	313,695	544,195	544,195	544,195

Notes: All the regressions use year dummies and country-pair fixed effects. Robust standard errors are in parentheses.
* significant at 10%; ** significant at 5%; *** significant at 1%.

for the "multilateral resistance" term in the theories of gravity model, as in Anderson and van Wincoop (2003), we include in the regressions some time-varying country variables, such as GDP and per capita GDP. We have also tried adding a "remoteness" variable, which is defined as the distance to the rest of the world weighted by all the other countries' GDPs in a given year. The results change little with this variable. Baier and Bergstrand (2009) use simulations to show that ad hoc remoteness variables are actually of little use in the gravity equation. Baldwin and Taglioni (2006), among others, suggest that time-varying country fixed effects can fully absorb the "multilateral resistance" effects in a panel data gravity regression. However, it is often computationally cumbersome and impossible to run regressions with such a large number of dummies. This method often offers unreasonable estimates possibly, possibly because of overcorrection by the time-varying country dummies (see, e.g., Clark et al. 2004;

Liu 2009). We did try including these dummies as well as country-pair fixed effects with the data sampled at ten-year intervals, but obtained unreasonably large and negative GATT effects.[22] Given that most major trading nations have already joined the GATT, much of the effect of the GATT might be picked up by these time-varying country dummies, which can magnify the effect of noise in the data and make it difficult to identify the effect of the GATT.

4.3 Conclusions

To address the "ineffectiveness puzzle" of the GATT raised by Rose (2004), Tomz, Goldstein, and Rivers (2007) consider the measurement error in formal GATT memberships. After considering the nonmember participants (NMPs) of the GATT, they find a much larger positive impact of the GATT on trade and that NMPs trade even more than formal members. Tomz, Goldstein, and Rivers (2007) gives the right answer to the questions it is designed to address. It contributes to the understanding of the measurement of GATT membership. It is difficult, however, to understand why the NMPs should trade even more than formal members. Rose is also skeptical about this result. In a survey paper, Rose (2010) says that "another uncomfortable feature of the results of Tomz et al. is that *informal participation* in the GATT consistently matters more for trade than *formal membership*. This doesn't seem wholly plausible to me (at least not without some explanation), and is a cause for concern. I simply don't understand why informal participation could create more trade than actual membership in the GATT." Rose (2010) also mentions the conflicting results between Tomz, Goldstein, and Rivers (2007) and Subramanian and Wei (2007). Tomz, Goldstein, and Rivers argue that the NMPs, mostly developing countries, seem to trade more than outsiders, while Subramanian and Wei say that the GATT is effective only for developed countries, not developing ones.

In this chapter, we have addressed both the "ineffectiveness puzzle" raised by Rose and the "NMP puzzle" raised by Tomz, Goldstein, and Rivers simultaneously. Estimating the gravity model using the Poisson regressions and a large dataset covering both positive and zero bilateral trade flows, we have shown that the GATT has been very effective at both the intensive and extensive margins, and NMPs turn out to be less liberalized than formal members, as we would expect. This chapter thus demonstrates the importance of considering zero trade flows and gravity model specification.

Appendix

Table 4.A1
Log-linear gravity regression, pooled data.

	T > 0			Full Sample		
	(1)	(2)	(3)	(4)	(5)	(6)
Both in GATT						
Both formal members	−0.046*** (0.010)	0.294*** (0.018)		1.711*** (0.022)	1.952*** (0.037)	
Formal and NMP		0.440*** (0.020)	0.354*** (0.018)		0.613*** (0.038)	1.284*** (0.035)
Both NMPs		1.311*** (0.042)			0.034 (0.052)	
Only One in GATT						
One formal member	−0.253*** (0.011)	0.074*** (0.018)	0.097*** (0.018)	1.116*** (0.022)	1.320*** (0.036)	0.823*** (0.035)
One NMP		0.239*** (0.027)			−0.487*** (0.041)	
Log product of GDP	0.913*** (0.002)	0.920*** (0.002)	0.907*** (0.002)	1.562*** (0.005)	1.558*** (0.005)	1.660*** (0.005)
Log product of GDP per capita	0.368*** (0.003)	0.359*** (0.003)	0.365*** (0.003)	0.802*** (0.007)	0.787*** (0.007)	0.736*** (0.008)
Log product of area	−0.085*** (0.002)	−0.082*** (0.002)	−0.083*** (0.002)	−0.240*** (0.004)	−0.236*** (0.004)	−0.245*** (0.004)
Log distance	−1.107*** (0.005)	−1.115*** (0.005)	−1.119*** (0.005)	−2.257*** (0.011)	−2.277*** (0.011)	−2.285*** (0.011)
Land border	0.576*** (0.023)	0.589*** (0.023)	0.593*** (0.023)	0.763*** (0.066)	0.776*** (0.066)	0.691*** (0.066)

(continued)

Table 4.A1
(continued)

	T > 0			Full Sample		
	(1)	(2)	(3)	(4)	(5)	(6)
Landlocked	-0.412***	-0.403***	-0.415***	-0.689***	-0.700***	-0.640***
	(0.008)	(0.008)	(0.008)	(0.016)	(0.016)	(0.016)
Island	0.045***	0.017**	0.039***	0.203***	0.170***	0.062***
	(0.008)	(0.008)	(0.008)	(0.018)	(0.018)	(0.018)
Common language	0.398***	0.398***	0.409***	0.963***	0.952***	0.947***
	(0.012)	(0.012)	(0.012)	(0.025)	(0.025)	(0.025)
Ever colonized	1.311***	1.314***	1.297***	2.209***	2.145***	2.192***
	(0.021)	(0.021)	(0.021)	(0.060)	(0.060)	(0.060)
Currently colonized	1.301***	1.279***	1.306***	-0.659*	-0.923**	-1.248***
	(0.094)	(0.093)	(0.094)	(0.385)	(0.386)	(0.385)
Common colonizer	0.457***	0.433***	0.438***	0.872***	0.821***	0.812***
	(0.013)	(0.013)	(0.013)	(0.026)	(0.026)	(0.026)
Common country	0.410*	0.412**	0.453**	0.552	0.311	-0.417
	(0.202)	(0.200)	(0.201)	(0.561)	(0.561)	(0.556)
RTA	0.643***	0.629***	0.617***	1.198***	1.166***	1.207***
	(0.013)	(0.013)	(0.013)	(0.031)	(0.031)	(0.031)
Currency union	0.868***	0.820***	0.826***	1.927***	1.926***	2.061***
	(0.024)	(0.024)	(0.024)	(0.053)	(0.053)	(0.053)
GSP	0.801***	0.794***	0.777***	2.841***	2.803***	2.887***
	(0.009)	(0.009)	(0.009)	(0.021)	(0.021)	(0.021)
Observations	313,695	313,695	313,695	544,195	544,195	544,195
R-squared	0.64	0.64	0.64	0.50	0.50	0.50

Notes: All the regressions use year dummies. Robust standard errors are in parentheses.
* significant at 10%; ** significant at 5%; *** significant at 1%.

Notes

I thank Alejandro Riaño, Robert Staiger, Benjamin Zissimos, and other participants at the 2015 CESifo Venice Summer Workshop on "The WTO and Economic Development" for comments and suggestions. All remaining errors are mine.

1. The trade data are based on the dataset used by Liu (2009).

2. Detailed definitions of these categories can be found in the footnote to figure 4.1.

3. This is based on the GDP and population data from standard sources as used in Liu (2009).

4. Country size may be related to the effectiveness of the GATT/WTO on trade, but the theoretical prediction can go either way. For example, Anderson and van Wincoop (2003, Implication 1) show in their comparative statics exercise that, conditioning on country size, big countries that liberalize are likely to have larger trade effects than small countries that liberalize. Shackmurove and Spiegel (2004), on the other hand, show in a duopoly model that a small country benefits more from the large market size of the integrated economy. Cabrales and Motta (2001) argue that large countries are more likely to become leaders after trade liberalization, but this can be reversed if small countries have huge cost advantages.

5. Rose (2004) drops zero trade because of his concern about missing regressor data for small countries. In a later survey paper, Rose (2010) discusses this issue and correctly envisions the possible effects of sample selection on the results of Tomz, Goldstein, and Rivers (2007), although he does not take this into account in his data.

6. A country is considered a trade partner of country A as long as country A imports from this country in a given year.

7. This was true before the Uruguay Round, which was completed in 1994. After that, the rule of "single undertaking" was adopted, meaning that all agreements were to apply to all members, and all members were to submit schedules of concessions and commitments. The special and differential treatments, however, still apply as stated explicitly in the Punta del Este Ministerial Declarations (GATT 1986, p. 7). Besides GATT Article XXXVI.8, other similar provisions regarding a de facto member status related to decolonization include Article XXVI.5(c) and Article XXXIII, as discussed by Tomz, Goldstein, and Rivers (2007).

8. The dependent variable is the total trade between two countries in a given year. Subramanian and Wei (2007), among others, suggest using only import data. No matter whether total trade or only import data are used, the main conclusions in this chapter always hold. Therefore, this chapter follows Rose and Tomz, Goldstein, and Rivers and uses total trade for easy comparison between our results and theirs.

9. Liu (2009) has data for 1948–2003. To be consistent with Rose (2004) and Tomz, Goldstein, and Rivers (2007), the last two years are not used in this chapter.

10. There are 175 countries in Rose (2004) and Tomz, Goldstein, and Rivers (2007).

11. More details on these data and sources can be found in Rose (2004), Tomz, Goldstein, and Rivers (2007), and Liu (2009).

12. The measurement error created is small because the unit of measurement of trade flows is *one* dollar.

13. The Gamma Pseudo Maximum Likelihood (GPML) method has also been used to address the zero trade issue in the literature. Santos-Silva and Tenreyro (2011), however, find that the GPML has a larger bias than the Poisson estimation. Martinez-Zarzaso (2013) also shows that the GPML estimation can be imprecise when the variance function is misspecified or the log-scale residuals have high kurtosis. We take Poisson estimation to be the preferred method in this chapter.

14. As shown by Wooldridge (1999), the fixed-effect Poisson estimator is consistent as long as the conditional mean assumption holds. The distribution of the dependent variable given X and the fixed-effects components is entirely unrestricted. In particular, this estimator is still consistent under overdispersion or underdispersion, and there is no restriction on the serial correlation of the dependent variable over time.

15. For example, countries may extend their MFN tariffs to many non-WTO members. For example, China enjoyed a "normal trading relationship" with the United States and some other WTO members for a long time before its formal entry into the WTO. As another example, an agreement signed at the Hong Kong WTO Ministerial Meetings allowed tariff-free access to WTO member markets for 97% of imported products from the world's 50 least-developed countries by 2008.

16. As Tomz, Goldstein, and Rivers (2007) document, Article XXXV [was] a clause signatories sometimes used to limit their obligations with respect to another signatory. Article XXXV states that the GATT "shall not apply as between any contracting party and any other contracting party if: (a) the two contracting parties have not entered into tariff negotiations with each other, and (b) either of the contracting parties, at the time either becomes a contracting party, does not consent to such application." They show that the use of this article by one country in a dyad reduces the benefit of the GATT by half on average, and the use of the article by both countries in a dyad wipes out the benefit completely. They also mention that some NMPs, such as provisional members, do not possess negotiating rights, which might have limited the obligations of concessions made between NMPs.

17. The definitions for developed and developing countries follow Rose (2004) and Tomz, Goldstein, and Rivers (2007). Developed countries, including Switzerland, Japan, Iceland, Malta, and Yugoslavia, were NMPs for some years during 1953–1965.

18. No fixed-effect Tobit procedure is available, as there is no sufficient statistic allowing the fixed effects to be conditioned out of the likelihood.

19. CU is also replaced with individual customs union dummies in the regressions. The dummy for current colonial relationship is dropped from the regressions because of collinearity, probably with some of the newly added RTA or CU dummies. The dyad fixed-effect Poisson regressions cannot converge with so many separate RTA dummies.

20. They do try using multiple years in the 1980s without including country-pair fixed effects or some traditional time-varying covariates (e.g., GDP and GDP per capita). Country-pair fixed effects could be included in the second stage, but this will introduce some complication into the first-stage probit regression. In probit, only random-effects regression is available, and this can complicate the probability prediction.

21. Santos-Silva and Tenreyro (2015) argue that this two-step estimation procedure is only valid under strong distributional assumptions, which are rejected by statistical tests. Moreover, their numerical experiments show that the two-stage estimator is very sensitive to departures from the assumption of homoscedasticity. In addition, we conjecture

that this can also be caused by the lack of good instrumental variables. Conceptually, it is difficult to find a valid instrument that is related to decision to trade but uncorrelated with the volume of trade. The regulation cost variables are often insignificant in the first stage. As shown by Bound, Jaeger, and Baker (1995), weak instruments in the first stage can lead to inaccurate estimation in the second stage.

22. The coefficients of *"both formal members," "both NMPs," "formal and NMP," "one formal member,"* and *"one NMP"* are -8.17, -4.33, -2.35, -4.10, and -2.41, respectively, and significant.

References

Anderson, J., and E. van Wincoop. 2003. "Gravity with Gravitas: A Solution to the Border Puzzle." *American Economic Review* 93(1): 170–192.

Bagwell, K., and R. W. Staiger. 1999. "An Economic Theory of GATT." *American Economic Review* 89(1): 215–248.

Bagwell, K., and R. W. Staiger. 2003. *The Economics of the World Trading System.* Cambridge, MA: MIT Press.

Baier, S. L., and J. H. Bergstrand. 2009. "Bonus Vetus OLS: A Simple Method for Approximating International Trade-Cost Effects Using the Gravity Equation." *Journal of International Economics* 77(1): 77–85.

Baldwin, R., and D. Taglioni. 2006. "Gravity for Dummies and Dummies for Gravity Equations." Working Paper. Graduate Institute of International Studies (HEI).

Bound, J., D. A. Jaeger, and R. Baker. 1995. "Problems with Instrumental Variables Estimation When the Correlation between the Instruments and the Endogenous Explanatory Variables Is Weak." *Journal of the American Statistical Association* 90(430): 443–450.

Cabrales, A., and M. Motta. 2001. "Country Asymmetries, Endogenous Product Choice and the Timing of Trade Liberalization." *European Economic Review* 45(1): 87–107.

Clark, P., N. Tamirisa, S.-J. Wei, A. Sadikov, and L. Zeng. 2004. "Exchange Rate Volatility and Trade Flows—Some New Evidence." IMF Policy Paper. Washington, DC: International Monetary Fund.

Eicher, Theo S., and Christian Henn. 2011. "In Search of WTO Trade Effects: Preferential Trade Agreements Promote Trade Strongly, but Unevenly." *Journal of International Economics* 83(2): 137–153.

Felbermayr, G. J., and W. Kohler. 2008. "Exploring the Intensive and Extensive Margins of World Trade." *Review of World Economics* 142(4): 642–674.

General Agreement on Tariffs and Trade (GATT). 1986. "Punta del Este Ministerial Declarations." http://www.sice.oas.org/trade/punta_e.asp.

Helpman, E., M. Melitz, and Y. Rubinstein. 2008. "Estimating Trade Flows: Trading Partners and Trading Volumes. " *Quarterly Journal of Economics* 123(2): 441–487.

Henderson, D. J., and D. L. Millimet. 2006. "Is Gravity Linear?" *Journal of Applied Econometrics* 23(2): 137–172.

Hoekman, B., and M. Kostecki. 1995. *The Political Economy of the World Trading System: From GATT to WTO*. Oxford: Oxford University Press.

Liu, X. 2009. "GATT/WTO Promotes Trade Strongly: Sample Selection and Model Specification." *Review of International Economics* 17(3): 428–446.

Maggi, G., and A. Rodríguez-Clare. 1998. "The Value of Trade Agreements in the Presence of Political Pressures." *Journal of Political Economy* 106(3): 574–601.

Martinez-Zarzoso, I. 2013. "The Log of Gravity Revisited." *Applied Economics* 45(3): 311–327.

Mitra, D. 2002. "Endogenous Political Organization and the Value of Trade Agreements." *Journal of International Economics* 57(2): 473–485.

Rose, A. K. 2004. "Do We Really Know That the WTO Increases Trade?" *American Economic Review* 94(1): 98–114.

Rose, A. K. 2007. "Do We Really Know That the WTO Increases Trade? Reply." *American Economic Review* 97(5): 2019–2025.

Rose, A. K. 2010. "The Effect of Membership in the GATT/WTO on Trade: Where Do We Stand?" In Z. Drabek (ed.), *Is the World Trade Organization Attractive Enough for Emerging Economies?* London: Palgrave Macmillan.

Santos-Silva, S., and S. Tenreyro. 2006. "The Log of Gravity." *Review of Economics and Statistics* 88(4): 641–658.

Santos-Silva, S., and S. Tenreyro. 2011. "Further Simulation Evidence on the Performance of the Poisson-PML Estimator." *Economics Letters* 112(2): 220–222.

Santos-Silva, S., and S. Tenreyro. 2015. "Trading Partners and Trading Volumes: Implementing the Helpman–Melitz–Rubinstein Model Empirically." *Oxford Bulletin of Economics and Statistics* 77(1): 93–105.

Shackmurove, Y., and U. Spiegel. 2004. "Size Does Matter: International Trade and Population Size." PIER Working Paper Archive 04-035, Penn Institute for Economic Research, Department of Economics. Philadelphia: University of Pennsylvania.

Staiger, R. W., and G. Tabellini. 1987. "Discretionary Trade Policy and Excessive Protection." *American Economic Review* 77(5): 823–837.

Staiger, R. W., and G. Tabellini. 1999. "Do GATT Rules Help Governments Make Domestic Commitments?" *Economics and Politics* 11(2): 109–144.

Subramanian, A., and S.-J. Wei. 2007. "The WTO Promotes Trade, Strongly but Unevenly." *Journal of International Economics* 72(1): 151–175.

Tomz, M., J. Goldstein, and D. Rivers. 2007. "Do We Really Know That the WTO Increases Trade? Comment." *American Economic Review* 97(5): 2005–2018.

Wooldridge, J. 1999. "Distribution-Free Estimation of Some Nonlinear Panel Data Models." *Journal of Econometrics* 90(1): 77–97.

Wooldridge, J. 2002. *Econometric Analysis of Cross Section and Panel Data*. Cambridge, MA: MIT Press.

5 Opportunities for Cooperation in Removing Prohibitive Trade Barriers

David R. DeRemer

5.1 Introduction

This chapter provides a distinct theory of how nations can achieve cooperation in eliminating prohibitive trade barriers. New theory is valuable here because such cooperation is not possible in the canonical two-good model of trade agreements with perfect competition and political economy (Bagwell and Staiger 1999, 2011). In the canonical model, cooperation in reducing import tariffs is possible only for industries for which trade already exists under noncooperative policies. That model permits extreme political economy forces that could cause governments to impose prohibitive protection for import-competing industries, but under such forces, the unilateral preference for prohibitive protection must imply a joint preference for prohibitive protection.[1] The possibility that cooperation can eliminate prohibitive barriers has been relatively unexplored.[2]

Cooperation in eliminating prohibitive trade barriers, particularly services trade barriers, is important for economic for development. Presently, trade barriers are higher for developing countries than for developed countries in goods (Kee, Nicita, and Olarreaga 2009) and in services (Jafari and Tarr 2017). The importance of removing services trade barriers for growth and development is the focus of a seminal survey by Francois and Hoekman (2010). The authors remark, "Evidence from the literature on both OECD and developing countries strongly suggests that producer services, in particular, play a critical role in productivity growth in general, including manufacturing competitiveness. The contribution of services in this regard is closely related to patterns of market segmentation, openness, and trade" (Francois and Hoekman 2010, p. 644). Consequently, distortions in global services trade are significant barriers to growth and development. Trade barriers in services often take the form of restrictions rather than tariffs in developing countries (Borchert, Gootiiz, and Mattoo 2014). For example, Laos, Nepal, and Zambia maintain barriers that limit foreign entry into telecommunications and air transport, and these restrictions exacerbate their economic isolation and enable monopoly and government rents (Borchert, et al. 2017). Though the WTO has achieved some success in reducing services trade barriers, most notably through China's WTO accession protocol (Mattoo 2004; Miroudot, Sauvage, and Shepherd 2013), overall there has been much less cooperation in services trade than in goods trade (Francois and Hoekman 2010). Theory focusing on cooperation over prohibitive barriers, more common in services, can then be helpful in addressing the challenges of services trade liberalization.

Prohibitive trade barriers are also relevant for import substitution industrialization (ISI), the textbook example of developing-country protectionism. Often associated with Latin American and Indian trade policy in the 1950s and 1960s, ISI sought to protect "infant" industries (Krugman, Obtsfeld, and Melitz 2014, chapter 11). Latin American ISI policy had an "emphasis on autarky" that limited integration even within the continent (Baer 1972). Whether such trade protection overall promoted industrial development is still debated (Rodrik 2001). Such trade protection fell into disrepute among policymakers in the 1980s, though some firms born in this era still survive and thrive (e.g., Brazil's Embraer in aircraft and Marcopolo S.A. in bus bodies). The chapter's theory helps to illuminate when developing countries could achieve cooperation in trade while seeking to promote such national champions. Such cooperation is important to free resources for development by reducing distortions from ill-advised promotion of national champions.

To develop theory for cooperation in eliminating prohibitive policies, there first must be an explanation for why governments would unilaterally impose prohibitive protection. We do not focus on models that rationalize the infant industry argument, because the success of infant industry policy has been questionable. Instead we model governments that weigh profits of particular firms in excess of national-income maximization, as is common practice in the trade agreement literature. Such a weight could result from government's political desire to promote a national champion like Embraer or a monopoly providing services. The best policies to maximize such government preferences are domestic subsidies (Dixit 1985), but developing nations are more likely to lack the state capacity for such transfers (Besley and Persson 2009).[3] Absent such subsidies, governments can use import protection to shift profits from abroad to favored domestic firms. The government trade policy choice thus imposes a profit-shifting externality on the trading partner, as in Venables (1985). This externality is distinct from the terms-of-trade externality that is the focus of the canonical trade agreement model. Because of the additional profit-shifting externality, cooperation over prohibitive trade policies may be possible, depending on how much governments value the profits.

This chapter's formal contribution is to solve for the political parameters in a two-country model such that prohibitive policies are unilaterally optimal for each government but free trade is jointly optimal for both governments. The model is then extended to consider how market characteristics affect the possibility of liberalization when prohibitive policies are unilaterally optimal. The chapter thus provides a comprehensive framework that could be used to evaluate which sectors have the greatest potential for cooperative gains from a starting point of prohibitive trade barriers.

To model cooperation in eliminating prohibitive policies, this chapter adopts a partial equilibrium framework of two countries with Cournot firms competing in segmented markets. The firms have constant marginal production costs and iceberg trade costs. Consumer demand for the Cournot product is linear with a choke price, and we can endogenize whether governments choose prohibitive barriers. Cournot competition is a typical choice for modeling import restrictions that shift rents between nations (e.g., Venables 1985). Though the model is stylized, it has relevance for trade both in goods and in services, though the parameter interpretation can differ across sectors. The trade cost for goods is easily interpreted as a transport cost, while the trade cost for services can be interpreted as a relative inefficiency for a domestic firm serving a foreign market.[4] The appropriateness and robustness of the model are discussed further in section 5.2.

Results are first derived for a baseline case in which marginal costs of production are equal across firms and destinations. In this setting, prohibitive policies are not optimal if governments maximize national income, but governments will impose a prohibitive policy if they assign an additional 50% weight on firm profits. It must still be verified that such political preferences do not also imply that barriers are jointly preferable to no barriers. We find that liberalization is desirable as long as the political weight is not considerably larger.

The model extensions in section 5.3 yield testable predictions for when trade cooperation is feasible. The model allows for three possible outcomes, depending on the governments' political weight on firm profit: (1) for a sufficiently low weight, governments always impose nonprohibitive policies; (2) for an intermediate weight, governments choose prohibitive policies noncooperatively and free trade cooperatively; and (3) for a sufficiently large weight, governments always choose prohibitive policies. The model can then help us identify the relative likelihood of being in state (2) conditional on observing that we may be in either state (2) or state (3); that is the relative likelihood of cooperative liberalization given that we are currently observing prohibitive policies. The model predicts how this likelihood varies conditional on market characteristics, which are likely to be more transparent than estimated parameters of a government's objective function.

The first extension considered here is symmetric trade costs. When trade costs are higher, the prohibitive tariff level is lower. Trade costs then lower the cutoff of the political parameter necessary to rationalize the imposition of prohibitive trade barriers. The larger the trade cost, the narrower the parameter range for which nations could cooperate even if prohibitive policies are unilaterally optimal. Though trade costs make a potential agreement less harmful to domestic profits, they make the agreement less appealing both in terms of consumer welfare and export profits. The results provide an explanation for why more distant countries could have more difficulty achieving trade liberalization.

Our baseline case allows for only procompetitive gains from trade, so an interesting extension is the possibility of Ricardian gains from trade when nations have different technologies. We extend the standard model by introducing a second imperfectly competitive sector in each country, and we consider the simplest case of two countries with mirror-image differences in productivity between the two sectors. Relative to the case of equal productivities across industries, a small cross-industry difference in productivity increases the political parameter necessary to rationalize prohibitive policy but causes little effect on the difference in payoffs between free trade and autarky—thus, a sufficiently small difference in productivity leads to less cooperation in eliminating prohibitive barriers. But for sufficiently large differences in productivity, industry profits flatten or even increase following liberalization. When profits increase from liberalization, free trade is preferable to autarky regardless of the political parameter.

We then consider the level of competition in each country, parameterized by the number of symmetric Cournot firms in each nation. We first consider a symmetric increase in competition in each country. This narrows the range of the political parameter for which cooperation is possible. When markets are already competitive, there are limited procompetitive gains from trade, so governments prefer to maintain protection relative to the case in which both nations have limited competition. Liberalization is then possible for national monopolies but impossible for perfect competition in this framework. We also consider the potential for cooperation between a nation with limited competition and a nation with high competition. In the limiting case, as the number of firms in the high-competition nation approaches infinity, there is zero potential for liberalization if prohibitive policies are unilaterally optimal, so the impossibility of liberalization is the same as in the perfectly competitive case.

Lastly, we consider the case of within-country firm heterogeneity in productivity among symmetric countries. The focus is on the simple yet rich case of asymmetry in productivity among two firms in each country. When there is a small asymmetry in productivity, the results approach those from competing duopolies, and with a large asymmetry, the results approach those from competing monopolies. With a more intermediate level of asymmetry, we obtain the most interesting case of firm heterogeneity. In this case, both consumer surplus and industry profits can increase upon cooperation, so liberalization is always preferable to autarky, regardless of political economy considerations. And if industry profits decrease somewhat, very strong political economy considerations are still necessary to rule out the possibility of liberalization. The results suggest that industries with such an intermediate level of heterogeneity are suitable targets for achieving liberalization.

To my knowledge, this is the first work to emphasize a class of two-country models and solve for parameters such that (1) prohibitive policies are unilaterally preferable to nonprohibitive policies and (2) nonprohibitive policies are jointly preferable to prohibitive policies. While the profit-shifting externalities considered here are also the focus of a large body of literature from the 1980s (surveyed in Brander 1995), that literature focuses on maximizing national income. The current chapter finds that for prohibitive tariffs to arise noncooperatively while free trade arises cooperatively, government preferences must depart from standard objectives of maximizing national income. Later literature that considers political-economic preferences (e.g., Bagwell and Staiger 1999) focuses on cases in which the unilaterally optimal import policies are nonprohibitive. More recent trade policy literature with imperfect competition maintains the focus on nonprohibitive policies (e.g., Ossa 2011). The current chapter focuses instead on the corner solutions, and in that sense it relates to Romer (1994) on the importance for development of policy that expands trade in new goods rather than expanding volumes of goods that are already traded. Concurrent work by Staiger and Sykes (2017) on services trade does mention the possibility of cooperation starting from prohibitive policies for a restricted version of their model. The relationship with their paper is discussed in more detail in section 5.2.

Several recent papers assume Cournot competition in addressing other trade agreement issues. Mrázová (2011) was the first to rationalize the principles of reciprocity and nondiscrimination in a Cournot framework. Bagwell and Staiger (2012a) show how a linear Cournot model can rationalize export subsidy bans under free trade, and Bagwell and Staiger (2012b, 2015) focus on how international externalities from imperfect competition can disappear when nations negotiate over both import and export policies. Horn and Levinsohn (2001) consider nations choosing the number of Cournot firms to model coordination over competition policy. Fung and Siu (2008) consider profit-shifting effects of entry restrictions on services. Lebrand (2016) considers agreements regarding a foreign direct investment (FDI) restriction on the number of identical Cournot firms allowed to operate abroad. Deardorff and Stern (2008) also consider profit shifting in the context of services trade when modeling the effects of a unilateral barrier to entry.

Lastly, the chapter mentions other related literature that provides alternative explanations for cooperation in eliminating prohibitive policies. There is literature in which trade agreements allow governments to tie their hands to avoid political pressure from import-competing special interests (Maggi and Rodríguez-Clare 1998, 2007). In such frameworks, political pressure absent an agreement could lead to prohibitive policies, while a trade agreement could commit governments to free trade. Though these papers already provide an explanation for how trade agreements could eliminate prohibitive policies, the legal literature expresses some doubt over whether the commitment theory can plausibly explain cooperation in services trade.[5] There is literature on prohibitive product standards in the presence of consumption externalities (Fischer and Serra 2000; Essaji 2010), but its focus is different from that of the current chapter. This chapter also relates to literature on why Latin American import substitution industrialization ended during macroeconomic crises of the 1980s. This work argues that liberalization can result after crises shift the domestic balance of political power (Drazen and Grilli 1993; Rodrik 1994). Our results suggest that liberalization can occur without any exogenous change that would alter either the unilaterally optimal policies or the jointly optimal policies absent contracting costs—common crises could spur change simply by reducing the costs of coordinating on the cooperative equilibrium.

The rest of the chapter proceeds as follows. Section 5.2 presents the baseline model and then derives the parameter restrictions for which liberalization from prohibitive policies is possible. Section 5.3 explores how various market characteristics affect the potential for trade cooperation. Section 5.4 then concludes by discussing further applications of the framework.

5.2   Model of Prohibitive Trade Policies

This section develops a tractable setting in which countries impose prohibitive trade policies noncooperatively but nonetheless can benefit from trade cooperation.

5.2.1   Baseline Model Structure

The baseline model is partial equilibrium with two countries, each with one firm. There is Cournot competition between firms in the two segmented markets. We call the nations Home and Foreign, with asterisks (*) denoting Foreign variables. Consumer demand is linear with prices $P(Q) = 1 - Q$ and $P^*(Q) = 1 - Q^*$ for aggregate domestic quantity Q and foreign quantity Q^*. The home tariff is τ and the foreign tariff is τ^*, and these are restricted to be nonnegative. Each firm can produce with constant marginal labor requirement c and iceberg trade cost ϕ. As is standard for partial equilibrium, there is an outside sector that is perfectly competitive with a unit labor requirement. Assumptions of costless trade in the outside sector and perfect labor mobility between sectors imply equal wages across sectors and countries, and we pick this wage as the numeraire.

The notation for firm-level variables is as follows. Throughout the chapter, lowercase q denotes the quantity sold by a single firm in a single market, and lowercase π denotes profits of a single firm in a single market. The subscript h is used for Home firms, and f is for Foreign firms. The asterisk (*) denotes outcomes in the Foreign market, while no asterisk denotes outcomes in the Home market. For example, q_f denotes a Foreign firm's exports to the Home market. Home market quantity Q is then the sum of quantities sold by either nation's firms in the Home market, and Q^* is defined similarly for the Foreign market.

Following a large body of political economy literature starting with Baldwin (1987), governments maximize national income, except they assign to firm profits a political economy weight $\alpha \geq 1$. Such preferences can be microfounded through a specific factor that absorbs profits in the outside sector (Helpman and Krugman 1989, section 7.3) and organized lobbying among owners of the specific factor that leads governments to give excess weight to specific factor rewards (Grossman and Helpman 1994). The Home government objective defined over its own import tariff τ, given α and the Foreign import tariff τ^*, takes the form

$$G(\tau; \alpha, \tau^*) = CS(\tau) + \alpha n(\pi_h(\tau) + \pi_f(\tau^*)) + TR(\tau), \tag{5.1}$$

where CS is Home consumer surplus and TR is Home tariff revenue. In our framework with partial equilibrium and segmented markets, the Foreign tariff does not affect Home's consumer surplus, domestic profits, or tariff revenue, and the Home tariff does not affect profits from Home's exports. The Foreign government objective takes a similar form.

Throughout this chapter, we maintain a similar set of assumptions, though we later vary trade costs, the number of firms, and firm productivities. Having laid out the model, this is an appropriate place to discuss the suitability and robustness of its structure.

One natural question is whether our results will be specific to Cournot competition, rather than a more general set of profit-shifting models. Based on related work, we can conclude that the possibility of cooperation eliminating prohibitive policies is not specific to Cournot, or even imperfect, competition. Staiger and Sykes (2017) also remark that cooperation in eliminating prohibitive policies is possible in their model of price-taking service producers, but only under certain restrictions. We consider here the common characteristics between their restricted setting and our model. One explicit similarity is that export subsidies are exogenously absent. A well-established result is that negotiating over both import policies and export policies can eliminate international externalities related to rent shifting (Bagwell and Staiger 2012a, 2012b), though the absence of export policies is a reasonable setting to consider under current WTO law, which prohibits export subsidies, as noted by Ossa (2011).[6] A key logical consequence is that a model in which rent shifting matters for trade agreements must fail to satisfy the conditions for Lerner symmetry—otherwise import and export policies would be equivalent. Failure of Lerner symmetry requires that there be multiple sectors with markups that are not equated by using domestic subsidies (Epifani and Gancia, 2011). Such is the case for any partial equilibrium model featuring a markup from imperfect competition and no corrective subsidies, because the outside sector has no markup.[7] Failure of Lerner symmetry can also be introduced in a perfectly competitive, partial equilibrium economy in which export sectors receive a political economy weight, supply curves slope upward, and firms make short-run profits (Bagwell and Staiger 2016).[8] So, to summarize, the absence of export subsidies and the failure of Lerner symmetry are more essential to our model than the specific mode of competition.

Another natural question is whether results will be sensitive to how we model the choice between prohibitive and nonprohibitive policies. One concern is that nonprohibitive policies might be infeasible—this can be true for certain types of services trade (Francois and Hoekman 2010). A second concern is whether a more appropriate model might involve firms that are unable to cover fixed costs of trade. Robustness here would be particularly important in applying the model to services trade delivered through foreign direct investment rather than exporting, though any exporting could involve fixed costs. A third concern is the extent to which prohibitive policies are maintained through local content requirements for intermediate goods rather than for final goods, and how much the economy's input-output structure matters (see Baer 1972 for specifics on Latin American ISI). Ultimately, the modeling choice here follows Bagwell and Staiger (2012a) in using a Cournot model with linear demand, and the model is highly tractable. Given the dearth of literature on how cooperation can eliminate prohibitive policies, the stylized approach here is a suitable starting point.

The final critical evaluation of the assumptions here relates to textbook criticisms of the strategic trade literature (e.g., Feenstra 2004, chapter 7). One concern is the robustness of our results on optimal unilateral policy, given that optimal unilateral export policy for third-market competition hinges on modeling assumptions.[9] The focus here, however, is on rents for import-competing firms, and there is no similar fragility in the claim that import-competing firms benefit from import protection. Other criticisms of the strategic trade literature include that rent shifting is not robust to free entry (Horstmann and Markusen 1986) or foreign ownership (Feeney and Hillman 2001), but we note that these corrective forces are more likely to fail in the developing-country context given higher barriers to entry and ownership restrictions for nationalized industries or services.

5.2.2 Baseline Model Results

For the baseline model, we assume $\phi = 0$. Using standard results and definitions from Cournot competition, we can derive outcomes in the home market under autarky (the usual monopoly case), free trade (the usual duopoly case), and a nonprohibitive tariff.[10] Each row of table 5.1 lists the results under the various policy choices. For all tables in this chapter, the "Free Trade" column contains outcomes for joint free trade, while the "Tariff" column contains outcomes for nonprohibitive Home and Foreign tariffs (τ and τ^*, respectively).

We write the Home government objective $G(\tau; \alpha, \tau^*)$ as a function of the Home trade policy choice τ, as well as the parameter α and the Foreign trade policy τ^*, and denote prohibitive tariff levels as $\bar{\tau}$ and $\bar{\tau}^*$, so Home's objective equals $G(\bar{\tau}; \alpha, \bar{\tau}^*)$ under autarky and $G(0; \alpha, 0)$ under free trade. To define the government objective as a function of the tariff τ, we must define it piecewise with a cutoff at the prohibitive tariff level. The tariff is prohibitive when $\frac{1}{3}(1 - c - 2\tau) \le 0$; that is,

Table 5.1
Results for the baseline model.

Outcome \\ Policies	Autarky	Free Trade	Tariffs
Home domestic sales q_h	$\frac{1}{2}(1-c)$	$\frac{1}{3}(1-c)$	$\frac{1}{3}(1-c+\tau)$
Foreign exports q_f	0	$\frac{1}{3}(1-c)$	$\frac{1}{3}(1-c-2\tau)$
Home exports q_h^*	0	$\frac{1}{3}(1-c)$	$\frac{1}{3}(1-c-2\tau^*)$
Market quantity Q	$\frac{1}{2}(1-c)$	$\frac{2}{3}(1-c)$	$\frac{1}{3}(2(1-c)-\tau)$
Market price P	$\frac{1}{2}(1+c)$	$\frac{1}{3}(1+2c)$	$\frac{1}{3}(1+2c+\tau)$
Consumer surplus CS	$\frac{1}{8}(1-c)^2$	$\frac{2}{9}(1-c)^2$	$\frac{1}{2}\left(\frac{2(1-c)-\tau}{3}\right)^2$
Home domestic profits π_h	$\frac{1}{4}(1-c)^2$	$\frac{1}{9}(1-c)^2$	$\left(\frac{1-c+\tau}{3}\right)^2$
Home export profits π_f	0	$\frac{1}{9}(1-c)^2$	$\left(\frac{1-c-2\tau^*}{3}\right)^2$
Tariff revenue TR	0	0	$\tau\left(\frac{1-c-2\tau}{3}\right)$
Government objective G	$\left(\frac{1+2\alpha}{8}\right)(1-c)^2$	$\left(\frac{2+2\alpha}{9}\right)(1-c)^2$	(given later)

$\tau \geq \frac{1}{2}(1-c)$. Using equation (5.1) and results in table 5.1, the Home government objective is

$$G(\tau; \alpha, \tau^*) = \begin{cases} \frac{1}{2}\left(\frac{2(1-c)-\tau}{3}\right)^2 + \alpha\left(\frac{1-c+\tau}{3}\right)^2 + \alpha\pi_f(\tau^*) + \frac{\tau(1-c-2\tau)}{3}, \\ \qquad\qquad\qquad \text{if } \tau \leq \frac{1}{2}(1-c), \\ \left(\frac{1+2\alpha}{8}\right)(1-c)^2 + \alpha\pi_f(\tau^*), \quad \text{if } \tau \geq \frac{1}{2}(1-c), \end{cases}$$

(5.2)

where we have written Home export profits as a function of the Foreign tariff. Observe that in this segmented market, partial equilibrium case, the effects of the Home tariff and Foreign tariff are additively separable. This greatly simplifies analysis, as there is no strategic interaction between the tariff choices, and the optimal tariff of this objective is a dominant strategy. Proving that a prohibitive tariff maximizes this objective is then sufficient to prove that autarky is the noncooperative equilibrium.

Under standard national-income-maximizing preferences with $\alpha = 1$, duopoly yields the payoff of $\frac{4}{9}(1-c)^2$, which is preferable to the payoff of $\frac{3}{8}(1-c)^2$ obtained under monopoly. So here we obtain a typical outcome of trade under imperfect competition: procompetitive gains from trade can result from the reduction in markups that arises from greater competition.

Under more general political-economic preferences with $\alpha \geq 1$, the difference between the free trade payoff and the monopoly payoff is

$$G(\bar{\tau}; \alpha, \bar{\tau}^*) - G(0; \alpha, 0) = \frac{7 - 2\alpha}{72}(1-c)^2,$$

(5.3)

so the governments acting jointly will strictly prefer free trade to autarky as long as $\alpha < \frac{7}{2}$. If autarky is the noncooperative outcome, then this upper bound on α implies that governments benefit from a trade agreement. Because tariffs serve to reduce joint production in the sector distorted by imperfect competition and political economy, it is immediately clear that either autarky or free trade must be the optimal joint outcome on the boundary of the policy space.[11] Which is optimal again depends on whether α is above or below the cutoff. When $\alpha = \frac{7}{2}$, the optimal joint policy is not unique—governments are indifferent between autarky and free trade.

To derive the optimal unilateral policies, first observe that

$$\frac{dG}{d\tau} = \tau\left(\frac{2\alpha - 11}{9}\right) + \left(\frac{2\alpha + 1}{9}\right)(1 - c), \text{ if } \tau < \frac{1}{2}(1 - c). \tag{5.4}$$

Substituting the cutoff τ for the prohibitive tariff into the first-order condition, we can easily derive that if $\alpha < \frac{3}{2}$, there is an optimal non-prohibitive tariff satisfying $\frac{dG(\tau)}{d\tau} = 0$ (the second-order condition is satisfied for $\alpha < \frac{11}{2}$). For $\alpha \in (\frac{3}{2}, \frac{11}{2})$, $\frac{dG(\tau)}{d\tau} > 0$ for all nonprohibitive tariffs, and the optimal unilateral trade policy is prohibitive. So the optimal unilateral policy satisfies

$$\tau^N(\alpha) = \begin{cases} \left(\frac{2\alpha+1}{11-2\alpha}\right)(1-c), & \text{if } \alpha < \frac{3}{2}, \\ \text{prohibitive} & \text{if } \alpha \in (\frac{3}{2}, \frac{11}{2}). \end{cases} \tag{5.5}$$

Notice that when $\alpha = \frac{3}{2}$, there is no unique optimal policy.

A second method for deriving the optimal policy involves writing the government objective as a function of equilibrium quantities, which depend on trade policy. This approach allows for easier economic interpretation. The Home government objective is

$$G(\tau; \alpha, \tau^*) = \frac{1}{2}(q_h(\tau) + q_f(\tau))^2 + \alpha(q_h^2(\tau) + q_h^{*2}(\tau^*)) + \tau q_f(\tau). \tag{5.6}$$

Observe that the left derivative at $\bar{\tau} = \frac{1}{2}(1-c)$ is

$$\frac{d_- G}{d\tau}\Big|_{\tau=\bar{\tau}} = q_h(\bar{\tau})(q_h' + q_f') + 2\alpha q_h(\bar{\tau})q_h' + \bar{\tau}q_f' \tag{5.7}$$

$$= \frac{1}{6}(1-c)(-3 + 2\alpha), \tag{5.8}$$

where from table 5.1, $q_h(\bar{\tau}) = \frac{1-c}{2}$, $q_h' = \frac{1}{3}$, and $q_f' = -\frac{2}{3}$. The three additive terms in equation (5.7) are the effects of Home's tariff on Home's consumer surplus, profits, and tariff revenue, respectively, as Home's tariff approaches the prohibitive level. Clearly, when $\alpha > \frac{3}{2}$, $\frac{d_- G}{d\tau}\Big|_{\tau=\bar{\tau}} > 0$. Given the satisfaction of the second-order condition ($\alpha < \frac{11}{2}$ derived earlier), the Home government objective is strictly increasing in τ over the domain $[0, \bar{\tau})$, and the prohibitive policy is unilaterally optimal.

Table 5.2 summarizes the optimal unilateral policies and optimal joint policies.

Table 5.2
Optimal unilateral and joint policies.

α range	Optimal Unilateral Policy	Optimal Joint Policy
$[1, \frac{3}{2})$	nonprohibitive tariff	free trade
$(\frac{3}{2}, \frac{7}{2})$	prohibitive trade policy	free trade
$(\frac{7}{2}, \frac{11}{2})$	prohibitive trade policy	prohibitive trade policies

The following proposition highlights the α interval of interest.

Proposition 5.1   For our baseline model, if governments assign a weight $\alpha \in (\frac{3}{2}, \frac{7}{2})$ to firm profits, then the unique Nash equilibrium trade policies are prohibitive, free trade is the unique joint optimum, and governments can benefit from a trade agreement.

To support the relevance of our first proposition, we argue that the political economy parameters in the interval of interest are empirically reasonable. Ossa (2014) estimates industry-level weights for agriculture and manufacturing industries. Though his largest weights are for industries in agriculture that do not easily fit into our imperfectly competitive framework, he does still find substantial variation across political weights for Chinese manufacturing industries: either textiles or motor vehicles have roughly a 50% larger political economy weight than transport equipment (a representative industry with a low weight). There is less variation in Brazilian manufacturing, but leather goods receive a 30% larger weight than electronic equipment. Since Ossa estimates his political weights for a single-factor model, we would expect the estimated political weights to be lower than in a model like ours, in which only the specific factor is politically weighted and the mobile labor factor has no excess political power. Moreover, as we extend the model in section 5.3, the minimum α necessary to explain the unilateral imposition of prohibitive policies will decline.

5.3   How Market Characteristics Affect Cooperation

This section extends our baseline model to illustrate how various market characteristics can affect the potential for cooperation. The extensions we consider are symmetric trade costs, mirror-image differences in productivity for two industries, increases in competition for symmetric nations, asymmetry in competition across nations, and firm heterogeneity in productivity for symmetric nations. As detailed in the chapter's introduction, these extensions can be useful to help identify when liberalization is more likely to be feasible if nations are starting from prohibitive policies. We will characterize how market characteristics impact the possibility of cooperation, based on whether changes in a market parameter lengthen or shorten the α interval of interest, in which prohibitive policies are unilaterally optimal but liberalization is still feasible.[12]

5.3.1 Trade Costs

We introduce symmetric trade costs $\phi > 0$ into the model. The autarky case is the same as in table 5.1, while payoffs for free trade and tariffs are listed in table 5.3.

For the standard case of $\alpha = 1$, free trade is welfare improving when $\frac{\phi}{1-c} < \frac{5}{22}$, while for $\frac{\phi}{1-c} \in (\frac{5}{22}, \frac{1}{2})$ competition from trade is detrimental to welfare.[13] Free trade is socially inefficient in this parameter range because of a well-known pathology. In models of intra-industry trade with homogeneous products and imperfect competition, "cross-hauling" trade costs can exceed the gains from trade (Feenstra 2004, chapter 7). We focus on the $\frac{\phi}{1-c} \in [0, \frac{5}{22})$ case throughout.

More generally, the difference between the free trade payoff and the monopoly payoff is

$$\frac{7-2\alpha}{72}(1-c)^2 - \left(\frac{2}{9} + \frac{2}{9}\alpha\right)(1-c)\phi + \left(\frac{1}{18} + \frac{5}{9}\alpha\right)\phi^2, \tag{5.9}$$

so free trade is jointly optimal, provided that

Table 5.3
Results with trade costs.

Outcome \\ Policies	Free Trade (duopoly)	Tariffs
Home domestic sales q_h	$\frac{1}{3}(1-c+\phi)$	$\frac{1}{3}(1-c+\phi+\tau)$
Foreign exports q_f	$\frac{1}{3}(1-c-2\phi)$	$\frac{1}{3}(1-c-2\phi-2\tau)$
Home exports q_h^*	$\frac{1}{3}(1-c-2\phi)$	$\frac{1}{3}(1-c-2\phi-2\tau^*)$
Market quantity Q	$\frac{1}{3}(2(1-c)-\phi)$	$\frac{1}{3}(2(1-c)-\phi-\tau)$
Market price P	$\frac{1}{3}(1+2c+\phi)$	$\frac{1}{3}(1+2c+\phi+\tau)$
Consumer surplus CS	$\frac{1}{2}\left(\frac{2(1-c)-\phi}{3}\right)^2$	$\frac{1}{2}\left(\frac{2(1-c)-\phi-\tau}{3}\right)^2$
Home domestic profits π_h	$\left(\frac{1-c+\phi}{3}\right)^2$	$\left(\frac{1-c+\phi+\tau}{3}\right)^2$
Home export profits π_f	$\left(\frac{1-c-2\phi}{3}\right)^2$	$\left(\frac{1-c-2\phi-2\tau^*}{3}\right)^2$
Tariff revenue	0	$\tau\left(\frac{1-c-2\phi-2\tau}{3}\right)$

$$\alpha < \frac{7(1-c)^2 - 16(1-c)\phi + 4\phi^2}{2(1-c)^2 + 16(1-c)\phi - 40\phi^2}. \tag{5.10}$$

Next we derive the set of parameters for which autarky is the non-cooperative equilibrium. We first derive the government objective as a function of the tariff τ. The tariff is prohibitive if $\tau \geq \frac{1}{2}(1-c) - \phi$.

$$G(\tau; \alpha, \phi, \tau^*) = \begin{cases} \frac{1}{2}\left(\frac{2-2c-\phi-\tau}{3}\right)^2 + \alpha\left(\frac{1-c+\phi+\tau}{3}\right)^2 + \alpha\pi_f + \frac{\tau(1-c-2\tau-2\phi)}{3}, \\ \qquad \text{if } \tau \leq \frac{1}{2}(1-c) - \phi, \\ \left(\frac{1+2\alpha}{8}\right)(1-c)^2 + \alpha\pi_f, \quad \text{if } \tau \geq \frac{1}{2}(1-c) - \phi. \end{cases}$$

The derivative for nonprohibitive tariff values is

$$\frac{dG}{d\tau} = \tau\left(\frac{2\alpha - 11}{9}\right) + \left(\frac{2\alpha - 1}{9}\right)(1-c) + (2\alpha - 5)\phi, \text{ if } \tau < \frac{1}{2}(1-c) - \phi. \tag{5.11}$$

Lastly, we derive the optimal unilateral policy conditional on α,

$$\tau^N(\alpha) = \begin{cases} \frac{(1+2\alpha)(1-c)+(2\alpha-5)\phi}{11-2\alpha}, & \text{if } \alpha < \frac{3}{2} - \frac{2\phi}{1-c}, \\ \text{prohibitive}, & \text{if } \alpha \in \left(\frac{3}{2} - \frac{2\phi}{1-c}, \frac{11}{2}\right). \end{cases} \tag{5.12}$$

Therefore, prohibitive policies are unilaterally optimal when

$$\alpha > \frac{3}{2} - \frac{2\phi}{1-c}. \tag{5.13}$$

To interpret inequalities (5.10) and (5.13), notice that both are at their threshold when $\frac{\phi}{1-c} = \frac{1}{5}$ and $\alpha = \frac{11}{10}$. When $\frac{\phi}{1-c} \in [0, \frac{1}{5})$, both are satisfied for $\alpha \in \left(\frac{7(1-c)^2-16(1-c)\phi+4\phi^2}{2(1-c)^2+16(1-c)\phi-40\phi^2}, \frac{3}{2} - \frac{2\phi}{1-c}\right)$. As $\frac{\phi}{1-c}$ increases from 0 to $\frac{1}{5}$, the length of the α interval for which free trade is jointly optimal while prohibitive policies are unilaterally optimal then decreases from 2 to 0. We summarize the result in the following proposition.

Proposition 5.2 If we extend the baseline model to allow for symmetric trade costs satisfying $\frac{\phi}{1-c} < \frac{1}{5}$, then there exists an interval of α such that governments unilaterally impose prohibitive policies and jointly prefer free trade. The length of this interval of α is strictly decreasing in the scaled trade cost $\frac{\phi}{1-c}$.

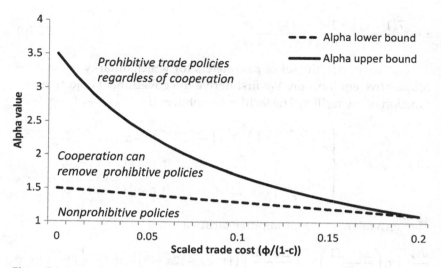

Figure 5.1
Effects of symmetric trade costs.

We plot the relevant bounds on α as a function of the scaled trade cost $\frac{\phi}{1-c}$ in figure 5.1. With trade costs, the lower bound of α for which prohibitive policies are unilaterally optimal decreases to $\frac{11}{10}$ from $\frac{3}{2}$. To the extent that a $\frac{11}{10}$ value is more empirically plausible than $\frac{3}{2}$, this finding improves the empirical relevance of the theory. In addition, the exercise provides an explanation for why distant markets could have difficulty achieving trade cooperation: because the range of cooperation over prohibitive policies narrows as the trade costs increase.

To understand the economic intuition for why the range narrows, the key is the $-\left(\frac{2}{9}+\frac{2}{9}\alpha\right)$ term in the expression (5.9) representing the first-order changes in payoffs from an increase in trade costs. The term is negative because the increase in trade costs leads to a reduction in export profits and consumer surplus from an agreement. The trade cost increase also mitigates the fall in domestic profits from an agreement, but this effect is dominated. The agreement as a whole becomes less appealing as trade costs increase, so the α upper bound in figure 5.1 decreases. The lower bound also decreases, but at a slower rate. This lower-bound decrease is the consequence of a lower tariff being sufficient to achieve prohibitive policies.

5.3.2 Mirror-Image Differences in Productivity

Because our baseline model allows for only procompetitive gains from trade, a worthwhile extension is to consider how cooperation is affected by other sources of gains from trade. One straightforward extension from our single-factor framework is to allow for Ricardian gains from trade. To explore this possibility, we allow for two imperfectly competitive sectors in each country plus the usual outside sector, and we allow costs to differ between the two imperfectly competitive sectors. We assume that utility is additively separable between the three sectors, so there is no complementarity or substitution between the imperfectly competitive sectors. To further simplify the analysis, we assume that each nation has an equal absolute advantage in production in exactly one of the two sectors, so there are mirror-image (i.e., antisymmetric) differences in productivity for the two nations. The technological differences imply that there are Ricardian gains from trade in this extension in addition to procompetitive gains. We capture the difference in productivities with a single parameter ψ and evaluate how the possibility of cooperation varies with ψ. Each nation produces with cost c in the sector for which it has absolute advantage, and cost $c + \psi$ in the other sector, for $\psi \in (0, 1 - c)$.

Based on our baseline results, we can easily derive that the value of either government objective in autarky is

$$\left(\frac{1+2\alpha}{8}\right)(1-c)^2 + \left(\frac{1+2\alpha}{8}\right)(1-(c+\psi))^2 \tag{5.14}$$

given that we have monopoly with cost c in one industry and cost $c + \psi$ in the other.

The value of the government objective under free trade takes a form similar to that of the trade cost extension in table 5.3. The cost difference ψ plays a role similar role to that of the trade cost ϕ, as both represent cost differences between competing firms in the same market:

$$\left(\frac{2(1-c)-\psi}{3}\right)^2 + \alpha\left(2\left(\frac{1-c+\psi}{3}\right)^2 + 2\left(\frac{1-c-2\psi}{3}\right)^2\right). \tag{5.15}$$

The difference between the autarky and free trade payoffs is

$$\frac{7-2\alpha}{36}(1-c)^2 + \left(\frac{2\alpha-7}{36}\right)(1-c)\psi + \left(\frac{62\alpha-1}{72}\right)\psi^2. \tag{5.16}$$

While the previous expression lacks any immediately obvious interpretation, it can be rewritten as

$$2\left[\frac{7-2\alpha}{72}(1-c)^2 - \left(\frac{2}{9}+\frac{2}{9}\alpha\right)(1-c)\psi + \left(\frac{1}{18}+\frac{5}{9}\alpha\right)\psi^2\right]$$
$$+ \left[(2(1-c)\psi) - \psi^2)\left(\frac{1+2\alpha}{8}\right)\right].$$

Notice the similarity between the left bracketed term here and the expression (5.9) from the trade cost extension. Each term reflects procompetitive gains from trade when there is a cost difference among the competing firms in a particular market postliberalization. This cost difference is the trade cost ϕ in subsection 5.3.1, and ψ in the previous expression. Since the current extension now has two imperfectly competitive sectors, these joint procompetitive gains from free trade are now achieved twice, hence the doubling of the bracketed term on the left. In addition to the procompetitive gains from trade, there is an additional strictly positive bracketed term on the right. This term represents the promised Ricardian gains from trade that result from gaining access to the producer abroad with lower costs.

We can then derive the following restriction on α for free trade to be jointly preferable to autarky:

$$\alpha < \frac{14 - 14(\frac{\psi}{1-c}) - (\frac{\psi}{1-c})^2}{4 - 4(\frac{\psi}{1-c}) - 62(\frac{\psi}{1-c})^2}. \tag{5.17}$$

We now have the cutoff for when free trade is preferable to autarky as a function of the scaled difference in productivities $\frac{\psi}{1-c}$. We plot this cutoff in figure 5.2—labeled as the alpha upper bound—as a function of $\frac{\psi}{1-c}$. To interpret this function, notice that it is a ratio of polynomials in $\frac{\psi}{1-c}$ and strictly increasing over the range of interest. Because the denominator has a root of $\frac{3\sqrt{7}-1}{31} \approx .224$, the cutoff function bends up toward a vertical asymptote at this value. When the scaled productivity difference exceeds this value, free trade increases profits for either nation, so there is no value of α for which autarky would be jointly preferable to free trade.

Next, we derive the lower bound on α for which prohibitive policies are unilaterally optimal. We derive a sufficiently high α to motivate a tariff large enough to choke off trade in both the high-productivity industry and the low-productivity industry. Naturally, a higher tariff is

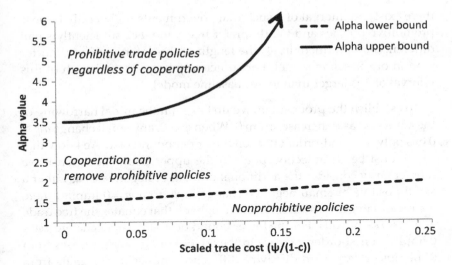

Figure 5.2
Effect of mirror-image differences in productivity.

necessary to choke off trade for the higher-productivity imports than for the lower-productivity imports, so we need only consider the cutoff α for imports from the higher-productivity industry. The derivation of this cutoff is then the same as in inequality (5.13), except the difference in costs for the relevant industry between the domestic producer and imports is now $-\psi$ instead of $+\phi$. This is because the total cost of imports is now cheaper by ψ because of the superior technology abroad in this sector, instead of being ϕ more expensive because of the trade cost. The lower bound on α for prohibitive tariffs is then

$$\alpha > \frac{3}{2} + 2 \left(\frac{\psi}{1-c} \right). \tag{5.18}$$

Figure 5.2 summarizes the results. The range of α for which cooperation removes prohibitive policies is represented by the area between the solid line (the upper bound for when cooperation is jointly preferable to autarky) and dashed line (the lower bound for which prohibitive policies are unilaterally optimal). The length of the α interval of interest initially shrinks as ψ increases from 0, but then it sharply widens. We summarize the results with the following proposition.

Proposition 5.3 If we extend the baseline model to allow for two industries with mirror-image costs of c and $c + \psi$, such that $\frac{\psi}{1-c} < 1$, there exists an interval of α such that governments unilaterally impose prohibitive policies and jointly prefer free trade. For sufficiently small differences in productivity ψ, the length of this interval of α is shorter than in our baseline model. For sufficiently large ψ, the length of this interval of α is larger than in our baseline model.

To establish the proposition, we first explain the initial narrowing of the α interval as ψ increases from 0. When $\psi = 0$, any small change $d\psi > 0$ has only a second-order effect on the upper bound of α. We know that $\psi = 0$ must be an inflection point in the upper bound function if we momentarily consider the additional domain of negative ψ, as either a small positive or small negative change in ψ from $\psi = 0$ implies there are Ricardian gains from trade and a higher α that equates the free trade and autarky payoffs. For the lower bound on α, any small change $d\psi > 0$ implies a first-order increase in the lower bound as ψ increases from 0, because a larger productivity difference implies larger gains from trade and a larger weight α for prohibitive policies to be unilaterally optimal. The first-order increase in the lower bound and second-order increase in the upper bound imply that the α range of interest initially narrows as ψ increases, but for larger ψ, the upper bound of α increases sharply as ψ approaches the asymptote where trade increases global profits rather than decreasing them. Because of this sharp increase in the upper bound of α, the α range of interest must widen for sufficiently large ψ.

5.3.3 Competition

The next extension we consider is when there are multiple homogeneous firms in each nation. Increasing the number of symmetric Cournot firms is a reasonable way to model the level of competition in each nation. For example, the international competition policy study of Horn and Levinsohn (2001) follows the same approach. Let n be the number of Home firms and n^* be the number of Foreign firms. The environment we consider again features only procompetitive gains from trade, so, to preview results, we should expect that there will be less benefit from trade liberalization as domestic competition increases.

Table 5.4 gives values of various economic quantities under Cournot competition, with some elements of the tariff column defined from previous rows. As before, the Home government objective is $G = CS + \alpha n(\pi_h + \pi_f) + TR$.

Table 5.4
Results with domestic competition.

Outcome \\ Policies	Autarky	Free Trade	Tariffs
Home domestic sales per firm q_h	$\frac{(1-c)}{n+1}$	$\frac{1-c}{n+n^*+1}$	$\frac{(1-c+\tau n^*)}{n+n^*+1}$
Foreign exports per firm q_f	0	$\frac{1-c}{n+n^*+1}$	$\frac{(1-c-\tau(1+n))}{n+n^*+1}$
Home exports per firm q_h^*	0	$\frac{1-c}{n+n^*+1}$	$\frac{(1-c-\tau^*(1+n))}{n+n^*+1}$
Market quantity Q	$\frac{n(1-c)}{n+1}$	$\frac{(n+n^*)(1-c)}{n+n^*+1}$	$\frac{((n+n^*)(1-c)-\tau n^*)}{n+n^*+1}$
Market price P	$\frac{(1+nc)}{n+1}$	$\frac{(1+(n+n^*)c)}{n+n^*+1}$	$\frac{(1+(n+n^*)c+\tau n^*)}{n+n^*+1}$
Consumer surplus CS	$\frac{n^2(1-c)^2}{2(n+1)^2}$	$\frac{(n+n^*)^2(1-c)^2}{2(n+n^*+1)^2}$	$\frac{1}{2}Q^2$
Domestic profits per firm π_h	$\frac{(1-c)^2}{(n+1)^2}$	$\frac{(1-c)^2}{(n+n^*+1)^2}$	$(P-c)q_h$
Export profits per firm π_f	0	$\frac{(1-c)^2}{(n+n^*+1)^2}$	$(P-c)q_h^*$
Tariff revenue TR	0	0	$\tau n^* q_f$
Government objective G	$\left(\frac{n^2+2\alpha n}{2(n+1)^2}\right)(1-c)^2$	$\frac{((n+n^*)^2+4\alpha n)(1-c)^2}{2(n+n^*+1)^2}$	(in text)

We first consider the case of symmetric firms in each country such that $n = n^*$. Consider the cutoff α for which free trade is jointly preferable to autarky. We find that

$$\alpha < \frac{4n^2 + 3n}{4n^2 - 2}. \tag{5.19}$$

To solve for the lower α bound at which point prohibitive policies are unilaterally optimal, notice first that the prohibitive tariff is $\tau = \frac{1-c}{1+n}$. The Nash equilibrium tariff equals the prohibitive level when

$$\left(\frac{2\alpha n + 1}{2(n+1)(2n+1) - n(1+2n\alpha)}\right)(1-c) > \frac{1-c}{n+1},$$

which then simplifies to the following simple inequality:

$$\alpha > 1 + \frac{1}{2n}. \tag{5.20}$$

We then plot the cutoffs as a function of n in figure 5.3. As n goes to infinity, thus increasing competition in both markets, there is a shorter interval of α values for which cooperation can eliminate prohibitive policies. The potential procompetitive gains become smaller as competition increases, so the agreement becomes relatively less appealing for any given value of α. In the limiting case, as $n \to \infty$, there is no potential

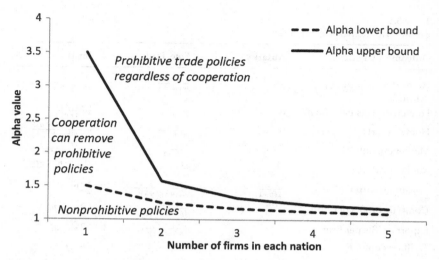

Figure 5.3
Effects of intranational competition.

for cooperation if prohibitive trade policies are unilaterally optimal. This result is expected because Cournot competition approaches perfect competition in the limiting case, and we know there is no possibility of cooperating to eliminate prohibitive policies under perfect competition with zero profits.

So far, we have considered cooperation only among nations with symmetric levels of competition. An interesting alternative possibility is cooperation between nations with different levels of competition. For example, we might imagine cooperation between a developed country with many firms because of low barriers to entry and a developing country with few firms because of high barriers to entry. For this asymmetry, a limiting case is again insightful. Consider a fixed number of firms n for Home and the limiting case as $n^* \to \infty$, so Home has the less competitive industry and Foreign has the more competitive industry. Consider the upper and lower bounds on α such that Home unilaterally prefers prohibitive policies but joint cooperation to free trade is possible. As $n^* \to \infty$, both the upper and lower bounds on α equal $1 + \frac{1}{2n}$ (which recall was the lower bound for α for the case with symmetric n plotted in figure 5.3), so if Home has a protected monopoly or oligopoly, Foreign has a perfectly competitive industry, and Home and Foreign each unilaterally prefer to impose prohibitive trade barriers, then there is no possibility for cooperation.

The results are summarized in the following proposition.

Proposition 5.4   Suppose we extend the baseline model to allow for n identical firms in Home and n^* firms in Foreign. As n and n^* increase symmetrically, there is a progressively shorter interval of α for which cooperation is jointly optimal and prohibitive policies are unilaterally optimal. As the number of firms in either nation approaches infinity, there is no potential for liberalization when prohibitive policies are unilaterally optimal.

We qualify the results on competition here in a few ways. First, notice that the results are highly sensitive to the possibility that there are significant domestic barriers to entry yet international liberalization is still possible. This is a strong assumption but one that could be more relevant in developing nations with high barriers to entry.

Another significant limitation is that this extension again only allows for procompetitive gains from trade. If we also allow for gains from trade as a result of comparative advantage, as in subsection 5.3.2, we no longer find that the gains from trade fall to zero as the number of firms increases. This suggests there could be additional insight in exploring how competition and comparative advantage jointly affect cooperation.

5.3.4   Firm Heterogeneity

The final extension that we consider is firm heterogeneity. We consider a simple kind of heterogeneity—two firms with different productivities within each nation but symmetry between nations—but the model is still rich in implications. We index the firms within each country as 1 and 2 with costs c_1 and c_2. Assume $c_1 \leq c_2$ so 1 indexes the superior firm and 2 indexes the inferior firm. We denote the equilibrium domestic quantity for the more productive Home firm as q_h^1 and the less productive Home firm as q_h^2. We denote Foreign exports to the Home market similarly as q_f^1 and q_f^2.

Table 5.5 reports the results of Cournot competition with heterogenous firms. As before, the first column describes outcomes under autarky and the second describes outcomes under free trade. The third column requires more explanation than our previous extensions. We include here results for the case in which Foreign imposes prohibitive barriers on Home firms and Home imposes a barrier that is prohibitive for the inferior Foreign firm but nonprohibitive for the

Table 5.5
Results with firm heterogeneity.

Outcome \\ Policies	Autarky	Free Trade	Home Tariffs
Domestic quantity q_h^1	$\frac{1-2c_1+c_2}{3}$	$\frac{1-3c_1+2c_2}{5}$	$\frac{1-2c_1+c_2+\tau}{4}$
Domestic quantity q_h^2	$\frac{1-2c_2+c_1}{3}$	$\frac{1-3c_2+2c_1}{5}$	$\frac{1-3c_2+2c_1+\tau}{4}$
Foreign exports q_f^1	0	$\frac{1-3c_1+2c_2}{5}$	$\frac{1-2c_1+c_2-3\tau}{4}$
Foreign exports q_f^2	0	$\frac{1-3c_2+2c_1}{5}$	0
Home exports q_h^{i*}	0	$\frac{1-3c_i+2c_j}{5}$	0
Market quantity Q	$\frac{2-c_1-c_2}{3}$	$\frac{4-2c_1-2c_2}{5}$	$\frac{3-2c_1-c_2-\tau}{4}$
Market price P	$\frac{(1+c_1+c_2)}{3}$	$\frac{1+2c_1+2c_2}{5}$	$\frac{1+2c_1+c_2+\tau}{4}$

more productive Foreign firm. This case will be most relevant in determining the lower bound on α such that the prohibitive policy is unilaterally optimal. The derivation of consumer surplus, profits, tariff revenue, and government objectives from the quantities in table 5.5 is straightforward, but these outcomes are not reported here.

To capture the extent of firm heterogeneity, we define the parameter $\omega \equiv \frac{1-c_1}{1-c_2}$. We focus on the $\omega \geq 1$ case without loss of generality. Using the definition of ω and the expressions for q_h^2 in table 5.5, we can derive that $\omega < 2$ is a necessary condition for both firms to be producing in autarky, and $\omega < \frac{3}{2}$ is a necessary condition for both firms to be producing under free trade.

We first derive the upper bound on α for which free trade is jointly preferable to autarky. When $\omega = 1$, all firms are active, and we have the same results as for the competing duopoly model from subsection 5.3.3. As ω increases from 1, the cutoff α initially increases. For a particular range of ω, however, no cutoff α exists, because liberalization increases total profits summed across all firms, in which case free trade is jointly preferable to autarky, regardless of α. The lower end of this range is $\bar{\omega} \equiv \frac{116-15\sqrt{7}}{109} \approx 1.43$, and the upper end of this range is $\frac{5}{3}$. The bounds on this domain of ω are plotted as gray vertical lines in figure 5.4. For $\omega \in \left(\frac{5}{3}, 2\right)$, an interval in which only the more productive firms are active under free trade, profits again begin to decline under liberalization, and the cutoff α declines as ω increases. As $\omega \longrightarrow 2$, the inferior firm output $q_h^2 \longrightarrow 0$, and the model approaches the baseline model. The complete results for the α upper bound, plotted as solid curves in figure 5.4, are as follows.

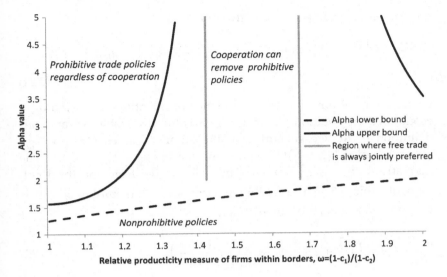

Figure 5.4
Effects of firm heterogeneity.

1. For $\omega \in [1, \bar{\omega})$, $\alpha < \frac{11(1+\omega)^2}{2(-109\omega^2 + 232\omega - 109)}$.

2. For $\omega \in [\bar{\omega}, \frac{5}{3}]$, free trade is always jointly preferable to autarky.

3. For $\omega \in (\frac{5}{3}, 2]$, $\alpha < \frac{3\omega^2 - 2\omega - 1}{6\omega^2 - 16\omega + 10}$.

As a check of our results, notice that, for $\omega = 1$, we obtain the same upper bound, $\alpha < \frac{11}{7}$, as in the symmetric duopolies model from subsection 5.3.3, which can be found by evaluating inequality (5.19) at $n = 2$. Similarly, for $\omega = 2$, we obtain the same upper bound, $\alpha < \frac{7}{2}$, as in the baseline model.

Next we derive the lower bound on α for which a prohibitive policy is unilaterally optimal. We first observe that for any $\omega \in (1, 2)$ there exists a tariff level such that both Home firms are active and only the superior Foreign firm is exporting.[14] For this set of active firms in the Home market, we derive the lower bound on α such that the Home government objective is strictly increasing. To confirm that we have indeed derived the optimum, we must also verify that if α is above the derived bound, then the Home objective is still strictly increasing in the tariff, even for tariff levels at which other sets of firms are active.

We follow the second method of deriving the α lower bound, similar to equations (5.6) and (5.7) in subsection 5.2.2. The left derivative of the government objective at prohibitive policies is

$$\frac{d_-G(\tau; \alpha, \omega, \tau^*)}{d\tau}\Big|_{\tau=\bar{\tau}} = Q(q_h^{1\prime} + q_h^{2\prime} + q_f^{1\prime}) + 2\alpha(q_h^1 q_h^{1\prime} + q_h^2 q_h^{2\prime}) + \bar{\tau} q_f^{1\prime},$$

(5.21)

where we have omitted the dependence of quantities on $\bar{\tau}$ and ω to economize on notation. From the first column of table 5.5 and our definition of ω, we substitute in the autarky values $Q = \frac{1}{3}(1 + \frac{1}{\omega})$ $(1 - c_1)$, $q_h^1 = \frac{1}{3}(2 - \frac{1}{\omega})(1 - c_1)$, and $q_h^2 = \frac{1}{3}(\frac{2}{\omega} - 1)(1 - c_1)$. The derivatives $q_h^{1\prime} = \frac{1}{4}$, $q_h^{2\prime} = \frac{1}{4}$, and $q_f^{1\prime} = \frac{-3}{4}$ derive from the third column of table 5.5. The prohibitive tariff level that implies $q_f^1 = 0$ is $\bar{\tau} = \frac{1}{3}(2 - \frac{1}{\omega})(1 - c_1)$. We then obtain

$$\frac{d_-G}{d\tau}\Big|_{\tau=\bar{\tau}} = \left(\left(\frac{2}{\omega} + 2\right)\alpha - \left(7 - \frac{2}{\omega}\right)\right)\left(\frac{1 - c_1}{12}\right).$$

(5.22)

This and the appropriate second-order conditions imply that the objective is increasing in τ for this set of active firms, provided that

$$\alpha > \frac{7\omega - 2}{2\omega + 2} \text{ for } \omega \in [1, 2).$$

(5.23)

This lower bound on α is the dashed curve plotted in figure 5.4. Notice that as ω increases, the size of the prohibitive tariff (scaled by $1 - c_1$) increases, so a larger political-economic weight is necessary to rationalize the choice of prohibitive policy.

To verify that the prohibitive policies are indeed unilaterally optimal when α satisfies this lower bound, we also need to check that the Home government objective is still increasing when other sets of firms are active. We can derive that when all firms are active, the Home government objective is increasing in the tariff level as long as $\alpha > \frac{33 - 23\omega}{4(3 - \omega)}$, which is always satisfied when inequality (5.23) holds for $\omega \in (1, 2)$. The other possible set of active firms is the two superior firms alone. Both inferior firms exit the Home market for a sufficiently large productivity difference and sufficiently small tariff level: $\omega > \frac{3}{2}$ and $\tau \in [0, \frac{2\omega - 3}{\omega}(1 - c_1)]$. We need to verify that the Home government objective is strictly increasing in this case. But indeed this is the competing monopolist case from the baseline model, and the objective is increasing whenever $\alpha > \frac{3}{2}$, which is always satisfied when (5.23) is satisfied and $\omega \geq \frac{5}{4}$. Other combinations of active firms are not possible. Lastly, we note that the Home government objective is always continuous over $\omega \in [1, 2]$. Consequently, inequality (5.23) indeed defines the lower bound on α such that prohibitive policies are unilaterally optimal.

As a check on our results, notice that for $\omega = 1$ the bound is $\alpha > \frac{5}{4}$. When we evaluate inequality (5.20) at $n = 2$ for the equivalent symmetric duopoly model, we obtain the same result. As $\omega \longrightarrow 2$, the lower bound approaches $\alpha > 2$. This may seem surprising because when $\omega = 2$ the inferior firms exit and the model becomes equivalent to our baseline model, for which the lower bound is $\alpha > \frac{3}{2}$. The reason for the distinction is that the derivative of the Home government objective does not exist at this point: for any $\omega < 2$, the derivative $q_h^{2\prime}$ is always $\frac{1}{4}$, but the right derivative at $\omega = 2$ becomes 0, as the inferior Home firm ceases to be active.

Figure 5.4 summarizes all the results. To interpret the figure, first observe that when the two firms are homogeneous, there is a narrow range of parameter values $(\frac{3}{2}, \frac{11}{7})$ for which liberalization would be feasible if prohibitive policies were unilaterally optimal. But as the productivity difference between the firms increases, the parameter range for which cooperation is possible increases dramatically, and cooperation is possible for all $\alpha > \frac{3}{2}$, provided that $\omega \in [\bar{\omega}, \frac{5}{3}]$. Taking the derivatives of the respective curves at $\omega = 1$, we verify that the interval of α between the bounds lengthens as ω increases from 1. When firms have a more intermediate level of heterogeneity, liberalization can lead to an increase in total profits for all Home firms and for all Foreign firms, even if liberalization causes the inferior firms to cease production. Though firms lose domestic sales when trade competition increases, exports can more than make up for those losses.

As ω increases beyond $\frac{5}{3}$, liberalization increasingly reduces profits relative to autarky. When the inferior domestic firm is providing sufficiently low competition for the superior firm in autarky, industry profits decrease once each de facto monopoly is exposed to trade. As the losses in profits from liberalization increase with ω, the political weight on profits necessary to ensure a joint preference for autarky over free trade decreases with ω, so liberalization is possible for a shorter α interval. The increase in the lower bound of α also contributes to the shortening of the α interval as ω increases.

A final proposition summarizes all these results.

Proposition 5.5 Suppose we extend the baseline model to allow for two firms in each country with asymmetric costs, and we maintain cross-country symmetry. Consider the interval of α for which cooperation is jointly optimal and prohibitive policies are unilaterally optimal. As firm heterogeneity increases, the length of this interval of α initially expands and then contracts.

The assumption that any lobbying would be at the industry level is crucial for this result. If the inferior firm could lobby more than the superior firm to protect its existence from trade liberalization, then results would be different. Empirical evidence suggests, however, that larger firms lobby more (Bombardini 2008).

5.4   Conclusion

The first contribution of this chapter is to show that cooperation is possible starting from prohibitive policies, even if there is no change in any nation's domestic political environment. This is a nontrivial result because such cooperation does not occur in the canonical trade agreement model with two goods, general equilibrium, and perfect competition. We then extend our baseline model to determine under which market characteristics liberalization from prohibitive policies is likely to be feasible. We find that such cooperation is more likely for lower levels of trade costs, sufficiently large cross-industry differences in productivity, weaker levels of intranational competition, and intermediate ranges of firm heterogeneity.

Our framework could be relevant in guiding future liberalization from prohibitive policies, though like any theoretical study, the results here motivate checks of empirical validity and theoretical robustness. As mentioned in section 5.2, an important check would be to consider prohibitive policies resulting from fixed costs of exporting rather than a choke price in linear demand. For empirical validity, a valuable exercise would be to test the model's predictions on prohibitive barriers that were later removed. A complete empirical treatment of cooperation in eliminating prohibitive barriers would have to consider both the motives described here and also the possibility of commitment motives for trade agreements. Another concern is that our exogenous political parameters could be related to market characteristics. Ideally, the framework can guide future trade negotiations by identifying which sectors with prohibitive barriers have the greatest potential for cooperation.

We conclude by discussing how the theory here relates to the limited success of developing countries in negotiations under the WTO and the

General Agreement on Tariffs and Trade (GATT), which preceded it. The liberalization in our theory—cooperation for industries and country pairs where trade does not already exist—does not fit well with prior GATT/WTO norms. Lamp (2015) argues that developed countries shut out developing nations on the basis of the *principal supplier rule*, as developing countries rarely had the capacity to be principal suppliers of any product. Consequently, developing countries rarely obtained liberalization that suited their interests. Indeed, Ludema and Mayda (2013) find that the Uruguay Round tariff reductions (negotiated between 1986 and 1994) are consistent with a theory in which negotiations internalize benefits only for the principal suppliers for any industry. As Bagwell and Staiger (2014) detail, the hope was that developing nations could nonetheless free ride off the nondiscriminatory (MFN) tariffs obtained by other nations' reciprocal negotiations, yet we should expect that developing nations would achieve limited gains unless they engage in reciprocal liberalization themselves. The principal supplier rule is one explanation for limited developing-country participation, particularly for the liberalization in our theory.

An additional obstacle facing developing countries is the "latecomers problem" described by Bagwell and Staiger (2014). This problem arises when developed countries have achieved their politically optimal tariffs and have no desire for further liberalization with developing nations that have yet to participate in reciprocal negotiations. The framework in the current chapter also suggests an additional possible dimension to the latecomers problem, when developed countries have already achieved all politically feasible cooperation in response to prohibitive policies through prior trade negotiations with other developed countries.

But, on a more optimistic note, the theory here suggests an alternative hypothesis, that more liberalization could be achieved if only there were better institutional norms that could facilitate cooperation in response to prohibitive policies. This possibility then offers a partial solution to the latecomers problem. Even if trade cooperation opportunities were exhausted under previous institutional norms for products and countries where trade already exists, there could still be potential cooperation between developed and developing countries where trade does not yet exist. There are then potentially significant gains from determining which institutional designs could aid the negotiation process for country pairs and industries in which trade is absent or severely limited.

Notes

The author is grateful to the editor, Ben Zissimos, and Mostafa Beshkar, Eric Bond, Chad Bown, Paola Conconi, Meredith Crowley, Alan Deardorff, W. Walker Hanlon, Arye Hillman, Balázs Muraközy, and Robert Staiger for helpful comments. Participants at the March 2015 DISSETTLE Warsaw workshop, the VSVK seminar at the Hungarian Academy of Sciences, the First Middle East and North Africa Trade Workshop, the CESifo Venice Summer Institute, the Annual Conference of the European Association for Research in Industrial Economics, and the European Trade Study Group provided excellent feedback. This chapter benefited from funding through the MTA Lendület program, the NSF-IGERT International Globalization and Development Program, and the project "Dispute Settlement in Trade: Training in Law and Economics" (DISSETTLE), a Marie Curie Initial Training Network (ITN) funded under the EU's Seventh Framework Programme, Grant Agreement No. FP7-PEOPLE-2010-ITN 264633.

1. This result is most transparent in equation (11) of Bagwell and Staiger (2011), which shows that cooperation has no effect on import tariffs if trade volume is zero under noncooperative policies.

2. This chapter follows the literature that presumes trade agreements' role is to correct global inefficiencies caused by nations' failure to internalize cross-border effects of their unilateral policy choices (Bagwell, Bown, and Staiger 2016). Another explanation for the elimination of prohibitive trade barriers could follow if trade agreements instead solve governments' commitment problem when facing pressure from domestic lobbies (Maggi and Rodríguez-Clare 1998). This possibility is discussed further at the end of this section.

3. Most literature on import restrictions and imperfect competition abstracts from the possibility of domestic subsidies that could correct distortions from imperfect competition (Bagwell, Bown, and Staiger 2016). The persistence of markup heterogeneity across industries (Epifani and Gancia 2011) suggests that nations are not actually imposing such best subsidies.

4. High trade costs for services are empirically plausible. Crozet, Milet, and Mirza (2016) find that French firms face large regulatory barriers for service exports, even those destined for other European Union members.

5. Marchetti and Mavroidis (2011) note the number of legal loopholes in WTO services agreements, and economists echo this concern (Francois and Hoekman 2010).

6. Introducing export subsidies would not be straightforward in our framework. For the strong political economy forces considered here, governments would seek unbounded transfers to the firms. A richer public finance framework that appropriately models the financing costs of subsidies would be necessary to develop reasonable predictions.

7. Lerner symmetry can also fail in a general equilibrium model with multiple sectors, but the discussion here mainly focuses on partial equilibrium examples, as this is the simplest way to introduce a second sector.

8. Under the standard long-run assumptions of perfect competition—perfect factor mobility and no barriers to entry—such profits would be dissipated, however.

9. Specifically, a subsidy is optimal for Cournot competition in homogeneous products (Brander and Spencer 1985), and a tax is optimal for Bertrand competition in differentiated products (Eaton and Grossman 1986).

10. Throughout the chapter, we regularly apply the following general Cournot-Nash equilibrium results For a given market with n active firms that can serve the market at costs $\{c_1, \ldots, c_n\}$ (here costs include trade costs and tariffs), the equilibrium quantity q_i produced by the firm that serves the market at cost c_i is $q_i = \frac{1 - c_i + \sum_{j \neq i}(c_j - c_i)}{n+1}$. Then the implied equilbrium market quantity is $Q = \frac{n - \sum_i c_i}{n+1}$ and the equilibrium market price is $P = \frac{1 + \sum_i c_i}{n+1}$ (see, e.g., Bagwell and Staiger 2012a).

11. Globally optimal policy here is then as in Ossa (2011), in which only import tariffs are available, and free trade is a corner solution. The policy space is thus distinct from that of Bagwell and Staiger (2012b, 2015), who allow for import and export subsidies and find interior solutions.

12. We acknowledge that this characterization does not fully solve for the likelihood of liberalization from prohibitive policies, conditional on market characteristics and a distribution of α. Such a solution would depend heavily on the distribution of α. We focus on the length of the α interval described earlier because it is a simple measure and still captures much of the variation of interest in the potential for liberalization from prohibitive policies.

13. To solve for the cutoffs, consider the difference between the free trade payoff and the monopoly payoff when $\alpha = 1$. The resulting polynomial, rescaled by $\frac{72}{(1-c)^2}$, is $5 - 32\left(\frac{\phi}{1-c}\right) + 44\left(\frac{\phi}{1-c}\right)^2$. The polynomial is negative between the two roots of $\frac{5}{22}$ and $\frac{1}{2}$.

14. A tariff that yields this combination of firms in the Home market must exist because (1) both Home firms are active under prohibitive tariffs for $\omega \in [1, 2)$ and (2) there exists some tariff range such that the inferior Foreign firm exits the Home market but the superior Foreign firm does not for $\omega \in (1, 2)$.

References

Baer, W. (1972), "Import Substitution and Industrialization in Latin America: Experiences and Interpretations," *Latin American Research Review* 7, 95–122.

Baldwin, R. (1987), "Politically Realistic Objectives and Trade Policy," *Economic Letters* 24, 287–290.

Bagwell, K., C. P. Bown, and R. W. Staiger (2016), "Is the WTO Passé?" *Journal of Economic Literature* 54, 1125–1231.

Bagwell, K. and R. W. Staiger (1999), "An Economic Theory of GATT," *American Economic Review* 89, 215–248.

Bagwell, K. and R. W. Staiger (2011), "What Do Trade Negotiators Negotiate About? Empirical Evidence from the World Trade Organization," *American Economic Review* 101, 1238–1273.

Bagwell, K. and R. W. Staiger (2012a), "The Economics of Trade Agreements in the Linear Cournot Delocation Model," *Journal of International Economics* 88, 32–46.

Bagwell, K. and R. W. Staiger (2012b), "Profit Shifting and Trade Agreements in Imperfectly Competitive Markets," *International Economic Review* 53, 1067–1104.

Bagwell, K. and R. W. Staiger (2014), "Can the Doha Round Be a Development Round? Setting a Place at the Table," in R. C. Feenstra and A. M. Taylor (eds.), *Globalization in an Age of Crisis: Multilateral Economic Cooperation in the Twenty-First Century*, 91–124, Chicago: University of Chicago Press for the NBER.

Bagwell, K. and R. W. Staiger (2015), "Delocation and Trade Agreements in Imperfectly Competitive Markets," *Research in Economics* 69, 132–156.

Bagwell, K. and R. W. Staiger (2016), "The Design of Trade Agreements," in K. Bagwell and R. W. Staiger (eds.), *Handbook of Commercial Policy*, volume 1, 435–529, Amsterdam: Elsevier.

Besley, T. and T. Persson (2009), "The Origins of State Capacity: Property Rights, Taxation, and Politics," *American Economic Review* 99, 1218–1244.

Bombardini, M. (2008), "Firm Heterogeneity and Lobby Participation," *Journal of International Economics* 75, 329–348.

Borchert, I., B. Gootiiz, A. G. Goswami, and A. Mattoo (2017), "Services Trade Protection and Economic Isolation,' *World Economy*, 40, 632–652. doi: 10.1111/twec.12327.

Borchert, I., B. Gootiiz, and A. Mattoo (2014), "Policy Barriers to International Trade in Services: Evidence from a New Database," *World Bank Economic Review* 28, 162–188.

Brander, J. A. (1995), "Strategic Trade Policy," in G. M. Grossman and K. Rogoff (eds.), *Handbook of International Economics*, volume 3, 1395–1455, Amsterdam: North Holland.

Brander, J. A. and B. J. Spencer (1985), "Export Subsidies and International Market Share Rivalry," *Journal of International Economics* 18, 83–100.

Crozet, M., E. Milet, and D. Mirza (2016), "The Discriminatory Effect of Domestic Regulations on International Trade in Services: Evidence from Firm Level Data," *Journal of Comparative Economics* 44, 585–607.

Deardorff, A. and R. M. Stern (2008), "Empirical Analysis of Barriers to International Services Transactions and the Consequences of Liberalization," in A. Mattoo, R. M. Stern, and G. Zanini (eds.), *A Handbook of International Trade in Services*, 169–220, New York: Oxford University Press.

Dixit, A. (1985), "Tax Policy in Open Economies," in A. J. Auerbach and M. Feldstein (eds.), *Handbook of Public Economics*, 313–374, Amsterdam: North Holland.

Drazen, A. and V. Grilli (1993), "The Benefits of Crises for Economic Reform," *American Economic Review* 83, 598–607.

Eaton, J. and G. Grossman (1986), "Optimal Trade and Industrial Policy under Oligopoly," *Quarterly Journal of Economics* 101, 383–406.

Epifani, P. and G. Gancia (2011), "Trade, Markup Heterogeneity and Misallocations," *Journal of International Economics* 83, 1–13.

Essaji, A. (2010), "Trade Liberalization, Standards and Protection," *BE Journal of Economic Analysis and Policy* 10, 1–21.

Feeney, J. and A. Hillman (2001), "Privatization and the Political Economy of Strategic Trade Policy," *International Economic Review* 42, 535–556.

Feenstra, R. C. (2004), *Advanced International Trade: Theory and Evidence*, Princeton, NJ: Princeton University Press.

Fischer, R. and P. Serra (2000), "Standards and Protection," *Journal of International Economics* 52, 377–400.

Francois, J. and B. Hoekman (2010), "Services Trade and Policy," *Journal of Economic Literature* 48, 642–692.

Fung, K. C. and A. Siu (2008), "Political Economy of Service Trade Liberalization and the Doha Round," *Pacific Economic Review* 13, 124–133.

Grossman, G. M. and E. Helpman (1994), "Protection for Sale," *American Economic Review* 84, 833–850.

Helpman, E., and P. R. Krugman (1989), *Trade Policy and Market Structure*, Cambridge, MA: MIT Press.

Horn, H. and J. Levinsohn (2001), "Merger Policies and Trade Liberalization," *Economic Journal* 111, 244–276.

Horstmann, I. and J. Markusen (1986), "Up the Average Cost Curve: Inefficient Entry and the New Protectionism," *Journal of International Economics* 20, 225–247.

Jafari, Y. and D. G. Tarr (2017), "Estimates of Ad Valorem Equivalents of Barriers against Foreign Suppliers of Services in Eleven Services Sectors and 103 Countries," *World Economy* 40, 544–573. doi: 10.1111/twec.12329.

Kee, H. L., A. Nicita, and M. Olarreaga (2009), "Estimating Trade Restrictiveness Indices," *Economic Journal* 119, 172–199.

Krugman, P. R., M. Obtsfeld, and M. Melitz (2014), *International Economics: Theory and Policy*, 10th edition, Boston: Pearson Education.

Lamp, N. (2015), "How Some Countries Became Special: Developing Countries and the Construction of Difference in Multilateral Lawmaking," *Journal of International Economic Law* 18, 743–771.

Lebrand, M. (2016), "Profit Shifting and FDI Restrictions," CESifo Working Paper No. 5885, Munich: CESifo.

Ludema, R. D. and A. M. Mayda (2013), "Do Terms-of-Trade Effects Matter for Trade Agreements? Evidence from WTO Countries," *Quarterly Journal of Economics* 128, 1837–1893.

Maggi, G. and A. Rodríguez-Clare (1998), "The Value of Trade Agreements in the Presence of Political Pressures," *Journal of Political Economy* 106, 574–601.

Maggi, G. and A. Rodríguez-Clare (2007), "A Political Economy Theory of Trade Agreements," *American Economic Review* 97, 1374–1406.

Marchetti, J. A. and P. C. Mavroidis (2011), "The Genesis of the GATS," *European Journal of International Law* 22, 689–721.

Mattoo, A. (2004), "The Services Dimension of China's Accession to the WTO," in D. Bhattasali, S. Li, and W. Martin (eds.), *China and the WTO: Accession, Policy Reform, and Poverty Reduction Strategies*, 117–140, Washington, DC: World Bank.

Miroudot, S., J. Sauvage, and B. Shepherd (2013), "Measuring the Cost of International Trade in Services," *World Trade Review* 12, 719–735.

Mrázová, M. (2011), "Trade Agreements When Profits Matter," mimeo, London School of Economics, February.

Ossa, R. (2011), "A New Trade Theory of GATT/WTO Negotiations," *Journal of Political Economy* 199, 122–152.

Ossa, R. (2014), "Trade Wars and Trade Talks with Data," *American Economic Review* 104, 4104–4146.

Rodrik, D. (1994), "The Rush to Free Trade in the Developing World: Why So Late? Why Now? Will It Last?," in S. Haggard and S. Webb (eds.), *Voting For Reform*, 61–88, New York: Oxford University Press.

Rodrik, D. (2001), "The Global Governance of Trade as If Development Really Mattered," United Nations Development Programme background paper, October.

Romer, P. (1994), "New Goods, Old Theory, and the Welfare Costs of Trade Restrictions," *Journal of Development Economics* 43, 5–38.

Staiger, R. W. and A. O. Sykes (2017), "The Economic Structure of International Trade-in-Services Agreements," mimeo, Dartmouth College, May.

Venables, A. J. (1985), "Trade and Trade Policy with Imperfect Competition: The Case of Identical Products and Free Entry," *Journal of International Economics* 19, 1–20.

6   China's Dual Export Sector

Fabrice Defever and Alejandro Riaño

6.1   Introduction

Over the last two decades, international trade theory has increasingly shifted its focus toward understanding an individual firm's decision to serve foreign markets, following, most notably, the seminal work by Melitz (2003). This paradigm change has been facilitated by the parallel emergence of a robust set of stylized facts that point to a substantial degree of heterogeneity across firms in terms of size and productivity within narrowly defined industries and according to their export status. More specifically, researchers have established three key empirical regularities that hold across a wide range of countries and time periods (Bernard et al. 2007; Melitz and Redding 2014):

(i) Relatively few firms engage in exporting.

(ii) Exporters tend to be larger and more productive than firms that only sell domestically.

(iii) The vast majority of exporting firms sell only a small share of their output abroad.

In this chapter, we ask whether these stylized facts also reflect the patterns observed in China's manufacturing sector after it joined the World Trade Organization (WTO) in 2001. We believe that this is a fruitful question to pose for three reasons. First, China has transitioned from being a quasiautarkic economy in the late 1970s to become the world's largest exporter in a little less than three decades while at the same time maintaining distinctive traits of a centrally planned economy (Naughton 1996, 2007; Xu 2011). Thus, it is not straightforward to expect its exporters to share the same traits as their counterparts operating in the United States, France, and other market-oriented economies for which the aforementioned stylized facts have been established.

Second, China is widely recognized for having followed an unconventional and heterodox approach to trade opening—placing a strong emphasis on encouraging exports while at the same time protecting its domestic market (Naughton 1996; Feenstra 1998; Rodrik 2010, 2014). Throughout its integration into the world economy, China has implemented a wide range of policy measures that have sought to facilitate its interaction with the rest of the world while minimizing disruptions to its socialist economy. This mixture of policy objectives has led Feenstra (1998) to aptly characterize China's trade policy regime as "one country, two systems": a large collection of export-oriented enclaves coexisting within a highly protected economy. Prominent examples of policy measures with these characteristics include free trade zones (FTZs)[1] (World Bank 2008; Wang 2013), the export processing duty drawback scheme (Feenstra and Hanson 2005; Ianchovichina 2007), and a broad range of tax concessions and subsidies featuring export share requirements (i.e., fiscal incentives conditioned on the recipient firm exporting more than a certain stated share of its output) (Defever and Riaño 2015, 2017a).

Third, China also stands at the heart of a long-standing debate on the role of FTZs as an industrial policy to foster economic development. On the one hand, FTZs have been very successful in promoting exports and may be the first step toward political-economic reforms. On the other hand, these policies have been shown to distort the market selection mechanism that lies at the heart of the observed performance premium of exporting firms (Chor 2009; Demidova and Rodríguez- Clare 2009; Defever and Riaño 2017a), and given the unprecedented scale of their implementation in China over the last three decades, it is only natural to wonder how similar Chinese exporters are to their peers elsewhere.

At first pass, our analysis suggests that exporters in China are not so different from exporters elsewhere. Only 28% of the firm-year observations in our data—which is a census of relatively large firms and is therefore likely to overestimate the share of exporting firms—report positive export sales. Furthermore, exporters' total shipments are, on average, more than twice as big as those of domestic firms and are also significantly more productive than the latter.

The most striking difference that we observe among Chinese manufacturing exporters against the backdrop of the stylized facts outlined earlier is the existence of a large number of exporters that sell almost all

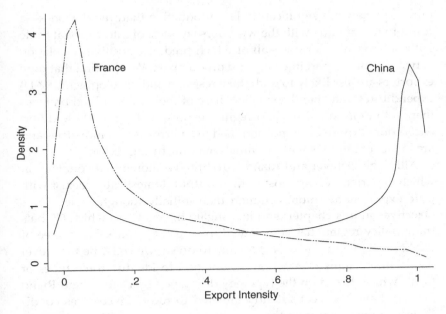

Figure 6.1
Export intensity distribution for Chinese and French manufacturing exporters. The figure depicts the kernel density of export intensity, defined as the share of exports in total sales, for firms reporting a positive value of exports. Data for Chinese manufacturing exporters are for the period 2000–2006 and are described in detail in section 6.3. Data on French exporters are from the Enquete Annuelle Entreprises, SESSI, for the year 2000.

their output abroad. To be more precise, between 2000 and 2006, more than one-third of Chinese manufacturing exporters sold 90% or more of their output in foreign markets. In contrast, only 1.9% of French exporters and 0.7% of US exporters display such high export intensity (Bernard et al. 2003). Figure 6.1 vividly illustrates this point by comparing the distribution of export intensity (i.e., the share of total sales accounted for by exports) for Chinese manufacturing exporters during our period of study with the equivalent distribution for French exporters in 2000.

Two major groups of exporters can therefore be identified in China: "pure exporters" (by which we mean firms that export more than 90% of their output), and "regular exporters," which sell most of their output domestically. Our empirical analysis reveals that these two types of exporters differ significantly from one another across several dimensions. First, although both pure and regular exporters are more productive than firms that only operate domestically, we find that pure exporters are significantly less productive than regular ones—a result that is at odds with the workhorse models of international trade with heterogeneous firms—all of which predict a positive correlation between firms' export intensity and productivity. We also find that pure exporters are less likely to undertake research and development (R&D) expenditures and spend a smaller share of their value added on taxes than both domestic firms and regular exporters. Despite these differences, pure exporters are not confined to a narrow set of industries and are in fact ubiquitous within China's manufacturing sector.

Although Defever and Riaño (2017b) have shown that countries in which exporters selling most of their output domestically coexist with pure exporters are more common than initially thought, one of our objectives in this chapter is to investigate the extent to which China's trade policy regime has contributed toward the remarkable degree of duality observed in its export sector. To do so, we combine firm-level data with customs transaction information to identify three types of firms, which, based on the typology developed by Defever and Riaño (2017a), have been consistently targeted to receive incentives conditioned on their exporting the majority of their output. These firms are foreign-owned enterprises, firms located in free trade zones, and firms exporting via the export processing regime.[2]

Our empirical analysis suggests that China's trade policies have played an instrumental role in fostering a dual export sector. Notably, nine out of ten manufacturing exporters in China are eligible to enjoy incentives contingent on export performance. Pure exporters are substantially more prevalent among the group of firms that are eligible to benefit from these policy measures. However, we show that pure exporters are also not confined to the export processing regime; a substantial number of them are foreign-owned firms not engaged in processing, and some are privately owned Chinese firms located in free trade zones. Lastly, we find that pure exporters pay on average 2.52% less taxes (as a share of their value added) than regular exporters. This result crucially holds even within each group of exporters (i.e., processing trade enterprises, foreign-owned firms not specializing in processing, and domestically owned exporters).

Related literature The previous literature studying the prevalence of high-intensity exporters in China has focused on the technological differences between pure and regular exporters (e.g., in terms of the magnitude of foreign market access costs faced by each type of exporter and their factor usage intensity) (Lu 2010; Dai, Maitra, and Yu 2016; Lu, and Tao 2014). In this chapter, we emphasize instead the role played by the heterodox trade policy regime in promoting pure exporters. We also contribute to the extensive body of work seeking to establish robust empirical regularities regarding the export behavior of firms, exemplified by the summaries by Bernard et al. (2007) and Melitz and Redding (2014), which we hope will inform future theoretical work regarding the effects of trade policy on firm-level outcomes.

The rest of the chapter is organized as follows. Section 6.2 provides an overview of the trade policies implemented in China that have fostered the development of its dual export sector. This section also discusses potential reasons for their persistent use. Section 6.3 describes the data we utilize. Section 6.4 presents our empirical findings, and section 6.5 gives our conclusions.

6.2   China's Heterodox Trade Opening

Since China's trade liberalization reforms have been amply described in several sources (Naughton 1996; Lardy 2002; Naughton 2007; Branstetter and Lardy 2008), our objective in this section is to highlight the key economic policy elements that have fostered dualism in China's export sector. Since, as we will argue, the initial objectives of policies fostering export dualism were quite rapidly achieved, we speculate about the potential reasons that could rationalize their use long after China had joined the WTO.

The death of Mao Zedong in 1976 marked a watershed moment in which the Chinese Communist Party (CCP) began its transition away from a command economy after the disastrous consequences of the Great Leap Forward (see Li and Yang 2005). The party's ideology was reoriented to emphasize economic development as the foundation for both socialism and the political monopoly of the CCP (Xu 2011).

The process of market reform relied on the establishment of a dual-track system in which the centrally planned economy coexisted with a market mechanism Lau, Qian, and Roland (2000). This approach was pursued more intensively in areas that were perceived to be least embedded in the socialist economy, such as international trade. Naughton (2007) notes that the main objective of this development strategy was not necessarily to reduce distortions but rather to experiment with reforms in a controlled environment. Doing so allowed policymakers to contain problems more easily and to undertake the necessary adjustments before rolling out policies at the provincial and national levels. Additionally, Xu (2011) argues that this setup also facilitated the implementation of schemes aimed at compensating interest groups opposing the reforms.

The creation of special economic zones in 1978, the establishment in 1986 of a separate corporate tax regime for foreign-invested enterprises, which provided tax breaks conditioned on a 50% export share requirement, and the institution of the processing trade regime in 1987 all conform to the general pattern outlined here. These three policy measures provided incentives for firms to export the majority of their output and, as a consequence, helped shield state-owned enterprises from import competition, as shown by Defever and Riaño (2017a). Of course, export subsidies foster exports, and import competition may increase to balance trade. However, subsidies associated with export requirements force firms that expand on the export market to also contract their domestic sales, which decreases domestic competition. By attracting multinational affiliates and compelling them to export all of their production, China has protected its low-productivity domestic companies from competition while simultaneously boosting exports. The promotion of processing trade enterprises and the establishment of FTZs are geared toward the same objective.

The reforms targeting pure exporters were initially implemented with the narrow objective of increasing and diversifying China's sources of foreign exchange—a goal that was very quickly achieved by the early 1990s (Naughton 2007). Why then has the use of incentives targeted toward firms exporting the majority of their output persisted so long after the early phases of transition? After all, it is well known that export promotion is not a desirable objective per se; as Krugman (1993) notes, exports are essentially just an input to acquire imports. Moreover, a large body of work has shown that policies that incentivize firms to export all their output can only be considered second-best policies from a welfare perspective in the presence of other distortions such as externalities, imperfect competition, or unemployment (Hamada 1974; Miyagiwa 1986; Davidson, Matusz, and Kreinin 1985; Rodrik 1987). Similarly, Defever and Riaño (2017a) show from a quantitative perspective that imposing export share requirements on export subsidies exacerbates their distortions relative to standard, unconditional subsidies.

Since all models listed here are set up in a static environment, they are not well suited to speak to the dynamic consequences of China's export promotion efforts. It is plausible that the policies targeted at pure exporters played a significant role in the rapid industrialization process observed in China, helping to ease the reallocation of labor from agriculture toward manufacturing, although, to the best of our knowledge, this hypothesis has not yet been formalized or quantified. Thus, static distortions in terms-of-trade or within-industry market shares could in principle be compensated by dynamic gains in physical capital and knowledge accumulation (Young 2003). A related advantage associated with maintaining tight control over its domestic market is that it allowed China's policymakers to successfully trade market access in exchange for technology transfers from foreign multinationals, as noted by Holmes, McGrattan, and Prescott (2015).

A second potential explanation for the continuing promotion of pure exporters—from a political economy perspective—relies on the regionally decentralized authoritarian nature of Chinese policymaking (Xu 2011). Local governments in China have enjoyed substantial autonomy in the design and implementation of rules and legislation affecting the export sector, grounded in the principle of reform experimentation described earlier. As the number of free trade zones expanded dramatically following their initial success,[3] an intense regional competition developed among local officials for bureaucratic promotion based on performance rankings, in which exports and foreign direct investment (FDI) growth featured prominently (Li and Zhou 2005; Xu 2011). Branstetter and Feenstra (2002), however, have shown that besides the promotion of international trade and foreign investment, local governments also placed significant importance on the performance of state-owned enterprises. Estimating a variant of Grossman and Helpman's (1994) seminal paper on protection for sale, extended to account for FDI and government ownership of domestic firms, Branstetter and Feenstra (2002) find that provincial governments in China assign a weight to consumer welfare of one-seventh to one-quarter of the weight applied to the output of domestic firms in their political objective function. This result is all the more striking since protection-for-sale models estimated across a wide range of countries usually imply that the weight assigned to consumer welfare in policymakers' objective function is substantially larger than that given to interest groups (Gawande and Krishna 2003). Defever and Riaño (2017a) show that subsidies with export requirements foster aggregate exports, but unlike unconditional export subsidies, they also increase the profitability of firms operating only in the domestic market. As noted, these two effects have a direct impact on key performance indicators' affecting the career progression of local officials. Maintaining the profitability of domestic producers is consistent with both the well-documented gradualist approach to transition followed by Chinese authorities (McMillan and Naughton 1992) and a desire to implement "reforms without losers," as suggested by Lau, Qian, and Roland (2000).

A third plausible motivation could be attributed to "strategic trade policy" objectives. The aggressive subsidization of pure exporters by China can be viewed as a means to increase its market share in international markets at the expense of its competitors, as illustrated by the seminal work by Brander and Spencer (1985). The fact that over the last decade China has been the most targeted country in terms of temporary trade barriers such as antidumping and countervailing duty measures attests to the popularity of this view across the world (Bown 2011). Rodrik (2013) argues that China has become the leading perpetrator of modern mercantilism. In his view, Chinese policymakers do not consider—as most economic models show—that the main source of gains from trade is the increased possibility of imported consumption. Instead, China has actively subsidized exports, perhaps at the expense of its own consumers, with the objective of supporting domestic production and employment.

Rodrik aptly summarizes the combination of export promotion and domestic protection elements underlying the Chinese approach to trade opening:

Rather than liberalize its trade regime in the standard way, which would have decimated the country's inefficient state enterprises, China allowed firms in special economic zones to operate under near-free-trade rules while maintaining trade restrictions elsewhere until the late 1990s. This enabled China to insert itself in the world economy while protecting employment and rents in the state sector. The Chinese Communist Party was strengthened and enriched, rather than weakened, as a result. (Rodrik 2014, p. 2000)

Although incentives targeted at pure exporters are one of the most important instruments of industrial policy deployed across developing countries—in no small part because of the perception of their success in China—their potential to foster economic development has been less convincing (Rodrik 2004; World Bank 2008; Farole and Akinci 2011). The encouragement of a dual export sector through the provision of subsidies conditioned on export performance limits the creation of productive linkages with the local economy, curtails the extent of potential knowledge spillovers, and can even harm the local economy, as shown by Rodríguez-Clare (1996).

6.3 Data

Our first data source is the annual survey of Chinese manufacturing firms compiled by the National Bureau of Statistics (NBS) for the years 2000 to 2006. This dataset includes both state-owned enterprises and private firms with sales above five million Chinese yuan and contains detailed balance sheet information as well as firms' ownership status and total export sales.

In order to clean the data, we follow Brandt, Biesebroeck, and Zhang (2012) and drop firms reporting less than eight employees or reporting missing or incoherent values for our key variables of interest. We drop observations that report missing, null, or negative values for total output, employment, intermediate inputs, fixed capital, and value added or if the export/sales, value-added tax/value added, output tax/output, or income tax/value-added ratios exceed 1. We also exclude firms with an operating status recorded as "inactive," "bankrupt," or "closed." Lastly, we drop a small number of observations in which firms report no exports in the manufacturing survey but for which we observe export transactions in the custom data (discussed later) in that particular year. After applying these filters, our final sample consists of 1,100,600 firm-year observations with 386,185 different firms. Our sample represents approximately 95% of China's industrial output and 98% of its manufacturing exports.

For the purposes of our empirical analysis, we define a *pure exporter* as a firm exporting more than 90% of its production in a given year, a firm reporting a positive value of export sales with an export intensity below 90% is classified as a *regular exporter*, and a *domestic firm* is a firm that does not export at all in a given year.

6.4 Empirical Analysis

Are exporters a minority in China? In a nutshell, yes. Table 6.1 presents a first cut at the manufacturing survey data. Column 2 reveals that only 28% of firm-year observations feature positive export flows. Since our survey is of large firms, it is likely that the share of exporters among the universe of Chinese manufacturing firms is even lower. Column 3 shows that, conditional on exporting, more than one-third

Table 6.1
Summary statistics for manufacturing survey, 2000–2006.

	Manufacturing Survey, 2000–2006		
	Number of Observations (1)	Percentage among	
		All Firms (2)	Exporters (3)
Pure exporters	105,543	9.59	34.37
Regular exporters	201,563	18.31	65.63
Domestic firms	793,494	72.10	
Total	1,100,600	100	100

of firms fall in the pure exporter category. This share is substantially higher than what has previously been documented in the United States, France, and Colombia—three countries that have figured prominently in the empirical literature on the decision to export at the firm level (Bernard and Jensen 1999; Bernard et al. 2003; Arkolakis 2010; Eaton, Kortum, and Kramarz 2011; Roberts and Tybout 1997)—none of which have a share of pure exporters (among exporting firms) that exceeds 8%.

Díaz de Astarloa et al. (2013) document the existence of a large number of "born-to-export" firms in the apparel sector in Bangladesh and argue that they could arise as a result of a lack of domestic demand for the specific products they manufacture. This explanation does not suit the Chinese case because (as shown) pure exporters in China are prevalent across a wide range of manufacturing industries and because domestic absorption in China exceeds exports in most manufacturing industries (Brandt and Morrow 2013).

Are exporters more productive than domestic firms?   In order to answer this question, we first estimate two-digit sector-specific production functions for the firms in the NBS survey over the period 2000–2006. Total factor productivity (TFP) is computed as the difference between a firm's observed and predicted output. We next regress our TFP measure on an export status dummy in order to estimate export performance premiums following Bernard and Jensen (1999) and Bernard et al. (2007), including year, four-digit sector, and prefecture-city fixed effects. The latter are included to capture potential productivity differences arising from a firm's location in an FTZ, as well as differences in cities' skill endowments, which might affect firm-level productivity, as shown by Cheng, Morrow, and Tacharoen (2012).

Total factor productivity for firm i in year t, denoted by φ_{it}, is estimated as the residual of the two-factor Cobb-Douglas production function

$$Q_{it} = \lambda_0 + \lambda_K K_{it} + \lambda_L L_{it} + \varphi_{it} + \epsilon_{it}, \tag{6.1}$$

where Q_{it}, L_{it}, and K_{it} denote firm i's value added before taxes, labor, and capital stock, respectively (all in logarithms), and ϵ_{it} stands for measurement error in output, λ_0 is a constant term, and λ_L and λ_K are the elasticities of output with respect to labor and capital, respectively. We use the deflators computed by Brandt, van Biesebroeck, and Zhang (2012) to calculate real values for intermediate inputs, capital, and output.[4] Real value added is obtained by subtracting the deflated value of intermediate inputs used in production from the firm's deflated output. As Feenstra, Li, and Yu (2014) note, it is preferable to estimate a valued added rather than a gross output production function in the case of China, because of the importance of processing trade. The production functions represented by equation (6.1) are estimated both by ordinary least squares (OLS) and using the semiparametric method proposed by Levinsohn and Petrin (2003) (LP). We cluster the standard errors at the firm level to account for any potential within-firm correlation over time.

The first three columns of table 6.2 reveal that Chinese exporters are indeed larger and more productive than domestic firms—just like their counterparts in other countries. More precisely, Chinese exporters are 128% larger in terms of sales and 76% more productive (using the LP estimator) than firms selling solely at home, with both differences being significant at the 1% confidence level.[5] Using the OLS-based TFP measure yields the same productivity ranking, although the magnitude of the productivity premium is lower. These results are in line with previous findings by Dai, Maitra, and Yu (2016), Ma, Tang, and Zhang (2014), and Feenstra, Li, and Yu (2014).

In columns 4–6, we present estimated performance premiums—again relative to domestic firms—for regular and pure exporters separately. We find that both types of exporters are larger and more productive than domestic firms. However, and more interestingly, we find that regular exporters are significantly larger and more productive than firms selling all their output abroad. This result is at odds with most workhorse models of international trade with heterogeneous

Table 6.2
Exporters' productivity premium.

	(1) log Sales	(2) TFP LP	(3) TFP OLS	(4) log Sales	(5) TFP LP	(6) TFP OLS
	Comparison Group: All Domestic Firms					
Exporter	0.824***	0.563***	0.151***			
	(0.005)	(0.004)	(0.003)			
• Pure exporters				0.575***	0.383***	0.073***
				(0.007)	(0.006)	(0.005)
• Regular exporters				0.917***	0.631***	0.181***
				(0.006)	(0.005)	(0.004)
Year fixed effects	✓	✓	✓	✓	✓	✓
Sector fixed effects	✓	✓	✓	✓	✓	✓
Prefecture-city fixed effects	✓	✓	✓	✓	✓	✓
# observations	1,100,600	1,100,600	1,100,600	1,100,600	1,100,600	1,100,600
# firms	386,185	386,185	386,185	386,185	386,185	386,185
R^2	0.217	0.265	0.313	0.221	0.268	0.314

Note: Robust standard error clustered at the firm level is in parentheses.
***significantly different from 0 at the 1% level; **significantly different from 0 at the 5% level;
*significantly different from 0 at the 10% level.

firms, such as Melitz (2003) (with more than two countries), Melitz and Ottaviano (2008), Arkolakis (2010), and Eaton, Kortum, and Kramarz (2011), all of which predict a positive correlation between a firm's productivity and its export intensity.[6]

Lu, Lu, and Tao (2014) show that adding a fixed cost to access both the domestic and foreign markets (over and above the fixed cost associated with setting up a production facility) to a partial equilibrium version of the Melitz (2003) model generates pure exporters that are less productive than regular ones, as long as the foreign market is larger than the domestic one. Another possibility is that the majority of pure exporters are engaged in processing activities, which are in turn associated with low fixed costs (Manova and Yu 2016) (e.g., if these firms do not engage in product design, marketing, or R&D or have lower search costs to find foreign buyers). While the two mechanisms outlined emphasize differences in "technology" between regular and pure exporters, lower fixed costs of servicing export markets can also be the result of incentives subject to export share requirements, as noted by Defever and Riaño (2017a). In this case, pure exporters enjoy advantages such as provision of utilities at below-market rates or priority access to infrastructure and land, which reduce the fixed cost of exporting relative to that faced by firms that choose to sell a substantial share of their output domestically. Firms that are relatively less productive elect to operate as pure exporters instead of regular exporters in order to save on fixed costs.

Is the prevalence of pure exporters the result of interindustry differences? It is plausible that the figures reported in table 6.1 are the result of a composition effect related to significant interindustry heterogeneity in market access costs. The standard Melitz (2003) model assumes that the fixed cost of servicing the foreign country—relative to the market's effective size—is higher than the corresponding cost of selling domestically. The implications following from this assumption are that the most productive firms select exporting and that all exporters sell some of their output domestically; in other words, it precludes the existence of pure exporters. Lu (2010) shows that in a multisector extension of the Melitz model, the sign of the selection condition can be reversed in the comparative advantage sector. Under these circumstances, the least productive firms in the comparative advantage sector export all their output, while the most productive sell both domestically and abroad. Conversely, domestic firms and regular exporters coexist in the comparative disadvantage sector. If this is the case, we would expect to see pure exporters disproportionately concentrated in certain sectors while being absent in others.

The data do not support this hypothesis. Figure 6.2 shows that pure exporters are not confined to a narrow set of industries; they coexist with regular exporters and domestic firms across all two-digit industries covered in the NBS dataset.[7] Pure exporters are less frequently observed in sectors such as printing, processing of ferrous metals, and paper, and are most prevalent in the manufacture of textiles, apparel, and sporting goods as well as in the production of electronics and electrical machinery.

Identifying firms eligible to receive support subject to exporting the majority of their output As noted in section 6.2, a key element of China's heterodox trade regime has been to actively incentivize firms that sell the majority of their output abroad. As documented in more detail by Defever and Riaño (2017a), policies favoring pure exporters have primarily targeted three groups of firms: foreign

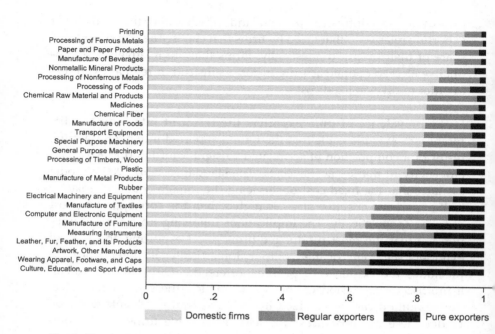

Figure 6.2
Distribution of firm types across two-digit industries.

invested enterprises (FIEs), processing trade enterprises (PTEs), and firms located in free trade zones (FTZs).

Although the NBS data provide information on firms' ownership status (with a further breakdown based on whether a firm's capital originates from Hong Kong, Macau, Taiwan, or other sources), it does not allow us to directly distinguish PTEs, because the survey does not record the value of exports sold through different customs regimes. To obtain information about a firm's reliance on processing exports, we merge the NBS dataset with a transaction-level customs dataset from the Chinese General Administration of Customs. We follow Manova and Yu (2016) and match the two datasets by using firms' names as a common variable. While each uses a different identifier, firms' names are a reliable matching variable since, by law, two firms cannot have the same name in the same administrative region. Table 6.3 provides summary statistics for the merged sample. We are able to successfully match approximately half the observations reporting a positive value of export sales in the NBS sample with their respective customs records. Nevertheless, it is reassuring that the share of pure exporters in the

Table 6.3
Summary statistics for matched data, 2000–2006.

| | Matched Data, 2000–2006 | | |
| | Number of Observations (1) | Percentage among | |
		All Firms (2)	Exporters (3)
Pure exporters	51,113	5.40	33.58
Regular exporters	101,104	10.69	66.42
Domestic firms	793,494	83.90	
Total	945,711	100	100

matched sample (column 3 of table 6.3) is almost identical to the one we find using the NBS data (column 3 of table 6.1).

We calculate the average share of exports sold under the processing trade regime in every year for each firm in the matched sample. The distribution of firms' export processing share is strikingly bimodal: 72.1% of firms use the processing regime for less than 10% of their exports, while 15.5% sell more than 90% of their exports under this regime. Therefore, we define processing trade enterprises as firms selling more than 90% of their exports through the processing trade regime. It is important to highlight the fact that, based on this definition, PTEs encompass firms that export all their output as well as firms selling domestically and using the processing regime to serve foreign markets. We then proceed to identify foreign invested enterprises as firms with a positive amount of foreign capital but that do not satisfy the criteria to be considered a PTE.

Although the NBS survey does not explicitly state whether a firm is located in a free trade zone, it does record firms' administrative location. We use this information to identify firms operating in a free trade zone as producers located in prefecture-level cities promoted as special economic zones, coastal development zones, or the Yangtze and Pearl River Delta economic zones. Our definition of FTZ excludes smaller industrial parks such as "economic and technological development zones," "new and high-tech industrial development zones," and "export processing zones," in which firms also enjoy preferential treatment. Many of these are located along the coast within prefecture-level cities already classified as FTZs in our definition.[8] The appendix provides the exact list of prefecture cities included in our definition of FTZs.

Table 6.4

Percentage of exporters and percentage of pure exporters by firm type and location.

Panel A: Percentage of Exporters

	PTE	FIE	Neither FIE nor PTE	Total
In an FTZ	22.63	35.79	24.08	82.51
Outside an FTZ	1.42	5.66	10.41	17.49
Total	24.06	41.45	34.49	100.00

Panel B: Percentage of Pure Exporters among All Exporters

	PTE	FIE	Neither FIE nor PTE	All Exporters
In an FTZ	52.63	34.67	22.49	36.04
Outside an FTZ	35.56	27.85	16.85	21.93
All locations	51.62	33.74	20.79	33.58

Prevalence of different firm types Panel A of table 6.4 presents the share of exporters across each category described (FIE, PTE, neither) and also according to firms' location in an FTZ. The main message from panel A is that approximately 90% of Chinese manufacturing exporters are potentially eligible to receive preferential treatment, conditional on exporting the majority of their output. Panel B shows the percentage of pure exporters among exporters across different firm groups. Pure exporters are highly concentrated among FIEs and PTEs, accounting for approximately one-half and one-third of all exporters in these categories, respectively. Table 6.4 also shows that pure exporters, regardless of their ownership status or the customs regime used to sell their output, are more likely to be located in an FTZ.

Figure 6.3 presents the distribution of export intensity across the four groups of exporters described in table 6.4. Pure exporters are significantly more prevalent among PTEs, whereas the distribution of export intensity for FIEs and firms located in an FTZ appears more bimodal. Interestingly, more than one-third of PTEs sell 30% or more of their output domestically. This challenges the commonly held view that firms engaged in processing activities are fully specialized in production for export (Brandt and Morrow 2013). The distribution of export intensity for the residual group of firms (i.e., exporters not located in an FTZ and are neither PTEs nor FIEs) shows a majority of firms selling a small share of their output abroad—the more common pattern documented

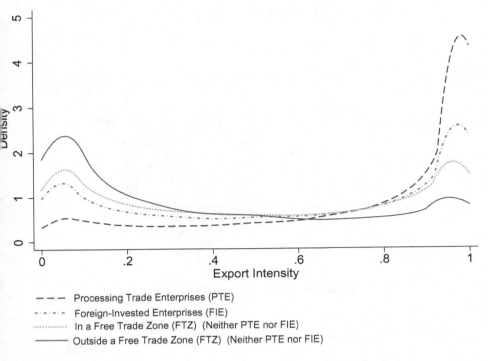

Figure 6.3
Export intensity distribution by firm type and location.

for manufacturing firms in other countries—although there is still a discernible hump in the upper bound of the export intensity distribution for this group of firms. This could result from the fact that our definition of FTZ excludes small industrial parks, which also provide preferential treatment for pure exporters, or because our firm grouping does not capture policies benefiting pure exporters enacted at the local level, such as the "Famous Brands" initiative or the "Auto Export Base" program.

Figure 6.4 presents the geographical distribution of FTZs and the distribution of the share of pure exporters among all exporting firms across prefecture cities (by quartiles); 25% of the prefectures have 33.6% or more of their exporters classified as pure exporters.[9] It can clearly be seen that pure exporters are highly concentrated along coastal areas, the same places where FTZs have been established. Unlike the traditional definition of a free trade zone, which stresses the fact that usually they are small, fenced-in, geographically delimited areas (World Bank 2008),

Free Trade Zones Established between 1979 and 2000

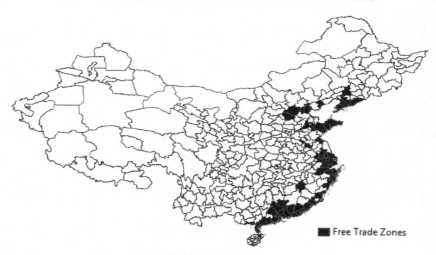

Quartiles of the Share of Pure Exporters

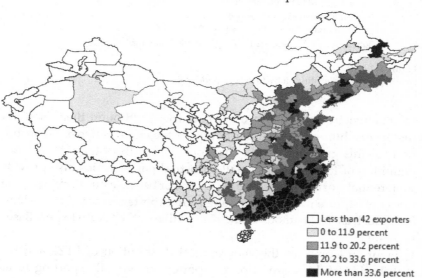

Figure 6.4
Free trade zones and share of exporting firms classified as pure exporters. A detailed description of the free trade zones is included in the appendix.

the scale of FTZs in China is unprecedentedly massive. They often encompass entire prefectures and in fact, as shown in figure 6.4, cover a substantial fraction of China's eastern seaboard.

Foreign affiliates from Hong Kong, Macau, and Taiwan Foreign direct investment (FDI) has played an instrumental role in China's integration into the world economy. A notable characteristic of FDI inflows into China, as Branstetter and Foley (2010) point out, is that a substantial share of them originate from Hong Kong, Macau, or Taiwan (HKMT). Anecdotal evidence suggests that an important share of HKMT-originated capital flows are the result of "round-tripping" (Prasad and Wei 2007), where Chinese investors create shell companies in HKMT to operate production facilities located in mainland China in order to enjoy preferential tax treatment as foreign investment, which is also often conditioned on export performance (Defever and Riaño 2017a).

Using the information available in the NBS data regarding firms' ownership, we now explore the role of HKMT foreign firms in China's export sector. The first column of table 6.5 shows that foreign-owned firms are extremely important in China's export sector, accounting for slightly less than half of exporters. To provide a reference point, Rodrigue (2008) finds that foreign-owned firms account for only

Table 6.5
Percentage of firms with capital originating in Hong Kong, Macau, or Taiwan by firm type.

| | Manufacturing Survey | Matched Data | | | |
| | All Exporters | FIEs | PTEs | Neither FIEs nor PTEs | |
				in an FTZ	outside an FTZ
Non-HKMT foreign affiliate	11.37	23.97	28.56		
Non-HKMT foreign joint venture	11.24	32.54	16.08		
HKMT foreign affiliates	12.25	20.30	33.43		
HKMT foreign joint venture	10.01	23.19	16.31		
State-owned enterprises	6.77		1.29	8.55	26.38
Chinese private firms	48.37		4.33	91.45	73.62
	100.00	100.00	100.00	100.00	100.00

19% of Indonesian exporters. FIEs are evenly distributed between wholly owned foreign affiliates and joint ventures and also across the sources of their capital. Columns 2–4, which are based on our matched sample, show first that PTEs are overwhelmingly foreign owned (only 5% of them are domestically owned) and second that approximately half of all PTEs and 44% of FIEs not specialized in processing activities are owned by HKMT-based investors. These figures provide suggestive evidence of the importance of round-tripping and its close association with incentives conditioned on export performance.

A recurring argument put forward by policymakers to rationalize the use of incentives to attract foreign-owned firms is that their activity generates knowledge spillovers that can be appropriated by domestic firms through technology transfer, imitation of best practices, worker flows, and access to new markets (Keller 2004). Inasmuch as HKMT-based FDI flows are targeted toward export-oriented activities with the objective of enjoying tax incentives, the potential for FDI spillovers for Chinese firms appears quite limited, as shown by Agarwal, Milner, and Riaño (2014). Table 6.6 presents the percentage of observations reporting a positive value of R&D in the NBS survey. Column 1 shows that the proportion of pure exporters reporting a positive level of expenditures on R&D is three times smaller than that among regular exporters. Similarly, large differences in the share of firms reporting any R&D expenditures can also be identified in the matched data for all firm categories presented in columns 2–5. Regulations such as the 2002 *Provisions on Guiding Foreign Direct Investment*, for example, can help explain the stark differences in R&D activity between pure and regular exporters, since they provide preferential treatment to foreign enterprises that are *either* technology intensive *or* export the majority of their production. As a result, foreign investors seeking access to the Chinese market might choose to invest in R&D in order to qualify as

Table 6.6
Percentage of observations featuring positive expenditures on R&D.

Year	Manufacturing Survey	Matched Data			
	All Exporters	FIEs	PTEs	Neither FIEs nor PTEs	
				in an FTZ	outside an FTZ
Pure exporters	6.99	7.35	7.40	11.71	14.04
Regular exporters	20.78	17.07	15.92	26.99	36.26

technologically intensive firms, whereas pure exporters would tend to concentrate on labor-intensive activities.

Firm-level tax outlays Defever and Riaño (2017a) document a wide variety of policy measures utilized in China (even after joining the WTO) that provide incentives to firms under the condition that they export the majority of their output. Although it is extremely difficult to obtain systematic information indicating which firms receive these incentives and how big these incentives are, we can investigate whether pure exporters pay fewer taxes than domestic firms and regular exporters. To do so, we use the information provided by the NBS survey regarding firms' income, value added, and sales tax outlays as reported on their balance sheet.

Table 6.7 presents the tax outlay premiums of pure exporters vis-à-vis other firms. The upper panel of the table uses domestic firms as a reference group, while the lower one presents a groupwise comparison with regular exporters. For instance, the latter compares pure exporters that rely primarily on the processing customs regime to export with PTE firms that sell less than 90% of their output abroad in terms of their share of value added devoted to each specific tax. Just as in the productivity premium regressions, we include year, four-digit sector, and province- and city-specific fixed effects and cluster standard errors at the firm level. The dependent variables used in the regressions reported in columns 1–3 are respectively the income tax, value-added tax, and sales tax outlays as a share of a firm's value added.

The coefficients reported in Table 6.7 can be interpreted as the difference in the share of value added devoted to the payment of each type of tax by pure exporters relative to the corresponding control group defined earlier. By adding the coefficients, we obtain the overall difference (in percentage points) of firms' value added spent on taxes. Domestic firms devote, on average, an additional 5.08% ($\approx 0.68 + 3.32 + 1.08$) of their value added to pay these taxes compared to pure exporters, while regular exporters spend 2.52% ($\approx 0.47 + 1.88 + 0.17$) more. Columns 4–6 present the difference in tax expenditures for each of the three groups of pure exporters (PTEs, FIEs, and the residual group) compared to domestic firms and regular exporters of each type. All the estimates except the one comparing the sales tax outlays of pure and regular exporters that are FIEs indicate that pure exporters pay significantly less taxes than other firms.

Table 6.7
Pure exporters' tax expenditure premiums relative to domestic firms and regular exporters.

		Comparison Group: Domestic Firms					
		Manufacturing Survey			Matched Data		
		(1) Income Tax	(2) VAT Tax	(3) Sales Tax	(4) Income Tax	(5) VAT Tax	(6) Sales Tax
		as share of value added			as share of value added		
		Comparison Group					
		All Domestic Firms			All Domestic Firms		
Pure exporter		−0.687*** (0.019)	−3.325*** (0.042)	−1.082*** (0.023)			
×	FIE				−1.110*** (0.036)	−5.914*** (0.080)	−2.095*** (0.033)
×	PTE				−1.092*** (0.034)	−8.621*** (0.072)	−2.023*** (0.032)
×	Neither FIE nor PTE				−0.194*** (0.052)	−3.239*** (0.102)	−0.859*** (0.050)
		Comparison Group					
		All Regular Exporters			Each Type of Regular Exporter		
Pure exporter		−0.471*** (0.020)	−1.881*** (0.043)	−0.171*** (0.023)			
×	FIE				−0.460*** (0.041)	−3.497*** (0.088)	−0.049 (0.039)
×	PTE				−0.330*** (0.047)	−4.299*** (0.103)	−0.236*** (0.043)
×	Neither FIE nor PTE				−0.413*** (0.056)	−0.501*** (0.107)	−0.183*** (0.054)
Year fixed effects		✓	✓	✓	✓	✓	✓
Sector fixed effects		✓	✓	✓	✓	✓	✓
Prefecture city fixed effects		✓	✓	✓	✓	✓	✓
# of observations		1,100,600	1,100,600	1,100,600	945,711	945,711	945,711
# of firms		386,185	386,185	386,185	348,860	348,860	348,860
R^2		0.060	0.103	0.120	0.061	0.122	0.118

Note: Robust standard error clustered at the firm level in parentheses.
***significantly different from 0 at the 1% level; **significantly different from 0 at the 5% level;
*significantly different from 0 at the 10% level.

6.5   Concluding Remarks: Is Dualism Here to Stay?

China's transition over the last 30 years to become the world's largest exporter has been nothing short of spectacular, spurring great interest in the economic reforms that made it possible. In this chapter, we have shown that China's heterodox approach toward trade opening, combining strong incentives for export promotion with domestic protection, has resulted in a starkly dual export sector.

In this chapter, we have shown that although Chinese exporters resemble their counterparts elsewhere—namely in terms of being a minority among manufacturing firms and being larger and more productive—economic policies favoring firms exporting the majority of their output have engendered a rather unique degree of dualism among them. Using a rich database of Chinese manufacturing firms for the period 2000–2006 matched with customs transaction data, we have shown that the vast majority of Chinese exporters belong to one of two groups: regular exporters (firms that sell most of their output domestically) and pure exporters (producers that sell almost exclusively abroad). A large share of pure exporters are engaged in processing activities (i.e., assembling imported inputs into final goods to be sold in foreign markets), but many of them also export through the ordinary trade customs regime. Pure exporters are primarily located close to the eastern seaboard, in prefectures with free trade zones, and are also likely to be foreign owned. Compared to regular exporters, pure exporters tend to be significantly smaller and less productive, less likely to engage in R&D activities, and, crucially, devote a smaller share of their value added to tax payments.

Incentives contingent on export performance have remained a prominent element of China's trade policy regime, even after it became a member of the WTO in 2001. For instance, tax concessions granted by the central government to foreign-invested enterprises conditioned on their exporting more than 70% of their output were maintained until 2008, despite several complaints voiced by WTO members during China's annual Transitional Review Mechanism (TRM). At the same time, while China was required to disclose any subsidy programs in place on a yearly basis under the provision of Article 1 of the Agreement on Subsidies and Countervailing Measures (ASCM), it ended up submitting just two notifications, in 2006 and 2011, when the TRM ended. Both notifications were deemed to be highly incomplete, since they failed to state the level and annual amount spent on a large number of subsidies listed (Haley and Haley 2013). Additionally, subsidies granted at the subnational, provincial, and local levels were not acknowledged in either notification.[10] Similarly, the "Famous Brands" initiative—a large umbrella of export support programs, which featured several subsidies contingent on export performance—was introduced in 2005 and was not abandoned until 2009, after being challenged by the United States and the European Union at the WTO one year earlier.

The persistence of export promotion policies and their protectionist implications after China's successful integration into the global economy brings to mind Matoo and Subramanian's (2011) allegorical portrayal of China and its trade policy as Penelope, Ulysses's wife, unraveling by night the shroud she wove by day to keep her suitors at bay. As member countries maintain pressure on China to abide by WTO rules, one natural question to ask is whether the dual nature of China's export sector will endure. In this respect, Defever and Riaño (2015) find, using data from the World Bank Enterprise Survey available for 2002 and 2013, that the importance of pure exporters in China has declined significantly over the last decade. These results suggest that China's trade policy might have shifted its focus away from the active promotion of firms exporting the majority of their output, thereby reducing the extent of dualism in its export sector.

Understanding the potential impact of ending policies that incentivize pure exporters is crucial for a large number of developing economies that rely on subsides with export requirements. Crucially, 19 developing countries had been exempted from complying with the Agreement on Subsidies and Countervailing Measures by the WTO until December 31, 2015.[11] Defever et al. (2019) have shown, however, that efforts to make free trade zones compliant with the subsidy disciplines of the WTO by removing explicit export performance requirements—specifically in the Dominican Republic—have not been very successful in reducing the extent of duality of the export sector.

Appendix
List of Free Trade Zones

A.1 Special Economic Zones

Special economic zones include the six prefectures Haikou, Sanya, Shantou Shi, Shenzhen, Xiamen, and Zhuhai, and the entire province of Hainan.

A.2   Coastal Development Zones

Coastal development zones include the Shanghai economic area established in 1982. This zone does not entirely cover the Shanghai
prefecture and notably does not include the city center of Shanghai.
We make use of the firm post code to exclude firms located in the
city center from our definition of FTZ (i.e., postal code starting with
2000).

Coastal development zones also include the prefecture cities of
Anshan, Baoding, Beihai, Dalian, Dandong, Fuzhou, Guangzhou,
Jinan, Langfang, Lianyungang, Nantong, Ningbo, Qingdao, Qinhuang-
dao, Quanzhou, Shenyang, Shijiazhuang, Tianjin, Weifang, Wenzhou,
Weihai, Yantai, Yingkou, Zhanjiang, Zhangzhou, and Zibo.

A.3   Yangtze River Delta Economic Zone

The Yangtze River Delta economic zone includes cities located in the
Yangtze River Delta but also some cities located outside the area as
a result of mutual economic development. In 1982, the Chinese government set up the Shanghai economic area. Besides Shanghai, four
cities in Jiangsu (Changzhou, Nantong, Suzhou, and Wuxi) and five
cities in Zhejiang (Hangzhou, Huzhou, Jiaxing, Ningbo, and Shaox-
ing) were included. In 1992, a 14-city cooperative joint meeting was
launched. Besides the previous 10 cities, the members included Nan-
jing, Yangzhou, and Zhenjiang in Jiangsu and Zhoushan in Zhejiang.
In 1998, Taizhou became a new member.

A.4   Pearl River Delta Economic Zone

The boundaries of the Pearl River Delta as an economic zone differ
from those associated with the geographic boundaries of the delta.
In 1985, the State Council designated the Pearl River Delta as an
open economic zone. It contained three special economic zones that
had been established earlier: Shantou, Shenzhen, and Zhuhai. Other
leading cities in the open zone are Dongguan, Foshan, Guangzhou,
Huizhou, Jiangmen, and Zhongshan. "Peripheral" cities that were
declared open cities include Chaozhou, Heyuan, Jieyang, Maoming,
Meizhou, Qingyuan, Shanwei, Shaoguan, Yangjiang, Zhanjiang, and
Zhaoqing.

Notes

We thank Ben Zissimos and Arye Hillman as well as participants at the CESifo Venice Summer Institute Workshop on "The World Trade Organization and Economic Development," held at Venice International University in July 2015. All remaining errors are our own.

1. Throughout the chapter, we use the term free trade zone to encompass special economic zones and other geographically defined areas of export promotion.

2. Export processing is a legal arrangement between a foreign partner and a local producer where all or part of the intermediate inputs are imported and the finished product is reexported after processing or assembly by enterprises within the mainland.

3. See Wang (2013) for a detailed account of the evolution of special economic zones.

4. Nominal values of output and capital are deflated using two-digit sectoral price indexes. The deflators are obtained from the system of national accounts of the Chinese Bureau of Statistics. The two-digit intermediate input deflators have been computed using both output deflators and the 2002 Chinese input-output table.

5. $\exp(0.824) - 1 \approx 1.28$ and $\exp(0.563) - 1 \approx 0.76$, respectively.

6. All exporting firms allocate the same share of their total sales to the export market in the Melitz (2003) model with two countries. With three or more countries, the most productive firms sell to more destinations and therefore exhibit a higher export intensity than firms selling in fewer markets.

7. Redoing figure 6.2 at the four-digit level of aggregation yields the same conclusion.

8. Using a word search on firms' addresses, Schminke and van Biesebroeck (2011) report 891 new firms established in "economic and technological development zones" between 1999 and 2005, and 47% of them were located either in the Yangtze or Pearl River Delta economic zone, already accounted for as an FTZ in our definition. Tracking firms located in an "export processing zone" in our data is easier since the customs data provide a special code identifying them. However, in 2006, only 166 firms could be classified as being located in any of these processing zones, 85% of which are located in a city already classified as an FTZ.

9. Locations with fewer than 42 observations have been excluded in order to avoid inaccuracies.

10. See "Request from the United States to China," October 11, 2011, reference G/SCM/Q2/CHN/42.

11. See General Council decision of July 31, 2007 WT/L/691. The beneficiaries of this extension were Antigua and Barbuda, Barbados, Belize, Costa Rica, Dominica, Dominican Republic, El Salvador, Fiji, Grenada, Guatemala, Jamaica, Jordan, Mauritius, Panama, Papua New Guinea, St. Kitts and Nevis, St. Lucia, Saint Vincent and the Grenadines, and Uruguay. The notification also lists the subsidy programs that need to be reformed.

References

Agarwal, N., C. Milner, and A. Riaño. (2014). "Credit Constraints and Spillovers from Foreign Firms in China," *Journal of Banking and Finance* 48, 261–275.

Arkolakis, C. (2010). "Market Penetration Costs and the New Consumers Margin in International Trade," *Journal of Political Economy* 118, 1151–1199.

Bernard, A. B., J. Eaton, J. B. Jensen, and S. Kortum. (2003). "Plants and Productivity in International Trade," *American Economic Review* 93, 1268–1290.

Bernard, A. B. and J. B. Jensen. (1999). "Exceptional Exporter Performance: Cause, Effect, or Both?" *Journal of International Economics* 47, 1–25.

Bernard, A. B., J. B. Jensen, S. J. Redding, and P. K. Schott. (2007). "Firms in International Trade," *Journal of Economic Perspectives* 21, 105–130.

Bown, C. P. (2011). "Taking Stock of Antidumping, Safeguards and Countervailing Duties, 1990–2009," *World Economy* 34, 1955–1998.

Brander, J. A. and B. J. Spencer. (1985). "Export Subsidies and International Market Share Rivalry," *Journal of International Economics* 18, 83–100.

Brandt, L. and P. M. Morrow. (2013). "Tariffs and the Organization of Trade in China," manuscript, University of Toronto.

Brandt, L., J. van Biesebroeck, and Y. Zhang. (2012). "Creative Accounting or Creative Destruction? Firm-Level Productivity Growth in Chinese Manufacturing," *Journal of Development Economics* 97, 339–351.

Branstetter, L. G. and R. C. Feenstra. (2002). "Trade and Foreign Direct Investment in China: A Political Economy Approach," *Journal of International Economics* 58, 335–358.

Branstetter, L. G. and C. F. Foley. (2010). "Facts and Fallacies about U.S. FDI in China," in *China's Growing Role in World Trade*, edited by R. C. Feenstra and S.-J. Wei, 513–539, Cambridge, MA: National Bureau of Economic Research.

Branstetter, L. G. and N. R. Lardy. (2008). "China's Embrace of Globalization," in *China's Great Economic Transformation*, edited by L. Brandt and T. G. Rawski, Cambridge: Cambridge University Press.

Cheng, W., J. Morrow, and K. Tacharoen. (2012). "Productivity as If Space Mattered: An Application to Factor Markets across China," manuscript, London School of Economics.

Chor, D. (2009). "Subsidies for FDI: Implications from a Model with Heterogeneous Firms," *Journal of International Economics* 78, 113–125.

Dai, M., M. Maitra, and M. Yu. (2016). "Unexceptional Exporter Performance in China? The Role of Processing Trade," *Journal of Development Economics* 121, 177–189.

Davidson, C., S. J. Matusz, and M. E. Kreinin. (1985). "Analysis of Performance Standards for Direct Foreign Investments," *Canadian Journal of Economics* 18, 876–890.

Defever, F., J.-D. Reyes, A. Riaño, and M. E. Sánchez-Martín. (2019). "Special Economic Zones and WTO Compliance: Evidence from the Dominican Republic," *Economica* 86, 532–568.

Defever, F. and A. Riaño. (2015). "Gone for Good? Subsidies with Export Share Requirements in China: 2002–2013," *World Bank Economic Review Papers and Proceedings* 29, S125–S144.

Defever, F. and A. Riaño. (2017a). "Subsidies with Export Share Requirements in China," *Journal of Development Economics* 126, 33–51.

Defever, F. and A. Riaño. (2017b). "Twin Peaks," Centre for Economic Performance Discussion Paper, London School of Economics and Political Science, London.

Demidova, S. and A. Rodríguez-Clare. (2009). "Trade Policy under Firm-Level Heterogeneity in a Small Economy," *Journal of International Economics* 78, 100–112.

Díaz de Astarloa, B., J. Eaton, K. Krishna, B. Y. Aw-Roberts, A. Rodríguez-Clare, and J. Tybout. (2013). "Born-to-Export Firms: Understanding Export Growth in Bangladesh," International Growth Centre Working Paper, International Growth Centre, London.

Eaton, J., S. Kortum, and F. Kramarz. (2011). "An Anatomy of International Trade: Evidence from French Firms," *Econometrica* 79, 1453–1498.

Farole, T. and G. Akinci. (2011). *Special Economic Zones: Progress, Emerging Challenges and Future Directions*, Washington, DC: World Bank.

Feenstra, R. C. (1998). "One Country, Two Systems: Implications of WTO Entry for China," manuscript, University of California, Davis.

Feenstra, R. C. and G. H. Hanson. (2005). "Ownership and Control in Outsourcing to China: Estimating the Property-Rights Theory of the Firm," *Quarterly Journal of Economics* 120, 729–761.

Feenstra, R. C., Z. Li, and M. Yu. (2014). "Exports and Credit Constraints under Incomplete Information: Theory and Evidence from China," *Review of Economics and Statistics* 96, 729–744.

Gawande, K. and P. Krishna. (2003). "The Political Economy of Trade Policy: Empirical Approaches," in *Handbook of International Trade*, edited by J. Harrigan and E. K. Choi, Oxford: Basil Blackwell.

Grossman, G. M. and E. Helpman. (1994). "Protection for Sale," *American Economic Review* 84, 833–850.

Haley, U. C. V. and G. T. Haley. (2013). *Subsidies to Chinese Industry: State Capitalism, Business Strategy and Trade Policy*, Oxford: Oxford University Press.

Hamada, K. (1974). "An Economic Analysis of the Duty Free Zone," *Journal of International Economics* 4, 225–241.

Holmes, T. J., E. R. McGrattan, and E. C. Prescott. (2015). "Quid Pro Quo: Technology Capital Transfers for Market Access in China," *Review of Economic Studies* 82, 1154–1193.

Ianchovichina, E. (2007). "Are Duty Drawbacks on Exports Worth the Hassle?" *Canadian Journal of Economics* 40, 881–913.

Keller, W. (2004). "International Technology Diffusion," *Journal of Economic Literature* 42, 752–782.

Krugman, P. R. (1993). "What Do Undergrads Need to Know about Trade?" *American Economic Review* 83, 23–26.

Lardy, N. R. (2002). *Integrating China into the Global Economy*, Washington, DC: Brookings Institution Press.

Lau, L. J., Y. Qian, and G. Roland. (2000). "Reform without Losers: An Interpretation of China's Dual-Track Approach to Transition," *Journal of Political Economy* 108, 120–143.

Levinsohn, J. and A. Petrin. (2003). "Estimating Production Functions Using Inputs to Control for Unobservables," *Review of Economic Studies* 70, 317–341.

Li, H. and L.-A. Zhou. (2005). "Political Turnover and Economic Performance: The Incentive Role of Personnel Control in China," *Journal of Public Economics* 89, 1743–1762.

Li, W. and D. T. Yang. (2005). "The Great Leap Forward: Anatomy of a Central Planning Disaster," *Journal of Political Economy* 113, 840–877.

Lu, D. (2010). "Exceptional Exporter Performance? Evidence from Chinese Manufacturing Firms," manuscript, University of Chicago.

Lu, J., Y. Lu, and Z. Tao. (2014). "Pure Exporter: Theory and Evidence from China," *World Economy* 37, 1219–1236.

Ma, Y., H. Tang, and Y. Zhang. (2014). "Factor Intensity, Product Switching, and Productivity: Evidence from Chinese Exporters," *Journal of International Economics* 92, 349–362.

Manova, K. and Z. Yu. (2016). "How Firms Export: Processing vs. Ordinary Trade with Financial Frictions," *Journal of International Economics* 100, 120–137.

Matoo, A. and A. Subramanian. (2011). "China and the World Trading System," Policy Research Working Paper No. 5897, Washington, DC: World Bank.

McMillan, J. and B. Naughton. (1992). "How to Reform a Planned Economy: Lessons from China," *Oxford Review of Economic Policy* 8, 130–143.

Melitz, M. J. (2003). "The Impact of Trade on Intra-industry Reallocations and Aggregate Productivity," *Econometrica* 71, 1695–1725.

Melitz, M. J. and G. I. P. Ottaviano. (2008). "Market Size, Trade, and Productivity," *Review of Economic Studies* 75, 295–316.

Melitz, M. J. and S. J. Redding (2014) "Heterogeneous Firms and Trade," in *Handbook of International Economics*, volume 4, edited by E. Helpman, K. Rogoff, and G. Gopinath, 1–54, Amsterdam: Elsevier.

Miyagiwa, K. F. (1986). "A Reconsideration of the Welfare Economics of a Free-Trade Zone," *Journal of International Economics* 21, 337–350.

Naughton, B. (1996). "China's Emergence and Prospects as a Trading Nation," *Brookings Papers on Economic Activity* 27, 273–344.

Naughton, B. (2007). *The Chinese Economy: Transitions and Growth*, Cambridge, MA: MIT Press.

Prasad, E. and S.-J. Wei. (2007). "The Chinese Approach to Capital Inflows: Patterns and Possible Explanations," in *Capital Controls and Capital Flows in Emerging Economies: Policies, Practices and Consequences*, edited by S. Edwards, 421–480, Chicago: University of Chicago.

Roberts, M. J. and J. R. Tybout. (1997). "The Decision to Export in Colombia: An Empirical Model of Entry with Sunk Costs," *American Economic Review* 87, 545–564.

Rodrigue, J. (2008). "Foreign Direct Investment, Exports and Aggregate Productivity," manuscript, Queen's University.

Rodríguez-Clare, A. (1996). "Multinationals, Linkages, and Economic Development," *American Economic Review* 86, 852–873.

Rodrik, D. (1987). "The Economics of Export-Performance Requirements," *Quarterly Journal of Economics* 102, 633–650.

Rodrik, D. (2004). "Industrial Policy for the Twenty-First Century," CEPR Discussion Paper No. 4767, Centre for Economic Policy Research, London.

Rodrik, D. (2010). "Making Room for China in the World Economy," *American Economic Review* 100, 89–93.

Rodrik, D. (2013). "The New Mercantilist Challenge," *Project* Syndicate column, January 9.

Rodrik, D. (2014). "When Ideas Trump Interests: Preferences, Worldviews, and Policy Innovations," *Journal of Economic Perspectives* 28, 189–208.

Schminke, A. and J. van Biesebroeck. (2011). "Using Export Market Performance to Evaluate Regional Preferential Policies in China," Center for Economic Studies Discussion Paper No. 11.33, Katholieke Universiteit Leuven.

Wang, J. (2013). "The Economic Impact of Special Economic Zones: Evidence from Chinese Municipalities," *Journal of Development Economics* 101, 133–147.

World Bank. (2008). *Special Economic Zones: Performance, Lessons Learned and Implications for Zone Development*, Washington, DC: World Bank Group.

Xu, C. (2011). "The Fundamental Institutions of China's Reforms and Development," *Journal of Economic Literature* 49, 1076–1151.

Young, A. (2003). "Gold into Base Metals: Productivity Growth in the People's Republic of China during the Reform Period," *Journal of Political Economy* 111, 1220–1261.

7 Compensation, Gradualism, and Safeguards

Eric W. Bond

7.1 Introduction

Although trade liberalization has the potential to lead to a more efficient allocation of resources, the cost of moving resources between sectors can be significant and require a substantial period of time. This is particularly true for developing countries, where adjustment frequently requires geographic relocation, as in the case of rural to urban migration associated with agricultural liberalization. For example, Dix-Carneiro (2014) finds that adjustment costs in Brazil could represent between 14% and 42% of the gains from trade and that the adjustment process can take five years or longer.

In addition to the resource costs of adjustment, trade liberalization also can result in substantial income redistribution, since factors initially located in the import-competing sector will be harmed by the increased competition from imported goods. The idea that the redistributive costs can be mitigated by gradually reducing tariffs goes back at least as far as Adam Smith (1776), who in discussing the gains from trade noted: "Humanity may in this case require that freedom of trade should be restored only by slow gradations and with a good deal of reserve and circumspection. Were those duties and prohibitions taken away all at once, cheaper foreign goods of the same kind might be poured so fast into the home market, as to deprive all at once many thousands of our people of their ordinary employment and means of subsistence."

Countries thus face a trade-off in choosing the time path of tariff reductions: slowing the pace of trade liberalization may mitigate the negative effects of trade liberalization on factor owners in the import-competing sector, but it may also slow the adjustment process of reallocating factors to more productive uses. The purpose of this chapter is to address the question of how rapid the rate of tariff reduction should be and how it should vary across sectors in the economy and across countries. Should developing countries be granted preferential treatment by allowing more lengthy phase-in periods, as was the case in the Uruguay Round of trade negotiations, or should they be encouraged to accelerate the liberalization process in order to achieve more efficient resource allocation more rapidly? Should the tariff reductions be front-loaded, in the sense that the largest reductions occur at the beginning of the adjustment period, or should they be back-loaded to occur largely at the end of the adjustment period? Should safeguard measures be included that allow countries to slow the adjustment process in the event of import surges that occur during the transition period?

Recent periods of trade liberalization illustrate a variety of approaches to this question. The Marrakesh Protocol, which implemented the tariff schedules negotiated in the Uruguay Round, called for countries to reduce their tariffs over a period of five years using five equal rate reductions. However, a number of countries (primarily developing ones) were allowed longer phase-in periods in some sectors. For example, Egypt and Pakistan used a 10-year transition period for tariff reductions in textiles and agriculture. India also followed a 10-year phase-in for clothing and textiles, with the fraction of the difference between the initial applied rate and the new tariff binding in each year of the phase-in illustrated by the solid line in figure 7.1. Note that India's tariff reductions were significantly back-loaded relative to a path with equal reductions in each period (illustrated by the dotted line in figure 7.1), with 45% of the total tariff reduction occurring in the last year of the phase-in period.

Mussa (1982) has shown that the fact that a small country faces costs of adjustment is not sufficient to justify gradual trade liberalization. If markets are complete and perfectly competitive and the government has a full set of policy instruments at its disposal, the income-maximizing path of resource reallocation is obtained by moving immediately to free trade. Adjustment will be gradual when there are increasing marginal costs of adjustment, but an immediate move to free trade provides the signal to move resources at the rate that maximizes national income. Distributional concerns can then be addressed using lump sum transfers. In order for gradual trade liberalization to be optimal, it is necessary to introduce some friction into this benchmark model.

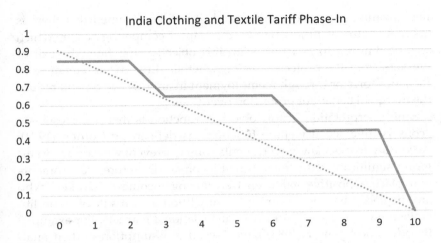

Figure 7.1
India phase-in (solid line) and equal increments phase-in (dotted line).

In this chapter, we investigate the optimal path of trade liberaliza-tion in an agreement between two large countries that would like to provide compensation to workers in the import-competing sector but lack the lump sum instrument to make this redistribution in a nondis-torting way. We initially consider the case in which the tariff is the only policy instrument, and then extend the analysis to add the ability to use a subsidy to factor owners that move between sectors. The absence of a lump sum instrument introduces a tension between income redistri-bution and factor mobility. Delaying tariff reductions provides greater compensation to import-competing factors, but slows the adjustment process.

The analysis in this chapter is primarily normative, since the objec-tive is to derive the optimal policy that should be followed if prefer-ences, technologies, and the access to policy instruments take the form that is assumed here. The results can then be used to discuss how policy should be designed in governments.

7.1.1 The Government Objective Function and Related Literature

In deriving the optimal phase-in period for trade liberalization, it will be assumed that the government maximizes a weighted social welfare function that puts greater weight on the welfare of factors who are initially in the import-competing sector at the time that the trade liberalization program is announced. It will be assumed that there is a single factor of production in the import-competing sector, which will be referred to as labor. With this objective function, the exit of workers from the protected sector, whether through retirement from the labor force or through reemployment in another sector, will reduce the marginal benefit of protection over time.

One interpretation of this objective function is that it represents a "conservative social welfare function" as defined by Corden (1974). According to this view, governments want to prevent workers from suffering significant reductions in real incomes. Therefore, governments will place a positive value on transferring income to workers who are displaced because of import competition as a result of trade liberalization or supply shocks from international markets. For example, Brander and Spencer (1994) have used this assumption in their analysis of the design of trade adjustment assistance programs, and Ethier (2002) uses it in his study of the role of unilateral actions in the presence of multilateral trade agreements.

A second interpretation of this objective function is that it reflects the political power of factors in the import-competing sector. The political economy model of Grossman and Helpman (1995) assumes that politicians put a greater weight on the welfare of factor owners in sectors that are organized as a result of their willingness to make campaign contributions to influence policy. In their model, the weight on organized interest groups is larger the greater the willingness of politicians to trade off reductions in national welfare in order to obtain campaign contributions. The model in this chapter differs from the standard political economy formulation because the extra weight is assumed to apply only to factors initially in the import-competing sectors and to decline as labor exits the sector. One justification for why governments may support declining industries is given by Hillman (1982), who points out that there is a stronger incentive to organize an industry when it is facing tariff reductions. Because firms in the import-competing sector will be earning below-normal returns during the period of liberalization, slowing the rate of tariff reduction will not induce additional entry. All returns from organizing will accrue to existing members of the industry. Once the industry has shrunk and factors are earning a market rate of return, there is no longer an incentive to organize, because additional entry would dissipate the returns from tariff increases.[1]

If the lobby in the import-competing sector is able to obtain a commitment to a particular level of compensation for its members at the time of the trade agreement, then the government will choose the path for its policy instruments to maximize social welfare subject to the promised compensation to the lobby. The Lagrange multiplier on this promised compensation will thus be equivalent to an additional weight placed on payoffs to the lobby members. Thus, either the conservative social welfare function or the political economy model with commitment can be used to motivate the payoff function we consider.

Given this objective function, we derive the optimal path of trade liberalization for an agreement between two large countries under the assumption of increasing marginal costs of moving workers between sectors and an exogenously given retirement of workers from the labor force. As in static models of trade agreements, the motive for a trade agreement in the dynamic model is to solve the prisoner's dilemma that arises from the adverse effect of tariffs on the partner's terms of trade. Therefore, in the absence of a government objective function that puts greater weight on the welfare of factor owners in the import-competing sector, the optimal path would result in immediate free trade.[2] We show that when government preferences reflect a compensation motive for workers initially located in the import-competing sector and workers are forward looking, the optimal policy involves a gradual tariff reduction at a rate that exceeds the retirement rate of workers.

The motivation for gradualism comes from two sources. One is the fact that the retirement of workers reduces the weight on the payoff to the import-competing sector, which reduces the incentive to raise the tariff over time. The second reason is that the time path of reductions can be used to influence moving decisions. Tariffs that are further in the future have a bigger impact on the mobility decision than tariffs immediately following the agreement, because they influence the decision to move between sectors for a larger number of periods. As a result, the optimal agreement will call for a decline in tariffs that exceeds the rate of retirement of workers from the labor force, and will reach free trade in finite time.

The approach taken here can be contrasted with that of two closely related papers that use dynamic models to analyze the optimal path of trade liberalization. Karp and Paul (1994) consider the case where the government is maximizing social welfare and there are convex adjustment costs of moving workers between sectors. They depart from the benchmark competitive model by assuming that there are externalities in the adjustment cost process, so that workers do not incur the full social cost of their decision to move between sectors. In this case, the optimal policy will depart from immediate free trade to mitigate this distortion rather than to redistribute income to workers affected by trade liberalization. Karp and Paul show that in the case where the government can commit to a time path for tariffs, the optimal policy will involve the phasing in and phasing out of tariffs in order to mitigate congestion of workers moving between sectors.

Maggi and Rodríguez-Clare (2007) consider a political economy model where the government is able to commit to tariffs in its trade agreement with the foreign country but is unable to commit in its deal with a domestic special interest group. They highlight the role of tariff ceilings under a trade agreement, because negotiated tariff ceilings act as a constraint on the negotiation between the government and the interest group over the setting of the tariff. They assume that an exogenously given fraction of the factor owners are allowed to move between sectors at a given point in time, so they do not allow factor owners to choose the timing of their move between sectors as in this chapter. Their approach also differs in that they examine Markov perfect equilibria, in which the tariffs under the agreement depend only on the state of the economy. In contrast, we consider the case where there is commitment to tariffs in calendar time.

We also consider the case in which the government has access to a labor market instrument in addition to the tariff. With both instruments available, the government uses the tariff to provide compensation to workers in the importable sector and a labor market subsidy to encourage exit from the importable sector. It is shown that when the government has a compensation motive, the tariff will decline at a rate equal to the rate of retirement of workers from the labor force in the optimal agreement. In this case, the tariff is assigned the role of compensating workers and the labor market instrument is used to provide the incentive to move workers out of the importable sector. The optimal path of employment in the importable sector is shown to be nonmonotonic, with employment in the importable sector falling below the level that maximizes national income in the early phase of the agreement and then rising asymptotically to the income-maximizing level.

The analysis in this chapter assumes that the parties to the trade agreements are able to commit to their promises to their trading partner. This approach contrasts with the literature, initiated by Staiger (1995), that examines how the requirement that trade agreements be self-enforcing can lead to gradual tariff reduction. In this literature, the incentives to deviate are larger the greater the stock of factors employed in the import-competing sector. As resources leave the sector, the no deviation constraint is relaxed, making further trade liberalization sustainable. Furusawa and Lai (1997) extended this approach to consider a model with adjustment costs of moving workers between sectors and show that the efficient trade agreement between welfare-maximizing governments will involve gradual tariff reduction.[3]

Section 7.2 of this chapter presents the basic model in the case where labor is fully mobile between sectors, and it characterizes the noncooperative equilibrium that exists prior to the signing of the trade agreement. Section 7.3 derives the features of the optimal trade agreement when only a tariff is used, and section 7.4 considers agreements over both tariffs and labor market policies. Section 7.5 offers some concluding remarks on the implications of these results for developing-country policy.

7.2 The Model

We consider an infinite-horizon two-country trade model in which each country produces a numeraire good (N) and two traded goods. We begin by examining equilibrium under the assumption of frictionless mobility of factors between production activities and then introduce adjustment costs of moving factors of production between sectors.

Home-country preferences are represented by the utility function $U = \sum_{s=0}^{\infty} u(d_{1s}, d_{2s}, d_{Ns})\beta^s$, where $\beta \in (0,1)$ is the discount factor, d_{is} is consumption of good $i \in \{1, 2, N\}$ in period s, and $u(d_1, d_2, d_N) = \sum_{i=1}^{2}(Ad_i - .5d_i^2) + d_N$. These preferences yield demand functions for the traded goods $i \in \{1, 2\}$ at each point in time of $d(p_{is}) = A - p_{is}$, where p_{is} is the home-country price of good i in period s. The indirect utility function is

$$V = \sum_{s=0}^{\infty} \sum_{i=1,2} s(p_{is})\beta^s + Y, \tag{7.1}$$

where $s(p_i) = .5(A - p_i)^2$ is the consumer surplus from consuming good i and Y is the present value of national income. Preferences in the foreign country have the same quasilinear form, with demand for trade goods given by $d^*(p_{is}^*) = A^* - p_{is}^*$ for $i \in \{1, 2\}$.

There are two types of labor, referred to as type m and type x, in each country. Type m labor can produce either one unit of good N or one unit of the importable good (good 1 in the home country and good 2 in the foreign country). Letting l^m denote the total supply of m labor in the home country and l_{1s} the quantity of m labor located in sector 1 in period s, the income of m labor at home in period s is $l^m + (p_{1s} - 1)l_{1s}$. A unit of type x labor can produce either good N or good 2. Type x workers are assumed to be of heterogeneous ability, resulting in a supply function for good 2 of $y_2(p_{2s}) = -a + \phi p_{2s}$.[4] The aggregate income of x labor in period s will be $l^x + R(p_{2s})$, where $R(p_2) = \frac{\phi(p_2 - a/\phi)^2}{2}$.

A similar production structure is assumed in the foreign country, so the foreign supply of good 1 is $y_1(p^*) = -a^* + \phi^* p_1^*$, which allows for differences in export sector productivity across countries. The following restrictions on parameters will be made throughout.

Assumption 7.1   The preference and technology parameters in sector 1 satisfy

(a) $\frac{A^* + a^*}{1 + \phi^*} < 1$, $\frac{A + a}{1 + \phi} < 1$,

(b) $A + A^* + a^* - 2 - \phi^* > 0$.

Part (a) is simply the requirement that the autarkic price of good 1 in the foreign country be less than that in the home country and that the autarkic price of good 2 be more, which is required for our identification of good 1 as the home-country importable and good 2 as its exportable. Part (b) ensures that there will be a positive level of employment of labor in sector 1 at home with free trade in the frictionless equilibrium. This assumption is not essential but reduces the number of cases to be considered.

These assumptions result in a separability between sectors for goods 1 and 2 so that we can solve for the equilibrium of sector 1 independently of policies in sector 2. Therefore, in the subsequent discussion, we focus on the market for the home-country importable, good 1. The analysis of the market for good 2 is similar.

We begin by characterizing the equilibrium when there is costless movement of factors between sectors and the home country's trade instrument is a specific tariff on imports of good 1, t. The home-country price of good 1 will satisfy $p = p^* + t$.[5] The foreign export supply is given by $x^*(p_s) = (\phi^* + 1)(p_s - t_s) - A^* + a^*$, which under assumption 7.1(b) is not sufficient to satisfy the domestic market at $p = 1$. The remaining demand that cannot be satisfied by imports at $p = 1$ will be

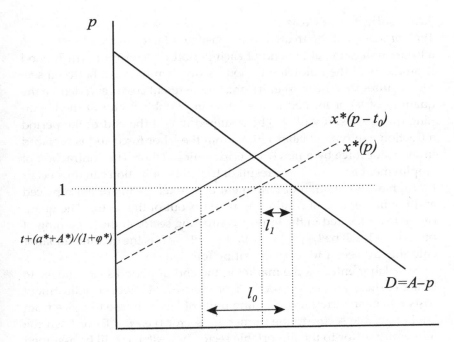

Figure 7.2
Home market for imported good 1.

met by domestic production, which results in employment of

$$\tilde{l}(t_s) = A + A^* + a^* - 1 - \phi^*(1 - t_s).\tag{7.2}$$

The effect of trade liberalization with costless factor mobility is illustrated in figure 7.2. At the initial nonprohibitive tariff t_0, the home country employs l_0 workers in production of good 1. The elimination of the tariff results in the reduction of home-country employment in sector 1 to $l_1 = d_1(1) - x^*(1)$.

In the presence of adjustment costs that restrict the movement of factors between sectors, the initial effect of trade liberalization will be to reduce the domestic price of good 1 below 1 because the domestic output will exceed l_1. As a result, labor that is initially allocated to sector 1 will suffer losses because the return in the import-competing sector will fall below that available in sector N until the time at which sector 1 employment declines to l_1. Subsection 7.2.1 introduces a specification of adjustment costs to moving factors between sectors to formalize that idea.

7.2.1 Adjustment Costs

Type m labor will be treated as a quasifixed factor, which must make a location decision at the end of each period to determine which good it produces in the following period. A decision to move between sectors requires that the worker incur an adjustment cost. Let l_s denote the quantity of labor located in the home importable sector at the beginning of period s. It will also be assumed that at the end of the period a fraction δ of type m labor retires from the labor force and is replaced in the labor force by a newly entering unit of labor. The contraction of employment in sector 1 as a result of trade liberalization can thus occur through a combination of retirement of workers who are not replaced and the movement of continuing workers out of the sector. The quantity of labor located in the import-competing sector at the beginning of period $s + 1$ will be $l_{s+1} = (1 - \delta)l_s + i_s$, where i_s is the quantity of labor entering the sector for $i > 0$ or exiting for $i < 0$.

New labor entering the market at the end of period s can choose to locate costlessly in either sector 1 or sector N. However, adjustment costs will be incurred if continuing units of labor choose to move from the importable sector to the numeraire sector (i.e., $i_s < 0$) or from the numeraire sector to the importable sector ($i_s > \delta l^m$). It will be assumed that there is congestion in the moving process so that there are increasing marginal costs of adjustment. The aggregate costs of adjustment (measured in units of the nontraded good) will be assumed to take the form

$$G(i) = \begin{cases} \frac{\gamma(i - \delta l^m)^2}{2} & i > \delta l^m \\ 0 & 0 \le i \le \delta l^m \\ \frac{\gamma i^2}{2} & i < 0 \end{cases} \tag{7.3}$$

where $\gamma > 0$.

Home-country imports of good 1 in period s will be $m(p_s, l_s) = A - p_s - l_s$. In order to simplify the presentation, we assume that type x labor is freely mobile between activities, so foreign exports of good 1 will be $x^*(p_s^*) = (\phi^* + 1)p_s^* - A^*$. We can then solve for the equilibrium prices as a function of home trade policy and the stock of labor:

$$p(t_s, l_s) = \frac{A + A^* + a^* + (1 + \phi^*)t_s - l_s}{2 + \phi^*} \tag{7.4}$$

The returns to m labor will not necessarily be equalized across sectors at a point in time because of the quasifixed nature of m labor, so it will be useful to denote the differential in returns to labor between sector 1 and sector N by

$$\Delta(t_s, l_s) = p(t_s, l_s) - 1, \tag{7.5}$$

which is increasing in t_s and decreasing in l_s.

A continuing worker will find it profitable to move between sectors at time s if the present value of wage gains exceeds the cost of moving. It will be assumed that there are no externalities in the labor adjustment process, which means that a worker moving at the end of period s faces a moving cost equal to the marginal social cost of adjustment, $G'(i_s)$. In periods where $i_s \in [0, \delta l^m]$, workers entering the labor force will be indifferent between sectors 1 and N and the present value of wage income in the two sectors will be equalized. In periods where workers move between sectors, the wage differential will equal the marginal cost of adjustment. Thus, at any time s, we have

$$\sum_{u=1}^{\infty} \Delta(t_{s+u}, l_{s+u})(1 - \delta)^{u-1} \beta^u = G'(i_s), \tag{7.6}$$

where worker forecasts of future tariffs and employment levels are assumed to be rational.

To illustrate how this adjustment process works, suppose that t is expected to be constant and initial employment l_0 in sector 1 is greater than $\tilde{l}(t)$ as defined in (7.2), so $\Delta(t_s, l_s) < 0$. All newly entering workers will enter the N sector until the wage differential is eliminated. Even if no continuing workers were to move out of sector 1, the allocation of new workers to the N sector would eliminate the wage gap in finite time by the attrition of workers in the import-competing sector. We refer to this as the attrition path. If $(l_0 - \tilde{l}(t)) > \delta l_0$, attrition will not be sufficient to close the wage gap in period 1. Since $G'(0) = 0$, the movement of workers out of sector 1 will accelerate the adjustment process relative to the attrition path. The intertemporal no arbitrage condition (7.6) must hold at s and $s + 1$, so

$$\Delta(t_s, l_s) = G'(i_{s-1})/\beta - (1 - \delta)G'(i_s). \tag{7.7}$$

Equation (7.7) requires that the wage loss from staying in sector 1 for an additional period equal the savings in expected adjustment costs from waiting an additional period to move.

7.2.2   Sectoral Payoff Functions

Because of the separability between sectors, we can use (7.1) to obtain an expression for the indirect utility derived by the home country from sector 1,

$$V = \sum_{s=0}^{\infty} \left[W^M(t_s, l_s) - G(l_{s+1} - (1 - \delta)l_s) \right] \beta^s, \tag{7.8}$$

where

$$W^M(t_s, l_s) = s(p(t_s, l_s)) + (p(t_s, l_s) - 1) + t_s m(p(t_s, l_s), l_s). \tag{7.9}$$

W^M is the sum of consumer surplus, producer surplus (the wage differential between sectors 1 and N), and tariff revenue associated with the home importable good. W^M is strictly concave in t_s and l_s.

The foreign indirect utility associated with its exportable sector 1 is the discounted sum of consumer and producer surpluses,

$$V^* = \sum_{s=0}^{\infty} \left[W^{X^*}(t_s, l_s) \right] \beta^s,$$

where

$$W^{X^*}(t_s, l_s) = s(p^*(t_s, l_s)) + R^*(p^*(t_s, l_s)).$$

W^X is decreasing and convex in t_s, reflecting the adverse effect of the home-country tariff on the exporter's terms of trade.

The impact of home tariff and employment choices on world welfare can be expressed as the sum of the payoffs to the home and foreign countries,

$$V^W = \sum_{s=0}^{\infty} [W^W(t_s, l_s) - G(i_s)] \beta^s, \tag{7.10}$$

where $W^W(t_s, l_s) = W^M(t_s, l_s) + W^{X^*}(t_s, l_s)$ is the sum of the surpluses in the home and foreign countries in good 1 plus the home-country surplus in the nontraded goods sector. The world surplus per period from sector 1 has the properties that

$$W_t^W(t_s, l_s) = -t_s \left(\frac{1 + \phi^*}{2 + \phi^*} \right), \quad W_l^W(t_s, l_s) = \Delta(t_s, l_s) - t_s \left(\frac{1 + \phi^*}{2 + \phi^*} \right). \tag{7.11}$$

An increase in the tariff reduces world welfare if $t_s > 0$, with the effect being proportional to the change in trade volume resulting from the tariff increase. An increase in employment in sector 1 at home affects world welfare through two channels: the first term is the effect on income of moving a worker from sector N to sector 1, and the second term is the impact of the move on trade volume. The private benefit of moving a worker into the import-competing sector, $\Delta(t_s, l_s)$, exceeds the social benefit when $t_s > 0$.

The existence of a negative spillover from the importing country's tariff means that if countries are setting tariffs unilaterally, they will choose tariffs that exceed the world welfare-maximizing level of 0. The noncooperative equilibrium will thus reflect a terms of trade driven prisoner's dilemma, so there will exist mutually beneficial tariff reductions, as has been emphasized by Bagwell and Staiger (2002).

7.3   Trade Agreements with Tariffs

We now turn to the case in which the two countries sign a trade agreement that commits them to a time path $\{t_s, t_s^*\}$ for tariffs. It will be assumed that the two countries are initially in a steady-state equilibrium with tariffs $\bar{t}, \bar{t}^* > 0$, which result in initial labor allocations in the respective import-competing sectors that are above the free trade level (i.e., $\bar{l} > \bar{l}(0), \bar{l}^* > \bar{l}^*(0)$). The expected lifetime income under the agreement of a worker who is initially located in the import-competing sector at home will be

$$\Omega_m = \sum_{s=0}^{\infty} p(t_s, l_s)(1 - \delta)^{s-1} \beta^s,$$

where future returns are discounted by $(1 - \delta)^{s-1} \beta^s$, reflecting the probability that the worker will still be in the labor force in period s.

As discussed, it is assumed that in negotiating the trade agreement the home-country government's objective function is $V + \lambda \Omega_m$, where $\lambda > 0$ reflects the additional weight the government places on the welfare of workers initially in the import-competing sector. In the case where the only instrument available to the government is the tariff, the objective function of the agreement is to choose the time path of tariffs to maximize $V^W + \lambda \Omega_m$ subject to the labor market adjustment constraint (7.6) for each period s. We assume that lump sum transfers of the numeraire good between countries are available ex ante, so that the goal of the agreement is to maximize the sum of welfare for the two countries. The solution to this contracting problem is obtained by choosing $\{t_s, l_s\}$ to maximize the Lagrangian

$$L = V^W + \lambda \Omega_m$$

$$+ \sum_{s=0}^{\infty} \mu_s \left(\sum_{u=1}^{\infty} \Delta(t_{s+u}, l_{s+u})(1-\delta)^{u-1}\beta^u - G'(l_{s+1} - (1-\delta)l_s)) \right) \beta^s,$$

(7.12)

where μ_s is the current value multiplier associated with the adjustment constraint at time s. If $\mu_s < 0$, the payoff under the agreement can be raised by inducing more labor to move to the numeraire sector, so an increase in Δ for $s' > s$ will tighten the labor mobility constraint at time s. If $\mu_s > 0$, the payoff can be raised by inducing more labor to move to the importable goods sector, so the increase will relax the labor mobility constraint.

In analyzing this problem, it is convenient to rewrite the last term in the Lagrangian as $\sum_{s=0}^{\infty} M_s \Delta(t_s, l_s)\beta^s - \mu_s G'(i_s)$, where $M_s = \sum_{u=0}^{s-1} \mu_u(1-\delta)^{s-1-u}$ summarizes the effect of an increase in Δ_s on the labor mobility constraint for all $s' < s$. $M_s < 0$ indicates that an increase in Δ_s will tighten the labor mobility constraint for $s' < s$, and when $M_s > 0$ it will relax the constraint. The definition of M_s then implies

$$M_{s+1} = (1-\delta)M_s + \mu_s, \quad M_0 = 0.$$

(7.13)

The multiplier M_s reflects the presence of commitment in the trade agreement, because it shows that the planner's decisions at time s incorporate the effects of these decisions on agent decisions at $s' < s$.[6] The initial condition $M_0 = 0$ results from the fact that the location of labor is predetermined at $s = 0$, so the time 0 tariff will not affect mobility decisions.

The necessary condition for the choice of t is

$$t_s = \lambda(1-\delta)^s + M_s.$$

(7.14)

An increase in the tariff transfers income to workers originally in the import-competing sectors, which is beneficial for world welfare when $\lambda > 0$. However, it will also make moving to the N sector less attractive, which tightens the labor mobility constraint when $M_s < 0$. The time path of the tariff will thus reflect the tension between these two effects. Utilizing (7.13), it can be seen that the rate of decline of the tariff along the optimal path will be $(t_{s+1} - t_s)/t_s = -\delta + \mu_s/t_s$. The tariff rate will decline at a rate greater than δ if $\mu < 0$ and $t_s > 0$, because the decline in the tariff is being used to relax the labor mobility constraint by encouraging labor to move out of the importable sector.

The necessary condition for the location of labor is obtained by differentiating the Lagrangian with respect to l_s and then substituting using (7.7), which yields the necessary condition

$$t_s = (1 - \delta)\mu_s G''(i_s) - \mu_{s-1}G''(i_{s-1})/\beta. \tag{7.15}$$

The left-hand side of (7.15) is the difference between the wage and the marginal social product of labor, which is equal to the tariff. The right-hand side of (7.15) is the impact on the labor mobility constraints of moving an additional unit of labor to sector 1. The optimal choice of labor thus trades off the static distortions against the dynamic distortions.

Equation (7.15) can be used to generate a second-order difference equation that can be solved for $\{M_1, .., M_{T-1}\}$ for a given terminal date of the phase-in, T. The resulting time path of tariffs can be substituted into the intertemporal arbitrage conditions for labor (7.6) to obtain a second-order difference equation for l_s. The optimal value of T is then determined as the time at which the adjustment of labor eliminates the sectoral wage differences. The necessary conditions for the optimal trade agreement can be used to obtain the following characterization of the optimal path of tariff and employment levels, which is proven in the appendix:

Proposition 7.1   When the tariff is the only instrument available to the government in the trade agreement, there will be a finite time T such that $t_s = 0$ and $l_s = \tilde{l}(0)$ for $s \geq T$.

(a) For $\lambda = 0$, the optimal trade agreement is the immediate removal of trade barriers.

(b) If $\lambda > 0$, $t_s > 0$ and the tariff declines at a rate exceeding δ for $s < T$.

(c) The level of employment in sector 1 is increasing in λ for $s < T$ for a given T, and the optimal length of the phase-in period is nondecreasing in λ.

The solutions for M_s and t_s are homogeneous of degree 1 in λ, which is used to establish part (a) of the proposition. Referring to

(7.14), a reduction in λ reduces both the incentive to transfer income to workers in the importable sector and the incentive to intervene in the labor adjustment process. If $\lambda = 0$, $M_s = 0$ for all s, because workers make the socially optimal location decisions and there is no incentive to alter the pace of adjustment. Mussa (1982) obtained the result that immediate elimination of trade barriers is optimal for a small-country model where there are no terms-of-trade effects. The optimality of immediate free trade also holds in the two-country model, because the trade agreement acts to neutralize terms-of-trade effects.

This front-loading of tariff reductions reflects the trade-off between compensating workers in the importable sector and providing incentives to move out. The retirement of workers from the labor force at rate δ means that the benefit of providing compensation will also decline at rate δ. However, the fact that future tariffs affect the incentive to move for a greater number of periods provides an additional incentive to front-load the tariff protection.

The optimal T is the value for which the path of employment eliminates the wage differential at T. The solutions for M_s, given T, will depend on the parameters of the adjustment process (δ, γ) and the discount factor but are independent of the demand and supply parameters for a given T. Thus, the demand and supply parameters affect the path of tariffs only through their effect on T.

Figure 7.3 illustrates how the desire to compensate workers in the import-competing sector affects the time path of their employment for a specific numerical example. The example assumes an initial tariff with an ad valorem equivalent of 12% and initial employment level of $l_0 = .7$, which corresponds to the level when the home country imposes its long-run Nash equilibrium. The dotted line in the left panel illustrates the path of employment when the adjustment is accomplished only by attrition of workers in the import-competing sector, where it is assumed that the attrition rate is $\delta = .05$ in each period. The attrition path achieves the employment level $\tilde{l}(0) = .4$, which is the free trade steady state, in period 11. The dashed line is the path of employment if the trade agreement were to result in an immediate elimination of the tariff in period 0, which results in the elimination of the wage differential between sectors in period 8. The solid line in figure 3 is the path associated with a value of $\lambda = .2$, which compensates the workers for half of the losses that they would have suffered if they had gone to immediate free trade. This path results in a slower rate of departure

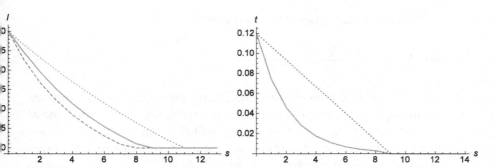

Figure 7.3
(left) Employment paths: optimal (solid line), free trade (dashed line), and attrition (dotted line); (right) tariff paths: optimal (solid line) and equal reductions (dotted line).

from sector 1 than does the path with immediate free trade, and reaches the steady state level in period 9.

The right panel in figure 7.3 shows the time path of tariffs in the optimal agreement (solid line) and the path under equal tariff reductions per period (dotted line). The optimal path front-loads the tariff reductions by cutting the tariff rate by approximately 40% in the first period of liberalization.

The preceding analysis focused on the case where the tariff setting is unconstrained and comes as a surprise to factor owners. If the government is constrained not to raise its tariff above the initial level, then the schedule derived in proposition 7.1 will be modified if the unconstrained path exceeds the initial tariff. In that case, the tariff will be kept at the ceiling for some period, after which the path will be determined by the preceding derivation.

7.3.1 Safeguards

We now extend the model to introduce uncertainty about the future volume of imports. Suppose that there is a probability π^H that there will be a permanent increase in the foreign-country supply of good 1 by an amount $e^H > 0$ from period $\tau < T$ onward. The foreign supply remains constant at its initial level with probability $\pi^L = (1 - \pi^H)$. We examine the optimal trade agreement, where the agreement can specify a state-contingent tariff t_s^i for $i = H, L$ and $s \geq \tau$. Since state H corresponds to an import surge in the home country, an agreement that specifies higher tariffs in state H can be interpreted as having a transitional safeguard.[7]

The equilibrium prices for state i will be

$$p(t_s, l_s, e^i) = \frac{A + A^* + a^* + (1 + \phi^*)t_s - l_s - e^i}{2 + \phi^*} \quad i = H, L, \ s \geq \tau, \quad (7.16)$$

where $e^L \equiv 0$. In the event of an import surge, the remaining factor owners in the import-competing sector will experience a loss in income at the initial tariff rate. The import surge will also require a greater movement of labor out of the import-competing sector to equalize wages between sectors at free trade, because $\tilde{l}^H(0) = \tilde{l}(0) - e^H$. The question is how tariff adjustments will be allocated over the life of the optimal agreement in response to an import surge.

Expressing the state-contingent wage differential as $\Delta(t_s^i, l_s, e^i) = p(t_s, l_s, e^i) - 1$, the labor mobility constraints will be

$$\sum_{u=1}^{\tau-s-1} \Delta(t_{s+u}, l_{s+u})(1-\delta)^{u-1}\beta^u$$

$$+ \sum_{i=L,H} \sum_{u=\tau-s}^{\infty} \pi^i \Delta(t_{s+u}^i, l_{s+u}, e^i)(1-\delta)^{u-1}\beta^u = G'(i_s) \quad s < \tau \quad (7.17)$$

$$\sum_{u=1}^{\infty} \Delta(t_{s+u}^i, l_{s+u}, e^i)(1-\delta)^{u-1}\beta^u = G'(i_s) \quad i = H, L, \ s \geq \tau, \quad (7.18)$$

where t_s^i is the tariff anticipated in state i for $s \geq \tau$. The labor market constraint shows that the promise of a higher tariff to compensate workers in the event of an import surge will have the effect of raising the return to workers from staying in sector 1 for $s < \tau$ and will deter labor reallocation.

Letting μ denote the multiplier associated with the labor mobility constraint (7.17) and μ_s^i the multiplier for the mobility constraint (7.18), we can define the accumulated effect of a relaxation of the mobility constraint in state i at time $s \geq \tau$ to be $M_s^i = \sum_{u=0}^{\tau-1} \mu_u(1-\delta)^{s-1-u} + \sum_{u=\tau-s}^{\tau} \mu_u^i(1-\delta)^{s-1-u}$. The necessary condition for the choice of a tariff will be

$$t_s = \lambda(1-\delta)^s + M_s \quad \text{for } s \leq \tau,$$

$$t_s^i = \lambda(1-\delta)^s + M_s^i \quad \text{for } s > \tau \text{ and } i = L, H.$$

The effect of λ on the setting of the tariff is the same in both the L and H state, because of the assumption of risk neutrality on the part of workers. Although the price is lower in the import surge state H, to workers the value of an additional dollar of income is the same in either state. Therefore, state H will have a higher tariff than state L iff $M_s^H > M_s^L$, which requires that the labor mobility constraint be more binding in state L than in state H.

The solutions for the M_s^i will be independent of the parameters of the export supply function for a given T. If the import surge is not large enough to lead to an increase in the optimal T^H, then there should be no adjustment in the tariff schedule in response to the import surge. In this case, the effect of the import surge can be handled by attrition of the workforce in the import-competing sector at $T - 1$ without requiring an adjustment in the tariff schedule. If the surge is sufficiently large, it will require an increase in the length of the transition period. Thus, an optimal safeguard will extend the transition period for shocks that are sufficiently large. However, the optimal safeguard will not increase the optimal tariff under the agreement at all points following the shock. Since workers are assumed to be risk neutral, the marginal utility of income for date $s > \tau$ is the same whether or not there is an import surge, and there is no reason to transfer income to the states where the surge takes place. The adjustments in the tariff schedule that occur following an import surge are done to achieve an efficient exit path for workers from the industry.

These points are illustrated in figure 7.4, which compares the optimal tariff path in the event of an import surge in period 1 (dashed path) with that without an import surge (solid path). The parameter values for the case without an import surge are the same as in figure 7.3, with the import surge chosen to be large enough that it extends the time required to eliminate the wage differential by four periods. Figure 7.4 illustrates that despite the significant magnitude of the import surge, it has virtually no effect on the optimal tariff path for these parameter values. The tariff policy in response to the import surge is a safeguard in the sense that it postpones the time until the tariff goes to 0, but the tariff path is also lower at some points. This could be interpreted as rotation of the tariff path in order to smooth out the larger adjustment required in response to an import surge. One reason the import surge has a minimal impact is that even though the adjustment period is extended, the optimal tariff is already so low near the end of the adjustment period that any extension of the path has minimal effect.

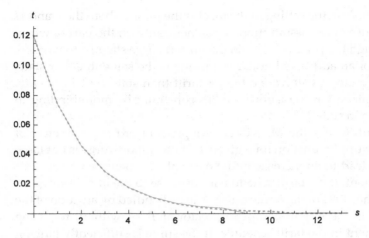

Figure 7.4
Tariff path with an import surge (dashed line) and without a surge (solid line).

This result contrasts with the common inclusion of safeguards in trade agreements that allow significant postponement of tariff reductions in the event of import surges. If the assumptions of the present model regarding the objective function of the government and its ability to commit to policies are correct, then the preceding result suggests that the emphasis on including safeguards in trade agreements is misplaced. Under the assumption that labor is risk neutral, state-contingent differences in tariffs are designed to alter the speed of adjustment rather than to affect the level of compensation to workers.

One extension that would justify a significant response of tariffs to import surges would be to introduce risk aversion on the part of workers. When workers are risk averse, the marginal utility of income is higher in states where there is an import surge, and the government could raise the expected utility of income by responding with an increase in the tariff.

7.4 Agreements with Trade Adjustment Compensation

Proposition 7.1 showed that the requirement of compensation for labor in the import-competing sector results in an exit from the import-competing sector that is less than the socially optimal level when the only available policy instrument is the tariff. In this section, we allow for the possibility of an additional instrument by allowing the government to use labor market policies that influence the movement of workers between sectors. A trade agreement will thus specify both a time path for the tariff and a time path for labor market policies.

We can formalize this problem by choosing l_s and t_s to maximize the weighted world welfare function, $V^W + \lambda \Omega_m$, given the initial employment level in sector 1. Note that this problem modifies (7.12) by dropping the labor mobility constraints, since the government can directly control the movement of labor through the use of labor market instruments. We will discuss the labor market policies required to implement the optimal path for labor.

The necessary condition for the time path of the tariff is

$$t_s^L = \lambda^L (1 - \delta)^s. \tag{7.19}$$

In contrast with the necessary condition when there is no labor market instrument (7.14), the tariff will be used only for compensation purposes when direct intervention in labor markets is possible. The labor market instrument will be targeted to influence the movement of workers out of the import-competing sector. As a result, the tariff will decline over time at rate δ because of the attrition from the labor force of workers initially employed in sector 1. Thus, the availability of the labor market instrument reduces the rate of tariff reduction for $s > 0$. In particular, the tariff will not be eliminated in finite time, in contrast to the result of proposition 7.1. A second effect of the labor market instrument is to reduce the distortion introduced by the existence of the payoff constraint, so that $\lambda^L < \lambda$. The multiplier on the payoff constraint reflects the reduction in world welfare resulting from an increase in the compensation paid to the workers in sector 1, which will be lower when the government has more policy instruments available.

The condition for the optimal choice of labor in sector 1 at time s is

$$\Delta(t_s, l_s) - t_s = G'(i_{s-1}) - \beta(1 - \delta)G'(i_s). \tag{7.20}$$

Condition (7.20) equates the loss in "social" value from delaying the move of a worker out of sector 1 to the savings in adjustment costs from delaying the move, where the "social" value of output in sector 1 is its value at the world price. This contrasts with the private no arbitrage condition, (7.7), which evaluates the value of moving at the domestic price. Workers value their wage in the import-competing sector at more than its social value when $t > 0$, which means that the optimal trade agreement will use a subsidy to workers moving out of the importable sector to speed up the adjustment process.

The adjustment process given by (7.20) will eventually reach a finite period T^L at which there is no movement of continuing workers between sectors. With no adjustment costs incurred by workers for $s > T^L$, the right-hand side of (7.20) will equal 0 and the market wage differential between sectors will satisfy $\Delta(t_s, l_s) = t_s > 0$. The optimal employment level in sector 1 will be

$$\tilde{l}_s^L = A + A^* + a^* - (2 + \phi^*) + \lambda^L(1 - \delta)^s \text{ for } s > T^L, \tag{7.21}$$

so employment in sector 1 will increase asymptotically to $\tilde{l}(0)$ as $t_s \to 0$. With a positive tariff, it will be optimal to hold employment in sector 1 below $\tilde{l}(0)$ because the domestic price of good 1 exceeds its social value.

For $s < T^L$, (7.20) can be used to obtain a system of equations that can be solved for $\{l_1, .., l_{T^L-1}\}$. It is shown in the appendix that the employment level in the import-competing sector will be decreasing in λ, with the $\lambda = 0$ resulting in the equilibrium with immediate free trade and no labor market intervention. This establishes that the adjustment path for labor in the import-competing sector will necessarily be nonmonotonic. The initial level of employment is above the optimal level given by (7.21), so there will be an exit of workers until the time T^L at which employment reaches $l^L(T^L)$. For the remaining time, employment will be increasing.

The following result, which is proven in the appendix, formalizes these observations.

Proposition 7.2   The optimal trade agreement when both tariffs and labor market instruments are available has the following properties:

(a)   The tariff at time s will be $t_s^L = \lambda^L(1 - \delta)^s$.

(b)   The time path of labor in the importable sector will be nonmonotonic. There will be a finite time $T^L \geq 1$ such that the labor stock in the importable sector will be increasing as given by (7.21) for $s > T^L$. For $s \leq T^L$, the labor stock will follow a path that reduces it from l_0 to $l^L(T^L)$.

(c)   Employment in the import-competing sector is increasing in λ^L for all s. There are no labor market interventions for $\lambda^L = 0$.

The adjustment process characterized in proposition 7.2 is illustrated in figure 7.5 using the same demand, supply, and adjustment

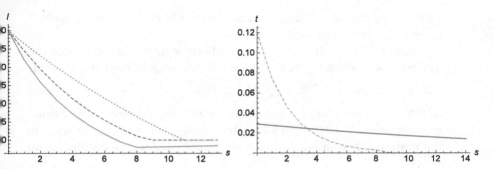

Figure 7.5
(left) Employment paths in optimal agreements: tariff and labor subsidy (solid line), tariff only (dashed line); (right) tariff path under optimal agreement with (solid line) and without (dashed line) labor subsidies.

cost parameters as in figure 7.3. Since the adjustment process is more efficient when the government can use a subsidy to labor that moves out of the import-competing sector, a given value of λ results in a higher payoff to workers in the import-competing sector when the subsidy to mobility is used. Therefore, the employment and tariff paths in figure 7.5 for the case with a mobility subsidy are derived using a value of $\lambda = .029$, which results in the same payoff to factors displaced by trade policy as in the case where the mobility subsidy is not available.

The left panel in figure 7.5 shows the adjustment paths for employment in the import-competing sector. The employment path in the optimal policy with a mobility subsidy (solid line) lies below the path when only the tariff is used (dashed line). The path with a mobility subsidy results in declining employment in the import-competing sector until period 9, at which point all sectoral labor adjustments are done through attrition and without incurring any adjustment costs. The employment level in the import-competing sector rises over time after period 9 and asymptotically approaches the free trade level.

The right panel in figure 7.5 compares the path of the tariff when the labor mobility subsidy is available (solid line) with that when only the tariff can be used (dashed line). When only a tariff is available, a high tariff in period 0 is used to transfer income to the workers adversely affected by the tariff, because it has the least impact on the mobility constraints. When the labor market subsidy is available, there is a substantial reduction in the tariff in period 0, followed by a decline at rate δ thereafter. The labor market subsidy is used to influence movements of workers between sectors, so the tariff can be used to compensate workers without having to worry about its impact on moving decisions.

To derive the labor market interventions required to implement the optimal path, observe that a worker in the import-competing sector will earn a return of $\sigma_s - \sum_{u=1}^{\infty} \Delta(t_{s+u}, l_{s+u})(1 - \delta)^{u-1}\beta^u$ from moving to the numeraire sector, where σ_s is the moving subsidy. The optimal moving subsidy will be the value that equates the return to moving to the marginal cost of adjustment when evaluated at the optimal path, $\{t_s^L, l_s^L\}$,

$$\sigma_s = \sum_{u=1}^{\infty} \Delta\left(t_{s+u}^L, l_{s+u}^L\right)(1 - \delta)^{u-1}\beta^u - G'\left(i_s^L\right) \ \text{if} \ i_s^L < 0. \tag{7.22}$$

Since $\Delta\left(t_s^L, l_s^L\right) = t_s > 0$ for $s > T^L$, the return to workers in the import-competing sector will exceed that in the numeraire sector at market prices for some $s > 0$. Therefore, to discourage additional workers from moving into the importable sector, it will also be necessary to impose a tax $v_s = \sum_{u=1}^{\infty} \Delta(t_{s+u}, l_{s+u})(1 - \delta)^{u-1}\beta^u$ for any s at which $v_s > O$.

Figure 7.6 shows the optimal subsidy to moving out of the import-competing sector (solid line) and the optimal tax on entry to the import-competing sector (dashed line). The tax on entry into the importable sector must be positive in periods where the present value of wages in the importable sector exceeds that in the numeraire sector. Referring to figure 7.6, it can be seen that the combination of tariff protection and the exit of workers from the importable sector means that the present value of wages in the importable sector exceeds that in the numeraire sector for $s > 0$, so it is necessary to tax entry into that sector to discourage new labor market entrants from locating there. This differential initially increases, and it reaches its maximum at the point where the exit of workers initially in the importable sector ceases. From period T_L onward, the labor tax will decline and asymptotically approach 0 as the tariff is reduced.

Figure 7.6 also illustrates that the optimal moving subsidy to encourage workers to exit the importable sector is relatively constant over the adjustment period. Observe from (7.22) that the optimal moving subsidy is the sum of the present value of the wage gap between the importable and numeraire sectors and the marginal cost of adjustment.

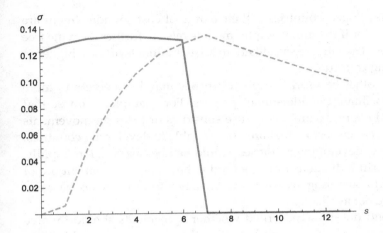

Figure 7.6
Subsidy to moving (solid line) and tax on entry to importable sector (dashed line).

As the adjustment period proceeds, the exit rate of workers from the importable sector decreases, which reduces the marginal adjustment cost. However, this effect is offset by the rising gain from remaining in the importable sector, as illustrated by the optimal wage tax. As a result of these offsetting effects, the subsidy to moving to the numeraire sector varies little over the adjustment period. Once period T_L is reached, it is no longer necessary to move workers out of the importable sector, and the moving subsidy is eliminated.

7.5   Discussion

The results of this chapter can be used to address the questions raised in the chapter's introduction concerning the optimal path of tariffs during the phase-in period. The first question concerned how phase-in periods for developing countries should compare with those in developed countries. The model showed that the desire of the government to compensate workers in the import-competing sector will result in tariff reductions being spread over the entire adjustment period until wage rates are equalized between sectors when the tariff is the only instrument being used. The length of the adjustment period will depend on the level of adjustment costs and on the difference between the initial employment level and the free trade employment level. It will be appropriate for developing countries to have longer phase-in periods than in developed countries if their marginal costs of adjustment are higher and/or if the initial employment levels are further from the free trade level. The latter case is likely to arise if initial tariffs are higher in developing countries.

On the other hand, developed countries may have access to more tools to facilitate the adjustment process. For example, suppose that developed countries are able to use subsidies or taxes on movements of labor between sectors that are not available to developing countries. In that case, developing countries should be liberalizing more rapidly, because tariff reductions must be used to encourage movement out of the import-competing sector when subsidies to movements between sectors are not available.

A second question concerned whether agreements should involve equal adjustments in each period, as in the phase-in of new bindings following the Uruguay Round. The results showed that when labor market instruments are not available, the tariff reductions should be front-loaded in order to accelerate the movement of factors out of the import-competing sector. This result contrasts sharply with the back-loading of tariff and quota liberalization that occurred in the phasing out of the Multi-Fibre Agreement.[8]

A final question concerned the use of safeguards that allow countries to slow the pace of liberalization if it results in a surge of imports. Under the assumption of risk neutrality of labor, it was shown that when the likelihood of an import surge is high, the response should be to have higher tariffs at all points along the path rather than to have them only when the surge occurs. With risk neutrality, the main goal of tariff changes in response to an import surge should be to facilitate adjustment rather than to redistribute income.

The results have also suggested ways in which the model could be extended to examine other factors that affect the pace of trade liberalization. The assumption that what workers pay for moving between is sectors equal to the marginal social cost of moving means that trade policy does not have to be concerned with correcting distortions in factor markets. When there are externalities in the adjustment process, the optimal pace of trade liberalization may be affected. Relaxing the assumption of risk neutrality for workers is also of interest, since it would provide an incentive to respond to negative price shocks by raising tariffs.

Appendix

Proof of Proposition 7.1 The world welfare function is concave in the choice variables and the constraints are linear in the choice variables, so the Lagrangian function (7.12) is concave.

The necessary conditions for optimization are given by

$$W_t^W(t_s, l_s) + (\lambda(1-\delta)^s + M_s) \, p_t(t_s, l_s) = 0,$$

$$W_l^W(t_s, l_s) + (\lambda(1-\delta)^s + M_s) \, p_l(t_s, l_s) + (1-\delta) \, (G'(i_s) + \mu_s G''(i_s))$$
$$- (1-\delta) \, (G'(i_{s-1}) + \mu_{s-1} G''(i_{s-1})) \, / \beta = 0.$$

Substituting from (7.11) and (7.7) yields the conditions (7.14) and (7.15) in the text.

Suppose that the optimal path has the property that there exists a time T such that wages are equalized between sectors for $s \geq T$. We characterize this path and then show that the optimal path must have this property. If $\Delta(t_s, l_s) = 0$ for $s \geq T$, then it follows from the labor mobility constraint (7.6) that $G'(i_{T-1}) = 0$ and hence $i_{T-1} \in [0, \delta l^m]$. Equalization of wages will imply $G'(i_s) = 0$ and $G''(i_s) = 0$ for $s \geq T-1$, so the necessary condition for choice of l_s in (7.15) yields $t_s = 0$. The result that free trade is achieved for $s \geq T$ yields $M_s = -\lambda(1-\delta)^s$ from (7.14). Thus, there is free trade with wages equalized between sectors 1 and N for $s \geq T$. The fact that $M_T < 0$ ensures that the labor mobility constraint is binding for policymakers for $s < T$.

For $s < T$, we use (7.13) in (7.15) to obtain the system of equations

$$- \beta(1-\delta)M_{s+1}G''(i_s) + (\beta + G''(i_{s-1}) + \beta(1-\delta)^2 G''(i_s))M_s$$
$$- (1-\delta)G''(i_{s-1})M_{s-1} + \beta\lambda(1-\delta)^s = 0 \quad \text{for } s = 1, \dots, T-1. \quad (7.23)$$

This system can be written in matrix form as $\mathbf{ZM} = -\lambda\mathbf{D}$, where $\mathbf{M}$ is the $T-1$ vector whose sth element is M_s and $\mathbf{D}$ is the $T-1$ vector with sth element $(1-\delta)^s$. Using the fact that $G''(i_s) = \gamma$ for $s = 1, \dots, T-1$ and $G''(i_T) = 0$, the matrix $\mathbf{Z}$ will have diagonal elements $z_{ss} = \left(1 + \frac{\gamma}{\beta} + \gamma(1-\delta)^2\right)$ for $s = 1, \dots, T-2$ and $z_{T-1,T-1} = \left(1 + \frac{\gamma}{\beta}\right)$. The off-diagonal elements are $z_{s,s+1} = -\gamma(1-\delta)$ for $i = 1, \dots T-2$, $z_{s,s-1} = -\gamma(1-\delta)/\beta$ for $i = 2, \dots T-1$, and 0 for all other elements.

Since the matrix $\mathbf{Z}$ is independent of λ, the solution $\mathbf{M} = -\lambda \mathbf{Z}^{-1}\mathbf{D}$ is homogeneous of degree 1 in λ. Also, since $\mathbf{Z}$ is a matrix with positive and negative off-diagonal elements and has positive column sums, $\mathbf{Z}$ has a dominant diagonal. It then follows from theorem 4.C.3 in Takayama (1974) that $\lambda \mathbf{D} < 0$ implies $\mathbf{M} \leq 0$. To show that $\mathbf{M} < 0$ in this case, suppose that $M_s = 0$ for some s. Then the sth element of $\mathbf{ZM}$ will be $\sum\limits_{j \neq s} z_{sj}M_j \geq 0$, since $z_{sj} \leq 0$ for $j \neq s$ and $M_j \leq 0$. However, this cannot be a solution, because it contradicts $\mathbf{D} < 0$. Therefore, we have $M_s < 0$ for all s. The necessary condition (7.14) can then be used to solve for the time path of tariff rates $\mathbf{t}$, which will be homogeneous of degree 1 in λ.

The system of equations (7.23) yields solutions $\mathbf{M}(T)$ and $t(T)$ that depend on the terminal time T. The optimal value of T will be the one for which $l_{T-1}(\lambda) \leq \bar{l}(0)/(1-\delta)$, which means that wages can be equalized between sectors in the following period because of attrition of workers in the import-competing sector. To solve for the path of employment levels for a given terminal time T, we note that for $s < T$, (7.7) yields a system of equations $\tilde{\mathbf{Z}}\mathbf{1} = \mathbf{B}$. The diagonal elements of $\tilde{\mathbf{Z}}$ are given by $\tilde{z}_{ss} = \left(\frac{1}{2+\phi^*} + \frac{\gamma}{\beta} + \gamma(1-\delta)^2\right)$ for $s = 1, .., T-2$ and $\tilde{z}_{T-1,T-1} = \left(\frac{1}{2+\phi^*} + \frac{\gamma}{\beta}\right)$. The off-diagonal elements of $\tilde{\mathbf{Z}}$ are identical to those in $\mathbf{Z}$. $\mathbf{1}$ denotes the vector of employment levels, and $\mathbf{B}$ is the vector with $b_1 = \frac{A+A^*+a^*-t_1(1+\phi^*)}{2+\phi^*} - 1 + \frac{\gamma(1-\delta)}{\beta}l_0$ and $b_s = \frac{A+A^*+a^*-t_s(1+\phi^*)}{2+\phi^*} - 1$ for $s = 2, .., T-1$.

Since $t(s)$ is increasing in λ, $\mathbf{B}$ is decreasing in λ, and we can use an argument similar to that used earlier to establish that $\mathbf{1}$ will be increasing in λ. Denoting the terminal point in the optimal agreement by $T^*(\lambda)$, the fact that $l_{T-1}(\lambda)$ is increasing in λ means that $T^*(\lambda)$ is nondecreasing in λ.

Proof of Proposition 7.2   The Lagrangian for this problem will be

$$\max_{l_s,t_s} L = \sum_{s=0}^{\infty} \left[W^W(t_s, l_s) - G(l_{s+1} - (1-\delta)l_s) + \lambda^L p(t_s, l_s)(1-\delta)^s\right]\beta^s.$$

The necessary conditions for the choice of t_s and l_s are

$$W_t^W(t_s, l_s) + \lambda^L p_t(t_s, l_s) = 0,$$

$$W_l^W(t_s, l_s) + \lambda^L p_l(t_s, l_s) + (1-\delta)G'(i_s) - G'(i_{s-1})/\beta = 0.$$

Substituting from (7.11) and (7.7) yields the necessary conditions (7.19) and (7.20) in the text.

The fact that $i_s < 0$ for $s < T^L - 1$ and $i_{T^L-1} \in (0, \delta l^m)$ means that $G'(i_s) = \gamma i_s$ for $s < T^L - 1$ and $G'(i_{T^L-1}) = 0$. Substituting these results into (7.20) gives the system of $T^L - 1$ equations that can be expressed in matrix form as $\mathbf{Z}\mathbf{l} = \mathbf{B}^L$, where $\mathbf{B}$ and $\mathbf{l}$ are as defined in the proof of proposition 7.1 and $b_1^L = \frac{A + A^* + a^* - \lambda^L(1-\delta)}{2+\phi^*} - 1 + \frac{\gamma(1-\delta)}{\beta} l_0$ and $b_s = \frac{A + A^* + a^* - \lambda^L(1-\delta)^s}{2+\phi^*} - 1$ for $s = 2, .., T - 1$. This system of equations will determine $l_1, .. l_{T-1}$, given l_0 and T^L. In order for this system to be consistent with reaching no adjustment costs at T^L, the solution must yield $l_{T^L-1} \in [l^L(T^L - 1)/(1 - \delta), l^L(T^L))$. Since $\mathbf{B}^L$ is decreasing in λ and $\mathbf{Z}$ has a dominant diagonal, we can use the same arguments as in the proof of Proposition 7.1 to show that employment in sector 1 is increasing in λ for $s < T^L$.

Notes

I thank Ayre Hillman, Ben Zissimos, and participants at the CESifo Venice seminar on the WTO and Economic Development for comments.

1. Baldwin and Robert-Nicoud (2007) formalize this argument in a monopolistic competition model.

2. This generalizes the results obtained by Lapan (1978) and Mussa (1978), (1982) for the small-country case to the large-country case.

3. Bond and Park (2002) show that gradual tariff reduction may arise without adjustment costs when countries are asymmetric and agreements must be self-enforcing.

4. Suppose that a worker can produce 1 unit of N or θ units of good 2. A linear supply function will be obtained if the distribution of ability is given by $f(\theta) = 2 (\underline{\theta}\overline{\theta})^2 \theta^{-3} / (\overline{\theta}^2 - \underline{\theta}^2)$ on $[\underline{\theta}, \overline{\theta}]$, which yields $\phi = 2 (\underline{\theta}\overline{\theta})^2 / (\overline{\theta}^2 - \underline{\theta}^2)$.

5. We drop the sectoral subscripts in the subsequent discussion to simplify notation.

6. This problem can also be formulated as a recursive saddle-point problem, as shown by Marcet and Marimon (2011).

7. See Beshkar and Bond (2016) for a survey on the role of safeguards in trade agreements.

8. Cassing and Hillman (1986) consider the case of a declining industry, and argue that the shrinking of the industry over time may result in a collapse in political support for protection.

References

Bagwell, Kyle and Robert W. Staiger (2002), *The Economics of the World Trading System*, Cambridge, MA: MIT Press.

Baldwin, Richard and Frederic Robert-Nicoud (2007), Entry and Asymmetric Lobbying: Why Governments Pick Losers, *Journal of the European Economic Association* 5(5), 1064–1093.

Beshkar, Mostafa and Eric W. Bond (2016), The Escape Clause in Trade Agreements in *Handbook of Commerical Policy: Volume 1b*, edited by Kyle Bagwell and Robert Staiger, Amsterdam: North Holland.

Bond, Eric W. and Jee-Hyeong Park (2002), Gradualism in Trade Agreements with Asymmetric Countries, *Review of Economic Studies*, 69(2), 379–406.

Brander, James and Barbara Spencer (1994), Trade Adjustment Assistance: Welfare and Incentive Effects of Payments to Displaced Workers, *Journal of International Economics* 36, 239–261.

Cassing, James and Arye Hillman (1986), Shifting Comparative Advantage and Senescent Industry Collapse, *American Economic Review* 76(3), 516–523.

Corden, W. M. (1974), *Trade Policy and Economic Welfare*, Oxford: Oxford University Press.

Dix-Carneiro, Rafael (2014), Trade Liberalization and Labor Market Dynamics, *Econometrica* 82(5), 825–885.

Ethier, Wilfred J. (2002), Unilateralism in a Multilateral World, *Economic Journal* 112, 266–292.

Furusawa, Taiji and Edwin Lai (1997), Adjustment Costs and Gradual Trade Liberalization, *Journal of International Economics* 49, 333–361.

Grossman, Gene M. and Elhanan Helpman (1995), Trade Wars and Trade Talks, *Journal of Political Economy* 103, 675–708.

Hillman, Arye (1982), Declining Industries and Political Support: Protectionist Motives, *American Economic Review* 72(5), 1180–1187.

Karp, Larry and Thierry Paul (1994), Phasing In and Phasing Out Protectionism with Costly Adjustment, *Economic Journal* 104, 1379–1392.

Lapan, Harvey E. (1978), International Trade, Factor Market Distortions, and the Optimal Dynamic Subsidy, *American Economic Review* 66, 335–346.

Maggi, Giovanni and Andres Rodríguez-Clare (2007), A Political Economy Theory of Trade Agreements, *American Economic Review* 97, 1374–1406.

Marcet, Albert and Ramon Marimon (2011), Recursive Contracts, unpublished manuscript.

Mussa, Michael (1978), Dynamic Adjustment in the Heckscher-Ohlin-Samuelson Model, *Journal of Political Economy* 86(5), 775–791.

Mussa, Michael (1982), Government Policy and the Adjustment Process, in *Import Competition and Response*, edited by J. Bhagwati, 73–122, Chicago: University of Chicago Press.

Smith, Adam (1776), *The Wealth of Nations*, London: W. Strahan and T. Cadell.

Staiger, Robert (1995), A Theory of Gradual Trade Liberalization, in *New Directions in Trade Theory*, edited by J. Lenvinsohn, A. Deardorff, and R. Stern, 779–795, Ann Arbor: University of Michigan Press.

Takayama, Akira (1974), *Mathematical Economics*, Hinsdale, IL: Dryden Press.

8 Price Controls versus Compulsory Licensing: Effects on Patent Holders and Consumers

Eric W. Bond and Kamal Saggi

8.1 Introduction

When the Doha Round of trade negotiations was launched in 2001, there was an expectation among developing countries that their interests would figure prominently in the ensuing negotiations. Indeed, the Doha Ministerial Conference explicitly stated that since a majority of the members of the World Trade Organization (WTO) were developing countries, the Doha work program would seek to place their needs and interests at its core. This was a welcome development from the viewpoint of developing countries, many of whom viewed the Uruguay Round (1986–1993) as having bequeathed a bargain that was biased in favor of developed countries. Perhaps the most problematic outcome of the Uruguay Round from the perspective of developing countries was the Agreement on Trade Related Aspects of Intellectual Property Rights (TRIPS)—a multilateral agreement that requires all WTO members, regardless of their level of economic development, to grant certain minimum levels of protection to all major forms of intellectual property.

Of course, by their very nature, intellectual property rights (IPRs) create monopoly power for rights holders. For example, the holder of a patent on an invention has the right to exclude others from making the invention, using it, or offering it for sale. The expansion in the global reach of such monopoly power via the worldwide enforcement of IPRs can be rather problematic in the realm of patented pharmaceuticals, at least some of which are frequently needed for addressing significant public health concerns. While the issue of affordability of patented pharmaceuticals takes on a special urgency in the context of poor developing countries, it is also relevant within the developed world. It is no surprise then that governments across the world use price controls and other such regulations to combat the monopoly power of firms selling patented pharmaceuticals.[1]

As one might expect, price regulation in the pharmaceutical industry has important consequences for consumers. For example, in her structural study of 155 pharmaceutical products sold in India during 2001–2003, Dutta (2011) found that consumers derived substantial benefits from price controls. Similarly, Chatterjee, Kobe, and Pingali (2013) argue that the removal of price controls in the oral antidiabetic segment of the Indian pharmaceutical market would have significant negative repercussions for consumers. While appealing, the use of price controls can become counterproductive if foreign pharmaceutical companies refuse to sell their patented medicines in markets where they find such controls to be too stringent. In her large sample study spanning 68 countries over the time period 1982–2002, Lanjouw (2005) found that the presence of price regulations in countries delayed pharmaceutical companies from introducing new drugs into their markets. Similar results were found by Kyle (2005) in her study of the 28 largest pharmaceutical markets in the world. Thus, while price controls can be effective in improving consumer access to patented pharmaceuticals conditional on local availability, they run the risk that patent holders will deliberately choose to make their products unavailable in countries that impose them.

An alternative strategy that governments can use for providing local consumers access to patented foreign pharmaceuticals that are not sold locally is to issue compulsory licenses for such products to local firms.[2] Multilateral rules governing the use of compulsory licensing (CL) by member countries of the WTO are contained in Article 31 of TRIPS, under which the use of CL is only justified if the entity seeking a compulsory license has failed to obtain a voluntary license from the patent holder on "reasonable" commercial terms. Furthermore, the government issuing the compulsory license has to ensure that "adequate remuneration" is paid to the patent holder in return for the right to produce its patented product locally.[3] While Article 31 requires that any sales under CL should be predominantly for the domestic market of the country issuing the license, the 2001 Doha Ministerial Conference relaxed this rule by allowing compulsory licenses for patented foreign products to be issued to producers in third countries. The objective of this modification was to bring CL within reach of those countries that lacked the technological capability to produce patented pharmaceuticals and other necessary products locally.

Building on related previous work (Bond and Saggi 2014), in this chapter we contrast the roles of price controls and CL as alternative instruments for improving consumer access to patented foreign products in developing countries. In the model, a developing country (called the South) sets the level of the price control while the patent holder chooses between direct entry and the voluntary licensing (VL) of its technology to a local firm. The model assumes that while the fixed costs incurred under VL are relatively lower, so is the quality of production. We compare two scenarios: one where the South attempts to improve consumer access via the use of a price control and another where it resorts to CL if the patent holder chooses not to work its patent locally. In accordance with the available case-study evidence pertaining to the implementation of CL in developing countries, we assume that the local firm's quality of production under CL is lower than that under entry.[4] For simplicity, we assume that there is no quality differential between the two types of licensing.

The analysis in Bond and Saggi (2014) focused on the case where the licensee's fixed-cost advantage is large relative to its quality disadvantage, and it showed that, depending on parameter values, the patent holder may choose to serve the Southern market by either VL or entry in the absence of price controls. In this chapter, we consider the case where the licensee's fixed-cost advantage is small relative to its quality disadvantage. The present case is likely to arise for sophisticated production processes in which a potential Southern licensee faces a significant handicap when attempting to undertake local production of the patented product and/or where the patent holder has a high degree of familiarity with the Southern market so that the fixed-cost disadvantage of entry is small. We show that in such a case, in the absence of a price control, the patent holder either directly enters the market or it stays out (i.e., VL does not emerge in equilibrium when monopoly pricing is permitted). However, it turns out that the use of a price control by the South tilts the patent holder's choice in favor of VL. Indeed, we find that there exists a range of price controls and fixed costs for which VL can end up emerging in equilibrium. Intuitively, because of the higher quality of production under entry, the monopoly price under entry exceeds that under VL, so that a price control penalizes the profitability of entry to a relatively larger degree.

Because of the presence of mode-specific fixed costs, both entry and VL can be unprofitable for the patent holder even when its pricing is completely unconstrained by the South. Clearly, in such a situation,

Southern consumers obtain no access to the product and the South's price control policy is rendered inconsequential. If only entry is profitable, it is optimal for the South to set the price control ($\bar{p}$) at a level that allows the patent holder to just break even (i.e., cover its fixed cost of entry)—anything more stringent simply results in complete loss of access to the product. A price control set at the break-even price hurts the patent holder by driving its net profit to zero but increases Southern welfare.

When both modes of supply are profitable, a given price control ($\bar{p}$) is more binding under entry relative to VL since the optimal monopoly price under entry is higher because of the lower quality of production under VL (i.e., $p_E^* \geq p_L^*$ since $q_E \geq q_L$). When the break-even price under entry ($\bar{p}_E$) is lower than that under VL ($\bar{p}_L$), it is optimal for the South to set the price control at $\bar{p}_E$ since entry is doubly preferable to VL: it not only offers a higher-quality product but does so at a lower price than VL. However, when $\bar{p}_L \leq \bar{p}_E$, the South has to decide whether to set a price control that just allows the patent holder to break even under VL (i.e., set $\bar{p} = \bar{p}_L$) or to set a sufficiently lax price control at which the patent holder prefers entry. Even though the patent holder earns profits under both modes, the entry-inducing price control $\tilde{p}$ is such that entry is marginally more profitable for the patent holder. Setting the price control at $\bar{p} = \bar{p}_E$ is not optimal when $\bar{p}_E \geq \bar{p}_L$ since doing so induces the patent holder to choose VL (under which it earns a profit). From the patent holder's viewpoint, the scenario where $\tilde{p} > \bar{p}_E$ is necessarily better, but the South also prefers it when the quality of production under VL is fairly low.

Our analysis shows that the option to use CL ensures that at least a lower-quality version of the patented good is available locally if the patent holder decides not to work its patent in the South. However, the very possibility of CL also makes it less likely that the patent holder will choose to sell in the South. The threat of CL reduces the patent holder's profits under VL by lowering the fee that the local licensee is willing to pay. Similarly, since the royalty payments under CL provide the patent holder a return from the Southern market if it chooses to stay out, entry becomes relatively less attractive as well. When CL *replaces* entry, it can lower Southern welfare because it not only delivers a lower-quality product to consumers but does so with some *delay*.

Overall, our results show that the social value of CL is very much context dependent. When the fixed cost of entry is high relative to the size of the Southern market, CL plays a socially useful role that can be to the advantage of both the South and the patent holder since the South obtains access while the patent holder receives royalties from a market that it would not have entered in the absence of CL. On the other hand, when fixed costs are of an intermediate level such that the patent holder prefers to wait for CL rather than entering itself, the South is made worse off by the option of CL. Finally, when fixed costs are so small that the patent holder chooses to enter regardless of whether the South has the option to issue CL, the threat of CL does not affect market outcomes and welfare.

The rest of the chapter is organized as follows. Section 8.2 introduces the model of the patent holder's choice between VL and entry and identifies the fixed cost/product quality trade-off between the two modes of supply. Section 8.3 analyzes the effect of price controls on the entry/licensing decision of the patent holder and derives the South's optimal price control. Section 8.4 considers the alternative case under which the South does not use a price control but has the ability to issue a compulsory license that is consistent with the relevant WTO rules. Here, we also compare the effects of price controls and CL on the patent holder's decision and on the welfare of the two parties. Section 8.5 provides some concluding remarks.

8.2   Model

Since the basic purpose of this chapter is to complete the analysis of the model of price controls and CL introduced in Bond and Saggi (2014), we begin by describing the basic structure of this model. Consider a Northern firm (referred to as the "patent holder") that produces a good protected by a patent for T periods. There is a continuum of Southern consumers of measure 1, each of whom buys (at most) one unit of the product. If a consumer buys the good at price p, its utility is $U = \theta q - p$, where q measures quality and $\theta \geq 0$ is a taste parameter that captures the willingness to pay for quality. For simplicity, θ is assumed to be uniformly distributed over the interval $[0,1]$. Normalizing utility under no purchase to zero, the demand per period in the South is $d(p,q) = 1 - p/q$.

If the patent holder decides to enter the Southern market and produce the good itself, then its quality level equals q_E. To be able to produce the good, the patent holder has to incur the fixed entry cost φ. The parameter φ captures the costs of obtaining any necessary approval from local authorities as well as the costs of establishing an effective marketing and distribution network.

The patent holder can also sell its product in the South by licensing its technology to a local firm. For simplicity, we assume that there is only a single local firm with sufficient capability to be an effective licensee. Since the purpose of the model is to analyze the role of compulsory licensing (CL), we refer to the patent holder's choice to license on its own terms as voluntary licensing (VL). Since VL allows the patent holder to use the local licensee's existing distribution and retail network, the fixed cost of VL is assumed to be lower than that of direct entry and is denoted by $\alpha\varphi$, where $0 < \alpha < 1$.[5] The parameter α captures the fixed-cost savings of VL relative to entry. The disadvantage of VL is that the quality of production under it (q_L) is lower than under entry, $q_L = \gamma q_E$, and $\gamma < 1$ captures the quality disadvantage of VL relative to entry.

Normalizing the cost of production under VL to zero, the monopoly price for the licensee equals $p_L^* = q_L/2$. The maximum gross profits accruing to the licensee over the life of the patent when facing the price control $\bar{p}$ are given by

$$v_L(\bar{p}, q_L) = (1 + \Omega)\pi_L(\bar{p}, q_L), \text{ where } \pi_L(\bar{p}, q_L)$$
$$\equiv \min[\bar{p}, p_L^*]\left(1 - \frac{\min[\bar{p}, p_L^*]}{q_L}\right), \tag{8.1}$$

where $\Omega = \sum_{t=1}^{T} \beta^t$ converts future profit flow to present value and $0 < \beta \leq 1$ is the per-period discount factor.[6]

Assuming that the marginal cost of production under entry is the same as that under VL, the present value of the maximum gross profit the patent holder earns by selling in the South via direct entry when facing the price control $\bar{p}$ equals

$$v_E(\bar{p}) = (1 + \Omega)\pi_E(\bar{p}), \text{ where } \pi_E(\bar{p}) \equiv \min[\bar{p}, p_E^*]\left(1 - \frac{\min[\bar{p}, p_E^*]}{q_E}\right), \tag{8.2}$$

where $p_E^* = q_E/2 > p_L^*$ is the unconstrained monopoly price under entry. The absence of a price control is then equivalent to $\bar{p} \geq p_E^*$.

Southern welfare under VL equals

$$W_L(\bar{p}, q_L) = (1 + \Omega)[S(\min[\bar{p}, p_L^*], q_L) + \pi_L(\bar{p}, q_L)] - \alpha\varphi - f, \tag{8.3}$$

where f denotes the licensing fee paid to the patent holder and $S(p, q_L) = (q_L/2)(1 - p/q_L)^2$ measures consumer surplus at price p and quality q_L. Southern welfare under entry (W_E) consists (solely) of consumer surplus that accrues to the South over the life of the (higher-quality) product sold by the patent holder:

$$W_E(\bar{p}, q_E) = (1 + \Omega)S(\min[\bar{p}, p_E^*], q_E). \tag{8.4}$$

Thus, while VL has the potential to provide the South with some benefits in terms of the profits of the local firm (net of the license fee), these benefits come at the cost of having a lower-quality product relative to entry. If the market is not served, the South receives a payoff of 0.[7]

We begin with the benchmark case where the only instrument available to the South for improving consumer access is the price control $\bar{p}$. Then, we allow the South to use CL in the event that the patent holder does not work its patent in the South.

8.3   Price Controls and Consumer Access

In what follows, we first analyze interaction between the patent holder and the Southern government (referred to simply as "the South" hereafter) in a two-stage game in which the South does not have the option to use CL if the patent holder refrains from selling locally.

In the first stage of the game, the South chooses its price control $\bar{p}$. To avoid any hold-up problem, we assume that once the price control has been set, the South is committed to it for the remainder of the game. Given the price control set by the South, the patent holder chooses between entry, VL, and not selling in the South. Under VL, the patent holder makes a take it or leave it offer to the Southern firm. If the Southern firm accepts the offer, it acts as a licensee and transfers the present value of its product market profit stream to the patent holder as the licensing fee $f_L(\bar{p})$. This is because if it rejects the offer, the Southern firm earns zero profit, since it lacks the right to produce the patented product independently.

8.3.1   Patent Holder's Decision
To determine how the patent holder's choice between VL and entry depends on the price control $\bar{p}$, first note that since $p_E^* > p_L^*$, a given price control either (1) binds under neither entry nor VL (i.e., $\bar{p} = p_E^*$);

(2) binds only under entry (i.e., $p_L^* \leq \bar{p} < p_E^*$); or (3) binds under both modes (i.e., $\bar{p} < p_L^*$).

Denote the present value of the patent holder's payoff under monopoly pricing by v_Z^*, where $Z = L$ or E. The present value differential between the two modes as a function of the price control $\bar{p}$ can be written as

$$\Delta v(\bar{p}) \equiv v_E(\bar{p}) - v_L(\bar{p})$$

$$= \begin{cases} \Delta v^* = v_E^* - v_L^* = \dfrac{q_E(1+\Omega)(1-\gamma)}{4} & \bar{p} \geq p_E^* \\[2ex] \Delta v_1(\bar{p}) = (1+\Omega)\left[\bar{p}(1 - \dfrac{\bar{p}}{q_E}) - \dfrac{q_L}{4}\right] & p_L^* \leq \bar{p} < p_E^* \\[2ex] \Delta v_2(\bar{p}) = (1+\Omega)\dfrac{\bar{p}^2}{q_E}\left(\dfrac{1-\gamma}{\gamma}\right) & \bar{p} < p_L^* \end{cases} \qquad (8.5)$$

Direct calculations establish the following lemma.

Lemma 8.1 (i) $\frac{\partial \Delta v(\bar{p})}{\partial \bar{p}} > 0$ for $p < p_E^*$; (ii) $\frac{\partial \Delta v^*}{\partial \bar{p}} = 0$; (iii) $\frac{\partial^2 \Delta v_1(\bar{p})}{\partial^2 \bar{p}} < 0$; and (iv) $\frac{\partial^2 \Delta v_2(\bar{p})}{\partial^2 \bar{p}} > 0$.

Part (i) of lemma 8.1 simply says that as the price control becomes less stringent, the present value differential between entry and VL increases for any price at which the control is binding for at least one mode of serving the market. For $\bar{p} \in (p_L^*, p_E^*)$, VL becomes relatively more attractive because the price control only binds under entry. For $\bar{p} < p_L^*$, a more stringent price control lowers profitability under both modes, but it is *more binding under entry* since $p_E^* > p_L^*$.

Part (ii) notes that if the price control lies above the optimal price under entry, the present value differential is independent of the price control since the patent holder is free to charge its optimal price under both modes of supply. Parts (iii) and (iv) say that if the price control binds only under entry, then the present value differential between entry and VL is concave in the level of the price control, whereas it is convex when it binds under both modes.

We now utilize the present value differential in (8.5) to derive the patent holder's optimal decision. We begin with the case where the price control is so lax that the patent holder can charge its optimal monopoly price under direct entry and VL (i.e., $\bar{p} \geq p_E^*$). The patent holder prefers entry to VL iff $v_E^* - \varphi \geq f_L(p_L^*) = v_L^* - \alpha$, which implies that entry is preferred by the patent holder iff

$$\varphi \leq \tilde{\varphi} \equiv \Delta v^* / (1 - \alpha). \tag{8.6}$$

Furthermore, each mode of selling in the South is profitable iff the fixed cost of each mode lies below the present value of the respective profit stream:

$$\varphi \leq \varphi_E \equiv v_E^* \text{ and } \varphi \leq \varphi_L \equiv v_L^* / \alpha. \tag{8.7}$$

The patent holder's choice between entry and VL depends on the following trade-off. Though the fixed cost of VL is lower than that of entry (since $\alpha < 1$), the revenue earned by the licensee is smaller because of the lower quality of its product (i.e., $q_L = \gamma q_E$, where $\gamma < 1$). When $\gamma \leq \alpha$, the fixed-cost saving under VL is dominated by the product-quality advantage of entry, and the break-even level of fixed cost for entry is lower than that for VL. Since the case where $\gamma > \alpha$ has been analyzed exhaustively in Bond and Saggi (2014), throughout the rest of the chapter we assume (assumption 8.1) that the cost advantage of licensing is dominated by its quality disadvantage.

Assumption 8.1 $\gamma \leq \alpha$.

Note that assumption 8.1 implies that $\varphi_L \leq \varphi_E$ (i.e., VL is profitable over a smaller range of fixed costs than for entry). In other words, whenever entry is unprofitable for the patent holder, so is VL. Using inequalities (8.6) and (8.7), we can show the following.

Proposition 8.1 Given assumption 8.1 ($\gamma \leq \alpha$), the patent holder chooses to enter for all $\varphi \in [0, \varphi_E]$, whereas it does not work its patent in the South for all $\varphi > \varphi_E$.

In other words, when the patent holder is free to charge its optimal monopoly prices under both modes, VL does not occur in equilibrium. However, it is still interesting to analyze VL since, as we will see, the use of a price control by the South tilts the patent holder's choice between entry and VL in such a way that VL can arise in equilibrium because of the imposition of a price control.

We are now ready to consider the case where the South imposes a price control that binds on the patent holder. It is useful to define the break-even price for entry $\overline{p}_E(\varphi)$ as the solution to $v_E(\overline{p}) = \varphi$. It is clear that $\overline{p}_E(\varphi)$ is continuous and increasing over $[0, v_E^*]$. Since there is no price at which the patent holder can break even for $\varphi > v_E^*$, we set $\overline{p}_E(\varphi) = \infty$ for $\varphi > v_E^*$. Similarly, the break-even price for VL is denoted by $\bar{p}_L(\varphi)$, which is continuous and increasing on $[0, v_L^*]$ and equal to ∞ for $\varphi > v_L^*$.

It is obvious that the patent holder does not serve the Southern market if $\bar{p} < \min[\bar{p}_L(\varphi), \bar{p}_E(\varphi)]$. If $\bar{p}_E(\varphi) \leq \bar{p}_L(\varphi)$, lemma 8.1 (i) ensures that entry is more profitable for the patent holder than VL for all price controls for which it is profitable (i.e., $\bar{p} \geq \bar{p}_E(\varphi)$). If $\bar{p}_L(\varphi) < \bar{p}_E(\varphi)$, then entry is the more profitable mode if

$$\Delta v(\bar{p}) \geq (1 - \alpha)\varphi. \tag{8.8}$$

If $\bar{p}_L(\varphi) < \bar{p}_E(\varphi)$ and $\varphi \leq \tilde{\varphi}$, there exists a price $\tilde{p}(\varphi)$ at which

$$\Delta v(\bar{p}) = (1 - \alpha)\varphi = 0.$$

We refer to $\tilde{p}(\varphi)$ as the *entry-inducing* price, since the patent holder prefers entry to VL if $\bar{p} \geq \tilde{p}(\varphi)$.[8]

We can show the following proposition.

Proposition 8.2 For all price controls $\bar{p} \in [0, p_E^*)$, there exists a threshold level of fixed costs $\varphi_0 \in (0, \varphi_L]$ such that the following hold:

(i) For $\varphi \in (0, \varphi_0)$, we have $\bar{p}_L(\varphi) < \bar{p}_E(\varphi) < \tilde{p}(\varphi)$ and the patent holder opts for VL if $\bar{p}_L(\varphi) \leq \bar{p} < \tilde{p}(\varphi)$; it enters if $\bar{p} \geq \tilde{p}(\varphi)$; and does not serve the Southern market otherwise.

(ii) For $\varphi \in (\varphi_0, \varphi_L]$, we have $\bar{p}_E(\varphi) \leq \bar{p}_L(\varphi)$ and the patent holder enters if $\bar{p} \geq \bar{p}_E(\varphi)$, whereas it does not serve the market otherwise.

(iii) The threshold value φ_0 has the property that $\frac{\partial \varphi_0}{\partial \alpha} < 0 < \frac{\partial \varphi_0}{\partial \gamma}$.

The intuition underlying this result follows from lemma 8.1 (i): as the price control $\bar{p}$ becomes more stringent, the profit advantage of entry over VL is reduced. Therefore, the fixed-cost advantage of VL starts to become more important as $\bar{p}$ falls, so that VL becomes a viable option over some range of fixed costs—that is, for $\varphi \in (\varphi_0, \varphi_L]$—when $\bar{p}$ is sufficiently low. The threshold value of the fixed cost (φ_0) below which VL is a viable option is higher if the licensee enjoys a greater fixed-cost advantage and a smaller quality disadvantage.

Figure 8.1 shows the relationship between the fixed-cost parameter φ and the relevant prices under the two modes for a specific example. For $\varphi > \varphi_E$, neither entry nor VL is profitable and the market is not served. When $\varphi \in (\varphi_L, \varphi_E)$, fixed costs are high enough that VL is not profitable at any price. Entry is the only possible mode of serving the market over this interval, and it is chosen by the patent holder as long

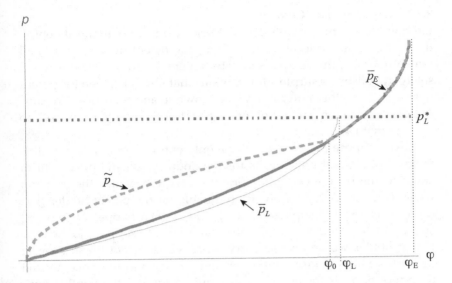

Figure 8.1
Price control thresholds.

as the price control is no less than $\bar{p}_E(\varphi)$. The example in figure 8.1 illustrates a case in which $\bar{p}_E(\varphi_L) < p_L^*$, so that there exists an interval of fixed costs $[\varphi_0, \varphi_L]$ for which $\bar{p}_E(\varphi) < \bar{p}_L(\varphi)$. Although there are prices at which both VL and entry are profitable over this interval, the patent holder always earns higher profits under entry. For $\varphi \in [0, \varphi_0]$, both VL and entry are profitable and entry is chosen by the patent holder iff the price control exceeds the entry-inducing price $\tilde{p}(\varphi)$.[9]

An interesting insight provided by a comparison of propositions 8.1 and 8.2 is that *the use of a price control by the South can make VL arise in equilibrium*. Given assumption 8.1, in the absence of a price control, the patent holder either chooses entry or stays out, whereas in the presence of a price control, it chooses VL when $\varphi \in (0, \varphi_0)$ and $\bar{p} \in (\bar{p}_L(\varphi), \tilde{p}(\varphi)]$. The intuition for this result comes from lemma 8.1: whereas a price control reduces profitability under both entry and VL, it is more binding under entry since $p_L^* < p_E^*$. As a result, when $\varphi \in (0, \varphi_0)$, for any price control $\bar{p} \in (\bar{p}_L(\varphi), \tilde{p}(\varphi)]$, the patent holder ends up choosing VL, whereas it never does so when the South allows it to charge its optimal monopoly prices under the two modes.

8.3.2   Optimal Price Control

We now derive the South's optimal price control assuming its objective is to maximize local welfare. Since the patent holder extracts all rents under VL, the comparison between entry and VL is determined solely by consumer surplus. It is obvious that if $\varphi > \varphi_E$, then the patent holder finds neither entry nor VL worthwhile and the price control is irrelevant since the patent holder stays out of the Southern market no matter what its level.

Next, suppose $\varphi_L \leq \varphi < \varphi_E$. Since only entry is profitable over this range, the optimal policy calls for the South to set the price control equal to the break-even entry price $\overline{p}_E$. Now consider the scenario where both modes of supply are profitable for the patent holder (i.e., $\varphi < \varphi_L$). Here, first suppose that $\overline{p}_E \leq \overline{p}_L$, which happens when $\varphi \in (\varphi_0, \varphi_L)$. Under this scenario, if the South were to set $\overline{p} = \overline{p}_E$, then the patent holder would choose entry, since VL does not break even at this price. Since quality is superior under entry and the price needed to induce entry is lower than that required for VL, the South's optimal policy is to set $\overline{p} = \overline{p}_E$ whenever $\overline{p}_E \leq \overline{p}_L$. Now consider the case where $\overline{p}_E > \overline{p}_L$. Here, to be able to induce entry, the South has to set the price control at the entry-inducing price $\tilde{p}$. Of course, it can alternatively set $\overline{p} = \overline{p}_L$ (the break-even price under VL), thereby inducing VL. Thus, the trade-off facing the South is clear: entry offers a higher-quality product but also requires a more lax price control. Thus, when $\overline{p}_E > \overline{p}_L$, the South prefers the entry-inducing price $\tilde{p}$ to the break-even VL price $\overline{p}_L$ iff

$$S(\tilde{p}, q) \geq S(\overline{p}_L, \gamma q). \tag{8.9}$$

We summarize the optimal price control policy as follows.

Proposition 8.3   The South's optimal price control policy is as follows:

(i) For $\varphi \in [\varphi_0, \varphi_E]$, the optimal price control equals the break-even entry price $\overline{p}_E$.

(ii) For $\varphi < \varphi_0$, the optimal price control equals the entry-inducing price $\tilde{p}$ if inequality (8.9) holds and the break-even licensing price $\overline{p}_L$ if it does not.

When both modes of supply are profitable for the patent holder and the break-even price for VL is higher, the South's choice between the two modes is clear-cut: entry is strictly preferable to VL since it offers a better product at a lower price. However, when $\overline{p}_E > \overline{p}_L$, whether entry is preferable to VL depends on how large a price premium is required to induce it. Further insight into this trade-off can be gained by solving for the price at which $S(p,q) = S(\overline{p}_L, \gamma q)$. This equation yields the highest price $p_S(\gamma)$ that the South is willing to pay to induce entry when VL can be induced at its break-even price. We have

$$p_S = q_E(1 - \sqrt{\gamma}) + \frac{\overline{p}_L(\gamma)}{\sqrt{\gamma}}, \qquad\qquad (8.10)$$

where $p_S \geq \overline{p}_L$ since $\gamma \leq 1$.

Differentiation of (8.10) establishes that

$$\frac{\partial p_S(\gamma)}{\partial \gamma} < 0$$

(i.e., the maximum price that the South is willing to pay to induce entry declines as the quality disadvantage of licensing decreases). Indeed, as $\gamma \to 1$, $p_S \to \overline{p}_L$, so that the South becomes unwilling to offer any price premium for entry and the patent holder ends up choosing VL. Furthermore, note that p_S increases in α (i.e., the Southern tolerance for a higher entry price increases when the cost advantage of VL declines).[10]

It is clear that the Southern price control necessarily makes the patent holder worse off: for $\varphi_L \leq \varphi < \varphi_E$, its net payoff from entry is driven all the way to zero. For $\varphi < \varphi_L$, it does earn some profits when the South chooses to implement the entry-inducing price $\tilde{p}$, but these profits are always lower than what it earns in the absence of the price control, since $\tilde{p} < p_E^*$. As we will see, unlike a price control, the use of CL does not always make the patent holder worse off.

8.4 Compulsory Licensing

We now examine how granting the South the option of using CL along the lines sanctioned by TRIPS affects the patent holder and Southern consumers. We do so by considering the following game. In the first stage, the patent holder chooses between VL and entry. Next, if the patent holder neither enters nor grants a voluntary license to the local firm, the South issues a compulsory license to the local firm, which produces the product for the duration of the patent. In return for the right to grant a compulsory license to the local firm, the South pays the per-period royalty R to the patent holder.

The TRIPS requirement that applicants for a compulsory license should have been unable to obtain a voluntary license on "reasonable commercial terms" is reflected in the assumption that the second stage of the game arises only if the patent holder neither enters nor issues a voluntary license to the local firm at the first stage. The per-period royalty R received by the patent holder captures the TRIPS requirement of providing "adequate remuneration" to the patent holder.

If the patent holder does not sell in the South in the first period, the South must decide whether to grant a compulsory license. A compulsory license granted at stage two provides the licensee with the right to produce the good for $T - 1$ periods and delays incurring the fixed cost by one period. We assume that the quality of the product produced by the Southern firm under CL is the same as that under VL, as is the required fixed cost. Thus, from a technological perspective, the two types of licensing are identical.[11] We allow the South to compensate the local licensee for any losses that it might suffer under CL. With these assumptions, the welfare of the South under CL equals

$$W_{CL} = \Omega \left[S(p_L^*, q_L) + \pi_L(p_L^*, q_L) - R \right] - \alpha\beta\varphi. \tag{8.11}$$

In order for CL to be a credible threat, we need $W_{CL} > 0$, which basically requires that the quality of production under CL not be so low that the total surplus generated in the South ends up being insufficient to cover the royalty payment made to the patent holder.

We denote the maximum level of fixed costs at which CL is a credible threat as

$$\varphi_C^m(R) = \frac{\Omega \left[S(p_L^*, q_L) + \pi_L(p_L^*, q_L) - R \right]}{\alpha\beta}.$$

8.4.1 Supply Mode

Given that CL is a credible threat, we are now ready to consider the patent holder's decision regarding whether and how to utilize its patent in the South. Under entry, the patent holder earns a return of $v_E^* - \varphi$. Under VL, the patent holder's payoff equals its licensing fee f_L^C and is determined as follows. We assume that the patent holder makes a take it or leave it offer to the Southern firm. If the Southern firm rejects the VL offer and the patent holder does not enter directly, then the Southern firm's outside option is no longer zero profit, since the government grants it a compulsory license in the next period while paying the per-period royalty R to the patent holder, the present value of which equals ΩR. Under CL, the licensee earns a return with a present value of $\max[\Omega \pi_L(p_L^*, q_L) - \alpha\beta\varphi, 0]$.

The highest fee that the patent holder can charge under VL is one that makes the Southern firm indifferent between agreeing to a VL in the first period and waiting for a compulsory license in the next period, which yields

$$f_L^C = v_L^* - \alpha\varphi - \max\{\Omega \pi_L(p_L^*, q_L) - \beta\alpha\varphi, 0\}. \tag{8.12}$$

When $\Omega \pi_L(p_L^*, q_L) > \alpha\beta\varphi$, the possibility of CL induces "profit shifting" from the patent holder to the local licensee since it reduces the license fee the patent holder can earn under VL. Note from earlier that $f_L^C \leq f_L(p_L^*)$ (i.e., if production under CL is profitable for the local firm, the threat of CL lowers the patent holder's payoff from VL; otherwise the payoff is not affected).

Given these payoffs, in the first period, the patent holder has to choose between the following options:

(i) enter with a return of $v_E^* - \varphi$;

(ii) issue a VL to collect the fee f_L^C; or

(iii) not work its patent and wait for CL, which yields royalties worth ΩR.

Recall from proposition 8.1 that because of assumption 8.1, absent the threat of CL, the patent holder necessarily prefers entry to VL. Note further that this conclusion remains unchanged when CL is an available option, since the threat of CL *further lowers* the payoff from VL. This means that the only remaining question is whether the patent holder prefers entry to CL. The patent holder prefers entry to CL iff

$$v_E^* - \varphi \geq \Omega R,$$

which yields the following proposition.

Proposition 8.4   The patent holder chooses entry if $\varphi \in [0, \varphi_E^C]$ where $\varphi_E^C \equiv v_E^* - \Omega R$, where $\varphi_E^C < \varphi_E$ for all $R > 0$; it does not work its patent otherwise, and the South resorts to CL in the second period.

Figure 8.2 illustrates proposition 8.4. A comparison of propositions 8.1 and 8.4 shows that the possibility of CL causes two types of switches in the patent holder's preferred mode of serving the Southern market. For $\varphi \in [\varphi_E^C, \varphi_E]$, the patent holder switches from entry to not serving

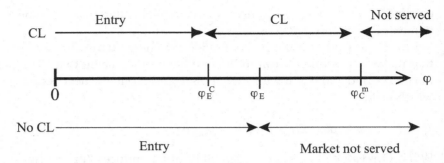

Figure 8.2
Effect of CL on market outcomes.

the market in order to obtain royalty payments under CL. This outcome represents a scenario where the patent holder's return from entry is dominated by the present value of royalty payments it receives under CL. For $\varphi \in [\varphi_E, \varphi_C^m]$, CL results in the patented product being produced locally, whereas the South would not have been served otherwise. As is clear from figure 8.2, the threat of CL expands the range of parameters for which Southern consumers enjoy access to the patented good while *simultaneously* reducing the range of fixed costs for which the patent holder chooses to enter the Southern market.

Thus, CL is similar to a price control in the sense that *both instruments reduce the absolute attractiveness of entry* for the patent holder. But the two instruments differ in two fundamental ways. First, unlike a price control, by reducing the fee paid to the patent holder under VL, the threat of *CL makes VL less attractive to the patent holder relative to entry*.[12] Second, if the patent holder chooses to stay out when facing a stringent price control, it earns no return from the Southern market, whereas it earns a strictly positive return when it decides to stay out and the South resorts to CL.

8.4.2 Welfare under CL

We now analyze the effect that the option to use CL has on Southern welfare and the patent holder. Figure 8.2 illustrates that three types of outcomes can be obtained when CL is a credible threat: the patent holder enters with or without CL for $\varphi \leq \varphi_E^C$, the patent holder switches from entry to waiting for the occurrence of CL for $\varphi \in [\varphi_E^C, \varphi_E]$, and the Southern market is served by the local firm acting as a licensee under CL for $\varphi \in [\varphi_E, \varphi_C^m]$.

Clearly, neither party is affected by the threat of CL for $\varphi \leq \varphi_E^C$. Now consider $\varphi \in [\varphi_E^C, \varphi_E]$. For this range of fixed costs, the possibility of CL *induces* the patent holder not to enter. As a result, Southern consumers experience a switch from consuming a product of quality q_E at its monopoly price of p_E^* to consuming a lower-quality product (of quality γq_E) at the price p_L^* (where $p_L^* = \gamma p_E^*$) with a delay of one period. These changes necessarily reduce the joint welfare of the two parties because not only is the quality of the product under CL lower than that under entry, it also becomes available after a one-period delay. The switch from entry to CL necessarily raises the welfare of the patent holder because the only reason it decides not to enter is that the royalty payments under CL offer a higher return than it can obtain under entry. Furthermore, since joint welfare decreases and the patent holder gains from its decision not to enter and wait for CL, the South necessarily loses from this switch. Thus, the mere observance of CL does not imply that the country using it is better off relative to a scenario where it does not have the option to use CL.

When $\varphi \in [\varphi_E, \varphi_C^m]$, both the South and the patent holder gain: here, CL grants access to a product that would otherwise not be sold in the South, and the South gets consumer surplus and profits of the licensee while the patent holder obtains royalty payments. Thus, over this range of fixed costs, the threat of CL yields a Pareto improving outcome— something that is not possible with a price control.

These results are summarized as the following proposition.

Proposition 8.5   The threat of CL affects equilibrium outcomes and the welfare of each party as follows:

(i) For $\varphi \in [\varphi_E, \varphi_C^m]$, the Southern market is served by the local firm under CL, whereas it would not be served without the threat of CL. As a result, the payoffs to both the South and the patent holder increase as a result of the option of CL.

(ii) For $\varphi \in [\varphi_E^C, \varphi_E]$, CL occurs, whereas the Southern market would have been served by entry if CL were not possible. In this case, the South loses, the patent holder gains, and joint welfare declines as a result of the option of CL.

8.5   Conclusion

Both price controls and CL have been used to improve consumer access to patented pharmaceuticals in developing countries. In this chapter, we have extended the analysis of Bond and Saggi (2014) to provide a comparison of the two instruments from the viewpoint of patent holders as well as consumers in developing countries. While the TRIPS agreement of the WTO is silent on the subject of price controls, it does lay down some clear conditions that a country seeking to use CL must satisfy. Our model is designed to capture actual WTO rules pertaining to the use of CL quite closely. In particular, the South is allowed to use CL only if the patent holder fails to work the patent locally either by entering directly or licensing its technology voluntarily to a local firm. It follows then that the patent holder can preempt CL by choosing to license its product or by entering the Southern market itself.

The model provides four main insights. First, from the perspective of the patent holder, the use of price controls increases the attractiveness of VL relative to entry, because the optimal monopoly price under VL tends to be lower. Second, the optimal price control of the South needs to account for the fixed cost of the two modes as well as the quality difference between them: while the patent holder's break-even price under VL tends to be lower relative to entry, so does the quality of production under it. Thus, it is sometimes worthwhile for the South to allow a higher price in order to ensure that the patent holder chooses entry over VL. The third insight provided by the model is that while the option of CL reduces the attractiveness of VL (by lowering the fee that the local licensee is willing to pay) relative to entry, it also makes staying out of the market more attractive to the patent holder since it can collect royalties under CL that result from its decision not to work its patent in the South. Fourth, CL ensures that local consumers have access to (a lower-quality version of) the product when the patent holder finds it unprofitable to sell locally. Indeed, it is possible that both the patent holder and the South are made better off by the option of CL. However, as we show in the chapter, when the option of CL induces the patent holder not to enter, the South loses while the patent holder benefits.

Appendix

Proof of Proposition 8.1   The break-even price under VL is the solution to $\pi(p, \gamma q_E)(1 + \Omega) - \alpha\varphi = 0$, which yields

$$\overline{p}_L(\varphi) = \frac{\gamma q_E}{2} \left(1 - \left(1 - \frac{\alpha\varphi}{v_L^*} \right)^{1/2} \right) \text{ for } \varphi \in \left[0, \frac{v_L^*}{\alpha} \right], \tag{8.13}$$

where $v_L^* \equiv \gamma q_E(1 + \Omega)/4$. We set $\overline{p}_L(\varphi) = \infty$ for $\varphi > v_L^*$, since fixed costs exceed monopoly profits and the licensee cannot earn zero profit at any price. Under entry, we have

$$\overline{p}_E(\varphi) = \frac{q_E}{2} \left(1 - \left(1 - \frac{\varphi}{v_E^*} \right)^{1/2} \right) \text{ for } \varphi \in [0, v_E^*], \tag{8.14}$$

where $v_L^* = \gamma v_E^*$ and $\overline{p}_E(\varphi) = \infty$ for $\varphi > v_E^*$. It is straightforward to establish that the respective break-even prices are increasing and convex in φ, with $\overline{p}_L(0) = \overline{p}_E(0) = 0$.

Since $\gamma \leq \alpha$, we have $v_L^*/\alpha \leq v_E^* \leq \Delta v^*/(1 - \alpha)$. To prove proposition 8.2(i), we show that there exists a unique $\varphi_0 \in (0, v_L^*/\alpha]$ such that $\overline{p}_L(\varphi) < \overline{p}_E(\varphi_0)$ for $\varphi \in (0, \varphi_0)$ and $\overline{p}_L(\varphi) \geq \overline{p}_E(\varphi_0)$ for $\varphi \in (\varphi_0, v_E^*]$. Differentiating (8.13) and (8.14) and evaluating at $\varphi = 0$ yields $\overline{p}_E'(\varphi) - \overline{p}_L'(\varphi) = (1 - \alpha)/(1 + \Omega)$, which ensures that $\overline{p}_L(\varphi) < \overline{p}_E$ in the neighborhood of $\varphi = 0$. Evaluating the break-even functions at v_L^*/α yields $\overline{p}_L(v_L^*/\alpha) > \overline{p}_E(v_L^*/\alpha)$ iff $\gamma < 2 - 1/\alpha$.

We then have two cases to consider: (a) $\gamma < 2 - 1/\alpha$ and (b) $\gamma \geq 2 - 1/\alpha$. First consider case (a). If $\gamma < 2 - 1/\alpha$, then $H(\varphi) = \overline{p}_E(\varphi) - \overline{p}_L(\varphi)$ is a continuous and differentiable function for $\varphi \in [0, v_L^*/\alpha]$ with $H(0) = 0$, $H'(0) > 0$, and $H(v_L^*/\alpha) < 0$. By the continuity of $H(.)$, there exists a $\varphi_0 \in (0, v_L^*/\alpha]$ such that $\overline{p}_L(\varphi) = \overline{p}_E(\varphi)$. Solving this equation yields the unique solution

$$\varphi_0 = \frac{\gamma q(1 - \gamma)(1 - \alpha)(1 + \Omega)}{(1 - \alpha\gamma)^2} \in (0, v_L^*/\alpha) \text{ for } \gamma < 2 - 1/\alpha. \tag{8.15}$$

For this range of parameter values, $\overline{p}_E(\varphi) > \overline{p}_L(\varphi)$ for $\varphi \in (0, \varphi_0)$ and $\overline{p}_E(\varphi) < \overline{p}_L(\varphi)$ for $\varphi \in (\varphi_0, v_L^*/\alpha)$. The fact that $v_L^*/\alpha < \Delta v^*/(1 - \alpha)$ ensures that lemma 8.1(iii) applies in the latter range.

Now consider case (b). For $\gamma \in [2 - 1/\alpha, \alpha]$, $H(v_L^*/\alpha) \geq 0$ and there is no solution for $H(\varphi) = 0$ on $(0, v_L^*/\alpha)$. Since $v_L^*/\alpha < \Delta v^*/(1 - \alpha)$, lemma 8.1(iii) applies and we have $\tilde{p}(\varphi) > \overline{p}_E(\varphi) > \overline{p}_L(\varphi)$ for $\varphi \in (0, v_L^*/\alpha)$. For $\varphi \in (v_L^*/\alpha, v_E^*]$, the licensee cannot break even at any price and lemma 8.1(i) applies.

(iii) This result follows from straightforward differentiation of the expression for φ_0 in equation (8.15) with respect to α and γ, respectively.

Notes

1. It is noteworthy that while TRIPS requires patented inventions to be protected from imitation for 20 years, it does not constrain countries from combating the market power of patent holders by using price regulations.

2. As Saggi (2016) notes, the right to issue a compulsory license is perhaps the most important flexibility that is available to WTO members under TRIPS.

3. Overall, Article 31 seems to grant a fair bit of discretion to countries seeking to use CL. For example, "reasonable commercial terms" remains undefined and open to different interpretations. Similarly, it is far from clear what level of remuneration to the patent holder should be considered "adequate" in the event of CL.

4. For a discussion of some of the relevant case studies, see Baron (2008), Lybecker and Fowler (2009), Daemmrich and Musacchio (2011), Bond and Saggi (2014), and Harris (2014).

5. Chatterjee, Kobe, and Pingali (2013) discuss how Novartis decided to license vildagliptin (an antidiabetic drug) to a local Indian firm called USV in order to take advantage of its established presence and reach in the market. A similar strategy was used by Merck to sell sitagliptin in India. Thus, one advantage of VL is that it allows patent holders to utilize the established marketing and distribution networks of their local licensees.

6. The distinction between first period and subsequent returns plays an important role in the analysis of compulsory licensing in section 8.4, since we interpret the first period as the waiting period required before a compulsory license can be imposed by the South. This period is intended to capture the time window granted by TRIPS for the patent holder to have an adequate opportunity to work its patent in the South.

7. Our analysis implicitly assumes that once the patent expires, the product is supplied by competitive generic producers so that Southern welfare equals the consumer surplus associated with the generic version of the product. We assume that the payoff following the expiration of the patent is independent of whether the product is supplied to the South and independent of the mode (entry or VL) via which it is supplied during the period when it is still under patent. This assumption allows us to simplify the exposition by dropping the welfare accrued after the expiration of the patent from the South's payoff function.

8. Of course, if $\tilde{p}_L(\varphi) < \tilde{p}_E(\varphi)$ and $\varphi > \tilde{\varphi}$, no entry-inducing price will exist. As with the break-even prices, we define $\tilde{p}(\varphi) = \infty$ in this case.

9. If $\tilde{p}_E(\varphi_L) \geq p_L^*$, then $\varphi_0 = \varphi_L$, and the break-even price for VL is lower than that for entry for all $\varphi < \varphi_L$. The threshold level φ_0 decreases as the licensee's quality disadvantage increases compared to its fixed-cost advantage. In either case, there can be only one such reversal of advantage in break-even prices for VL and entry.

10. If the Southern government has the ability to set two different price controls (one for entry and another for VL), it does not have to pay a premium to induce entry since it can drive the patent holder's net payoff under VL to zero by setting the price control under VL at $\overline{p}_L^C(\varphi, R)$. The abiltiy to set two different price controls makes entry more attractive to the South.

11. Intuitively, we are assuming that the quality of production under either type of licensing reflects the technological capability of the local firm and that this capability is unaffected by whether the patent holder grants a license voluntarily or is forced to do so by the South.

12. Beall and Kuhn (2012) provide an overview of international episodes of CL observed during 1995–2011. All in all, during this time period, there were 24 episodes where CL was either publicly considered or actually implemented by governments of developing countries. VL was the end result in only three of these episodes, CL resulted in 12 of them, and the patent holders agreed to sell their products at reduced prices in the other cases.

References

Baron, David. 2008. "Compulsory Licensing, Thailand, and Abbott Laboratories." Stanford Graduate School of Business Case No. P-66.

Beall, Reed and Randall Kuhn. 2012. "Trends in Compulsory Licensing of Pharmaceuticals since the Doha Declaration: A Database Analysis." *PLos Medicine* 9(1): 1–9.

Bond, Eric and Kamal Saggi. 2014. "Compulsory Licensing, Price Controls, and Access to Patented Foreign Products." *Journal of Development Economics* 109: 217–228.

Chatterjee, Chirantan, Kensuke Kobe, and Viswanath Pingali. 2013. "The Welfare Implications of Patent Protection, Pricing, and Licensing in the Indian Oral Anti-diabetic Drug Market." Indian Institute of Management Working Paper No. 408. Bangalore: Indian Institute of Management.

Daemmrich, Arthur A. and Aldo Musacchio. 2011. "Brazil: Leading the BRICs." Harvard Business School Case No. 9-711-024.

Dutta, Antara. 2011. "From Free Entry to Patent Protection: Welfare Implications for the Indian Pharmaceutical Industry." *Review of Economics and Statistics* 93(1): 160–178.

Harris, Gardiner. 2014. "Medicines Made in India Set Off Safety Worries." New York Times, Feb. 14.

Kyle, Margaret. 2007. "Pharmaceutical Price Controls and Entry Strategies." *Review of Economics and Statistics* 89(1): 88–99.

Lanjouw, Jean. 2005. "Patents, Price Controls and Access to New Drugs: How Policy Affects Global Market Entry." NBER Working Paper No. 11321. Cambridge, MA: National Bureau of Economic Research.

Lybecker, Kristina M. and Elisabeth Fowler. 2009. "Compulsory Licensing in Canada and Thailand: Comparing Regimes to Ensure Legitimate Use of the WTO Rules." *Journal of Law, Medicine and Ethics*, Spring, 222–239.

Saggi, Kamal. 2016. "Trade, Intellectual Property Rights, and the WTO," in *Handbook of Commercial Policy*, edited by Kyle Bagwell and Robert W. Staiger, 433–512. Amsterdam: Elsevier.

9 Estimating a Model of Settlement Bargaining in the World Trade Organization

Mostafa Beshkar and Mahdi Majbouri

9.1 Introduction

The establishment of a legalized dispute settlement process (DSP) was one of the most important reforms introduced to the old GATT system in its transition to the World Trade Organization (WTO). Under the GATT, dispute settlement was merely a political process for the negotiation and rebalancing of reciprocal state-to-state trade concessions (Shaffer 2003). In contrast, the DSP under the WTO is quite similar to a domestic legal system in that it involves dispute panels that act as a court of law and an appellate body that reviews the rulings of the panels. There is an ongoing debate on whether a "legalized" dispute settlement process creates a more level playing field that favors the less powerful members or whether this process is used as an instrument by powerful members to put pressure on developing countries to fulfill their liberalization promises.

One of the concerns about a legalized process of dispute settlement is its high cost, which may have an adverse effect on the bargaining position of developing countries against developed countries.[1] For example, in a recent survey, the WTO delegations from developing countries cited the high cost of litigation as one of the main reasons for not pursuing a complaint (Busch, Reinhardt, and Shaffer 2008).

Developing and developed countries show divergent behavior in their use of the dispute settlement process. More than half of all initiated disputes are resolved without litigation (i.e., without the establishment of a dispute panel), which may reflect the parties' desire to avoid the high costs of litigation in the WTO.[2] Disputes that involve developed countries, however, are more likely to result in litigation. To show this, we divide countries into developing and developed.

Table 9.1
Settlement rate and the sizes of the defending and complaining parties.

	Complainant Economy		
Defendant Economy	Developing	Developed	All
Developing	75%* (69)	62%† (71)	69% (140)
Developed	44% (66)	45% (142)	45% (208)
All	60% (135)	51% (213)	54% (348)

Notes: The numbers in parentheses show the number of disputes. Disputes that were the same and filed multiple times are combined. *Developing* includes all countries with GDP per capita $\leq$ \$10,000 and *Developed* contains all countries with GDP per capita above \$10,000. For more information, please see Tables 9.A1 and 9.A2. Using \$7,000, \$12,000, or even \$15,000 as the threshold does not change the results.
* This is statistically significantly different from 50% (the average settlement rate when the defendant is developed and complainant is developing, $p < 0.01$).
† This is statistically significantly different from 46% (the average settlement rate for when the defendant and complainant are both developed, $p < 0.01$). It is also statistically significantly different from 50% (when the defendant is developed and the complainant is developing, $p < 0.02$).

Countries whose GDP per capita (in 2005 dollars) is larger than \$10,000 are categorized as developed and those below this threshold as developing.[3] Using \$7,000, \$12,000, or even \$15,000 as the threshold does not change the results.[4] As demonstrated in table 9.1, being a developed country rather than a developing country as the defending party decreases the likelihood of pretrial settlement by 24 percentage points (from 69% to 45%; see the right column of the table). Similarly, being a developed defendant decreases the likelihood of settlement by 9 percentage points (from 60% to 51%; see the bottom row of the table).

A more curious pattern is that in a dispute between a developed and a developing country, litigation is more likely if the developed country is the defending party. As table 9.1 shows, 62% of disputes in which a developed country presses charges against a developing country are settled without establishing a dispute panel. In contrast, only 44% of disputes are settled without establishing a dispute panel if a developing country disputes against a developed country.

In this chapter, we provide a model of dispute settlement in the WTO that explains the preceding patterns. The model is a modification of the classic models of dispute settlement, namely Bebchuk (1984) and Reinganum and Wilde (1986). The point of departure from this tradition is the assumption that disputing parties are restricted to using policy adjustment as a means of compensation in their settlement negotiations. In disputes between private parties, a settlement normally involves a cash transfer from the defending party to the complaining party. However, cash transfer has rarely been used in the WTO to settle a trade dispute.[5] Instead, a complaining country is usually compensated through policy adjustments, such as a reduction in import tariffs in the defending country. The types of compensation mechanisms available determine the payoff structure in the bargaining process, which may also affect the outcome of the process. In particular, while cash transfer is a zero-sum transaction, a policy adjustment is not necessarily zero-sum. For example, as is well known in the trade literature, a reduction in import tariffs in an importing country generates more gains for the exporting country than losses to the importing country.

This chapter shows that because of differences in methods of compensation in private and intergovernmental disputes, classic models of settlement bargaining cannot correctly explain the settlement pattern in the WTO. To show this, we extend those models to study the determinants of out-of-court settlement under situations where the available compensation mechanism features a positive-sum transaction. This added feature alters some of the important predictions of the classic models. In particular, the models of Bebchuk (1984) and Reinganum and Wilde (1986) imply that the allocation of litigation costs between disputants has no bearing on the likelihood of settlement. In contrast, we show that under a positive-sum compensation mechanism, the likelihood of settlement is more sensitive to the defendant's litigation costs than to the complainant's litigation costs. This analysis has important policy implications, as it suggests that allocating the burden of proof to the defending party should lead to a higher settlement rate.[6]

This study provides a novel explanation for the divergent settlement behavior of developing and developed countries, which is based on the relative litigation costs of these countries. We construct a measure of litigation costs based on the assumption that the cost of pursuing a dispute in the DSP is greater for poorer and smaller countries. It is a widely held view among observers of the WTO that less developed countries have higher costs of legal work in the dispute settlement process. For example, Shaffer (2003) points out that "lack of legal expertise in WTO law and the capacity to organize information concerning trade barriers and opportunities to challenge them [... and] lack of financial resources, including for the hiring of outside legal counsel" are challenges faced by the developing countries in using the WTO legal system effectively.[7] In fact, to address this issue, in 2001, the Advisory Centre on WTO Law (ACWL) was established to provide subsidized legal counseling to developing countries.

In addition to whether the dispute had multiple complainants or third parties, we use the following measures of real value of trade one year before the violation to capture "stakes at dispute": (1) the real value of the defending country's imports from the complaining country in the disputed sector and (2) the real value of the defending country's imports from the rest of the world. The real value of total exports from the defending country to the complaining country in the year of the dispute is used as a measure of the retaliation capacity of the complaining country. We show that, controlling for these measures, the probability of settlement is positively correlated with the litigation costs of the disputants and statistically significant for the defending party, prior to 2001. It is also empirically verified that before 2001 the litigation costs of the defending party had a significantly larger effect on the likelihood of settlement than the litigation costs of the complaining party. While consistent with the prediction of our model, this latter observation is at odds with the prediction of the classical settlement bargaining models, where the total litigation costs of the disputants—not the distribution of costs—are what matters for the likelihood of settlement.

The fact that these results hold for the pre-2001 sample further strengthens our hypothesis that litigation costs of parties play a critical role in the settlement process. This is because if litigation costs are the key, they should not have mattered (or have mattered less) after the establishment of ACWL in 2001, which offered subsidized legal expertise to developing countries to help them overcome the challenges of the dispute settlement process.

We also show that the larger the defending party's imports from the complaining party in the disputed sector (i.e., the greater the stakes at dispute), the lower the likelihood of a pretrial settlement. The defending country's imports in the disputed sector from third parties (rest of the world), however, have no statistically significant effect on the likelihood of pretrial settlement. Multiplicity of complainants in the bargaining process and the existence of third parties in the dispute, however, reduce the chance of pretrial settlement. But, the retaliatory capacity of the complaining party, measured by total exports from defendant to complainant, has no statistically significant relation with the probability of settlement.

In the past decade, there have been a growing number of empirical studies of the dispute settlement process of the GATT and the WTO.[8] Guzman and Simmons (2002) consider the relationship between the nature of the dispute and the likelihood of an early settlement. They hypothesize that if the subject matter of the dispute has an all-or-nothing character and leaves little room for compromise (for example, health and safety regulations), the parties' ability to reach an agreement is limited and a higher rate of litigation is expected. They find empirical support for their hypothesis only among democratic states. Busch and Reinhardt (2003) consider the success of developing countries as complainants in this process by investigating the level of concessions that they have been able to induce from defending countries. In particular, they find that the introduction of a more legalized system of dispute settlement under the WTO has exaggerated the gap between developed-country and developing-country complainants with respect to their ability to get defendants to liberalize disputed policies. Nevertheless, Bown (2004) provides evidence that developing-country complainants have had more economic success in resolving trade disputes under the WTO than was the case under the GATT.

A number of papers study the determinants of the decision to initiate a formal dispute. Bown (2005) investigates the determinants of participation in the DSP and examines whether the new regulations of the DSP under the WTO discourage active engagement by developing countries. He finds that the size of the exports at stake and legal capacity are important factors in deciding whether to initiate a dispute. Wilckens (2009) also finds that a country is more likely to file a complaint if its retaliatory capacity is large. Horn Mavroidis, and Nordström (1999), however, argue that the bias in the pattern of disputes that have been initiated under the WTO is caused by the fact that developed countries have a larger diversity of imports and exports, which naturally leads to more disputable trade policies and more frequent use of the DSP by the developed countries.

In a more recent study, Kuenzel (2017) finds a relationship between the likelihood of a dispute and the degree of unilateral policy flexibility that a country has in any particular sector. As documented by Beshkar, Bond, and Rho (2015), Beshkar and Bond (2017), and Beshkar and Lee (2018), in a substantial fraction of sectors worldwide, the negotiated tariff bindings are above the tariffs applied by the government. The difference between applied tariffs and the negotiated bindings, known as tariff overhang, provides governments with a degree of flexibility to adjust their tariffs unilaterally. Kuenzel (2017) shows that a WTO dispute is more likely to arise in sectors with lower tariff overhangs. While we focus on the determinants of early (i.e., pretrial) settlements, many interesting questions regarding the later stages of the dispute settlement process, namely the WTO trial and posttrial negotiation, remain unexplored in this study. Moreover, in this chapter, we do not explicitly model tariff adjustments in the dispute settlement process. These issues are studied in various papers, including Park (2011), Beshkar and Park (2017), Maggi and Staiger (2011, 2015, 2017, 2018), and Beshkar (2010b, 2016). Park (2016) provides a comprehensive review of this literature.

In sections 9.2 to 9.4 of this chapter, we focus on disputes under the allegation of direct breach. In section 9.2, we introduce our assumptions regarding the costs and benefits of settlement to the disputing parties. In section 9.3, we set out a screening model of pretrial bargaining, which is a modified version of the Bebchuk (1984) model. Similarly, in section 9.4, we follow the approach of Reinganum and Wilde (1986) to model the pretrial settlement bargaining in the WTO as a signaling game. We turn our attention to nonviolation cases in section 9.5 and show that the effects on the settlement outcome of litigation costs and the stake at dispute are similar in violation and nonviolation cases. Section 9.6 provides a brief discussion of the datasets and explanatory variables. The empirical models and results are presented and discussed in section 9.7. Section 9.8 gives our conclusions.

9.2   Basic Setup

In this section and sections 9.3 and 9.4, we focus on the case of direct breach. In a direct breach, the dispute is on the nature of the prevailing contingency. If such a case is litigated, the court issues its opinion on the nature of the contingency and rules whether the defendant is in violation of its obligation. If the ruling is against the defendant, the defendant is supposed to reduce its tariff rate to a lower level (possibly the agreed-upon level) as specified by the court. Similarly, a settlement schedule is a tariff rate (lower than the disputed tariff rate) offered by one of the two parties.

The defendant's tariff rate on the imports from the complainant at the time of the dispute is denoted by τ^d, while τ^a $\left(\leq \tau^d\right)$ denotes the tariff rate that the defendant should adopt in order to be in compliance with its obligations. When a dispute arises, *renegotiation* takes place in order to find a "mutually agreed solution." A settlement proposal is characterized by a new tariff rate, τ $\left(< \tau^d\right)$, to be adopted by the defending country. If a mutually agreed solution is not achieved, the case will escalate to the dispute panel. If at the panel stage the defendant is found to be in violation of its obligations, it should reduce its tariff from τ^d to τ^a. Otherwise, the defending party can continue to adopt the disputed tariff rate, τ^d.

Let $W_D\left(\tau\right)$ and $W_C\left(\tau\right)$ denote the welfare of the defendant and the complainant, respectively, as functions of the defendant's tariff rate, where $W_D'\left(\tau\right) > 0$ and $W_C'\left(\tau\right) < 0$. Then the defendant's welfare loss from lowering its tariff from the disputed level (i.e., τ^d) to τ is given by

$$\Omega\left(\tau\right) \equiv W_D\left(\tau^d\right) - W_D(\tau).$$

Similarly, the complainant's benefit from this policy adjustment is given by

$$\Delta\left(\tau\right) \equiv W_C\left(\tau\right) - W_C\left(\tau^d\right).$$

Assuming there are gains from trade, an increase in tariff rates by one party would decrease the two parties' aggregate payoff.[9] Therefore, if deviation from the agreement benefits one party, it should hurt the other party to a larger extent. Similarly, the defendant's loss from reducing its tariff rate is smaller than the complainant's benefit from this policy adjustment; that is, $\Omega\left(\tau\right) < \Delta\left(\tau\right)$. For the sake of the tractability of the model, we impose more restrictions on the functions Ω and Δ as follows.

Assumption 9.1 $\Omega\left(\tau\right) = \alpha\Delta\left(\tau\right)$ *for all* $0 \leq \tau \leq \tau^d$, *where* $\alpha < 1$.

As will be seen in the subsequent sections, modifying the classical models of settlement bargaining (e.g., Bebchuk 1984 and Reinganum and Wilde 1986) reveals some interesting features of the settlement bargaining in the WTO.

9.3   A Screening Model

Consider a case in which the defendant has better information about the dispute case. In the case of implementing safeguard measures, for example, the defendant is better informed about the economic conditions surrounding its import-competing industries. Therefore, the defendant can make a better prediction about the ruling of the dispute panel in case of litigation. On this basis, we assume that the probability of an adverse ruling against the defendant, p, is private knowledge of the defendant, while the complainant knows only that p is distributed over interval $\left[\underline{p}, \overline{p}\right]$ by a distribution function $F(.)$. Here, p is interpreted as the defendant's type.

Bebchuk's (1984) framework can be easily adapted to this situation. Suppose that the complainant demands that the defendant adopt τ^s rather than τ^d. If the defendant fulfills this demand, the case is settled, the complainant earns $\Delta(\tau^s)$, and the defendant incurs a cost of $\Omega(\tau^s)$. On the other hand, if the defendant does not accept this offer, the parties bring the case before the dispute panel, in which case each of them should pay their respective legal fees, namely c_D and c_C.

Assuming that the panel's ruling is enforceable, the defendant accepts τ^S if and only if

$$\Omega(\tau^s) \le (1 - p) \times 0 + p\Omega(\tau^a) + c_D, \tag{9.1}$$

or, equivalently, if and only if

$$p \ge \frac{\Omega(\tau^s) - c_D}{\Omega(\tau^a)}. \tag{9.2}$$

Hence, the defendant will accept τ^s if and only if its type p is equal to or higher than $q(\tau^s)$, where $q(\tau^s)$ is the marginal defendant type defined by

$$q(\tau^s) = \frac{\Omega(\tau^s) - c_D}{\Omega(\tau^a)}.$$

On the other hand, the complainant's expected payoff from demanding τ^s is given by

$$A(\tau^s) = \{1 - F[q(\tau^s)]\}\Delta(\tau^s)$$

$$+ F[q(\tau^s)]\left\{-c_C + \frac{\Delta(\tau^a)\int_{\underline{p}}^{q(\tau^s)} pf(p)\,dp}{F[q(\tau^s)]}\right\}.$$

Therefore, the first-order condition is given by $A'(\tau^S) = 0$, where

$$A'(\tau^s) = -f[q(\tau^s)]q'(\tau^s)\Delta(\tau^s) + \{1 - F[q(\tau^s)]\}\Delta'(\tau^s)$$

$$- f[q(\tau^s)]q'(\tau^s)c_C + \Delta(\tau^a)q(\tau^s)f(q(\tau^s))q'(\tau^s)$$

$$= \{1 - F[q(\tau^s)]\} \Delta'(\tau^s) - f[q(\tau^s)] q'(\tau^s)$$
$$[\Delta(\tau^s) + c_C - \Delta(\tau^a) q(\tau^s)].$$

Substituting $q(\tau^s) = \frac{\Omega(\tau^s) - c_D}{\Omega(\tau^a)}$ and $q'(\tau^s) = \frac{\Omega'(\tau^s)}{\Omega(\tau^a)}$ in this equation and then applying assumption 9.1, that $\Omega(\tau) \equiv \alpha\Delta(\tau)$, yields

$$A'(\tau^s) = \left\{ \{1 - F[q(\tau^s)]\} - f[q(\tau^s)] \frac{c_C + \frac{c_D}{\alpha}}{\Delta(\tau^a)} \right\} \Delta'(\tau^s).$$

Thus, the first-order condition can be written as

$$\frac{f[q(\tau^s)]}{1 - F[q(\tau^s)]} = \frac{\Delta(\tau^a)}{c_C + \frac{c_D}{\alpha}}. \tag{9.3}$$

Moreover,

$$A''(\tau^s) = -\left\{ f\left[q\left(\tau^s\right)\right] + f'\left[q\left(\tau^s\right)\right] \frac{c_C + \frac{c_D}{\alpha}}{\Delta(\tau^A)} \right\} q'\left(\tau^s\right) \Delta'\left(\tau^s\right)$$

$$= -\left\{ f\left[q\left(\tau^s\right)\right] + f'\left[q\left(\tau^s\right)\right] \frac{c_C + \frac{c_D}{\alpha}}{\Delta(\tau^A)} \right\} \frac{\left[\Delta'\left(\tau^S\right)\right]^2}{\Delta(\tau^A)}.$$

Therefore, the second-order condition, $A''(S) < 0$, is given by

$$f[q(\tau^s)] + f'[q(\tau^s)] \frac{c_C + \frac{c_D}{\alpha}}{\Delta(\tau^a)} > 0. \tag{9.4}$$

Assuming a monotonic and increasing hazard function for the distribution function, F, the second-order condition will always be satisfied, and the first-order condition given in (9.3) yields a unique equilibrium.

9.3.1 Litigation Costs and the Likelihood of Settlement
Under the baseline model of Bebchuk (i.e., when $\alpha = 1$ in this setting), the settlement rate is equally sensitive to the changes in the litigation costs of either party. However, under the current model (i.e., when $\alpha < 1$), the settlement rate is more responsive to changes in the defendant's costs than to changes in the complainant's costs. To see this, denote the equilibrium value of $q(\tau^s)$ by q^* and rewrite the first-order condition (9.3) as

$$\frac{f(q^*)}{1 - F(q^*)} = \frac{\Delta(\tau^A)}{\frac{c_D}{\alpha} + c_C}. \tag{9.5}$$

Since we assume a monotonically increasing hazard function, an increase in the right-hand side of this equation results in a higher equilibrium value for q^* or, equivalently, a lower equilibrium settlement rate. Therefore, we have the following proposition.

Proposition 9.1 The equilibrium settlement rate is increasing in the litigation costs of either party and decreasing in the stake at dispute.

Moreover, since $\alpha < 1$, a reduction in the defendant's litigation costs reduces the likelihood of settlement to a greater extent than does a reduction in the complainant's costs. Formally, we can state the following proposition.

Proposition 9.2 The equilibrium settlement rate is more sensitive to changes in the defendant's costs than to changes in the complainant's costs.

To obtain an intuition for this result, consider the relative cost of litigation to concessions for each party. Because of gains from trade (assumption 9.1), a marginal change in tariffs has a greater impact on the welfare of the complaining country than on the welfare of the defending country. Therefore, the opportunity cost of litigation is relatively higher for the defending party.

Denoting the equilibrium settlement rate by R^*, propositions 9.1 and 9.2 imply

$$\frac{dR^*}{dc_D} > \frac{dR^*}{dc_C} > 0.$$

Example 9.1 Suppose that p is beta distributed with shape parameters given by $(2, 2)$,

$$f(p) = \frac{\Gamma(4)}{\Gamma(2)\,\Gamma(2)} p(1 - p),$$

where $p \in [0, 1]$ and Γ is the gamma function. The hazard function of this probability distribution is given by

$$\frac{\frac{\Gamma(4)}{\Gamma(2)\Gamma(2)} p(1-p)}{1 - \frac{\Gamma(4)}{\Gamma(2)\Gamma(2)} \int_0^p t(1-t)\,dt} = \frac{6p}{1 + p - 2p^2}.$$

Using this hazard function, the equilibrium condition (9.5) can be written as

$$\frac{6q^*}{1+q^*-2q^{*2}} = \frac{\Delta\left(\tau^A\right)}{\frac{c_D}{\alpha}+c_C}.$$

Solving for q^* yields

$$q^* = \frac{\Phi-6+\sqrt{-12\Phi+9\Phi^2+36}}{4\Phi},$$

where Φ is equal to the right-hand side of (9.5). Thus, the likelihood of settlement, $R^* = 1 - F\left(q^*\right)$, is given by

$$R^* = 1 - \frac{\Gamma\left(4\right)}{\Gamma\left(2\right)\Gamma\left(2\right)} \int_0^{q^*} t\left(1-t\right) dt$$

$$= 1 - \frac{3}{16\Phi^2}\left(\Phi-6+\sqrt{9\Phi^2-12\Phi+36}\right)^2$$

$$+ \frac{1}{32\Phi^3}\left(\Phi-6+\sqrt{9\Phi^2-12\Phi+36}\right)^3.$$

As is depicted in figure 9.1, R^* is a decreasing function of $\Phi \equiv \frac{\Delta\left(\tau^A\right)}{\frac{c_D}{\alpha}+c_C}$, and propositions 9.1 and 9.2 are verified.

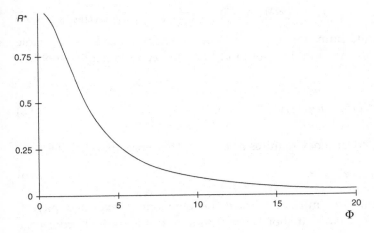

Figure 9.1
Equilibrium settlement rate, R^*, as a function of $\Phi \equiv \frac{\Delta\left(\tau^A\right)}{\frac{c_D}{\alpha}+c_C}$.

9.4   A Signaling Model

In section 9.3, we assumed that in the settlement bargaining game the uninformed party offers a settlement proposal and the informed party decides whether to accept or reject this proposal. In contrast, in this section, we assume that the informed party is the one that offers a settlement and the uninformed party may accept or reject the offer.

The model presented in this section is a modification of the signaling model of Reinganum and Wilde (1986). As in section 9.3, we assume that the defendant has private information about its probability of losing the case in court, denoted by p. The signaling game is as follows. The defendant offers a reduction in its import tariff from τ^d to τ^s. The complainant's strategy, on the other hand, is a function, $r(\tau^s)$, that specifies the probability that it rejects the defendant's policy adjustment proposal. If the complainant chooses a rejection probability of ρ, her expected payoff is given by

$$\Pi_C(\tau^s, \rho; b) = [1 - \rho]\,\Delta(\tau^s) + \rho\,[b(\tau^s)\,\Delta(\tau^a) - c_C], \tag{9.6}$$

where $b(\tau^s)$ represents the complainant's belief about p given the defendant's offer, τ^s.

Given function $r(.)$, the expected payoff of the defendant from offering τ^s is

$$\Pi_D(\tau^s; r(.)) = -[1 - r(\tau^s)]\,\alpha\Delta(\tau^s) - r(\tau^s)\,[p\alpha\Delta(\tau^a) + c_D]. \tag{9.7}$$

An equilibrium for this problem is characterized by a triple (b^*, r^*, τ^{s*}). An interior solution for the complainant's problem requires

$$\frac{\partial \Pi_C}{\partial \rho} = -\Delta(\tau^s) + b(\tau^s)\,\Delta(\tau^a) - c_C = 0. \tag{9.8}$$

Moreover, consistency requires $b(\tau^s) = p$. Therefore, (9.8) implies

$$\Delta(\tau^{s*}) = p\Delta(\tau^a) - c_C. \tag{9.9}$$

Furthermore, τ^{s*} must maximize the defendant's expected payoff, given $r^*(\cdot)$. That is, it should satisfy the defendant's first-order condition

$$r'(\tau^{s*})\,\alpha\Delta(\tau^{s*}) - [1 - r(\tau^{s*})]\,\alpha\Delta'(\tau^{s*}) - r'(\tau^{s*})\,[p\alpha\Delta(\tau^a) + c_D] = 0.$$

or, equivalently,

$$-\alpha \Delta' (\tau^{s*}) + \alpha \Delta' (\tau^{s*}) r (\tau^{s*}) - [\alpha c_C + c_D] r' (\tau^{s*}) = 0. \tag{9.10}$$

Equation (9.10) has a one-parameter family of solutions $r^* (\Delta' (\tau^s)) = 1 + \lambda \exp \left\{ -\frac{\Delta'(\tau^s)}{\alpha c_C + c_D} \right\}$. The appropriate boundary condition is $r^* (\Delta' (\underline{\tau}^s)) = 0$, where $\Delta' (\underline{\tau}^s) = \overline{p} \Delta' (\tau^a) - c_C$.[10] This implies that

$$\lambda = - \exp \left\{ \frac{\overline{p} \Delta' (\tau^a) - c_C}{\alpha c_C + c_D} \right\}.$$

Therefore, the equilibrium probability of rejection as a function of τ^s will be given by

$$r^* (\tau^s) = 1 - \exp \left\{ \frac{\overline{p} \Delta' (\tau^a) - c_C}{\alpha c_C + c_D} \right\} \exp \left\{ -\frac{\Delta' (\tau^s)}{\alpha c_C + c_D} \right\} \tag{9.11}$$

$$= 1 - \exp \left\{ \frac{\overline{p} \Delta' (\tau^a) - \Delta' (\tau^s) - c_C}{\alpha c_C + c_D} \right\}. \tag{9.12}$$

Finally, for a particular value of p, the equilibrium settlement rate, $R^* = 1 - r^*$, can be obtained by substituting $\Delta (\tau^{s*})$ from (9.9) into (9.11), namely

$$R^* = \exp \left\{ \frac{\overline{p} - p}{\alpha c_C + c_D} \Delta' (\tau^a) \right\}. \tag{9.13}$$

In contrast with the Reinganum and Wilde (1986) original model, in the present formulation, the probability of trial depends on the allocation of litigation costs. In particular, the probability of trial is more responsive to changes in the defendant's litigation costs than to complainant's litigation costs. Therefore, propositions 9.1 and 9.2 hold under the signaling model as well.

9.5 Settlement Bargaining under the Allegation of Indirect Breach

In this section, we consider disagreements over policies that are not explicitly restricted by the trade agreement but can potentially nullify or impair the benefits of a contracting party that were intended under the agreement. Such actions, if proved to nullify the effect of the agreement, may be categorized as an indirect breach of the contract. In an indirect breach, the defendant, while keeping its tariff rates fixed at the agreed-upon levels, adopts a policy, such as subsidies, that potentially nullifies or impairs the complainant's benefits from the agreement. If such a case is litigated, the court determines the extent to which the defendant's policy has nullified the complainant's gains from the agreement. If the court's ruling is against the defendant, the defendant is supposed to take mitigating actions that restore the complainant's benefits from the agreement.

In this type of disagreement, the dispute is over the extent of damages imposed on the complaining party. Such disagreements may arise from asymmetric information of the disputing parties about the size of the compensation, denoted by Δ, that the dispute panel would award to the complainant in the case of litigation. We assume that Δ is the private information of the complaining party, while the defending party only knows that Δ is distributed according to $G(\cdot)$ on the interval $(\underline{\Delta}, \overline{\Delta})$. We also maintain assumption 9.1, which implies that the cost to the defendant of conforming to an adverse ruling by the panel is given by $\alpha \Delta$, where $0 < \alpha < 1$.

Once again, we employ the signaling model of Reinganum and Wilde (1986) to analyze the settlement bargaining problem. More specifically, we consider a bargaining process in which the informed party, the complainant, demands a policy adjustment by the defendant in exchange for settlement. Let S denote the benefit of the proposed policy adjustment to the complaining party. We continue to maintain assumption 9.1, which implies that the cost of this policy adjustment to the defending party is given by αS.

The complainant's strategy is to demand S to maximize its expected payoff. The defendant's strategy, on the other hand, is a function, $r(S)$, that specifies the probability that it rejects the complainant's policy adjustment proposal. The expected payoff of a defendant who has received a settlement demand S and has a rejection probability of ρ is given by

$$\Pi_D(S, \rho; b) = -[1 - \rho]\alpha S - \rho[\alpha b(S) + c_D],\tag{9.14}$$

where $b(S)$ represents the defendant's belief about Δ given the complainant's demand, S.

The expected payoff of a complainant who would receive an award of the size Δ by the dispute panel, demands S to settle, and takes as given the strategy $r(S)$ of the defendant, is given by

$$\Pi_C(S; r) = [1 - r(S)]S + r(S)[\Delta - c_C].\tag{9.15}$$

An equilibrium for this problem is characterized by a triple (b^*, r^*, S^*). An interior solution for the defendant's problem requires

$$\frac{\partial \Pi_D}{\partial \rho} = \alpha S - \alpha b\,(S) - c_D = 0. \tag{9.16}$$

Moreover, consistency requires $b\,(S) = \Delta$. Therefore, (9.16) implies

$$S^* = \Delta + \frac{c_D}{\alpha}. \tag{9.17}$$

Furthermore, S^* must maximize the complainant's expected payoff, given $r^*\,(\cdot)$. That is, it should satisfy the complainant's first-order condition

$$[1 - r\,(S^*)] + [1 - r'\,(S^*)]\,S^* + r'\,(S^*)\,[\Delta - c_C] = 0,$$

or, equivalently,

$$1 + S^* - r\,(S^*) - \left(c_C + \frac{c_D}{\alpha}\right) r'\,(S^*) = 0. \tag{9.18}$$

Equation (9.18) has a one-parameter family of solutions $r^*\,(S) = 1 + \lambda \exp\left\{-\frac{S}{c_C + \frac{c_D}{\alpha}}\right\}$. Applying appropriate boundary conditions, the equilibrium probability of rejection as a function of S will be given by:

$$r^*\,(S) = 1 - \exp\left\{-\frac{S - \Delta - \frac{c_D}{\alpha}}{c_C + \frac{c_D}{\alpha}}\right\}. \tag{9.19}$$

Finally, for a particular value of Δ, the equilibrium settlement rate, $R^* = 1 - r^*$, can be obtained by substituting S^* from (9.17) into (9.19), namely

$$R^* = \exp\left\{-\frac{\Delta - \underline{\Delta}}{\frac{c_D}{\alpha} + c_C}\right\}. \tag{9.20}$$

Note the similarity between this result and equation (9.13), which is the equilibrium settlement rate in the signaling model of section 9.4. In both cases, the equilibrium settlement rate is more responsive to changes in the defendant's litigation costs than to the complainant's litigation costs, and propositions 9.1 and 9.2 continue to hold.

9.6   Data

The dataset used in this study is from Bown and Reynolds (2014). It contains 427 disputes from 1995 to 2011. For each case, the respondents, complainants, dispute initiation date, whether the dispute was over imports or exports, and the dates and nature of violations are reported. Of all the disputes, 308 cases target imports of specific products. The innovation of this dataset is the inclusion of bilateral trade volumes and values at the time of violation as well as the time of implementation of these disputes. Moreover, these trade data are included for two years before and after those dates.[11]

Note that some of these 308 cases are multiple filings of the same disputes.[12] These multiple filings are marked in the dataset with a variable that gives them the same dispute number. This helps us to combine these multiple filings into single disputes. But, since disputed product codes between a pair of countries might have been repeated across these multiple filings, one needs to eliminate these duplicate observations so that trade values are not counted twice in these combined disputes.

Measure of settlement   Settlement can happen before or after the panel's establishment. We call settlements that take place before panel establishment "early settlements" and those after it "late settlements." This study considers only early settlement. Cases for which panels were not established (i.e., where the date of panel establishment is missing in their data) are considered as settled early. The data on the dates of panel establishment are taken from the WTO dispute settlement dataset (Horn and Mavroidis 2008).

Measure of litigation costs   It is a widely held view among the observers of the WTO that less developed countries have relatively higher costs of legal work in the dispute settlement process. For example, Shaffer (2003) points out that little expertise in WTO law and the opportunities it offers, coupled with financial constraints in obtaining legal expertise from outside, are challenges faced by the developing countries in using the WTO legal system effectively.[13] In fact, in response to concerns about the relatively high costs of legal work for poorer countries, the Advisory Centre on WTO Law (ACWL) was established in 2001 to provide developing countries with subsidized legal aid for participation in the DSP.[14]

On this basis, we divide countries into high cost and low cost based on their GDP per capita. All countries whose GDP per capita is beyond a threshold are considered low cost and those below the threshold are high cost. $10,000 is chosen as the threshold, but the results do not change when we use $7,000, $12,000, or even $15,000 as the threshold.[15] Tables 9.A1 and 9.A2 rank countries based on their GDP per capita and report what percentage of the time they settled their disputes as a defendant or a complainant. For the defendants, a dummy is defined that is equal to 1 if the defendant belongs to the high-cost countries and 0 otherwise. A similar dummy is defined for the richest complainant in a dispute. This measure only depends on the disputing party's GDP per capita and not on the characteristics of the case (e.g., the complexity of the legal issues involved). While it would be interesting to include case-specific factors in the construction of this measure, it has been pointed out by observers that litigation costs are more or less independent of the commercial stakes involved in a dispute (Shaffer 2003).

Measure of the stake at dispute　Stake at dispute affects the chance of settlement negatively and should be included in any regression of dispute settlement. We use the value of the defendant's imports of the disputed products from the complainants one year before the violation as one measure of stakes at dispute. Products are measured using six-digit HS codes. The stake at dispute may also be affected by the size of the defending country's imports from third countries. In a three-country model of trade where the defending party imports from the complaining party as well as the rest of the world, it can be shown that the stake at dispute for the defending party is decreasing in its import value from the rest of the world. To account for this effect, we also include in the regression the value of imports in the disputed sector from the rest of the world one year before the violation.[16]

Measure of retaliation capacity of the complainants　The complainants in a dispute may want to retaliate by raising their tariff rates on imports from the defendant. The size of this threat may affect the likelihood of the settlement. Therefore, we control for the total value of exports from the defendant to all complainants.

Other control variables　Some disputes involve multiple complaining parties that join the dispute as interested parties. In some instances, third parties also join the dispute. The existence of multiple parties

Table 9.2
Summary statistics of variables.

	Observations	Mean	St. Dev.	Min.	Max.
Settlement prior to panel establishment	252	0.54	0.50	0	1
Defendant is high cost	252	0.44	0.50	0	1
Richest complainant is high cost	252	0.46	0.50	0	1
ln(imports from complainants in disputed sectors)	252	3.24	2.86	0	10.25
ln(imports from the rest of the world in disputed sectors)	252	5.52	2.98	0	11.48
ln(total exports to all complainants)	252	16.15	2.94	9.00	20.95
Multiple complainants	252	0.11	0.31	0	1
Third-party complainants	252	0.61	0.49	0	1

Notes: "Settlement prior to panel establishment" is a dummy that is 1 if the dispute is settled before the panel is established. Import variables have the real value of imports of the defendant from the complainants and from the rest of the world one year before the violation. "Real imports from the complainants" only includes imports from complainants who filed the dispute in the year before the violation. "Total exports to all complainants" are exports from the defendant to all complainants in the year the dispute is filed. We added one to all trade values so that zeros do not become missing values after taking logarithms. "Multiple complainants" is equal to 1 if more than one complainant filed the dispute. "Third-party complainants" is a dummy that is equal to 1 if at least one third party joined the dispute before the panel was established and 0 otherwise.

as well as the existence of third parties who joined before the panel was established can affect the settlement of a dispute. Therefore, we define and include two dummies in the regressions: (1) a multiple-complainants dummy that is 1 if the dispute has multiple complainants and 0 otherwise and (2) a third-party complainants dummy that is 1 if at least one of the third parties joined the dispute before the panel was established and 0 if there was no third party or all of them joined after the panel was established. The third-party complainants dummy is defined this way, which is different from the third-party variable already in the dataset, because not all parties that join a dispute can be considered a third party. Most third parties join a dispute after pretrial negotiations break down. Therefore, one can argue that it is the breakdown of pretrial negotiations that attracts third parties to join the dispute and not the other way around. Hence, only third parties that joined before the panel's establishment should be considered. Summary statistics of all variables are reported in table 9.2.

9.7 Empirical Results

In this section, we evaluate the following hypotheses that are derived from propositions 9.1 and 9.2.

Hypothesis 1A: The settlement rate is positively correlated with the measures of litigation costs.

Hypothesis 1B: The settlement rate is negatively correlated with the trade volume between the disputing parties in the disputed sector prior to violation.

Hypothesis 2: The settlement rate is more sensitive to changes in the litigation costs of the defending party than to changes in the litigation costs of the complaining party.

Hypotheses 1A and 1B correspond to proposition 9.1, and hypothesis 2 refers to proposition 9.2. In addition to these hypotheses, we will also be able to discuss other factors that may influence the outcome of settlement negotiations, including the retaliation capacity and the existence of co-complainants.

Table 9.3 reports the probit estimates for the likelihood of settlement in a dispute. Similar results are obtained from a linear probability model, logit model, and maximum likelihood estimation assuming a beta distribution. The dependent variable is a dummy that is equal to 1 if the panel is not established (i.e., the dispute is settled prior to panel establishment). Column 1 has the probit estimation for all disputes regardless of whether they are on imports, exports, goods, or services. It contains 349 disputes. Columns 2 through 6 restrict the results to those disputes that are about the import of goods in a specific disputed sector for which import data are available. They have 252 disputes.

Estimations for the whole data (column 1) and all import cases (columns 2 and 3) support hypothesis 1A, which states that the likelihood of settlement is positively correlated with the litigation costs of each party. The coefficient of the defendant's cost is statistically significant in all of them, but the coefficient of the richest complainant's cost, although positive, is not statistically significant. The results are robust when we control for different variables that are potentially related to settlement in column 3. The last row in the table reports the p-value for testing the null hypothesis of whether the coefficient of "the defendant is high cost" is smaller than the coefficient of "the richest complainant is high cost." The results in columns 1 through 3 reject the null and therefore support hypothesis 2.

Table 9.3
Probit estimation of the settlement likelihood.

	(1)	(2)	(3)	Pre-2001 (4)	Post-2001 (5)	(6)
Defendant is high cost	0.609***	0.619***	0.740***	1.591**	0.376	0.376
	(0.143)	(0.165)	(0.274)	(0.664)	(0.288)	(0.288)
Richest complainant is high cost	0.156	0.162	0.309	0.458	0.046	0.046
	(0.143)	(0.164)	(0.262)	(0.610)	(0.331)	(0.331)
ln(imports from complainants in disputed sectors)			−0.131***	−0.150*	−0.150***	−0.123***
			(0.042)	(0.081)	(0.051)	(0.042)
ln(imports from the rest of the world in disputed sectors)			0.065	0.151	0.045	0.028
			(0.047)	(0.112)	(0.056)	(0.044)
ln(total exports to all complainants)			0.058	0.175	−0.060	−0.015
			(0.055)	(0.116)	(0.063)	(0.043)
Multiple complainants			−0.773*	−2.763**	−0.083	−0.701*
			(0.448)	(1.099)	(0.496)	(0.413)
Third-party complainants			−2.726***	−4.019***		−2.625***
			(0.290)	(0.468)		(0.267)
Constant	−0.200**	−0.251**	0.808	−1.485	1.160	2.550***
	(0.099)	(0.125)	(0.993)	(2.049)	(1.199)	(0.632)
Observations	349	252	252	114	138	252
p-value for $H_0: \beta_{Def.} \le \beta_{Comp.}$	0.019	0.034	0.102	0.065	0.180	0.180

Notes: For the definitions of variables, see the notes to table 9.2. The dependent variable is "settlement prior to panel establishment." "Third-party complainants" is dropped from column 5, as it predicted success of probit perfectly. The last row reports the p-value of testing whether the coefficient of "defendant is high cost" is smaller than the coefficient of "richest complainant is high cost."
* $p < 0.10$, ** $p < 0.05$, *** $p < 0.01$.

Column 4 reports the results only for disputes prior to 2001, and column 5 depicts them for disputes filed in and after 2001. In 2001, the Advisory Centre on WTO Law was established to subsidize the cost of litigation for the developing countries. As a result, it became easier for these countries to press charges against their trade partners, especially the developed countries, and defend their cases in the DSP. As figure 9.2 shows, the share of disputes in which a developing country is a complainant substantially increased after 2001. This share was about 30% between 1995 and 2000 and increased to about 50% between 2001 and 2011. Hence, based on the model presented in this study, one may expect that the estimated results would only hold (or would be stronger) for disputes prior to 2001. The estimates in columns 4 and 5 are in line with this conjecture and show that hypotheses 1A and 2 are only supported by data from before 2001. In other words, with the advent of ACWL and the subsidization of litigation costs of developing countries, being a developing country is no longer correlated with the likelihood of settlement. This further supports the theoretical model of this chapter, that the litigation cost of developing countries is an important predictor of settlement.

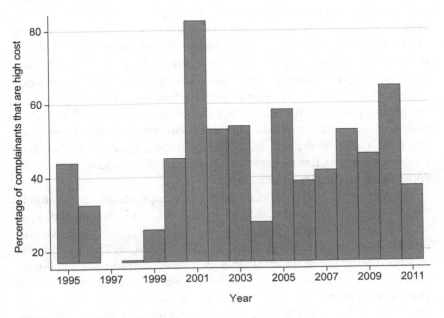

Figure 9.2
Percentage of complainants that are high cost over time.

The estimates for the pre-2001 period are similar to those for the whole sample. The coefficient of litigation costs for both the defendant and the richest complainant increases, but, similarly to columns 1 through 3, it is statistically significant only for the defendant. The test rejects that the correlation for the cost of the defendant is smaller than for the complainant, which confirms hypothesis 2 (for the pre-2001 sample).

Stake at dispute, retaliation capacity, and co-complainants The value of the defendant's imports from the complainants in the disputed sector one year prior to violation is a measure of stake at dispute. As shown in columns 3 through 6, the likelihood of settlement is negatively correlated with this variable. The coefficient remains statistically significant even after 2001. This supports hypothesis 1B, that the larger the trade value, the greater the stake at dispute and the harder the settlement. The value of the defendant's imports from the rest of the world, however, has no statistical correlation with the probability of settlement.

The dispute settlement process of the WTO does not provide any external enforcement of the agreement. Instead, the system relies on the retaliatory power of the injured countries against the offending countries to enforce trade agreements. Therefore, the retaliatory capacity of the complaining parties may influence the outcome of the pretrial negotiations. Retaliatory actions are normally in the form of import restrictions in the injured country against the products from the offending country. Thus, the volume of exports from the defending country to the complaining countries can be used as a measure of the complainants' retaliation capacity. Our empirical observation suggests that the total value of exports from the defending country to the complaining countries has no correlation with the likelihood of settlement, controlling for the size of imports.

On the other hand, having multiple complainants is negatively correlated with the probability of settlement, and the correlation is statistically significant. Columns 4 and 5 show that this negative correlation is pronounced only prior to 2001. Hence, in that period, the existence of multiple complainants may have reduced the likelihood of settlement by increasing the stake at dispute. This result is robust even if we control for measures of the stake at dispute such as the disputed trade values between the defendant and the complaining parties.

Busch and Reinhardt (2006) hypothesize that third parties under-mine pretrial negotiations by increasing the negotiation costs. In fact, they point out, "61 percent of disputes with no third parties ended in early settlement, in contrast to 26 percent of disputes with third parties. Likewise, nine percent of disputes without third parties ended in a ruling, whereas fully 45 percent of disputes with third parties went the legal distance." But it is important to note that most third parties join a dispute after pretrial negotiations break down. Therefore, one can argue that it is the breakdown of pretrial negotiations that attracts third parties to join the dispute and not the other way around. To analyze the effect of third parties on the pretrial negotiations, we define third-party complainants as a dummy variable that is equal to 1 if at least one third party joined the negotiations *prior to* the establishment of a WTO dispute panel. The coefficient of third-party complainants supports the Busch and Reinhardt (2006) hypothesis at least prior to 2001.

9.8 Conclusion

Our objective in this chapter was to highlight the effect of the compen-sation mechanism that is available to disputing parties on the outcome of pretrial negotiations. In particular, we considered trade disputes among the WTO members in which trade policy adjustments, rather than cash payments, are used to transfer wealth among the member countries. As opposed to cash payments, policy adjustments are not zero-sum transactions, in the sense that the payee receives a different amount than is paid by the payer. The classical settlement bargaining models, which consider cash payments as the method of compensation, are modified to study settlement bargaining in an environment where compensation is implemented through policy adjustment.

We showed that when policy adjustment is the only compensation mechanism, the litigation costs of the defending party have a pro-nounced effect on the likelihood of pretrial settlement. Thus, the classic result regarding the independence of the settlement likelihood and the allocation of litigation costs does not follow under this alternative com-pensation mechanism. This result suggests that legal procedures that allocate a larger fraction of the burden of proof on the defending party should result in a higher settlement rate.

This theory can explain some stark differences between the behavior of these developed and developing countries in the dispute settle-ment process of the WTO. In a dispute between a developed and a developing country, the likelihood of settlement is significantly lower when the developed country is named as the defending party. Assuming that developing countries in the dataset have higher litigation costs, this observation can be interpreted as an indication of the pronounced effect of the defending countries' litigation costs in pretrial negotiations.

Appendix

Table 9.A1
Settlement rate and the size of the defending and complaining parties with low litigation costs.

Country (from richest to poorest)	No. of Settled/All Disputes as a	
	Defendant	Complainant
Norway		1/2
Switzerland		2/3
Denmark	1/1	
United States	33/94	50/88
United Kingdom	0/1	
Netherlands	1/1	
Japan	6/12	2/10
Ireland	2/2	
Belgium	2/3	
Canada	5/15	11/23
Sweden	1/1	
France	2/2	
Australia	6/10	1/6
New Zealand		1/6
European Union	22/49	41/79
Singapore		1/1
Hong Kong		1/1
Greece	2/2	
Portugal	1/1	
Korea	5/12	4/14
Antigua and Barbuda		0/1

Table 9.A2
Settlement rate and the size of the defending and complaining parties with high litigation costs.

Country (from richest to poorest)	No. of Settled/All Disputes as a	
	Defendant	Complainant
Czech Republic	2/2	1/1
Croatia	1/1	
Hungary	2/2	5/5
Slovakia	3/3	
Trinidad and Tobago	1/1	
Mexico	8/14	6/15
Poland	1/1	2/3
Chile	7/10	6/10
Turkey	5/7	1/2
Venezuela	2/2	0/1
Argentina	9/16	9/13
South Africa	3/3	
Panama	1/1	1/3
Malaysia	1/1	0/1
Uruguay	0/1	1/1
Brazil	7/11	11/22
Costa Rica		2/3
Dominican Republic	2/4	
Romania	2/2	
Colombia	2/3	5/5
Ecuador		1/3
China	10/15	2/7
Peru	4/4	1/3
Thailand	1/3	6/13
Guatemala	0/2	3/5
Ukraine	1/1	2/2
Armenia	1/1	
Indonesia	0/1	1/4
Honduras		2/5
Egypt	3/4	
Philippines	3/4	2/4
Nicaragua	2/2	1/1
Moldova	1/1	1/1
Vietnam		0/1
Sri Lanka		1/1
India	8/13	8/18
Pakistan	2/2	1/3
Bangladesh		1/1

Notes

We are grateful to Ben Zissimos, Alejandro Riaño, Eric Bond, Andrew Daughety, Bob Hammond, James Hartigan, David Hummels, Sangsoo Park, Jennifer Reinganum, Drew Saunders, Robert Staiger, Chad Bown, and seminar participants at the CESifo workshop on the WTO and Economic Development, the Midwest International Economics Meetings, and Purdue University for their useful comments and discussions. Mostafa Beshkar acknowledges the funding provided by the Vice Provost for Research through the Faculty Research Support Program at Indiana University. The authors especially thank Ben Zissimos for organizing and editing this volume.

1. We use the commonly used keywords developing and developed *countries* to refer to all WTO members, although some members, such as the European Union, are not countries.

2. The main stages of the DSP are consultation (pretrial negotiations between disputants), dispute panel, and appellate body. See Beshkar and Bond (2008) for a summary of the DSP.

3. Income is measured in 2005 US dollars. The $10,000 threshold for classifying developed and developing countries is comparable to the World Bank threshold for high-income countries in 2005 dollars, $10,725 (GNI per capita). Moreover, using the World Bank threshold and GNI per capita leads to almost identical results. Lists of developed and developing countries can be found in Tables 9.A1 and 9.A2, respectively. For more information on the World Bank threshold, see "How Are the Income Group Thresholds Determined?" on the World Bank website (https://datahelpdesk.worldbank.org /knowledgebase/articles/378833-how-are-the-income-group-thresholds-determined).

4. $7,000, $12,000, and $15,000 are chosen to check the robustness of the results if one digresses from the World Bank definition of high-income countries.

5. See Limão and Saggi (2008) for a discussion of why cash compensation is rarely used as a means of settling disputes among WTO members.

6. The DSP can influence the allocation of litigation costs by adopting appropriate rules about the allocation of the burden of proof, for example.

7. For developing countries, the absolute marginal cost of pursuing a dispute—not just the relative marginal cost, for example, as a share of GDP—is larger than for the developed countries. For instance, developed countries have a large mission at the WTO that is available to litigate disputes when they happen, but developing countries have small missions that are insufficient or would be overwhelmed by the litigation at the margin. Therefore, their marginal costs of litigation are larger than for developed countries in absolute terms.

8. Busch and Reinhardt (2003) provide a survey of this literature.

9. This assumption is consistent with various trade models, but it may fail if there is a shock to the preferences of the parties that changes the jointly optimal tariff rate. In the framework of our chapter, this assumption always holds, as we assume away shocks to preferences. For models of dispute settlement that consider preference shocks, see Beshkar (2010a, 2010b) and Maggi and Staiger (2015, 2018, 2011).

10. For a discussion of this boundary condition, see Reinganum and Wilde (1986).

11. See Bown and Reynolds (2014) for more information on the dataset.

12. One example is when the same dispute between a pair of member countries is filed multiple times. Another is that when several parties have similar complaints against a defending party, they may file a single complaint as co-complainants or may file separate complaints. In either case, similar complaints are addressed as a single case by the DSP.

13. See the quotation from Shaffer (2003) in section 9.1.

14. Developing countries can access legal aid through ACWL for an hourly charge that ranges from $25 for the least developed countries to $200 for the highest-income developing countries (see www.ACWL.ch).

15. Some may argue that even though China, India, and Brazil are developing countries with low income levels, their capacity to litigate in the WTO is similar to that of the developed countries. This may be apparent from the fact that they are strong and active members of the WTO. Including these countries among the low-cost countries does not change the result qualitatively.

16. The Bown and Reynolds (2014) dataset includes the size of the defendant's imports from all countries, so the imports from the complainants and from the rest of the world are calculated based on these data. Moreover, when the complainant is the European Union, we calculate the size of the defendant's imports by adding the size of the imports from countries that were in the European Union in the year the dispute was initiated.

References

Bebchuk, L. (1984). Litigation and Settlement under Imperfect Information. *Rand Journal of Economics* 15(3), 404–415.

Beshkar, M. (2010a). Optimal Remedies in International Trade Agreements. *European Economic Review* 54(3), 455–466.

Beshkar, M. (2010b). Trade Skirmishes and Safeguards: A Theory of the WTO Dispute Settlement Process. *Journal of International Economics* 82(1), 35–48.

Beshkar, M. (2016). Arbitration and Renegotiation in Trade Agreements. *Journal of Law, Economics, and Organization* 32, 586–619.

Beshkar, M. and E. Bond (2017). Cap and Escape in Trade Agreements. *American Economic Journal-Microeconomics* 9(4), 171–202.

Beshkar, M., E. Bond, and Y. Rho (2015). Tariff Binding and Overhang: Theory and Evidence. *Journal of International Economics* 97(1), 1–13.

Beshkar, M. and E. W. Bond (2008). The Theory of Dispute Resolution with Application to Intellectual Property Rights. In K. Maskus (ed.), *Intellectual Property, Growth and Trade*, 391–422. Amsterdam: Elsevier.

Beshkar, M. and R. Lee (2018). How Do Terms-of-Trade Effects Matter for Trade Agreements? Department of Economics, University of Indiana at Bloomington typescript.

Beshkar, M. and J. Park (2017). Dispute Settlement with Second-Order Uncertainty: The Case of International Trade Disputes. Department of Economics, University of Indiana at Bloomington typescript.

Bown, C. (2005). Participation in WTO Dispute Settlement: Complainants, Interested Parties, and Free Riders. *World Bank Economic Review* 19(2), 287–310.

Bown, C. P. (2004). Developing Countries as Plaintiffs and Defendants in GATT/WTO Trade Disputes. *World Economy* 27(1), 50–80.

Bown, C. P. and K. M. Reynolds (2014). Trade Flows and Trade Disputes. World Bank Policy Research Working Paper No. 6979. Washington, DC: World Bank.

Busch, M. and E. Reinhardt (2003). Developing Countries and General Agreement on Tariffs and Trade/World Trade Organization Dispute Settlement. *Journal of World Trade* 37(4), 719–735.

Busch, M. and E. Reinhardt (2006). Three's a Crowd: Third Parties and WTO Dispute Settlement. *World Politics* 58(3), 446–477.

Busch, M. L., E. Reinhardt, and G. Shaffer (2008). Does Legal Capacity Matter? Explaining Patterns of Protectionism in the Shadow of WTO Litigation. Issue Paper, International Centre for Trade and Sustainable Development, Geneva, Switzerland.

Guzman, A. and B. A. Simmons (2002). To Settle or Empanel? An Empirical Analysis of Litigation and Settlement at the World Trade Organization. *Journal of Legal Studies* 31, 205–235.

Horn, H. and P. C. Mavroidis (2008). The WTO Dispute Settlement Data Set 1995–2006: User's Guide. Version 2.0. London: Center for Economic Policy Research.

Horn, H., P. C. Mavroidis, and H. Nordström (1999). Is the Use of the WTO Dispute Settlement System Biased? Discussion Paper Series No. 2340. London: Center for Economic Policy Research.

Kuenzel, D. J. (2017). WTO Dispute Determinants. *European Economic Review* 91, 157–179.

Limão, N. and K. Saggi (2008). Tariff Retaliation versus Financial Compensation in the Enforcement of International Trade Agreements. *Journal of International Economics* 76(1), 48–60.

Maggi, G. and R. Staiger (2011). The Role of Dispute Settlement Procedures in International Trade Agreements. *Quarterly Journal of Economics* 126(1), 475–515.

Maggi, G. and R. W. Staiger (2015). Optimal Design of Trade Agreements in the Presence of Renegotiation. *American Economic Journal: Microeconomics* 7(1), 109–143.

Maggi, G. and R. W. Staiger (2017). Learning by Ruling and Trade Disputes. Technical report. Cambridge, MA: National Bureau of Economic Research.

Maggi, G. and R. W. Staiger (2018). Trade Disputes and Settlement. *International Economic Review* 59(1), 19–50.

Park, J. (2011). Enforcing International Trade Agreements with Imperfect Private Monitoring. *Review of Economic Studies* 78(3), 1102–1134.

Park, J.-H. (2016). Enforcement and Dispute Settlement. In K. Bagwell and R. W. Staiger (eds.), *Handbook of Commercial Policy*, volume B1, 3–67. Amsterdam: Elsevier.

Reinganum, J. and L. Wilde (1986). Settlement, Litigation, and the Allocation of Litigation Costs. *Rand Journal of Economics* 17(4), 557–566.

Shaffer, G. (2003). How to Make the WTO Dispute Settlement System Work for Developing Countries: Some Proactive Developing Country Strategies. ICTSD resource paper. Resource Paper No. 5. Geneva: International Center for Trade and Sustainable Development.

Wilckens, S. (2009). The Usage of the WTO Dispute Settlement System: Do Power Considerations Matter? In J. C. Hartigan (ed.), *Trade Disputes and the Dispute Settlement Understanding of the WTO: An Interdisciplinary Assessment*, 213–241. Bingley, UK: Emerald Group.

International Problems Facing Developing Nations. Development...

...the WTO Dispute Settlement...

Contributors

Mostafa Beshkar Department of Economics, Indiana University Bloomington (USA)

Eric W. Bond Department of Economics, Vanderbilt University (USA)

Chad P. Bown Peterson Institute for International Economics (USA)

Fabrice Defever Department of Economics, City, University of London (UK)

David R. DeRemer International School of Economics and Social Sciences, Kazakh-British Technical University (Kazakhstan)

Xuepeng Liu Department of Economics and Finance, Kennesaw State University (USA)

Rodney D. Ludema Department of Economics, and School of Foreign Service, Georgetown University (USA)

Mahdi Majbouri Economics Division, Babson College (USA)

Anna Maria Mayda Department of Economics, and School of Foreign Service, Georgetown University (USA)

Jonathon C. F. McClure Department of Economics, Georgetown University (USA)

Alejandro Riaño School of Economics, University of Nottingham (UK)

Kamal Saggi Department of Economics, Vanderbilt University (USA)

Robert W. Staiger Department of Economics, Dartmouth College (USA)

Ben Zissimos Department of Economics, University of Exeter Business School (UK)

Index

Printed in the United States
by Baker & Taylor Publisher Services